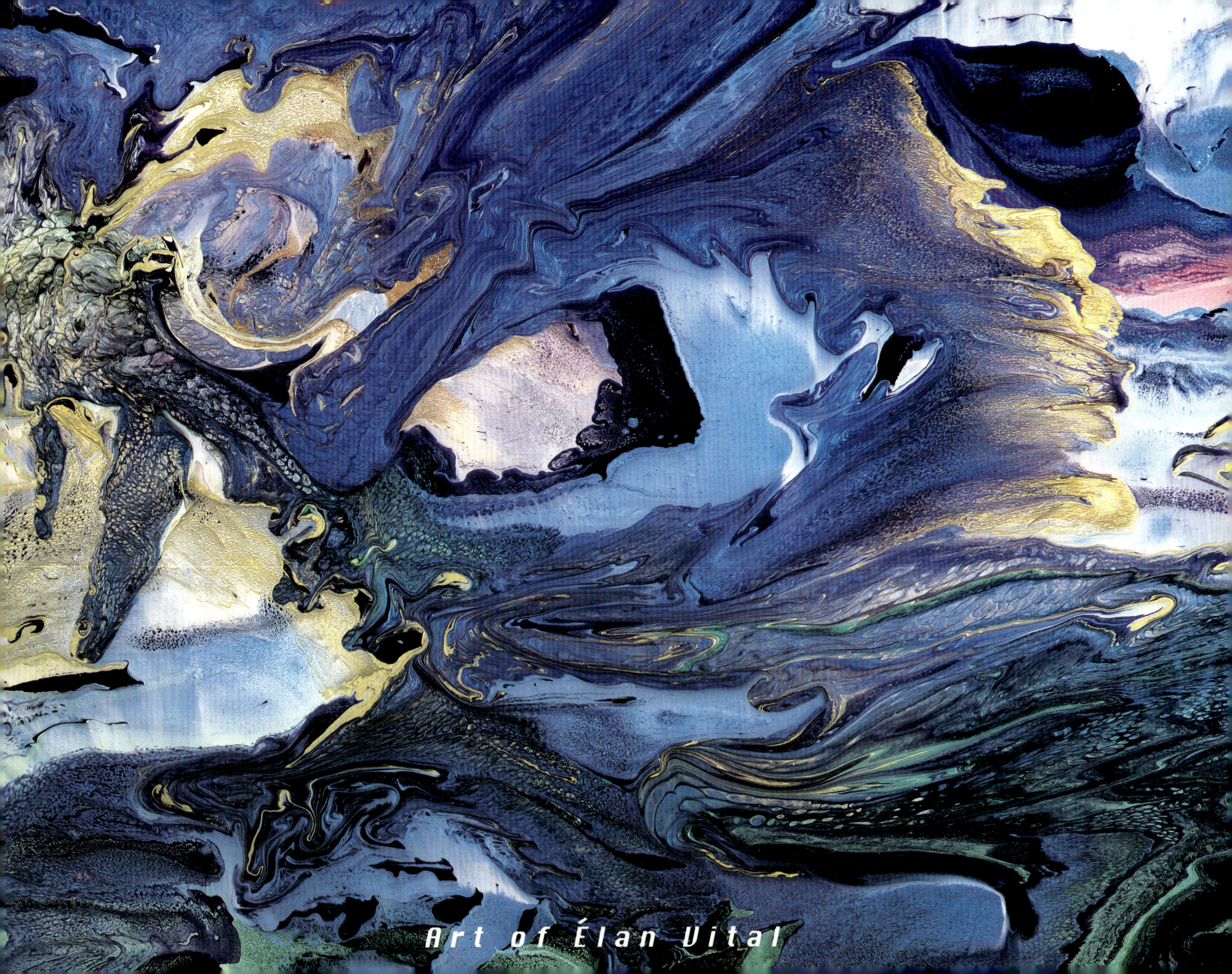
Art of Élan Vital

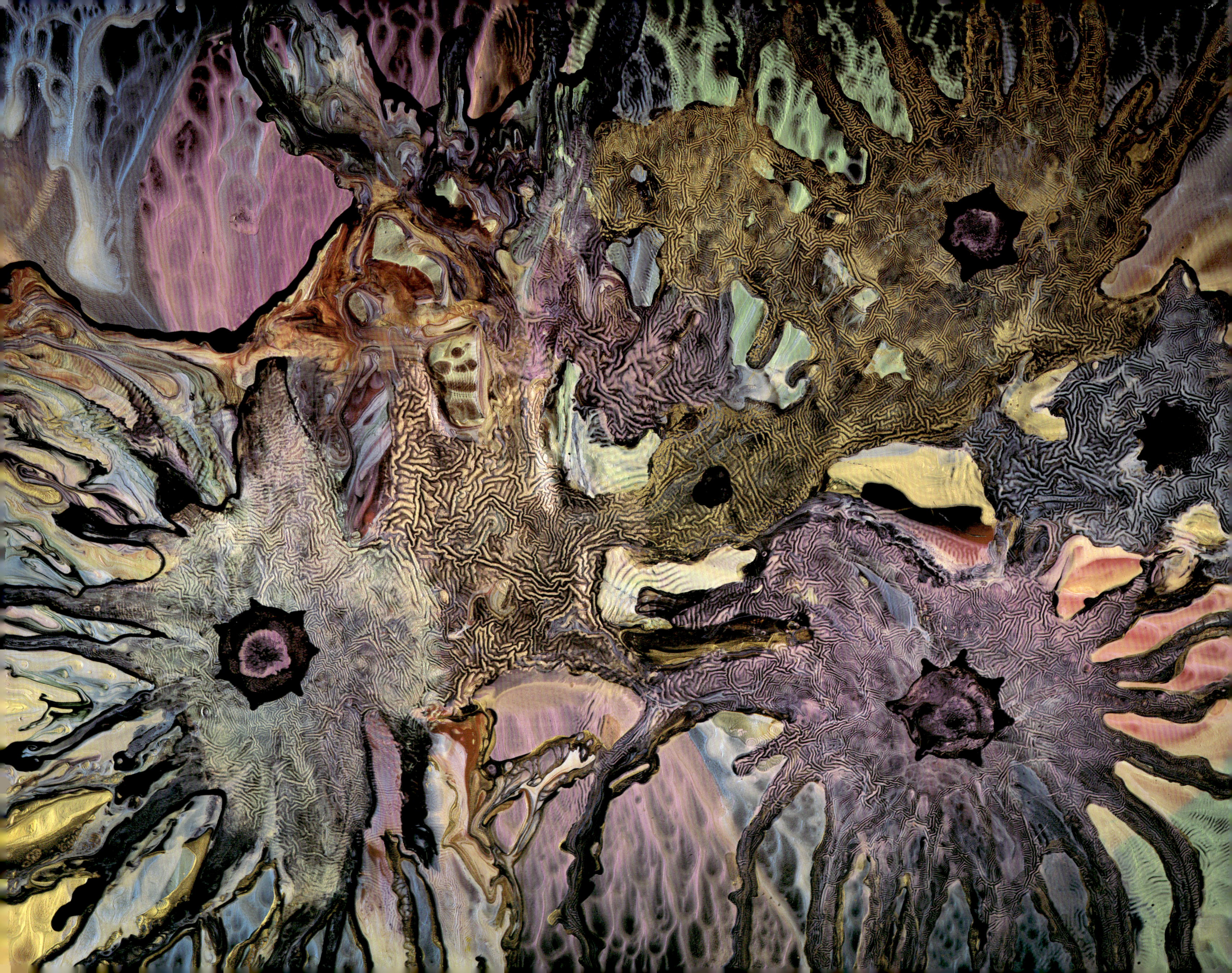

Artists in Hawaii

The Book

TABLE OF CONTENTS

Artists in Hawaii

The Book

Hawaii is a place of incomparable beauty and exotic cultural diversity that has attracted artists from around the world. It is not, therefore, surprising to find a thriving art community of extraordinary depth. Like many artists' work, the art community itself is a complex layering of styles and techniques woven into an integrated fabric of talent.

More than two years in the making, Artists In Hawaii is a cooperative effort between Printech Hawaii and the Hawaii art community, culminating in a publication that represents a wide range of art styles and mediums. Alone, it may not define the Hawaii art scene, but it is certainly an excellent opportunity for the art scene to define itself.

We thank all those artists involved for their participation and also to the corporations that have supported our distribution efforts.

Paul Vogelsberger, **Publisher**

About Printech Hawaii
Printech Hawaii is a publishing and graphic arts company specializing in the production and distribution of quality books, magazines and fine art reproductions.

Note to Hawaii's Artists:
For more information on being included in our next edition of "Artists in Hawaii", call: **(808) 733-2800.**

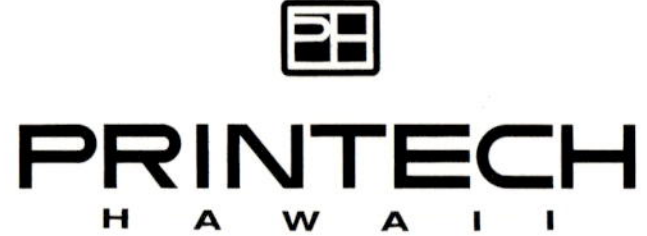

Published By:
Printech Hawaii
4614 Kilauea Avenue, Suite 528
Honoluu, HI 96816
(808) 733-2800 Fax (808) 733-2805

Publisher: Paul Vogelsberger
Book & Cover Design: Cliff Sorensen
Editors: Frances Vogelsberger & Lark T. Church
Contributing Writers: Zella Jackson & Loren Malenchek

First Edition, 1st printing October 1994

ISBN No. 1-878101-02-1

Artists in Hawaii

If enduring love, incomparable beauty, and cultural diversity inspire great art, then it is little wonder the Hawaiian Islands have spawned some of the greatest contemporary art in the world today.

First, the extraordinary beauty of our islands attracts artists from around the globe. Once here, the exotic loveliness of our diverse people alongside the bluest sky in the world, provide the backdrop for a love affair destined to last a lifetime. Put simply, great artists come here to visit and never leave.

Our great artists have painted, sculpted, and carved their way across our Hawaiian islands, creating works of art that stimulate and inspire the creative energies in us all.

Thus, whether you are an art admirer visiting the islands for the first time or a seasoned "kamaaina", sit back, relax, and enjoy this visual tour of "Artists in Hawaii".

Oahu is often referred to as the "main island" of the six most visited islands in our Hawaiian chain. Literally translated, Oahu means "the gathering place", and indeed it is the home of nearly one million people and the center for academy and museum caliber art. It is also the home of many "out-of-the-way galleries", artists' cooperatives, art events, as well as some major gallery chains. So, if you love the arts, have an eye for adventure, and don't mind driving in the city, get ready for an art journey that shall no doubt prove unforgettable.

Our adventure starts at the Honolulu International Airport. At several highly visible locations throughout the facility, all you have to do is look around to experience the art of Pegge Hopper. Her murals grace vast, expansive areas with her earthy renditions of Hawaiian women. We'll take a closer look at her work in Chinatown. In addition, there is a tiny little showroom at the foot of United Airline's main terminal. It sits diagonally across from Burger King and has a rotating exhibit featuring some local emerging artists. Sometimes the new talent there can be both refreshing and stimulating.

Now, let's journey out of the airport, to the newly renovated Gentry Pacific Design Center located at 560 North Nimitz Highway. You won't be able to miss its bright fuchsia awning and huge parking lot fronting this massive complex. The center sports what Honolulu Magazine calls "one of the best restaurants on Oahu" - ***Angelica's Cafe and Gallery.*** And now, the gallery portion of this establishment is taking a turn from a decidedly gift shop format to an artists' cooperative. Look for emerging artists of long standing in the islands as well as those who are brand-new, looking for a start. Right next door is a brand new art and jewelry showroom, ***Return to Paradise Galleries.*** The owners plan to add elements of "entertainment" to their new showroom concept. Bargain hunters should stop by and pick up their events calendar and schedule to attend one of their art auctions, jewelry shows, or private brunches.

Return to Paradise Galleries currently features the work of The Makks, Thomas and H. Leung, Nisla, Jeff Wilke, David Miller, and many others. While you are in the Return to Paradise Galleries showroom, treat yourself to the art of the ***Makk family.*** The Makks in every way could very well be our state's most important artists. Three nations claim them as their own, but in the United States, the Makks are considered a national treasure. Eva Makk, Americo, her husband of 42 years, and their son A.B., are America's first family of artists.

The Makks have met with kings, cardinals, and presidents; have journeyed to the heart of the Amazon and have painted their way across four continents. In the past 40 years, the Makks have completed five Presidential portraits, garnered over 100 gold medals from the United States, Italy, Hungary, and England; completed historic and personal treasures which grace museums, cathedrals, embassies, and homes all over the world.

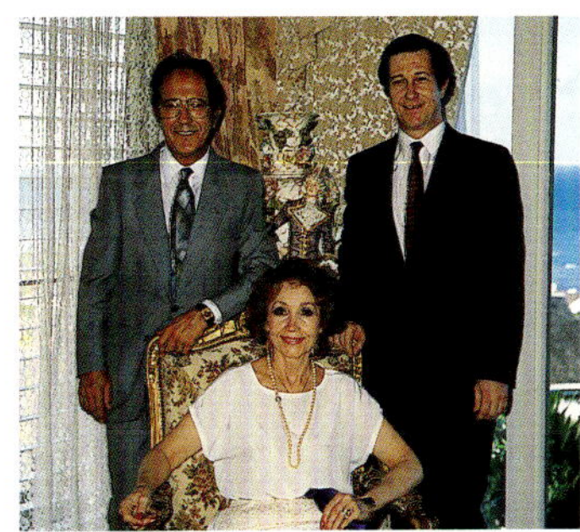

Americo Makk, Eva Makk, and A.B Makk

Eva Makk is a master impressionist painter and is best known for her serene landscapes, soft portraiture often depicting children, and vibrant florals. Americo is also a master impressionist painter and is most famous for his romantic European street scenes, powerful western scenes, and provocative portraits. Finally, their son, A.B., is inspired by the soft palettes of Monet and creates paintings which evoke serenity and supreme grace.

Now that you are comfortably "on foot", you can enjoy your adventure in the heart of Chinatown which is the home of many curio shops, galleries, and antique stores. One notable gallery is the ***Pegge Hopper Gallery*** located at 1164 Nuuanu Avenue, which features the artwork of one of Hawaii's most famous artists, Pegge Hopper. Many say she is to the Pacific what R.C. Gorman is to the Southwest.

Another must-see in Chinatown is the ***Robyn Buntin Galleries*** at 900A Maunakea Street on the corner of Maunakea and North Nimitz Highway (which becomes Ala Moana Boulevard). This gallery is a feast for the senses. It reflects the years of travel and eye for the rare, valuable, and exotic that owner Robyn Buntin, has lavished into his business.

When you first walk in, you don't know if you have come across a rare book store, antique shop, or art gallery – or perhaps it is all three. You also get the sense of being transported back in time to a collector's haven long before the advent of cookie cutter chain stores and malls. In short, this is a place where you can spend hours.

Robyn Buntin features many artists but most notably, ***Ho Hung Wong***. Ho Hung Wong is a Chinese-European impressionist painter and will delight your senses with his soft images and serene compositions.

Further on down in the direction of Waikiki is the ***Honolulu Academy of Arts*** on the corner of Ward Avenue and Beretania Street. The Academy was founded in 1927 by Mrs. Charles M. Cooke, who desired to share her collections and interest in art and art education with the children and adults of Hawaii. It is dedicated to the education and cultural enrichment of the entire community. A private, non-profit institution accredited by the American Association of Museums, the Honolulu Academy of Arts is the only general art museum in the state of Hawaii.

The Contemporary Museum

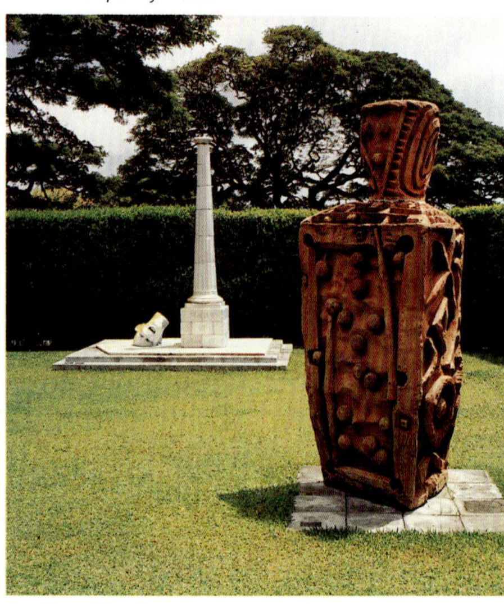

The Academy is internationally recognized for the excellence of its holdings, including one of the country's finest collection of Asian art, the James Michener Collection of Japanese Prints, the Kress Collection of Italian Renaissance paintings, American and European paintings and decorative arts, contemporary art, and an extensive graphics collection of 17,000 works on paper. In its main collection, the museum maintains a 22,000-piece (and growing) collection of art from cultures around the world and throughout history.

The Honolulu Academy of Arts is registered as a national and state historical place in recognition of the significant architecture of its buildings. Indeed, as you walk up to the Academy, you will experience a sense that this is an important place. The carefully manicured grounds, the meticulously maintained stucco facade and tile roof all bespeak of the care and love it's supporting members and staff provide. For a city the size of Honolulu, this truly is a labor of love.

The Academy is the state's largest private presenter of visual arts programs. It presents its collection in 30 galleries, surrounding six garden courtyards. There are over 40 temporary exhibitions each year. The Honolulu Academy of Arts is a must-see on your art journey through Hawaii. Its roster of supporting events is so lengthy, it would fill a small book, so please stop in to get the latest events calendar.

One new annual show you will want to take note of is co-sponsored by the Academy and celebrated its inaugural event on August 20 and 21, 1994. The ***ARTS Hawaii Festival*** is billed as the largest arts and crafts event in the state. The exhibition venues span Thomas Square Park, the Academy Art Center, and the Blaisdell Exhibition Hall. Top local visual and performing artists alongside our finest craftspersons display their art, as well as entertain and educate the public through children's workshops, a printmakers exhibition, and craftmaking seminars. So, if your art trek occurs in August, call the Academy and definitely schedule this event in.

Another must-see event is entering into its forty-fourth year: ***The Honolulu Academy of Arts 44th Annual Artists of Hawaii Exhibition***. This is a juried show and attracts Hawaii's best and brightest artists featuring paintings, drawings, prints, photographs, collages, sculpture, constructions, assemblages, wall hangings, video, light images, open and closed ceramic, glass and plastic forms, furniture, fiber arts, jewelry, and more! This delightful menagerie of artforms will be on display from the first of December until the first week in January.

The Contemporary Museum

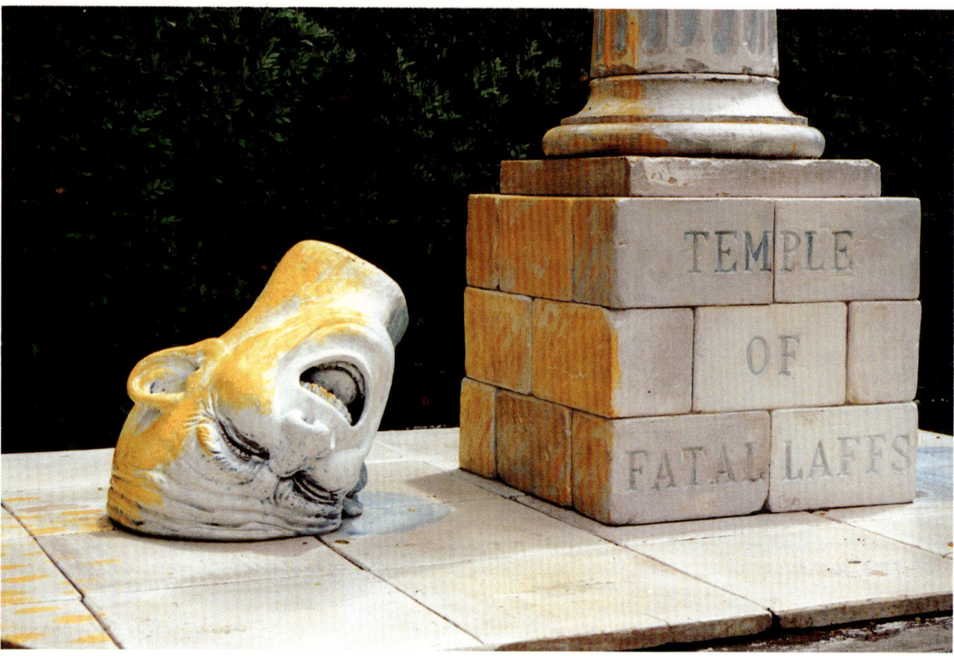

Although it can be quite difficult to find, head up in the "mauka" direction and visit ***The Contemporary Museum,*** located in Honolulu's scenic Makiki Heights. It is a cultural oasis combining exhibitions of contemporary art with the natural beauty of Hawaii. Surrounded by rolling lawns and lush foliage on a sprawling three and a half acre site, the museum offers spectacular views from its terraces of the Pacific Ocean, Diamond Head, and the Honolulu skyline. In addition, the beautiful gardens provide the perfect backdrop for sculpture from the museum's permanent collection. Many find this mesh of natural and man-made beauty to be the perfect place for contemplation and renewal.

Inside the Contemporary Museum, you will find five interconnected galleries in the main building, as well as the Milton Cades Pavillon. The museum's principal activity is the presentation of temporary exhibitions of works in all media by artists of local, national, and international reputation. Summer 1994 saw the art of Massachusetts artist, Robert Cummings, on display at the museum in an astonishing variety of media, including paintings, drawings, prints, sculpture, photographs, and even a giant inflatable "sculpture".

Selections from the museum's permanent collection are shown periodically in the exhibition schedule. Changing exhibitions are also presented in ***The Contemporary Cafe*** and at ***The Honolulu Advertiser Gallery,*** the museum's annex exhibition space in the News Building in downtown Honolulu.

You can make an afternoon of strolling through the gardens and art while enjoying the spectacular view. You can even indulge yourself in The Contemporary Cafe which offers museum visitors an opportunity to have lunch either indoors in a gallery-like atmosphere amid changing displays of art or outside in a pleasant garden setting.

Not too far from downtown Honolulu and right before the hustle and bustle of Waikiki is Ala Moana Shopping Center, Hawaii's largest and busiest shopping mall (and quite possibly the biggest mall in the central Pacific). Located on the mauka (mountain) side of the mall at the mall level is one of Oahu's best-known galleries, ***Images International of Hawaii***. Among the local artists represented here are Maui artist Robert Lyn Nelson and Japanese - born Hasashi Otsuka, a Hawaii resident since 1979. Other former Hawaiian resident artists on exhibit at Images include Caroline Young and Gary Hostallero, as well as the local talent of Raymond McCabe.

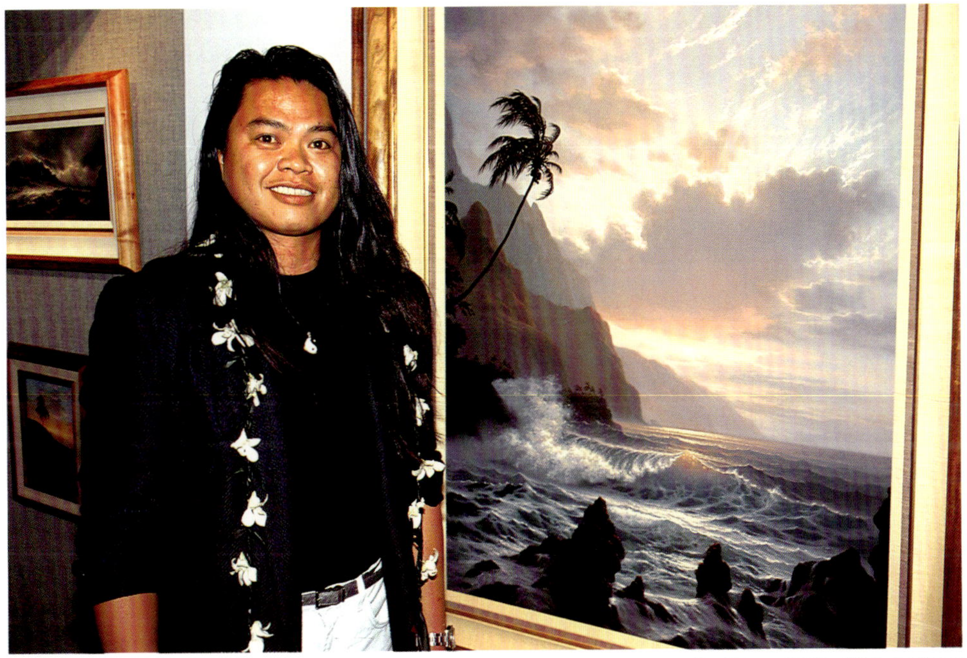

Roy Tabora at Wyland Galleries Hawaii

Just a few blocks Koko Head bound (east) of Ala Moana is one of the nicest little galleries in Waikiki located in The Hilton Hawaiian Village: ***Return to Paradise Galleries***. Having experienced their artists at their Gentry Pacific Design Center Showroom, you will have yet another view of some great art. This is where the artists do their book signings, painting demonstrations, and major shows. You will have the opportunity to meet many artists throughout the year. Occasionally, entertainment and food is provided to enhance your art experience. In short, now that you are in one of Hawaii's first class resorts, you can expect to be treated, well... first class!

Mark your calendars for a new annual art event scheduled to premier June 2 - June 11, 1995: **ARTFEST *Hawaii*.** This art event is the first of its kind to celebrate the diverse cultures of the Pacific through the visual, performing, and culinary arts. The goal in developing ARTFEST Hawaii was to create an art, wine, and food festival that would provide visitors and residents a unique interactive and "edutainment" event that is both fun and educational.

Famous chefs, wine connoisseurs, visual and performing artists will all come together to offer good food, wine, entertainment, educational seminars, sunset cruises with famous artists, and much more to make a visit to Waikiki a truly memorable occasion. This will all be done throughout the property, with focusing on the main lawn area, amidst planned fireworks at the lagoon and a May Day Parade. Return to Paradise is co-sponsoring the event with Hilton Hawaiian Village.

When you leave the village, turn left, then right back onto Ala Moana Boulevard. Turn right onto Kalakaua Street and make the trek through Waikiki's "main street". You will pass a menagerie of shops, specialty stores, and galleries. Some are tucked away inside the hotels which front the beach. Continue on until you reach Kapahulu Avenue. Turn left and make an immediate right into the Honolulu Zoo's parking lot. Feed the meter and put your walking shoes back on, because there is so much to see.

First stop is the beautifully restored Sheraton Moana Surfrider Hotel at 2353 Kalakaua Avenue. Originally built in 1901, this Victorian beauty with its stately columns still looks grand as it waltzes into the next century. Take a walking tour through this well dressed Victorian lady and enjoy the majesty of ***Lau Chun's*** exquisite art. Born in China over a half century ago, Lau Chun creates soft impressionistic paintings of oriental gardens, lovely fields of wild flowers, a gazebo nearly lost in an overgrown meadow, and other scenes restful to the eye and spirit.

Lau Chun's masterful landscape interpretations are both soft and magnificent at the same time due, in part, to the grand scale in which he loves to work. His canvases are so large they almost give the illusion of murals and beautifully fill the vast wall areas of this grand hotel. You will see more of Lau Chun in the "Pink

Lady" coming up a little later.

As you leave the main entrance of the hotel, look across the street for the large sign fronting the International Market Place. This gem of a shopping experience reminds many of "old Waikiki" where most merchants had open air, outdoor shops or stalls. Follow your nose to the Food Court, then look up because right next door on the second level is the ***Arts of Paradise Gallery***. This 3,000-square-foot gallery features fifty of Hawaii's top professional artists in an open-air, tropical setting; an art oasis in Waikiki. Every third Thursday of each month, the artists give demonstrations to the public, talk about their techniques, and answer questions.

A must-see is the artwork of ***Susie Brooks*** who uses abstract and loose impressionistic styles to "leave much to the admirer's imagination". When you gaze upon her "Lavascape" or feel one of her three dimensional loose and colorful hangings, you know you are visiting with an artist of considerable talent and originality.

Next stop is down the avenue at the Hyatt Regency Hotel at 2424 Kalakaua Avenue. This hotel has an inner sanctum a world away.

James Coleman

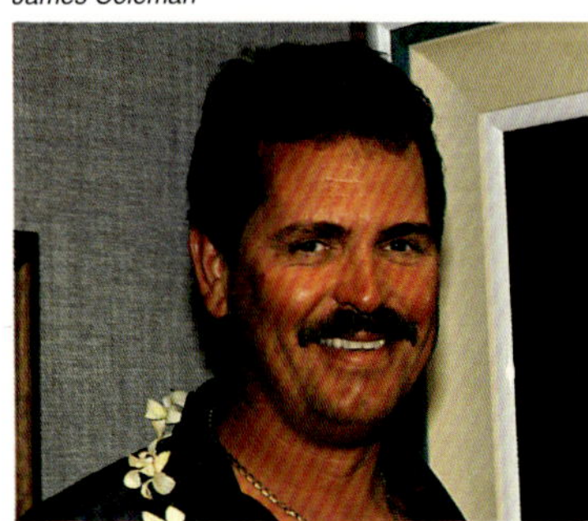

Amongst waterfalls, exotic birds, sidewalk cafes, lush foliage, and shops awaits the art adventure of a lifetime: ***Wyland Galleries***. Immediately you are struck by the koa wood cases filled to the brim with exotic hand made treasures, the bigger than life mural display backlit for drama, and, of course, some of the most spectacular art in Hawaii displayed in a most spectacular way. Wyland Galleries features some of Hawaii's most successful artists of this decade including ***Wyland, Roy Tabora, James Coleman, Scott Hanson,*** and many others.

Wyland openings are legendary in that the artist is always present to greet his admirers. Book signings, fine art poster dedications, elaborate finger foods, luscious fresh fruits, wine, and cheeses all come together for a memorable art event. Often the artist will share his or her experiences briefly with a breathless crowd of one to two hundred people. Once, Roy Tabora, the internationally renowned seascape artist, held us in the palm of his hand as he described his inspiration to paint what many believe are the finest seascapes created today.

"I see the energy of life ebb and flow in the waves. Even the fiercely powerful waves in a storm, which are ominous to some, are exquisitely beautiful to me. And for many of us, being successful in life requires learning to navigate in both stormy seas and tranquil waters. I am driven to the sea as my metaphor of life itself - everchanging, deeply mysterious, frightening at times, and yet, somehow always magnificently beautiful."

His pulsating ocean waves have captured the imagination of an entire world. Tabora's prominent collectors include President and Hilary Clinton, sporting goods magnate, J.R. Spalding, and Scotland's Lady Pauline Ogilvy, as well as everyday people like Kenji Higashi (Japan), Glinkau Wolfgang (Germany), and Stephanie Molyneux (London) from all over the world.

Wyland is Hawaii's premier marine artist and has completed sixty-one life-size "Whaling Walls" throughout the world, including one which at 116,000 square feet and ten stories high, qualifies in the **Guinness Book of World Records** as the largest mural in the world. He has championed the protection of endangered marine life and their habitat for more than two decades. His murals, in fact, have been his personal monument to the undersea world's plight and his prayer for their survival. Instead

Whaling Wall XLIV
Wyland with Bottlenose Dolphins in Wilmington, Delaware

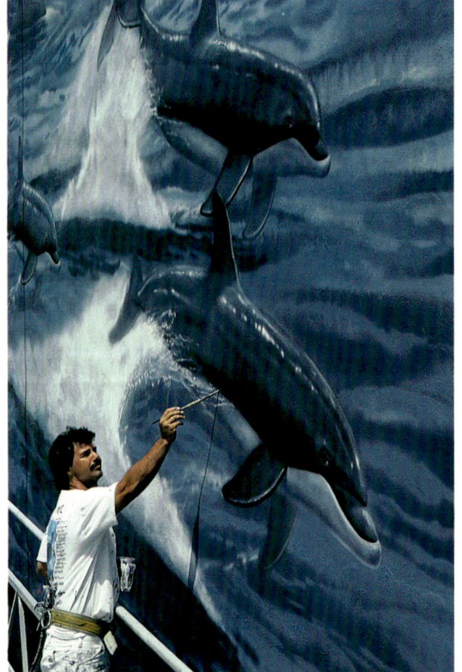

of preaching to us, he simply put these grand animals right up "front and center" with the hopes that we would finally see what he has known all along; these animals need our protection if they are to survive in the next century. Wyland certainly struck a chord and the people of the world began to listen and much has been accomplished in the way of strict laws and changing attitudes that will help see these animals through this challenging decade.

Wyland paints and sculpts marine life with the same love that inspired his murals. His signature imagery depicts a majestic humpback whale as the central figure surrounded by a beam of light in the haunting semi-darkness of the sea. Often the area fades into mysterious blackness as if to express the potentially bleak uncertainties that surround the animal itself. Wyland's art is an important commentary of our times, as well as profoundly beautiful. Anyone who has ever seen a humpback leap from the ocean and seem to dance playfully atop the waves, will surely be stilled at the sight of a Wyland painting or sculpture. Wyland Galleries Hawaii also has a great spot on the rural North Shore of Oahu in the small surfing town of Haleiwa. The Haleiwa location is Wyland's premiere Hawaii gallery – stroll in almost any day, and you may just see Wyland himself or perhaps Roy Tabora or James Coleman hanging about, "talking story" with some of the patrons!

Just down Kalakaua Avenue is what residents affectionately call "The Pink Palace", The Royal Hawaiian Hotel. Opened on February 1, 1927, it was described by the press as "the first resort hostelry in America" and has served as an elegant beachside getaway for nearly seventy years. Princess Kawananakoa, who might have been Queen if the monarchy had survived, was the first registered guest. Now registered as an Historic Landmark Structure, it is also the home of Lau Chun's impressionist art. His art graces the hallways of "The Pink Palace". In addition, you may view more than two dozen of his lovely works in the ***Lau Chun Gallery*** located in front of the lobby.

The last treat in Waikiki is not another elegant gallery, but rather a bargain hunter's paradise: ***The Zoo Fence.*** Almost every city which appeals to tourists has its very own year-round outdoor art fair which features local artists for affordable prices. Paris has Mon Martre, New Orleans has Jackson Square, and Honolulu has the Zoo Fence. From seascapes to landscapes; impressionism to realism; oriental to fantasy - you are likely to see most styles, shapes, and sizes of art modestly framed and unpretentiously displayed.

Follow the road oceanside until it curves around Diamond Head; turn right and complete your driving tour of one of the island's most prestigious neighborhoods, Kahala. In the bargain, you will also catch a glimpse of Hawaii's premier gate sculptor, ***Gregory Craft***. His signature art fronts Kahala's finest homes forming a bas relief sculpture of massive proportions. Copper is sculpted into peacocks, maile leaves, and palm fronds to form dramatic gateways for his patron's homes.

This ends our tour of Oahu's art scene but the journey continues for those venturing on to visit our lovely neighbor islands.

The Big Island

The island of Hawaii is known as "The Big Island" to visitors and its 120,300 residents alike and has a soul of diversity. Anyone who has landed at the Kona Airport, knows that eerie feeling of seeming to have just landed on the moon. And yet, just a scant few miles away, lies a coastal area lined with palm trees and lush foliage. A drive Hilo-side yields nearly impenetrable tropical jungles; while the nearly 14,000-foot-high top of Mauna Kea may sport snow and ice.

The cover of ***Artists in Hawaii*** was painted by an artist now residing on Maui but who until recently lived on the Big Island of Hawaii – ***Avi Kiriaty***. Born in Israel, Kiriaty was so taken by the idea of sculpting lava, he took molten run-off from tributaries on the slopes of Kilauea to make his lava art. Kiriaty's lava art is provocative and has been featured on the highly regarded PBS series, "Spectrum Hawaii".

Now, his decidedly "Gauguin-line" style of painting has captured the imagination of Hawaii and the rest of the world. He seems to infuse everyone and everything in his paintings with an aura of importance which is at the heart of his imagery. This, fused with bright colors, indigenous people, and tropical backgrounds make him that rare artist who can capture both the dignity and beauty of simpler cultures.

If you indeed landed in Kona, make your way to the Hilton Waikoloa Hotel. It is a short, twenty-minute drive from the airport and will be a thrill for anyone who loves fantasy. This is the Disney equivalent of a hotel resort complete with dolphins, boat rides, tram rides, waterfalls, lush tropical gardens, and an art walk that will intrigue and delight you. The art walk is a self-guided tour that rims the major walkways throughout the property and features sculptures, paintings, and tapestries from around the world. In addition to the art walk, you can stop by ***Wyland Galleries*** and get their show schedule of up-coming events. A famous artist might be in town the very weekend of your "art tour".

Less than a half hour drive from the Hilton Waikoloa Hotel in the north-central part of the Big Island is the quaint town of Waimea. Resembling the windswept plains of Montana more closely than a tropical Hawaiian paradise, the world's largest privately-owned cattle ranch, Parker Ranch, has been flourishing here for well over a century. Long-time Waimea resident ***Mary Koski*** is an artist well-known for her images of the children of Hawaii. She paints a romantic view of children that will enchant you as you become enthralled with their play, or simply watch a young child gaze at a flower. Mrs. Koski's work can be viewed in Waimea at the ***Gallery of Great Things*** as well as ***The Collectors Gallery,*** in Kailua-Kona. Once you have cooled off in the rural Waimea hills, head back to Kona for a quaint, coastal town experience. Another branch of ***Wyland Galleries*** awaits you on Alii Drive at the edge of town. If your excursion is scheduled in early August, make certain to attend the ***Pacific Ocean Research Foundation Art Exhibition*** held in conjunction with the Hawaiian International Billfish Tournament. This invitational fishing tournament attracts competitors from around the world who go on a quest for the biggest marlins in Hawaiian waters. Going into its thirty-seventh year, the accompanying art exhibit is featured for fourteen days in the King Kamehameha Hotel right next to the harbor. This art exhibit features some of the finest wildlife artists the islands have to offer including, of course, Wyland.

There is much more to experience on this vast island but for the traveler eager to see the islands through the eyes of our artists, let us move on to Kauai, "The Garden Isle".

Kauai

Kauai is nicknamed "The Garden Isle" and for good reason: due to its rainy climate, it stands out with lush tropical gardens, waterfalls, and forests. Indeed, Kauai has the wettest spot on earth, which gets over 100 inches of annual rainfall. However, most visitors to Kauai as well as its 51,000 residents find this island's beauty and slow pace simply intoxicating.

This tiny island can be thought of in terms of three primary areas: Lihue, Kapaa, and Poipu. Road signs are reliable for getting you directly and easily to either of these three regions. In the first, we find the earthy Kauai Museum.

Lihue

Lihue is the main town of Kauai and is the home of the ***Kauai Museum*** located on Rice Street. The mission of the Kauai Museum is to "perpetuate the living history of Kauai". And certainly, there are many who feel Kauai has some of the last vestiges of "old Hawaii" unique to an earlier time and those unique qualities are being swept away. The museum has on-going exhibits featuring Kauai resident artists.

Each fall, the museum hosts the Kauai Society

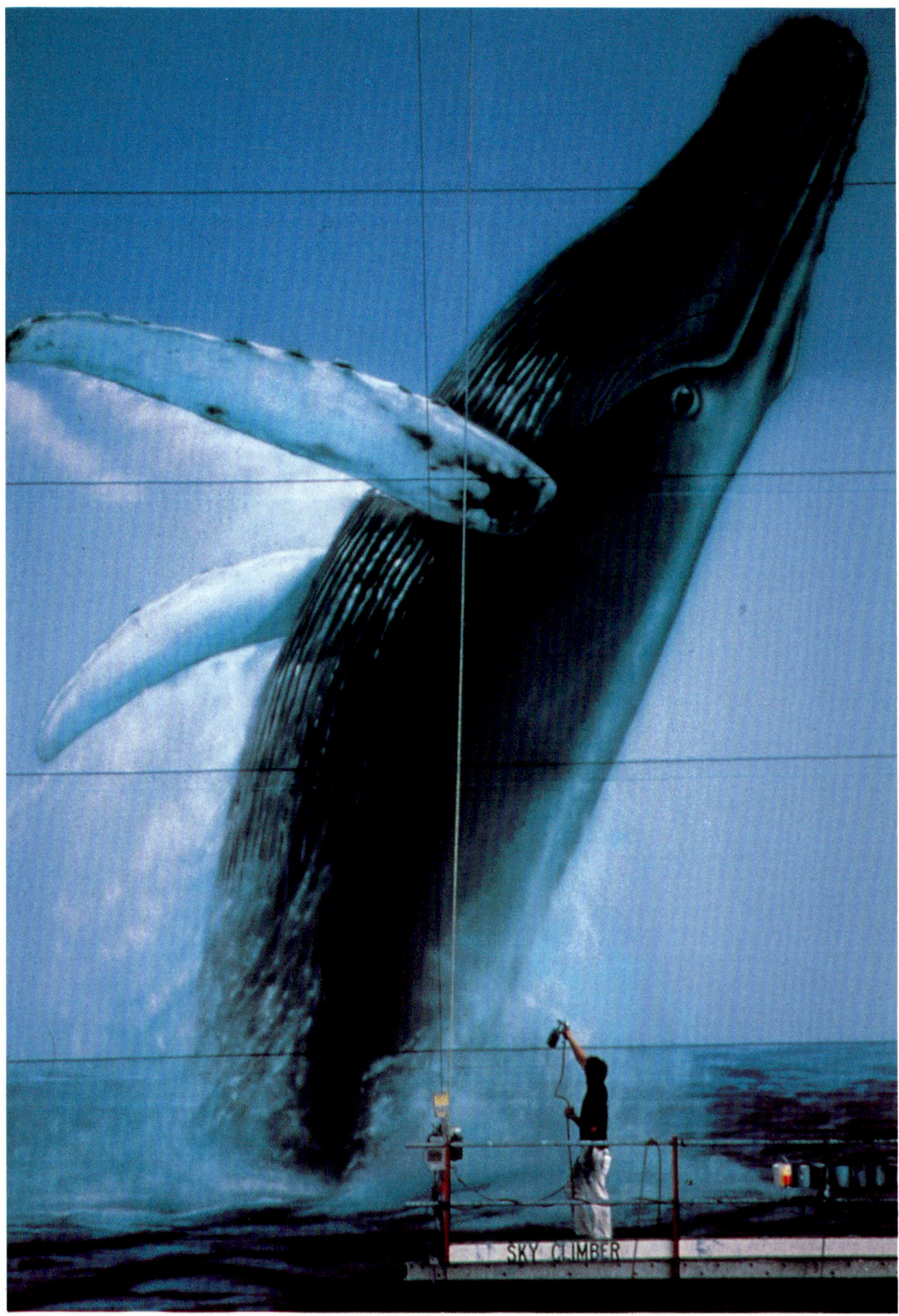

Whaling Wall VI
Wyland Working on Mural in Honolulu, Hawaii

of Artists' Annual Show, entitled this year ***Art Kauai '94***. Forty to fifty of Kauai's best and brightest visual artists display their work in this annual juried event.

Kapaa

Kapaa is the home of ***Wyland Galleries*** and ***Kahn Galleries***. Once in Kapaa, you can't miss Wyland Galleries. It is located in the Kauai Village Shopping Center back behind one of his famous "Whaling Walls" which fronts the main thoroughfare in town. Visit their Coconut Marketplace location for a schedule of personal appearances because their shows are done in a first-class yet Kauai-style, friendly manner. Another location you will not want to miss is the Kilohana Plantation which is on the main road as you drive towards Poipu. It is located on the right as you pass the only mainland-style shopping mall on the island.

Kilohana

The Kilohana Plantation is a grand estate that is now the home of one of the finest restaurants on Kauai, lovely shops and the Kahn Galleries where an exquisite show of Makk art continues. Their romantic impressionist styles are right at home here where you can wander through thirty-five acres of magnificent countryside, take a tour of the grounds in an old fashioned carriage pulled by an impressive Clydesdale horse, or bask in the grandeur of the 8,000 square foot mansion which takes you back to an earlier era.

Poipu

Once in Poipu, you must visit the Poipu Shopping Center. Live entertainment, shops, and eateries featuring outdoor dining are all nestled around a large tropical courtyard. ***Wyland Galleries*** is located on the far corner of the center and, as always, deserves a visit. Finally, Kauai is the home of one of the most intriguing art events in the islands: ***The Mokihana Festival***. This annual event is scheduled around the end of September to early October every year. Its site changes over the years, so call the Kauai Arts Relief Project at (808) 245-4561 weekday mornings for the location and dates which coincide with your visit.

You will find some paintings and sculpture here but the main focus is on "live folk art". Let us end our tour of the arts in Hawaii with the people of Kauai who celebrate folk art in its many forms through friendly competitions and workshops: music composer's contests, flowerless lei contests, Hawaiian language workshops, slack-key guitar workshops, nose flute workshops, Hawaii's only all-male hula contests, as well as folk art workshops. Perhaps the most fascinating event scheduled this year is the "most ukeleles played at one time in one place" event which is expected to make the **Guinness Book of World Records!**

Here's hoping you will always remember your time in the islands and especially your tour of the art and artists of Hawaii.

– By Zella Jackson

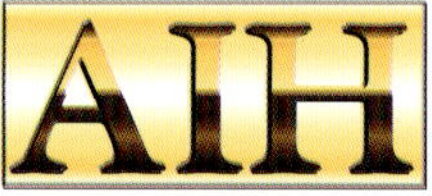

Maui, The Valley Isle

Maui is Hawaii's most popular neighbor island, visited by over one million visitors annually. Named the Valley Isle because it is formed by a verdant valley connecting two volcanoes, this double blessing creates Maui's varied geographical characteristics that exist closely in natural harmony. Haleakala, the largest volcano and an important experience for all visitors to Maui, has been dormant since the 1790s. Home to 100,000 residents on its 728 square miles, Maui epitomizes country living. Naturally, it attracts artists of all types whose souls respond to the clarity of light and free-form lifestyle.

Most visitors arrive on Maui at Kahului airport, located in central Maui. Destinations spread out like the spokes of a wheel from the Kahului hub so almost everyone passes through Kahului on their way to many other sights during their sojourn on Maui.

For the visitor, the first stop is near the airport — the recently unveiled Maui Arts & Cultural Center, a $28 million facility funded by the state, the county, the National Endowment for the Arts, and private sector donations. It was built to serve the entire community with a state-of-the art 1,200-seat main theater, 300-seat studio theater, a 4,100-square-foot visual arts gallery, adjoining classrooms and performing art studios, outdoor amphitheater that accommodates 4,000, and a community hall/rehearsal space. There is also a Pa Hula, a rock-faced hula mound that is traditionally reserved for the practice of native Hawaiian art and culture. This is the only Pa Hula on the island of Maui in recent history.

With a list of facilities like that, you can be sure something is always going on. The local newspaper lists the current programs, including plays, music and dance performances, art exhibitions, and cultural demonstrations such as Obun dancing, Kodo drums, and tea ceremonies, all of which typify the melting-pot population of the Hawaiian islands.

If you're a visitor headed over to the West Maui resorts of Kapalua and Kaanapali, you can return to Kaahumanu Avenue and drive up through Wailuku on your way. It is a quaint town of older homes and narrow streets that serves as the county seat. Nestled among the antique stores and clothing boutiques is the ***Olde Wailuku Gallery*** at No. 28. A mellow little spot, the paintings, prints, and sculptures each reflect a true Maui style and attitude. The informal setting invites browsing among the collection of artists that are just coming into their own. There is a nice cross section of traditional realists who are all residents of Maui and who paint *au plein air*.

Stroll the length of Market Street and enjoy an eclectic assortment of stores, mom-and-pop travel agencies, a bowling alley that was lost in a time warp for thirty or forty years, a tuxedo rental shop, the historic Iao Theater (which still functions as a performance space, albeit in need of some tender loving care), and a nice sampling of inexpensive restaurants for lunch and dinner. Wailuku is the Hawaii of yesteryear — you'll be nostalgic for its slower and gentler ways.

Two blocks away on Central Avenue is ***Elan Vital's*** studio. Look for his rustic house-cum-studio on the right side of the street. Guests need to call ahead for an appointment, or can view his finished works at ***Addi Gallery*** in Lahaina. Elan has created "metarealistic" visions of liquid colors flowing across a slick, shiny surface. He back lights them much the way a projector lights film and the abstract shapes of gem-like colors fairly dance on the canvas. This is a highly creative blend of several cutting edge technologies crafted into visionary works of art.

Just up from Wailuku, the Iao Needle is a natural rock formation in a lushly verdant gorge that is worth visiting if the sun is shining in the mountains! If the mountains are shrouded in mist, return another day.

The most important area of art in Hawaii is the historic whaling port of Lahaina. This charming town was once the state capital and certainly the favorite spot of many of Hawaii's royal family. Now it is the thriving center of the art scene on Maui. In fact, cognoscenti claim it to be the fourth largest art market in the United States. The main street is literally lined with galleries and a slew of some of the most famous restaurants in the world.

On Dickenson Street, near the museum home of missionary Dwight Baldwin, the unpretentious original location of ***Village Galleries*** is still Maui's premier address for island artists of integrity and vision. Established in 1970 by Lynn Shue, it is the oldest gallery on Maui, and has expanded in recent years to locations in the Lahaina Cannery and The Ritz-Carlton, Kapalua.

George Allan has been with Lynn Shue since the beginning, and his smooth style has garnered him many accolades. His series of koi fish in serene green ponds and wildly colorful bougainvillea are trademarks, but he captures all subjects with warmth and skill. ***Betty Hay Freeland*** is another Village Galleries treasure, more impressionistic than George in style, yet equally fond of local vistas. ***Margaret Bedell*** hails from Southern California but has been visiting her Maui home for over thirty years. Her embossed and hand-enhanced engravings of flowers and leaves become three-dimensional in their substance and texture. Her works are also on exhibit at Village Galleries in Lahaina.

Across from the seawall (which is an ocean-front promenade dating from the late 1800s) and down the block on Front Street is ***Lahaina Galleries,*** home to an array of locally and internationally acclaimed Maui and mainland artists.

Loren Adams is perhaps the most collectible artist to be found here, long known for seascapes of haunting beauty. Also a brilliant musician, Loren's other interests in theology, history and social issues weave a strong influence into his Classic Surrealistic images. He is currently creating an Accelerated Evolution Series that brings wildly disparate ages of time into a single frame and seems to catapult us into another dimension. Also exhibiting is ***Bruce Turnbull***, Maui's pre-eminent sculptor. Working in wood and bronze, he captures the flight of an eagle or the flow of a dolphin in form and spirit. Bruce has also created several large bronzes for public spaces, such as the beachfront lawns of the Hyatt Regency Maui.

Lahaina deserves a lingering look - be sure to

head in on Friday night for Art Night. Held every Friday as the sun goes down, the galleries join in a whirl of delightful festivities including exhibition openings, artists in residence, strolling musicians, and various other fun. It's a great excuse to stop in each and every gallery to see what is going on. Partake in some good cheer and hopefully you will purchase some art!

The triumvirate of painters in the Maui-born genre of underwater scenes have spaces on Front Street. Robert Lyn Nelson is in the forefront of the Two-Worlds look at Maui sea life/street life, and his airy gallery at the corner of Lahainaluna and Front Street features a full spectrum of his paintings and prints. ***Wyland,*** best known for his 100 whaling walls (see Oahu) has four galleries on Maui, three in Lahaina and one in Whaler's Village, that include works by other ecologically-minded artists who love the sea and its denizens. In addition, Christian Reese Lassen has several ***Gallerie Lassen*** from one end of Front Street to the other, each one a state-of-the-art multimedia showcase for his internationally marketed images of superslick sea life.

In the heart of Lahaina, the art scene beats beside the harbor in a historic building that was once the courthouse. Under the swooping arms of the world's largest banyan tree, the Lahaina Arts Society is an artists' collective established in 1965 that has nurtured and displayed the works of Maui's up and coming as they ply their talent and wait for much-deserved recognition. Under the tree, an open-air arts and craft fair is host on Saturdays to a variety of artists who put up a table and mingle with the crowds. In addition, the artists conduct workshops and classes for children and adults year-round and most sit in attendance at their exhibitions and those of their colleagues.

Bruce Turnbull in the Sculpture Garden

The ***Old Jail Gallery*** is their commercial space, but it's the least commercial gallery you'll find and a perfect place to cool off. The subterranean former jail is made of white painted stones and the old, barred cells are mini-galleries within the gallery.

Further north beyond the bustling Kaanapali resort, Kapalua is a casually elegant community that is fast becoming an art colony. Home to two of the finest hotels in Hawaii, this 1,500-acre resort also boasts The Art School. The Art School at Kapalua is a non-profit organization that was founded in memory of Sandra Buffet, a long-time resident of the community who believed in the power of art. The school is located in an historic area of Kapalua that was once a center of camp life that will open its doors for classes, programs and workshops in visual and performing arts. All ages and levels of experience will benefit from a broad curriculum taught by professional staff and visiting artists.

Kapalua Bay Hotel is the grand dame, reigning over Kapalua Bay's pristine waters since 1978. Gracing the sweeping lobby and public spaces are the glorious paintings of ***Jan Kasprzycki***, Maui's most exuberant painter. Huge canvases vibrate with color and energy even though the subject matter is usually native plants and flowers.

The new Ritz-Carlton, Kapalua is emerging as a center for cultural and artistic exploration. Early in spring, usually around Easter, the annual Celebration of the Arts takes place. This festival encourages all to share in the creative spirit and aloha of the Hawaiian culture. In a blend of traditional and contemporary Hawaiian elements, workshops in painting, ceramics, basket weaving, quilting, woodcarving, ti leaf art, tapa making and Hawaiian music are scheduled over four days.

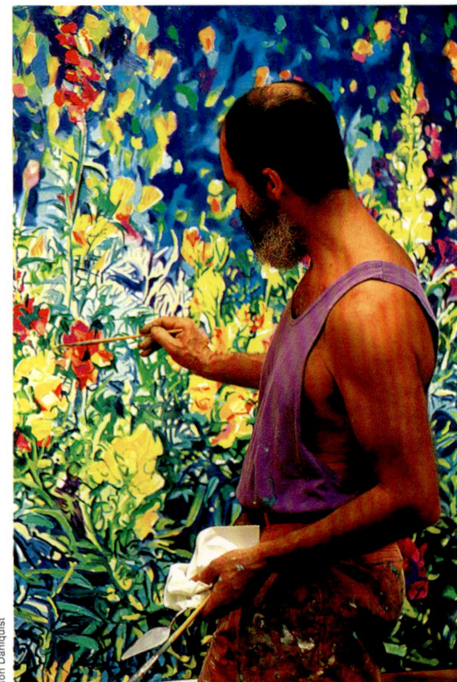

© Ron Dahlquist

Jan Kasprzycki

Later in the summer, the Rainbow Within You is a weekend of art and music co-sponsored by Hawaiian musician Henry Kapono, The Nature Conservancy and The Village Galleries. Celebrating the children and art of our multi-cultural islands, its goal is to raise the awareness of Hawaii's endangered rain forests. (Kapalua's founder, the late Colin C. Cameron, has dedicated a 28,000-acre rain forest in the West Maui Mountains above Kapalua as a preserve in perpetuity.) The event includes a hands-on art and music fair, Hawaii children's art exhibit showcasing winning entries from a state-wide contest, and an oceanside family concert by the acclaimed slack-key guitarist, Henry Kapono.

The Ritz-Carlton commitment to art is year-round, with an ongoing artist-in-residence program featuring Maui artists in informal settings conducting workshops and discussing methods and media. In fact, this is the only Ritz-Carlton to feature local artwork in their guest rooms and public areas in addition to the traditional Old Masters style of artwork found in all other Ritz-Carltons.

Beyond Kapalua is a wonderfully twisting road that goes to the tiny hamlet of Kahakuloa, a trip that is reminiscent of the road to Hana, but not as demanding. There's a blow hole, menehune statues, and cattle grazing on the dramatic cliffs that some say resemble Ireland.

You can continue around the island that way if you like and eventually arrive in Wailuku. If you do continue, you can visit ***Bruce Turnbull's*** sculpture garden. Bruce resides on the undeveloped back side of West Maui past Kahakuloa and has his workshop, sculpture garden, and home-turned-gallery on a beautiful spot high above the ocean. Give him a call!

A sunrise trip to Haleakala is a must. Be sure to stop at the intriguing town of Makawao on your way down the mountain. Once considered a cowboy hangout and nothing more, the town today is a charming blend of sophistication and genteel shabbiness. Hard to define, easy to love.

The pulse of the art scene in Makawao can be taken at ***Viewpoints Gallery***, the centerpiece of a courtyard filled with shops and a deli cafe that makes heaping sandwiches to consume under shady trees on the brick patio. Inside, Viewpoints is an artist-owned, artist-operated collective committed to free expression. Begun when watercolorist, ***Joelle Chicheportiche***, a huge influence in Lahaina Arts Society, spoke with painter Margaret Leach about bringing the same concept upcountry, it boasts the most impressive roster of Maui artists on the island. Bright and sparkling, the gallery offers you a chance to speak to the on-duty artists about their own art or the art of their colleagues – from an insider's viewpoint.

A painter's painter, ***Tony Walholm*** speaks to the viewer in abstract dialogue. He covers large surfaces with fast strokes of subtly metallic hues that reveal strength of composition with inherent structure that seems structureless. On the other end of the spectrum, Honolulu-born ***Douglas Chun***, a long-time architectural illustrator in California, retired here and now captures the landscapes of Maui with incredible detail and understanding of the play of light. Serene yet exhilarating, his watercolors display technical expertise beyond compare. Other artists of note include ***Terry McDonald*** and ***Peter & Madeline Powell***. Out back of Viewpoints is a glassblowing studio, transforming molten glass into shapes of flowing beauty by blowing through a gently spinning rod. Across the street is David Warren's studio, housed in a mini-cottage painted white and green. David's work has been on the Maui scene since the '70s and he is most noted for his swirling monoprints and etchings of figures caught in the movement of dance.

Mosey up the street and right next to the unexpected grove of whispering bamboo is the new state-of-the-art workshop/studio of designer/goldsmith, ***David Sacco***. David's extraordinary fine art jewelry is hand made from precious metals with gem and designer stones, often with screws and hinges as design elements. He'll work with you to customize your fantasy or you can choose from his one-of-a-kind finished pieces right there in the shop.

By now, you'll have felt the esprit de corps that permeates the atmosphere. Those who live in Upcountry feel they have the answer to life and that feeling is even more pronounced in the artist community. Couple that with the current trend of artists towards self-representation, and serious admirers can be privy to personal showings (by appointment) in many Maui studios. David Warren was a frontrunner of this trend. ***Jan Kasprzycki***, ***Tom Faught***, and ***Loren Adams*** have perfected it.

You'll remember Jan is the artist in the Kapalua Bay Hotel. He also hangs his works at several island restaurants, Mama's Fish House, David Paul's Lahaina Grill, SeaWatch in Wailea, and more. Once his art has spoken to you, you'll need to speak to Jan, who will ask you up to the very top of Olinda Road for a visit. The incredible vista as you step out of the car, the lofty workshop, and lush grounds will inspire you as they have inspired Jan for these many years.

His good friend Tom Faught is a sculptor who has the largest kiln in Hawaii for firing the enormous ceramic urns and vases he's famous for. Most are taller than he is. He also casts in metal and combinations of the two. A visit to his studio is an eye-opening experience.

Head down towards the ocean on Baldwin Avenue and you'll happen upon ***Hui Noeau Visual Arts Center***, the leading multi-disciplinary visual resource and art education center on Maui. The twelve acre historic estate was built in 1917 for Harry and Ethel Baldwin. She and a small group of friends formed the Hui in 1934. The current center was opened in 1976. With workshops, classes, lectures, and open studios, it is perhaps best known as the home of Art Maui, the extremely controversial show that is Maui's only juried exhibition and a true mark of distinction for the chosen entries.

Spilling out onto Hana Highway, on the corner of Baldwin and Hana Highway, ***Maui Sculpture Gallery*** is devoted to metal, clay, stone, wood, glass etching, koa furniture, and other forms of sculpture. Randy Joseph carves on site and there's even an abstract ceramic fountain by Piero Resta.

Across the street, ***Hana Hou Gallery*** is located at 65 Hana Highway in the Art & Antique Center, half hidden behind a gas station turned real estate office. A home-grown gallery run by a former "top cat" in the commercial art scene of Lahaina, you'll find works of integrity by as yet undiscovered artists mixed with pieces by established artists in an unpretentious setting. From the doorway, your eye is immediately drawn to an oil painting by ***Lisa Kasprzycki,*** Jan's daughter, whose expressive paintings draw their power from their softness.

There's a wall of juicy pen and ink drawings by ***Kirsten Bunney***. Absolutely refreshing in their whimsy, the images are gradually woven together with under and over layers of watercolor and fine cross-hatching to produce a rich tapestry of organic form and dream imagery. The Australian-born artist is contemporary in style and tropical in feeling, having lived in Bali prior to moving to Maui. American Savings Bank has chosen Kirsten as their 1995 calendar artist, joining the ranks of such renowned artists as Pegge Hopper, Susan MacGovney Hansen, and James Hoyle.

Down from Makawao is Paia, home to the ***Maui Craft Guild,*** the third in the triple crown of artists' collectives on Maui. Serious basketry, silk painting, jewelry, ceramics, wood carving, and the like are on display in this, Paia's first gallery.

On the other side of the island in Wailea, visit the ***Coast Gallery*** in the Hotel Inter-Continental. Director Sabrina Davis has created a gallery featuring local artists, similar to the Village Galleries on the other side of the island. ***George Allan***, ***Margaret Bedell***, ***Mary Faustine***, ***Betty Hay Freeland***, ***Mary Koski***, and ***Karen Bierce*** are among the artists on exhibit at the Inter-Continental gallery.

For those exploring the Kihei/Wailea area, the ***Na Pua Gallery*** at the Grand Wailea hotel tempts us with esoteric and traditional arts and crafts. Tony Walholm (from Viewpoints Gallery) hangs side by side with other cutting-edge Maui artists. Wailea is also home to an annual art festival, ***The Maui Marine Art Expo***, featuring over twenty mainland and island artists in paint, watercolor, ceramics, jewelry, sculpture, etchings, and more. Running from January through March, the show is in its second decade of prominence.

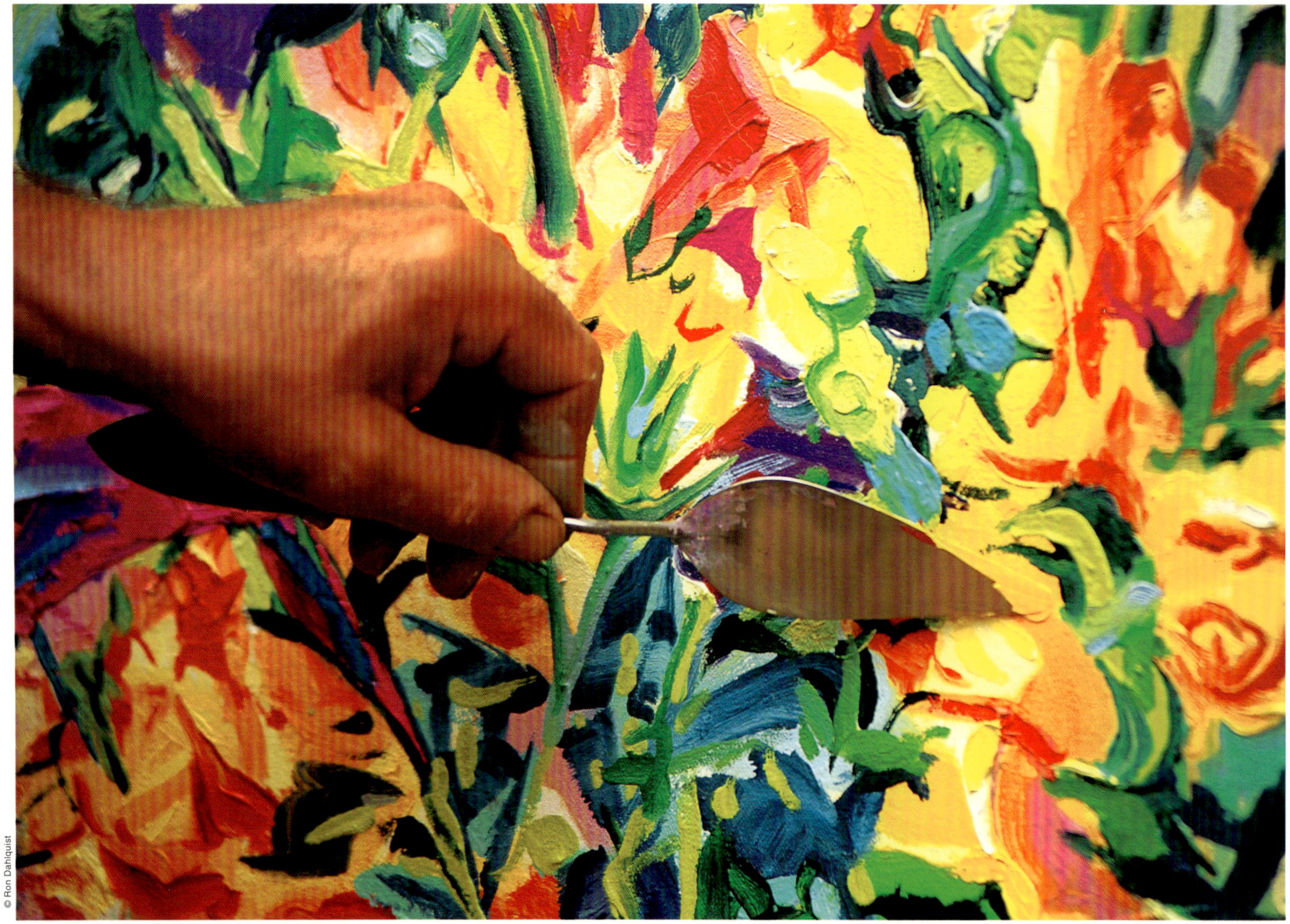

© Ron Dahlquist

The creative process is alive and well on Maui

Hana is a destination unto itself - this is Maui's most Hawaiian community, but if you have to ask "Is it worth the drive?" please don't go there. Over 300 curves make the two-hour thirty mile drive from Huelo a problem for the weak of heart or tummy, but the vision of other worldliness that spreads before you at the Seven Pools is sensational. ***The Coast Gallery*** has an outpost in the Hotel Hana Maui, where you'll find many of the same artists that hang in the ***Coast Gallery*** in the Wailea Inter-Continental Hotel, but with a reverence for the untouched Hana atmosphere.

Well, we've done it — completed an artistic adventure on an island in the middle of the Pacific. By the time we're ready to return, Maui will have spawned and inspired many more artists - another opportunity to explore it all over again!

– *By Loren Malencheck*

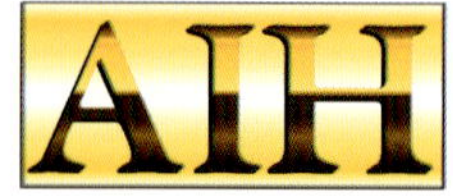

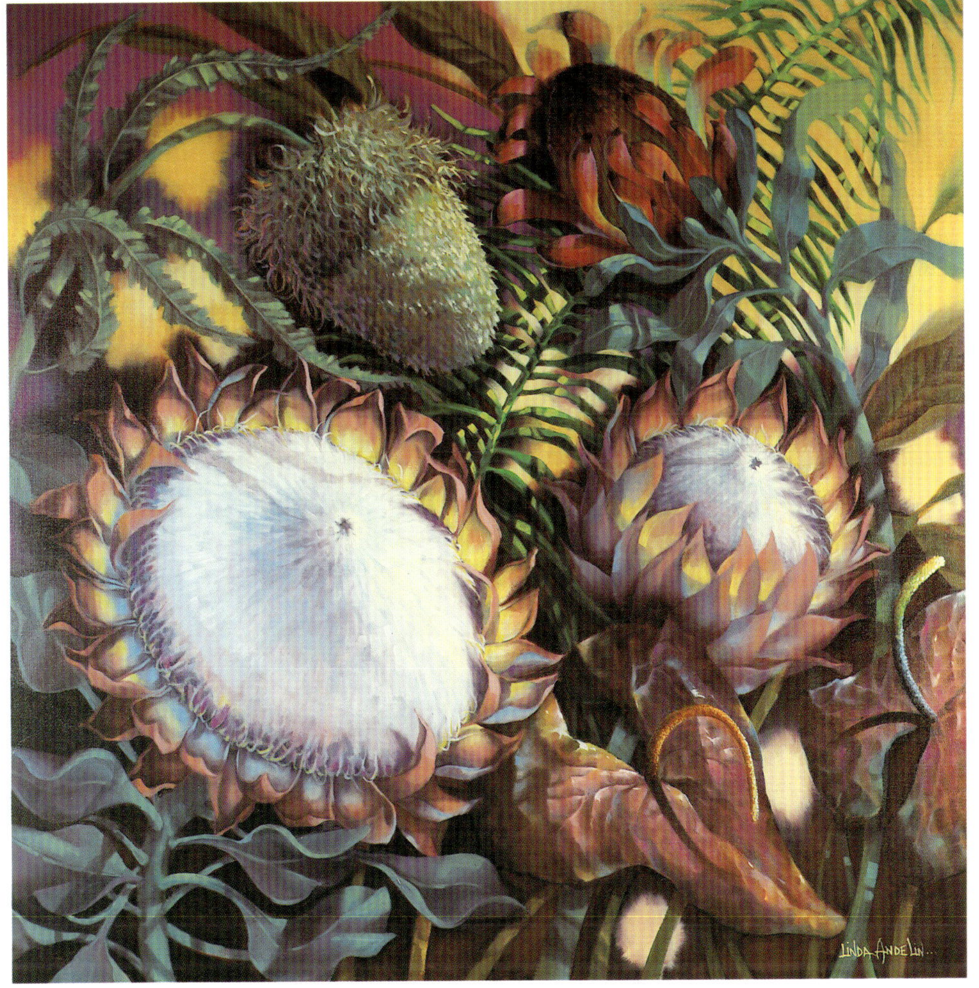

"Protea Passion"
Oil/Canvas 40 x 40

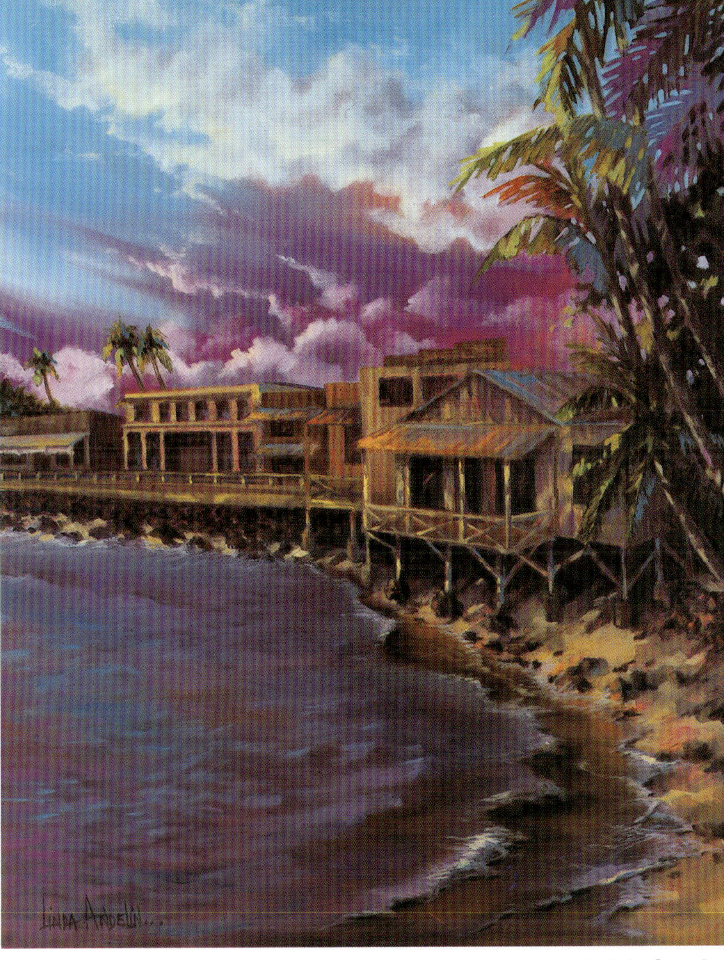

"Lahaina Sunset"
Oil/Canvas 30 x 40

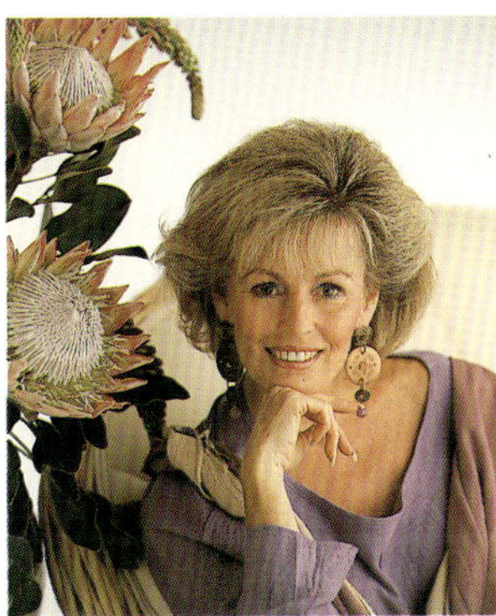

LINDA ANDELIN

Maui artist, Linda Andelin, born in Southern California, knew from the time she was a child that she wanted to be a painter. Her first achievement in the world of art was at age twelve, when her painting "The American Circus" was chosen to represent the United States on a world tour.

As her formal training began, she was drawn to Impressionists such as Cezanne, Gaugin and Monet. Linda received her initial education at Brigham Young University and

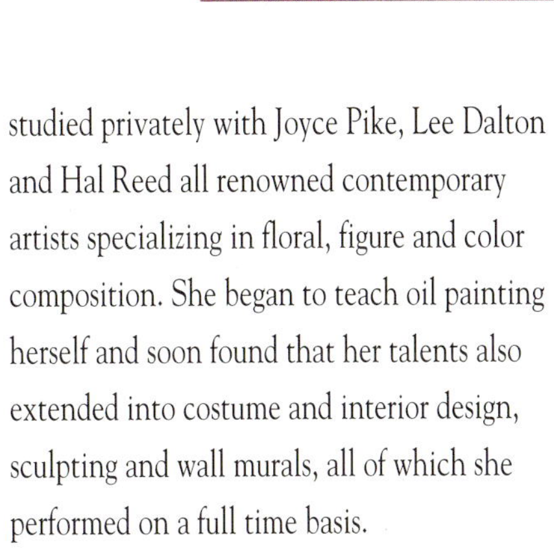

studied privately with Joyce Pike, Lee Dalton and Hal Reed all renowned contemporary artists specializing in floral, figure and color composition. She began to teach oil painting herself and soon found that her talents also extended into costume and interior design, sculpting and wall murals, all of which she performed on a full time basis.

Linda creates paintings glowing with warmth and vibrancy, highlighting the play of light and color. Linda is a member of the new generation of realists. Her style is uniquely her own. Her command of color allows her to capture the world in soothing, yet vibrant and daring combinations. Her works have been exhibited throughout the United States, England and Mexico, and may be seen at the ROYAL ART GALLERY, Maui, Hawaii.

The Royal Art Gallery
752 Front Street
Lahaina, Maui, HI 96761
(808) 667-1982
(800) 367-6925
FAX (808) 661-5198

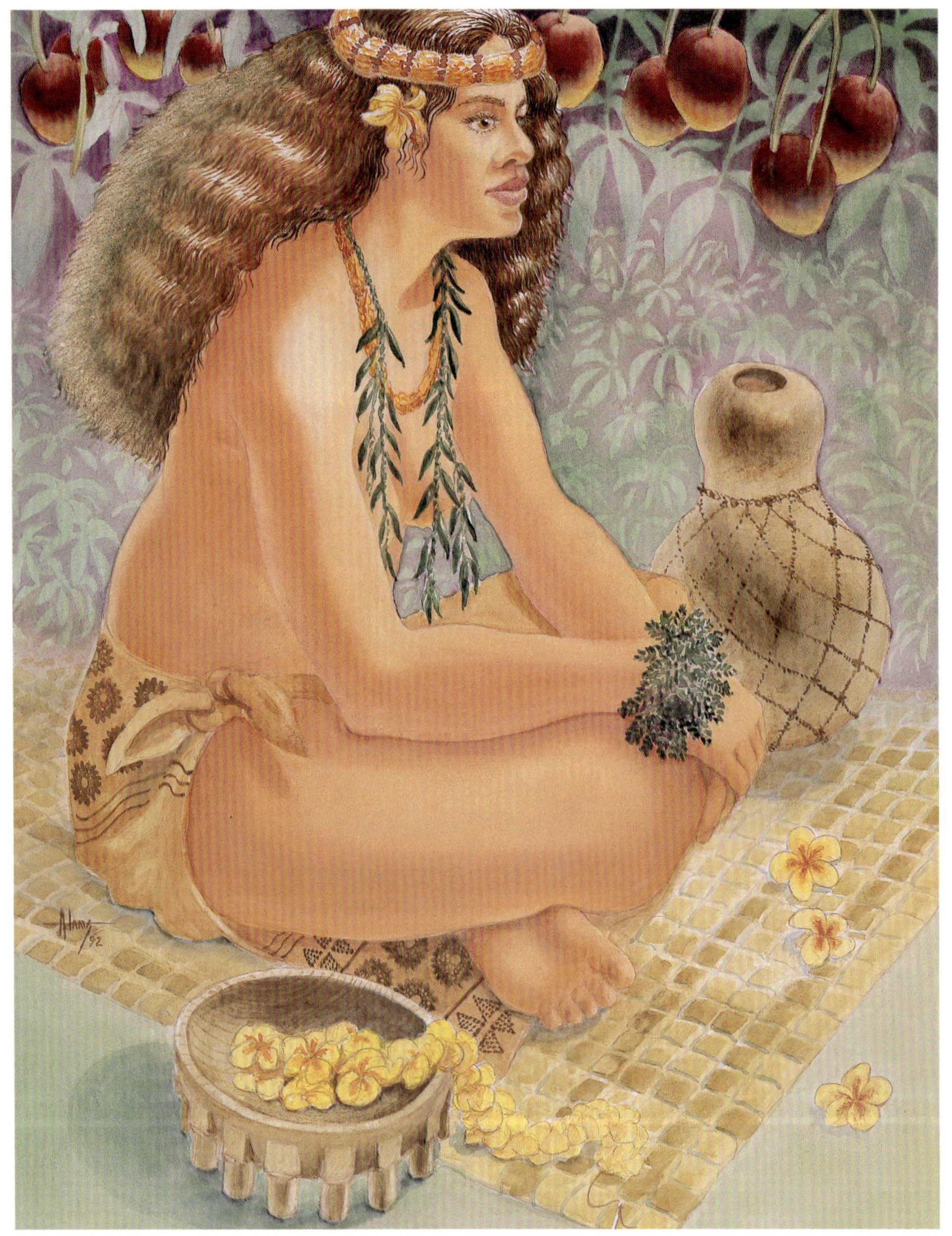

"Ripe Mango" 18" x 24"
Limited Edition Print

The design work of Jack Adams has been well known since he established his own interior design firm in Honolulu in 1976. Adams Design is listed in "Who's Who" as one of the top 100 interior design firms in the nation and is known for imaginative and dramatic work in both commercial and residential spaces.
Through Adams' years as a designer he has kept his art alive, and is now able to bring it to the forefront.

Adams' painting reflects his more personal side, and is represented in his watercolors of historic architecture in Hawaii as well as in his mixed media paintings. In early 1992, Robyn Buntin Galleries in Honolulu presented Adam's show, "Nudes: Fantasies and Realities". This consisted of 40 works on paper and 3 pieces of sculpture. In 1994, he was featured in a one man show at Ramsey's Gallery. Some of the works on paper are done in classical drawing form, with sepia and conte, and others are carried forward from the drawings with watercolor or acrylic.

All of Adams' works are studio drawings, done with live models. He has been greatly influenced by Japanese art from the 1920's art deco period, Japanese woodblock prints and the French printmaker, Paul Jacoulet, who combined European and Japanese influences. "I'm very much inspired by the blend of Eastern and Western culture in art".

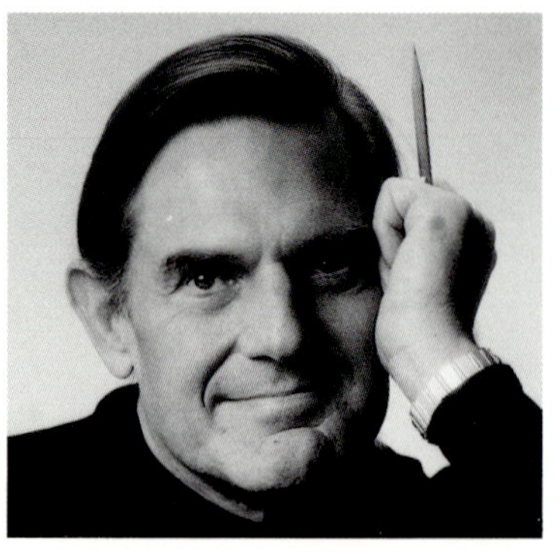

JACK ADAMS
1415 Kalakaua Avenue, Room 204
Honolulu, Oahu, HI 96826
(808) 955-6100
FAX (808) 947-4311

JACK ADAMS

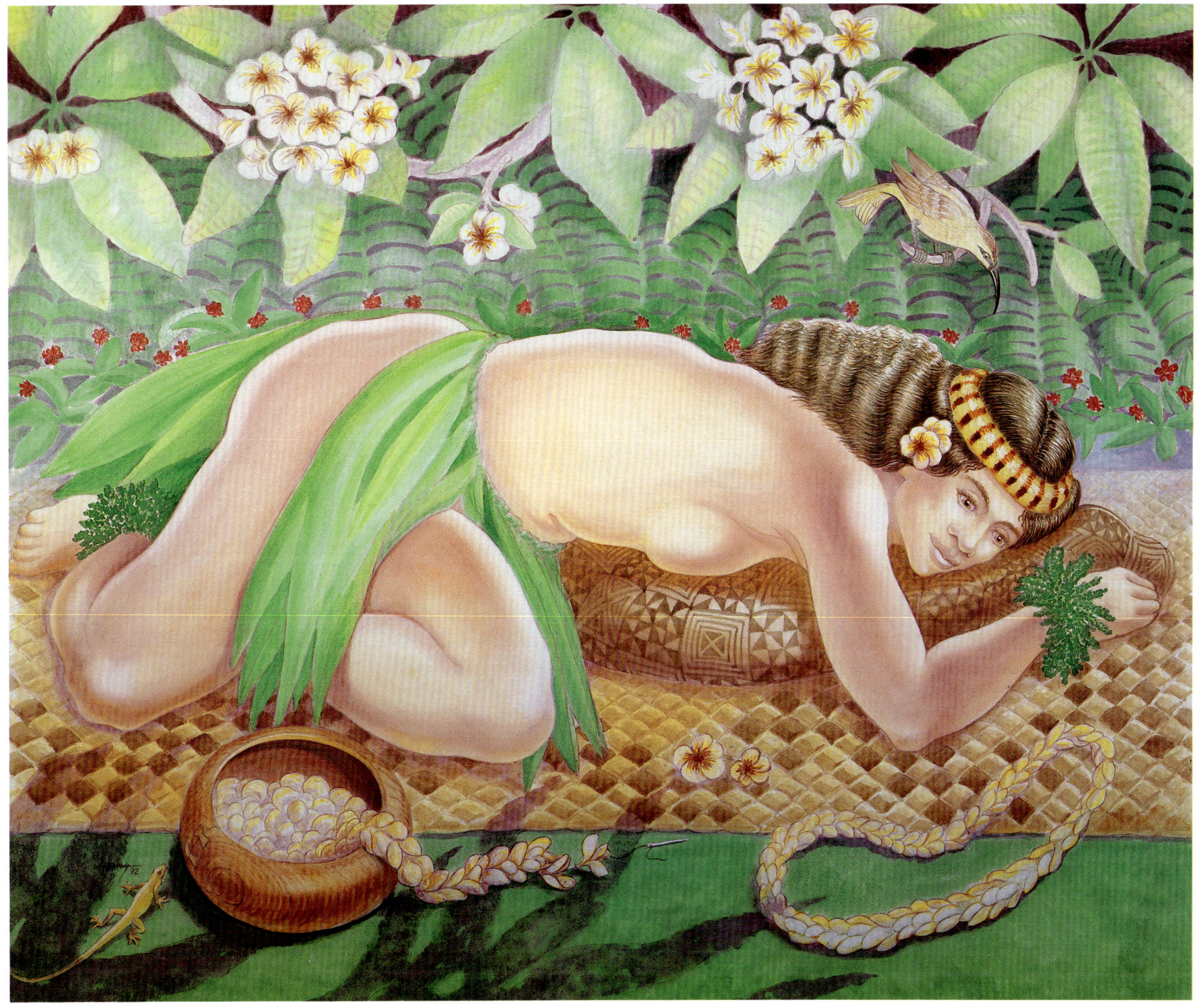

"Aki Aloa" 18" x 24" Limited Edition Print

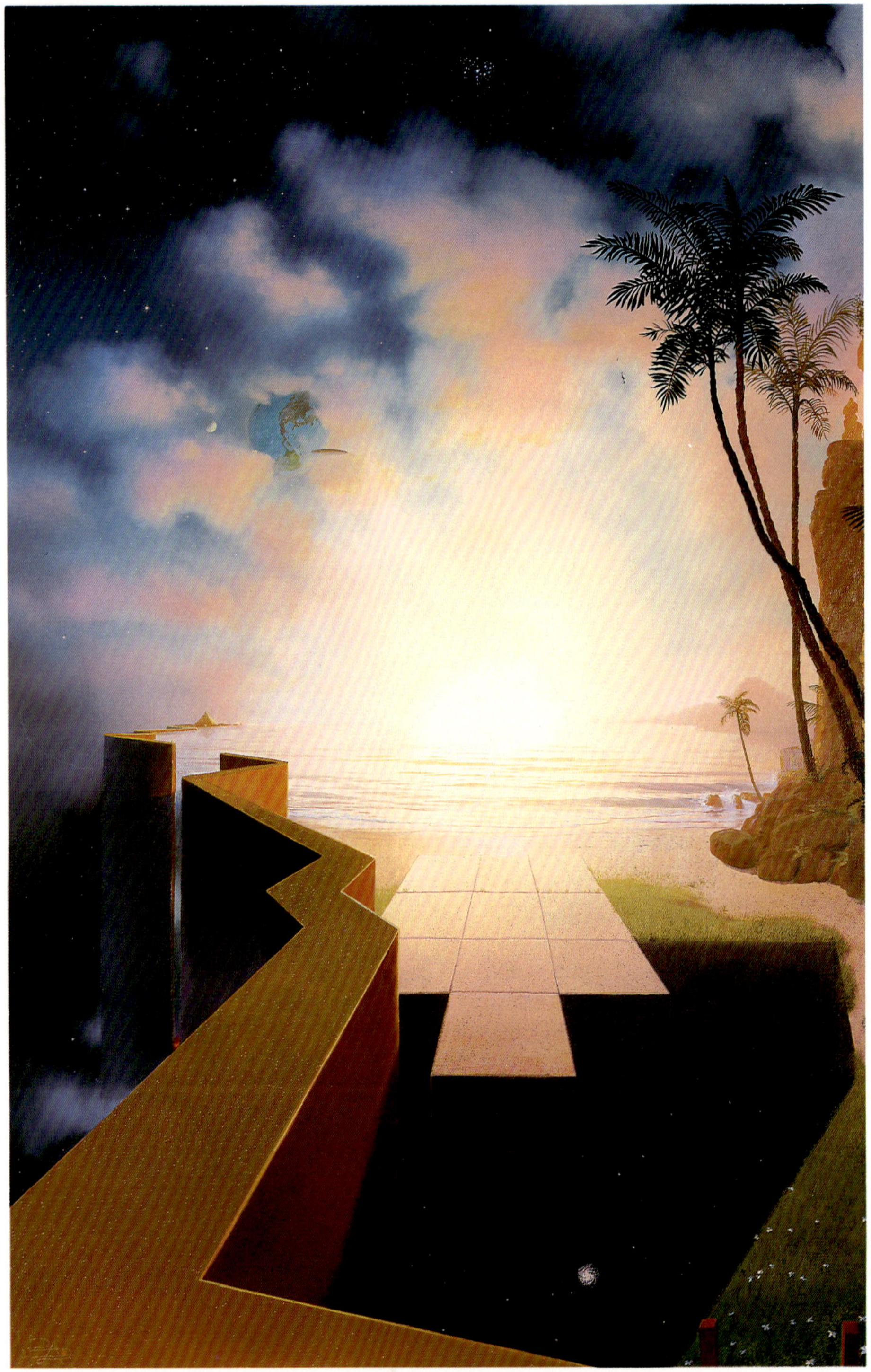

"Terra Incognita" 24" x 36" Original Oil Painting and Cibachrome®- Limited Edition Prints S/N 150

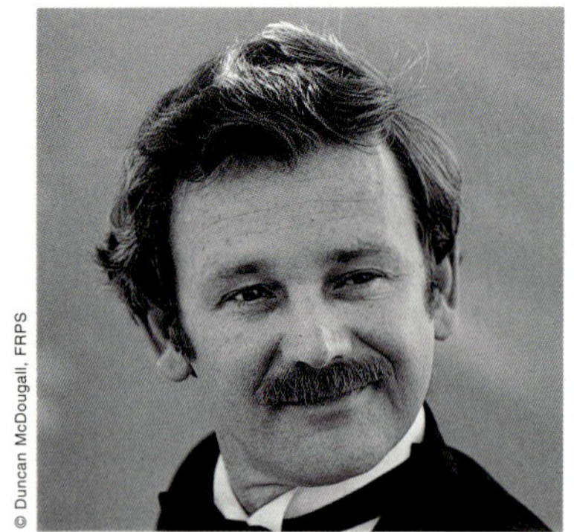

LOREN D. ADAMS

The Dream Awake…

A brief look at one of his paintings will reveal that Loren D. Adams, Jr. is a deep and perceptive human being. His interests, aside from painting, cover theology, music and fine art identification. He is versed in the 20th century masters and is involved in two think tanks that ponder various social issues.

Adams is an artist who pays attention. He is a lover of the natural world and approaches painting with a reverence for light, color and detail, dependably portraying nature at her finest. To varying degrees, the sea or a significant body of water is ever-present in each of his works. Waves with a delicate translucence move through mystical oceans. Light is used to create rapturous moments as Adams deftly orchestrates majestic dreams and visions.

Looking through the R.W. Norton retrospective collection of Adams' work, it is obvious he reached a level of technical excellence that left him nowhere to go but "through". By the early 1980's, his art entered a new dimension with the "Accelerated Evolution Series". Adams took a step from a grand and magnificent realism into a world that seems to exist just slightly beyond our normal perception. He calls this artistic genre "Classic Surrealism".

The "Accelerated Evolution" works are filled with symbolism from all ages, revealing the artist's own fascination with archeology and ancient cultures, religions and sacred writings. Many of his images seem to be generated from a dimension very close to our daily reality; elements of the pictures are easily recognizable and make one feel at home, although there is a vague sense that we are witnessing something extraordinary. "The Augmented Sea…" and "Telos Mu" are classic examples of this particular phenomenon.

The largest work in his Accelerated Evolution Series is the "Crystal Cave", a new form of stabile. It is a large, multi-dimensional, free-standing art object, hand carved from wood panels, then gold-leafed and painted on the surface. It depicts the last perfect day of mid-summer in Mu, the Motherland - the day the mountains were raised. When completed, the stabile will incorporate laser beams, crystals and electronic equipment.

Opposite Page:
"The Augmented Sea, Garden of Eden, the Motherland"
48" x 36" Original Oil Painting and 40" x 30" Cibachrome®- Limited Edition Prints S/N 100

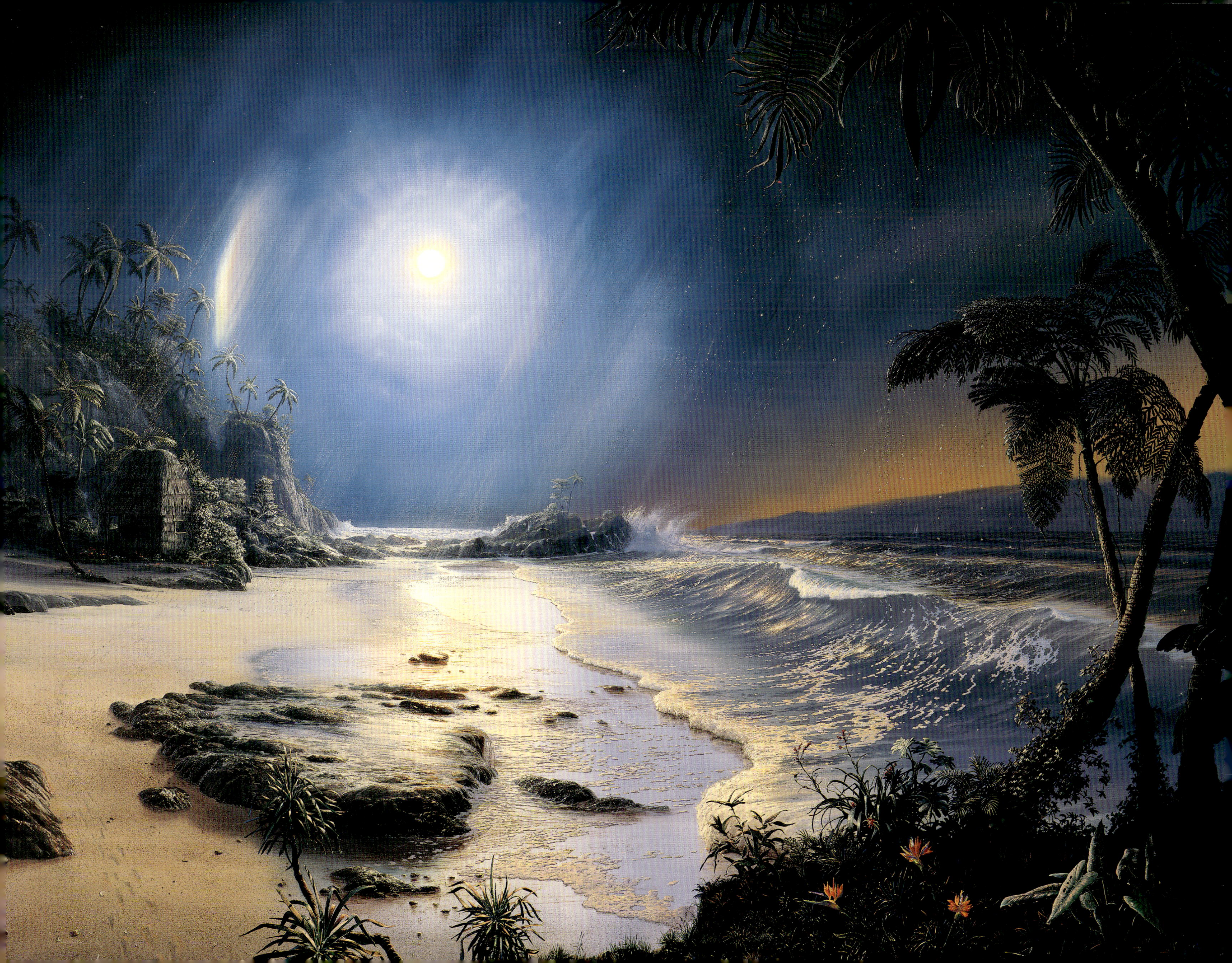

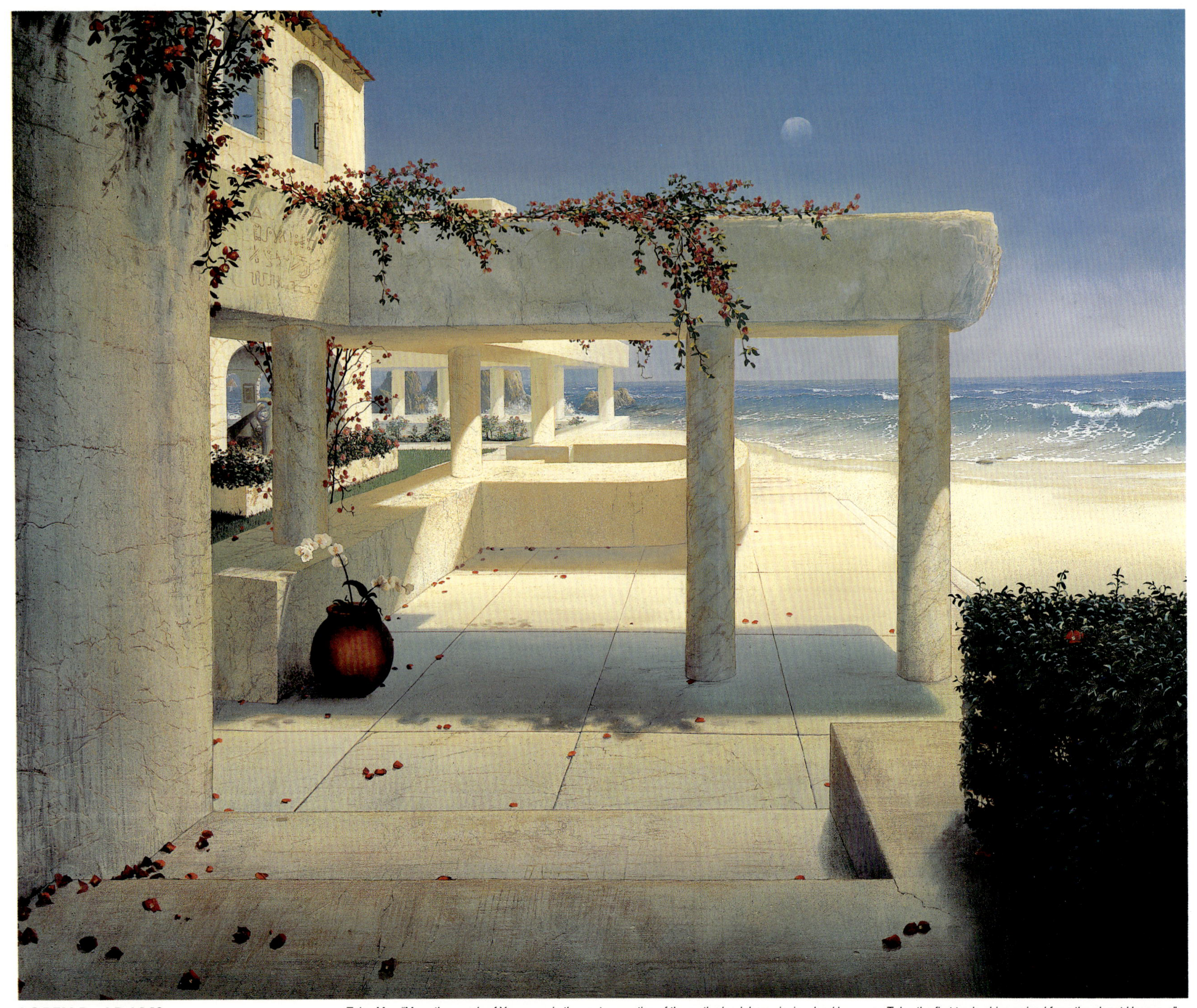

LOREN D. ADAMS

Telos Mu - "Many thousands of Years ago in the eastern section of the motherland, Lemuria, in a land known as Telos the first trade ships arrived from the planet Hesperus"
36" x 30" Original Oil Painting and Cibachrome® - Limited Edition Prints S/N 100

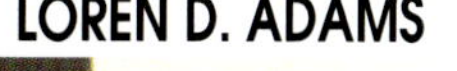

Adams is a very exacting painter who believes that "...a painting is only as beautiful as a single brush stroke". Planning his paintings meticulously, he sees them completed in his mind before he even lifts a brush. At times he feels as if he's only the instrument of a creative force painting through him. "I'm lucky enough to be the guy who holds the brush."

To illustrate his point Adams says, "...a painting is a song made visible - one sour note would spoil a symphony." In typical Adams style, the artist is an accomplished musician. He continually finds correlation between color and music and points out that each note on a musical scale vibrates at a frequency that corresponds with a color on the chromatic scale. In other words, each tone has its own color.

Adams synthesizes information from his various interests to provide inspiration and substance for his paintings. He is a pure artist, approaching each work with a curious combination of wisdom and child-like innocence.

To him, an artist has a right and a responsibility to paint what he feels, and he fiercely defends and upholds that right. He and his wife, Patty, spend considerable amounts of time researching statutes and laws that define and protect fine artists and their works.

"I think of my paintings as having a life separate from my own and a destiny independent from my own. I am pleased that quite a few museums have shown my works and several have purchased them. I think of the longevity of the art, and my collectors know that I think of the art as being held in sacred trust for the future. There is a responsibility attached to collecting Fine Art that is undeniable."

He views his works almost like they were his children, and is very reluctant to part with them. He feels that for someone to buy one of his paintings," ...they have to want it more than I do. My paintings are like spiritual children to me; my collectors don't acquire, they adopt".

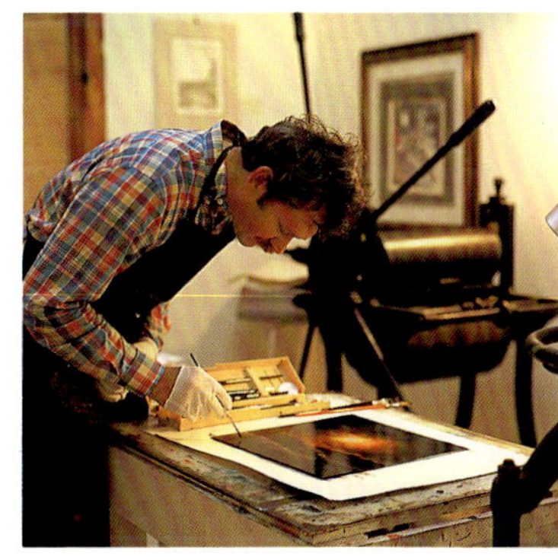

The limited editions that he does release are done in Cibachrome®, which is a highly accurate photographic process that yields full intensity of color and image, and is more colorfast than traditional print material. Loren embellishes each print with original handwork to elevate its status to a higher category and to meet his exacting standards.

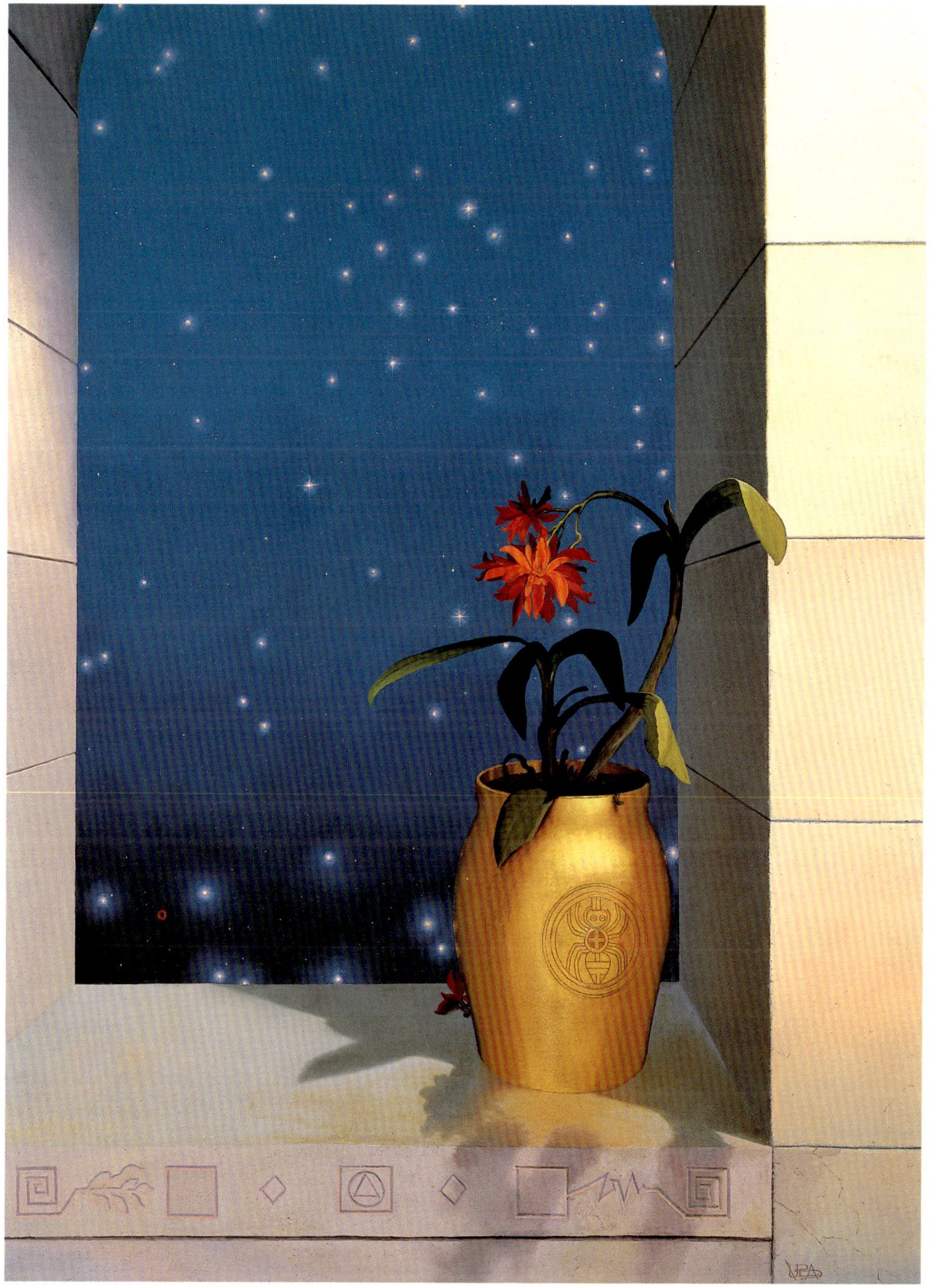

"The Return of the Lords of Light in Glory"
30" x 40" Original Oil Painting
and Cibachrome®- Limited Edition Prints S/N 150

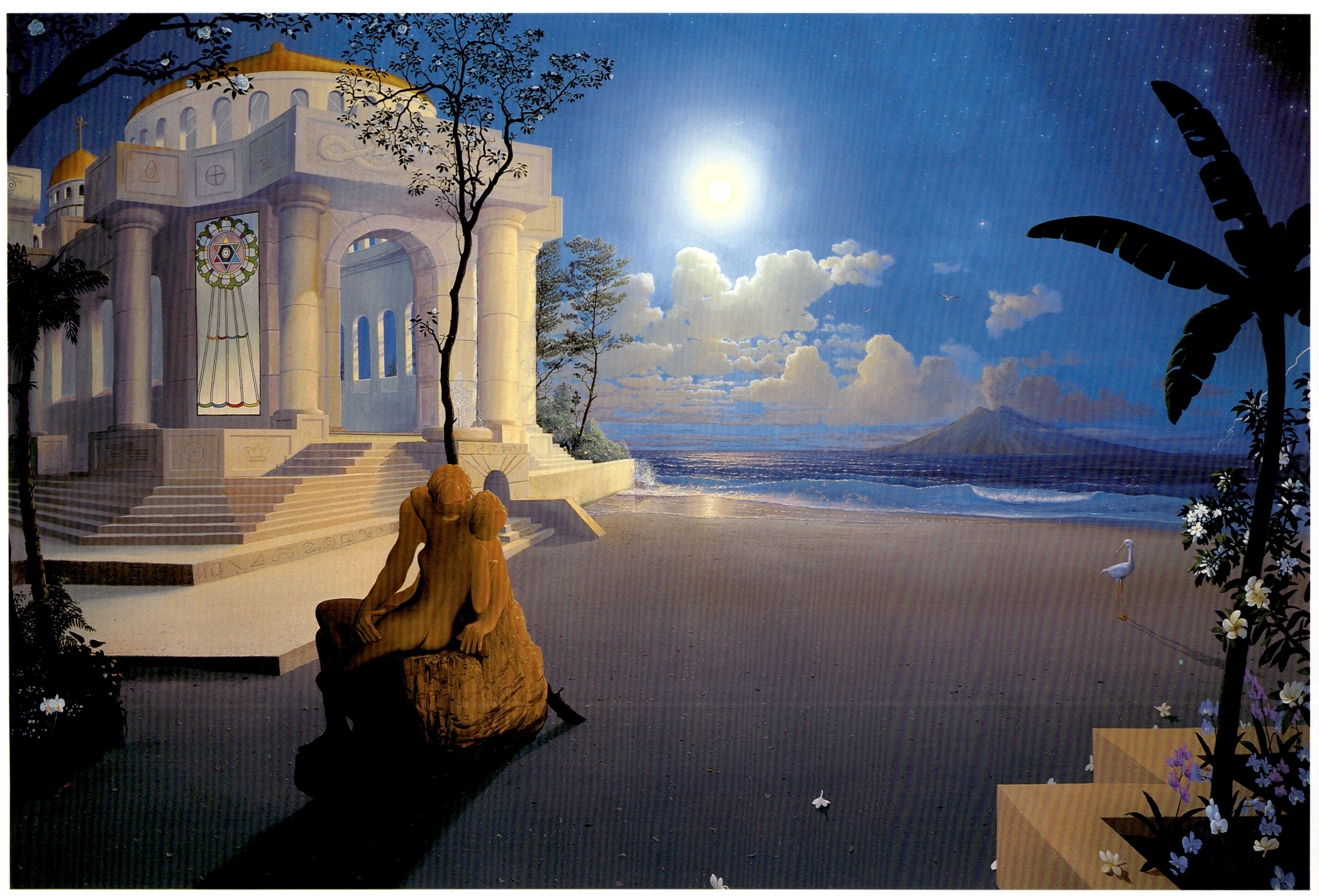

"Of Rhyme and Reason, Time and Season"
54" x 36" Original Oil Painting and 48" x 10" Cibachrome®- Limited Edition Prints S/N 100

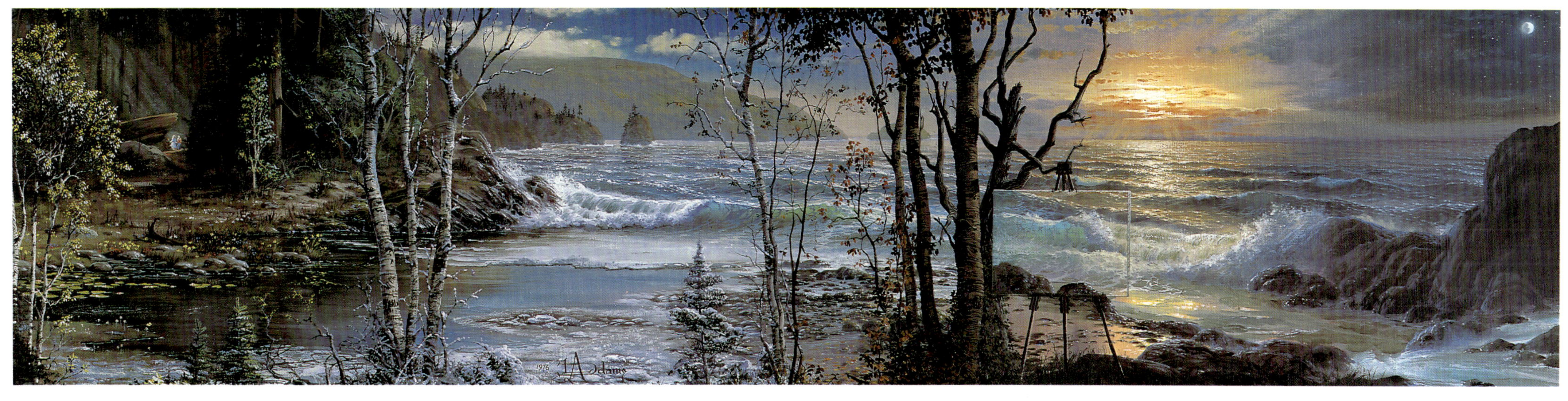

"Divine Right of Passage"
60" x 40" Original Oil Painting and 45" x 30" Cibachrome®- Limited Edition Prints S/N 150

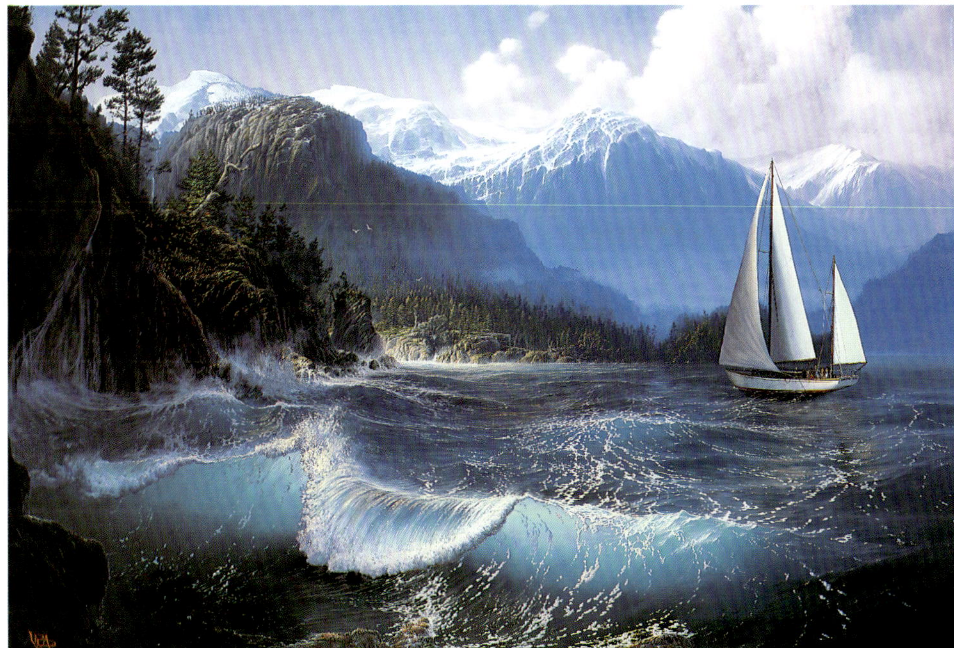

"Beside the Still Waters"
24" x 16" Original Oil Painting and 30" x 20" Cibachrome®- Limited Edition Prints S/N 100

Loren lists among his artistic influences the Old Masters and the Renaissance Masters - Raphael, Vermeer, Velazquez and Van Eycke and also Paul Klee, Vasarely, Aivazovsky, J.M.W. Turner; members of the Hudson River School, particularly Fredrich Church and Albert Bierdstadt; and finally the Surrealists, Salvador Dali, Magritte and Escher.

Having established his place in history, Loren Adams plans to continue expanding beyond the realm of paper and canvas to other mediums-

Opposite Page:
"The Naacal Temple of the Pristine Wilderness"
54" x 36" Original Oil Painting and 42" x 28" Cibachrome®- Limited Edition Prints S/N 150

LOREN D. ADAMS

"Madam Pele and the Rain Forest"
16" x 24" Original Oil Painting and Cibachrome® - Limited Edition Prints S/N 100

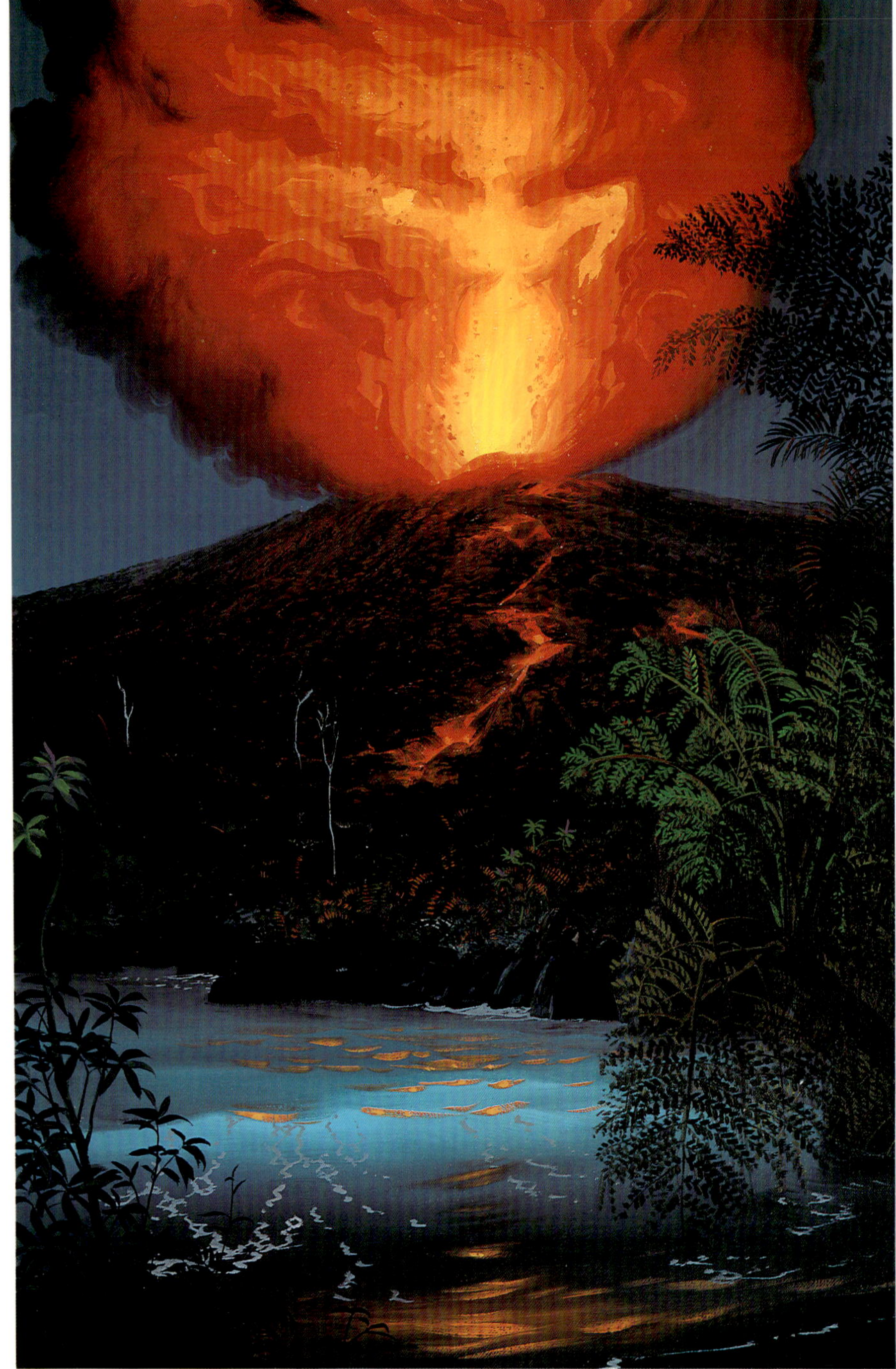

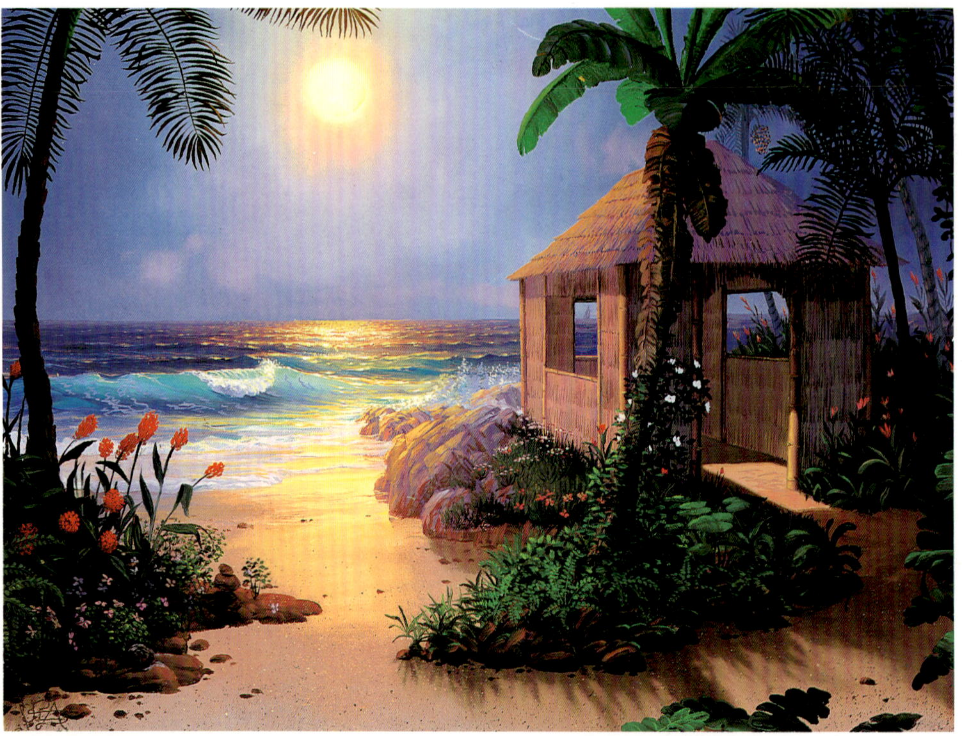

"Coming Home"
16" x 12" Original Oil Painting - Private Collection

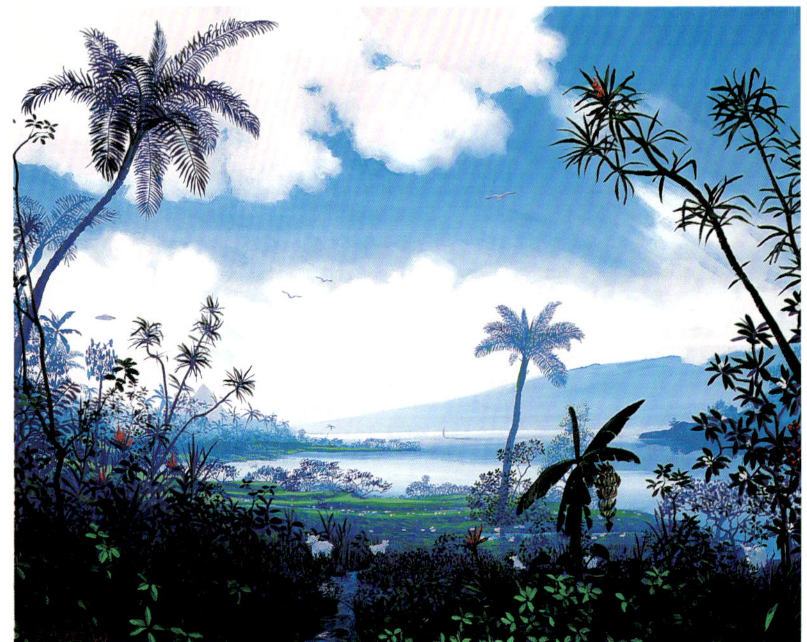

"Variations on Where Sheep May Safely Graze"

20" x 16"
Original Oil Painting -
Artist's Collection

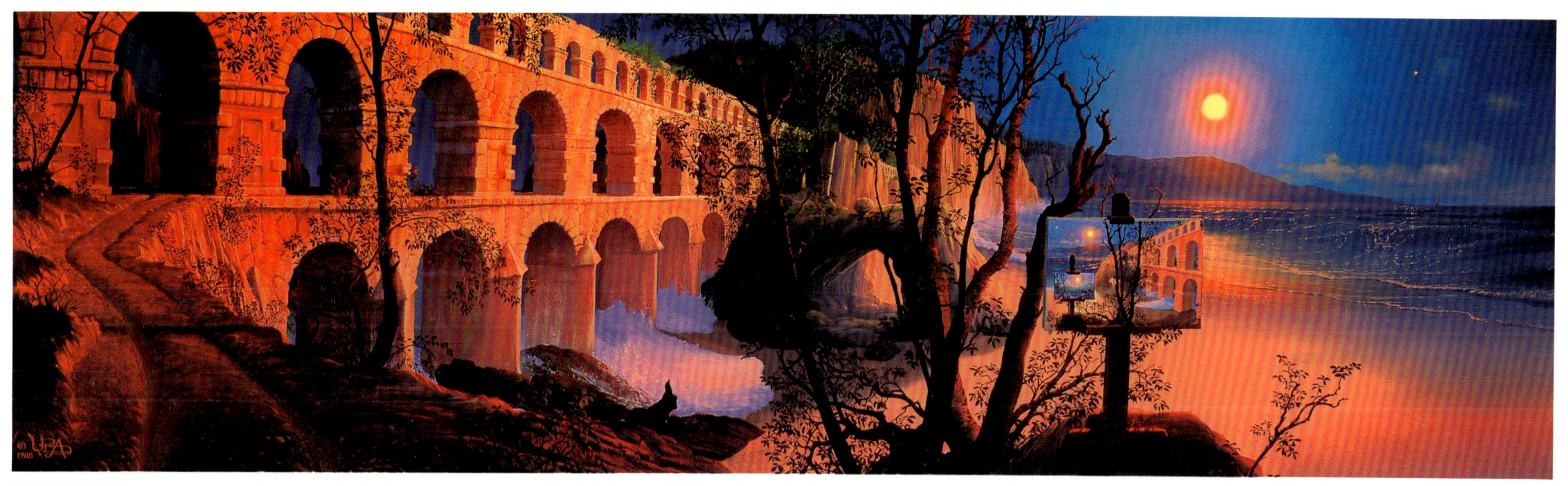

"La Mia Prerogitiva"
60" x 20" Original Oil Painting
and 45" x 14" Cibachrome®- Limited Edition Prints S/N 100

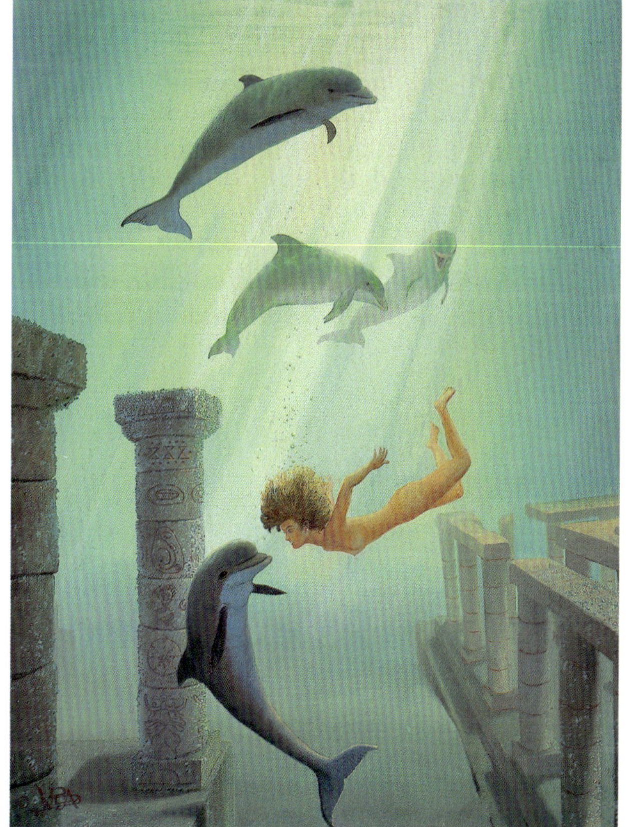

"The Story of Creation"
12" x 16" Original Oil Painting - Private Collection

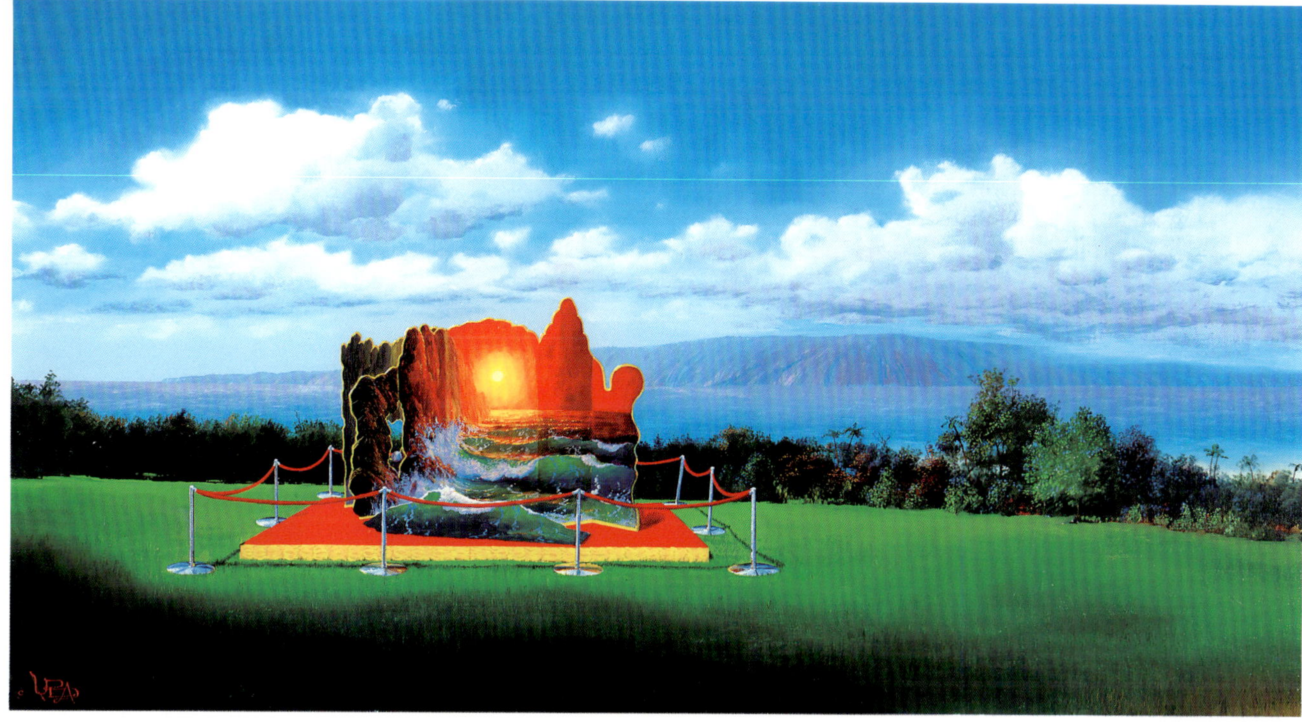

"Painting of the Loren D. Adams Stabile as seen on the Kapalua Golf Course, Overlooking Molokai"
24" x 16" Original Oil Painting

LOREN D. ADAMS

LOREN D. ADAMS

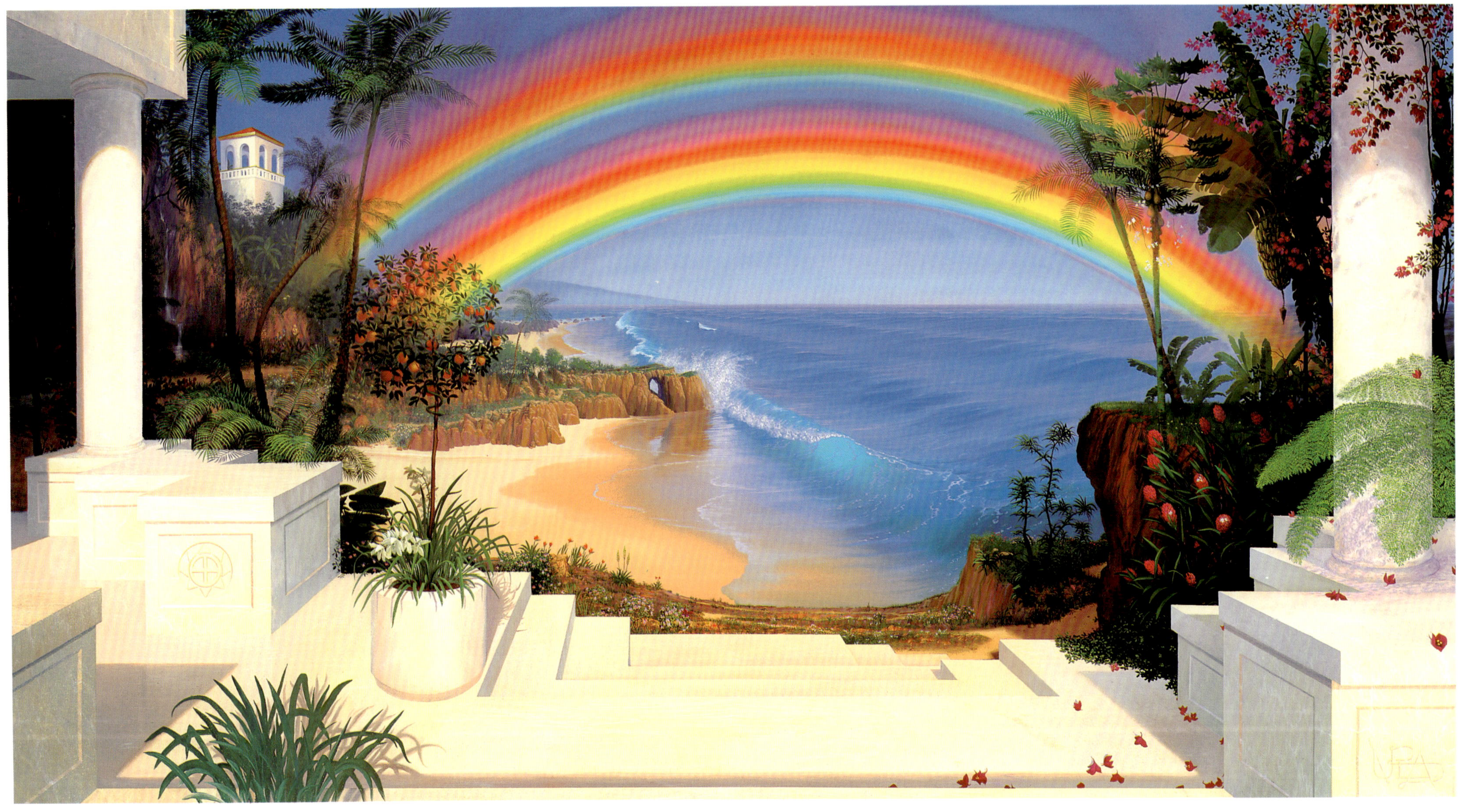

"The Lost Continent of Mu...
an Open Entrance to the Closed Palace
of the King and Queen"

76" x 42" Original Oil Painting

and 10 Full Size, 15 Half Size Cibachrome®

-75 Other Size & medium TBD - Limited Edition Prints S/N

silks, jewelry, tapestries, textiles, objets d'art. "You want to create something that is only found in that medium and nowhere else in nature - then it is art." To excel in all mediums? Why not? Because, as the artist says, "If you don't dream big, it damn for sure won't happen."

Adams' work has been the subject of numerous magazine articles and museum shows and is featured in some very notable private collections. Many awards and accolades have

LOREN D. ADAMS

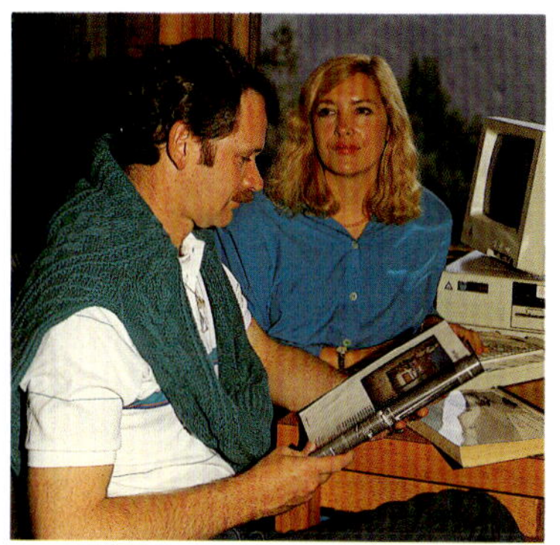

Loren and Patty Adams
Doing Research and Documentation

come Loren's way because of his artistry, including recognition in the European version of "Who's Who". Though Loren is a young man, there have already been several retrospectives of his work; the most notable by the R.W. Norton Museum in Shreveport, Louisiana.

Louis Miller and Loren D. Adams - Critical Acclaim

In a 1990 videotaped interview with an arts organization think tank, Louis Miller, senior appraiser and noted art authority termed Loren Adams' artworks, "Recognized Quality". Mr. Miller believed that "Art is an emotional language in that it must first have meaning to the artist before it can communicate anything to anyone else". He appreciated Mr. Adams deep involvement with his artworks; "They're great, Loren; they're all great. I believe you love every bit of the work you do!"

He dedicated an original work of his own poetry to Loren; and confided to the artist's wife Patty that "Loren paints things the way they ought to be."

Louis Miller was highly regarded as an art appraiser. He was also an attorney and vitally concerned with Fine Arts Legislation; he directly contributed with his ideas, to much of the legislation on state and national levels that protect fine artists and their creative works of mind.

He believed, and the legislation on the arts states that artists are a natural resource to our culture and as such should be protected.

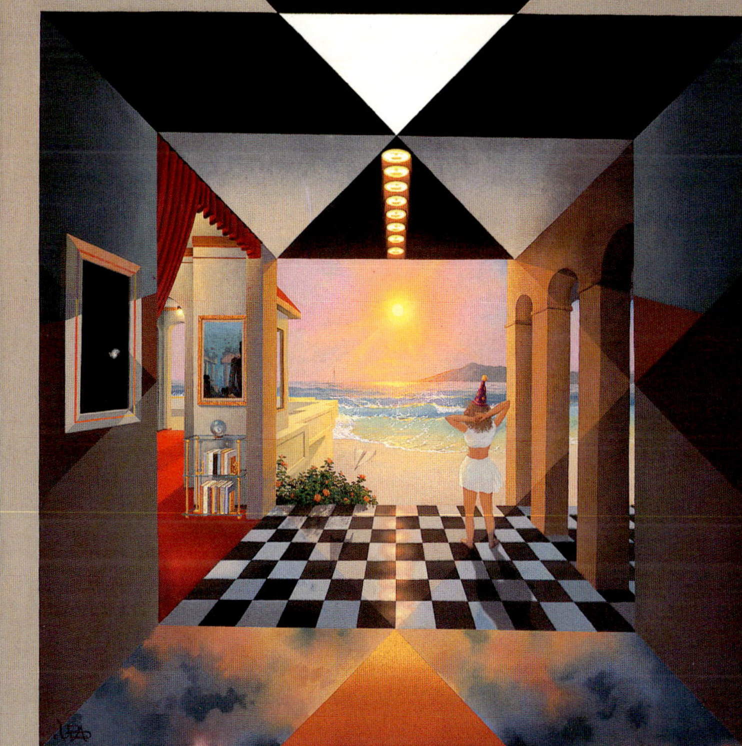

"The Magic Spell of Sun Lady"

44" x 44" Original Oil Painting and 40" x 40" Cibachrome® - Limited Edition Prints S/N 100

Round and round they go
the figures on the wall
and I upon my carousel
a master of them all.

I see what is, I see what was
I see what's going to be
but best of all I can recall
the things that ought to be...

Mr. Miller passed away in 1991.

Loren Adams' art can be seen primarily at Lahaina Galleries locations on Maui and at the Mauna Lani Resort on the Big Island of Hawaii and Wyland Galleries on Oahu and Kauai. For serious collectors, presentations at his Upcountry studio can be arranged by appointment only.

Loren D. Adams Studio
880 Front Street, #881
Lahaina, Maui, HI 96761
(808) 572-0239
FAX (808) 572-3579

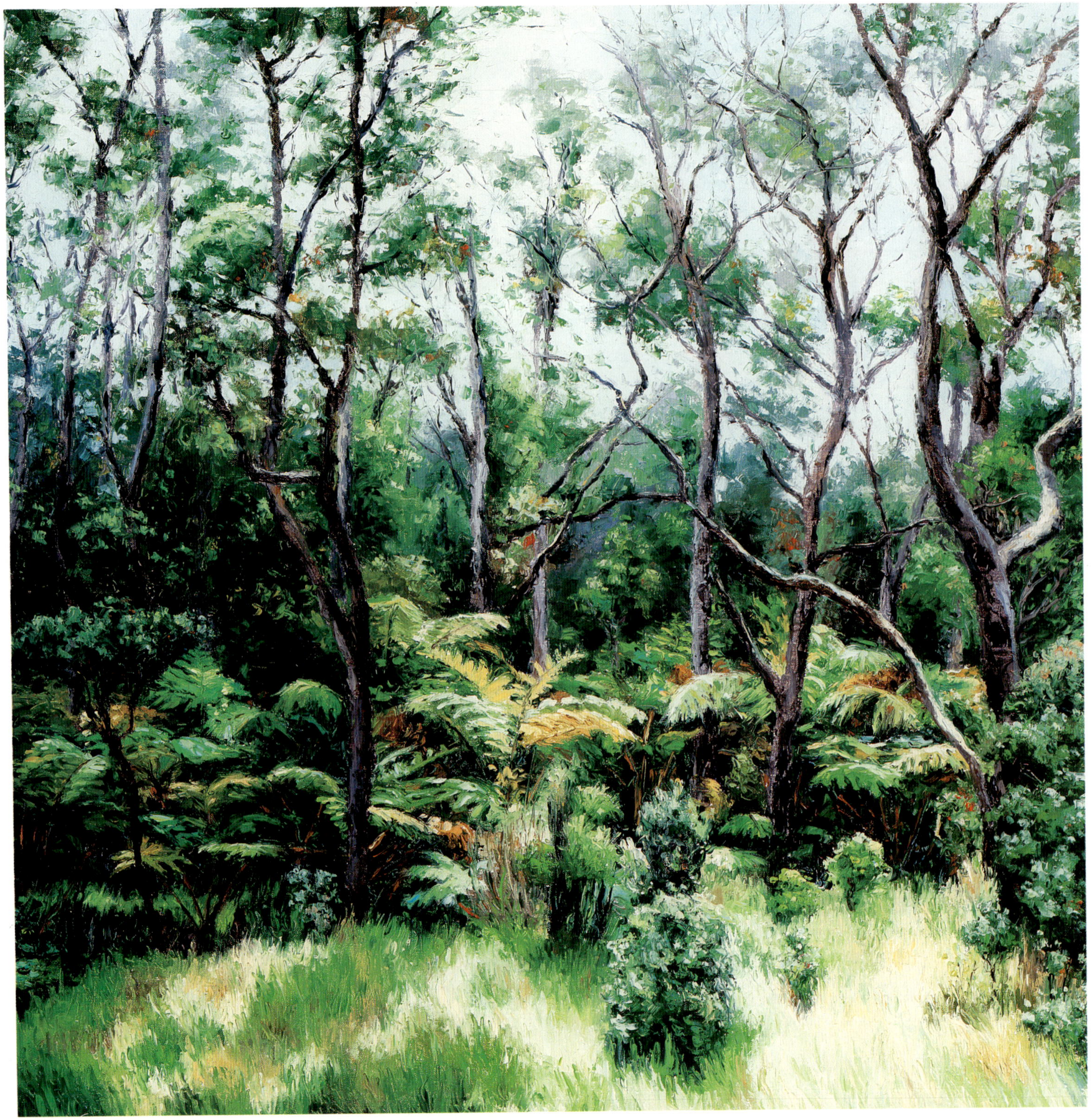

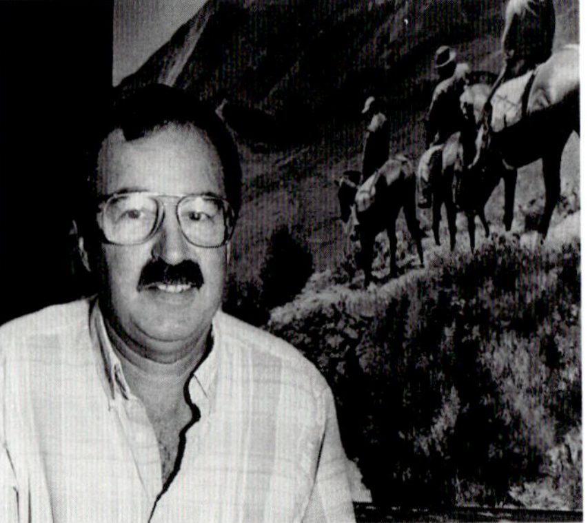

GEORGE ALLAN

Often called Maui's premier artist by art aficionados, George Allan prefers understatement and calls himself a "painter who's still growing". Though he has won many awards and honors, he's reluctant to talk about all the accolades. Born in Melbourne, Australia, in 1937, he attended the Royal Institute of Technology, then traveled for 12 years throughout the South Pacific, North and South America, Europe and Russia. George resided in St. Anton, Austria for 8 years, where he studied art every summer in European museums. Moving to Maui in 1973, he began his art career in earnest.

"George Allan captures light!" This recent headline tells everything about his oil paintings. Light-filled canvases now grace the walls of corporate offices, government buildings, and the homes of luminaries all over the world.

"Ohia Forest, Crater Rim Trail" 33" x 33" Original Oil Painting

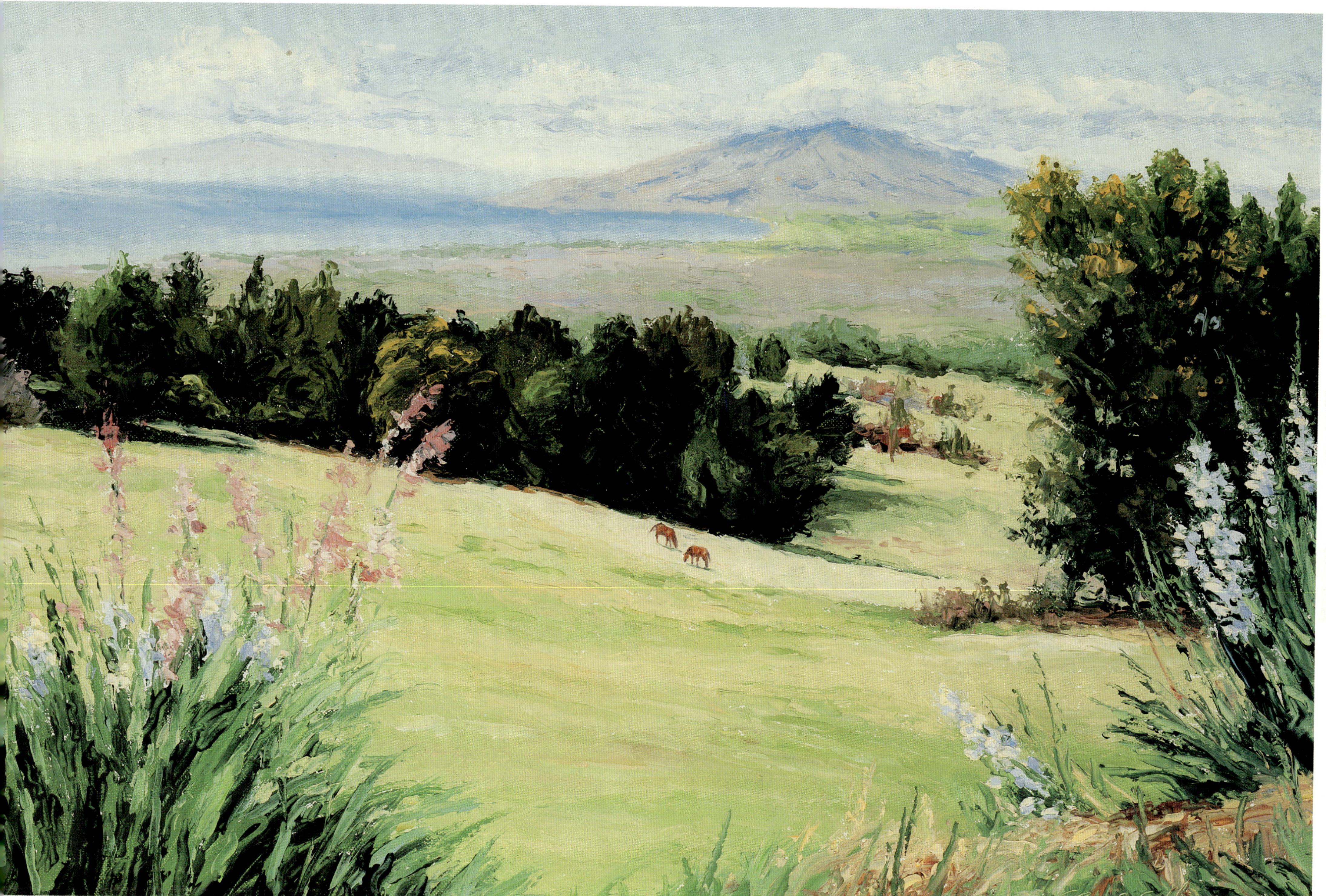

w to West Maui" Oil on Canvas 14" x 21"

ORGE ALLAN

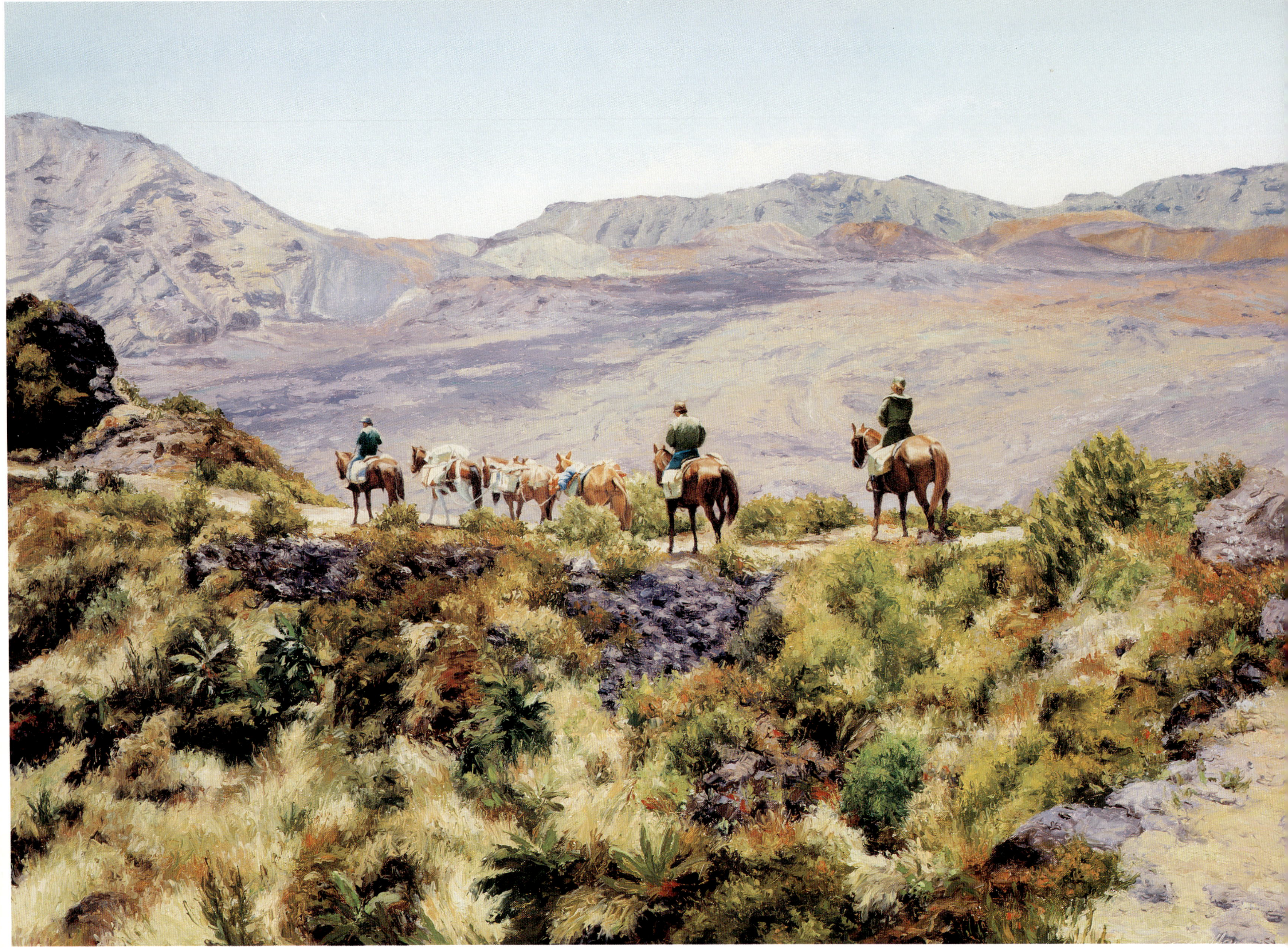

GEORGE ALLAN

"Halemau'u Trail" 27" x 40" Original Oil Painting

GEORGE ALLAN

"Pardner and Crescendo" Original Oil Painting 40" x 27"

George is represented by:
Village Gallery, Lahaina & Cannery Coast Gallery,
Wailea & Hana Kral Fine Arts ,
Oakland, California Viewpoints Gallery,
Makawao, Volcano Art Center,
Hawaii Volcanoes National Park, Hawaii

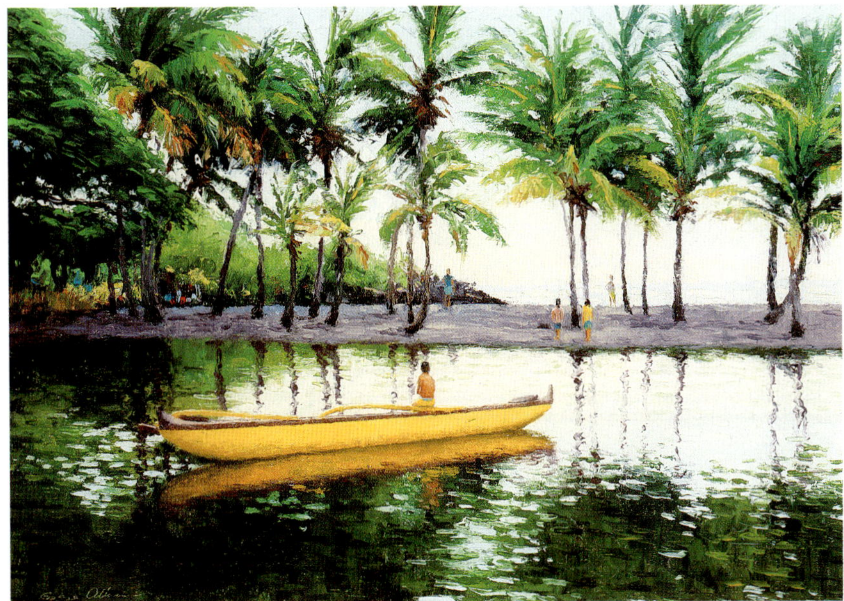

"Kiko's Canoe" Original Oil Painting 18" x 27"

"Braiding Ti" Original Oil Painting 10" x 15"

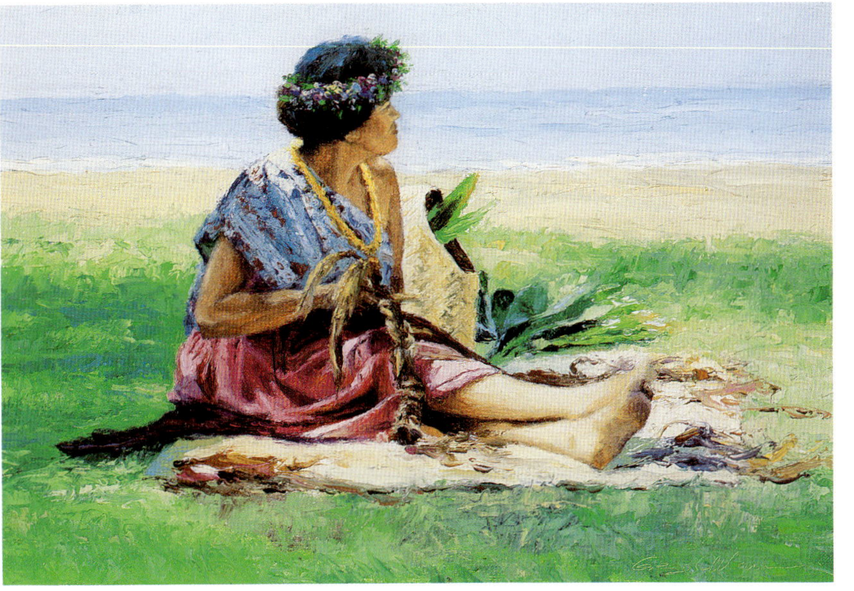

His successful shows in California and Hawaii in the past 18 years have earned him a long list of avid admirers. Many of them commission him to paint subject matter they admire, and he tackles the waiting list between other commitments. He appreciates everyone of his hundreds of collectors and their enthusiastic endorsement of his work.

Besides the many solo exhibits over the years, George has also been accepted in five Artists of Hawaii exhibitions at the Honolulu Academy of Arts. The annual Art Maui juried exhibition also included George's oils for 13 years in a row; so far, that's a record for any Maui artist.

George enjoys supporting civic and art groups on Maui. He also enjoys the challenge of jurying art exhibitions around the State, as well as teaching in the Artists-in-the-Schools program.

In any spare time, George plays the piano, either alone or with a group of musician friends. It's a pastime that has gained him friends all over the world.

It's no wonder Pacific Art & Travel Magazine called George Allan, "Renaissance Man"!

37 Haliu Street
Lahaina, Maui, HI 96761
(808) 669-8271
FAX (808) 669-7728

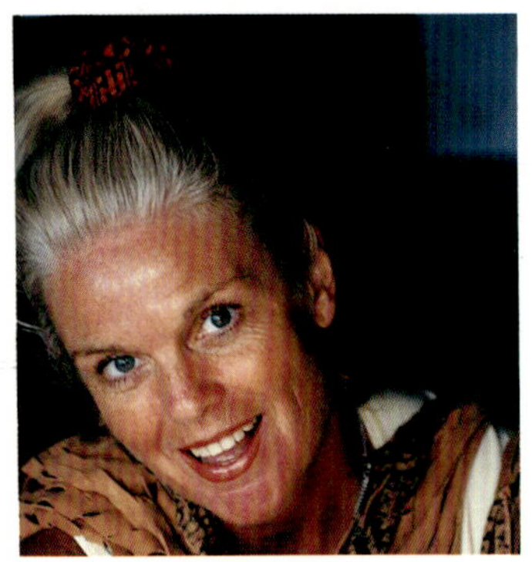

RAE ANDREWS

Born and raised near the ocean in Sydney, Australia, Rae Andrews was introduced at an early age to a myriad of outdoor activities, helping her to appreciate the wonder of nature. Coupled with her artistic family influence, it comes as no great surprise that Rae chose to uproot herself in 1991, marrying and moving to one of the most scenic spots in the world — the island of Maui.

This artist's background and qualifications are impressive. In 1987 she received her Bachelor of Arts in visual arts; then completed her training in professional art studies with a major in drawing at the City Art Institute, Sydney, Australia. In the '80s Rae's career took off rapidly. She made many appearances as a lecturer at various art schools & universities in Australia, and had her first solo exhibition in 1982 in Sydney. From 1984-1989, she entered and won numerous awards for both painting and drawing, as she continued to exhibit her works at universities and galleries throughout Sydney. In 1990, Rae became an entrepreneur, opening her own 400-student art school in Sydney.

Her marriage to an American brought this gifted artist to the Hawaiian Islands shortly thereafter. Upon moving to Maui, Ms. Andrews almost immediately became an art consultant for Studio Blue Galleries on Maui, as well as being a featured watercolor artist at the same location. Ever adventurous, in 1992 Rae established her own art studio & gallery in Kihei and also exhibited at the Art Maui Exhibit.

As an artist, her search for the new and exciting led Rae Andrews to the world of watercolor and mixed media. With this combination of media, she is able to work and rework her watercolors, building and layering the surface. Rae enjoys the sense of ambiguity of this process, as it allows her to balance the subject somewhere between abstraction and realism. Viewers are enticed to linger and inquire. It is quite apparent from her work that this artist has discovered much of the beauty of the Hawaiian rainforests and marine life. Ms. Andrews' journey has led her to a fresh and vivid outlook. She says, "I hope the viewers of my paintings derive great pleasure from them, because the pleasure has been all mine."

1941 S. Kihei Road
Kihei, Maui, HI 96753
(808) 879-4181

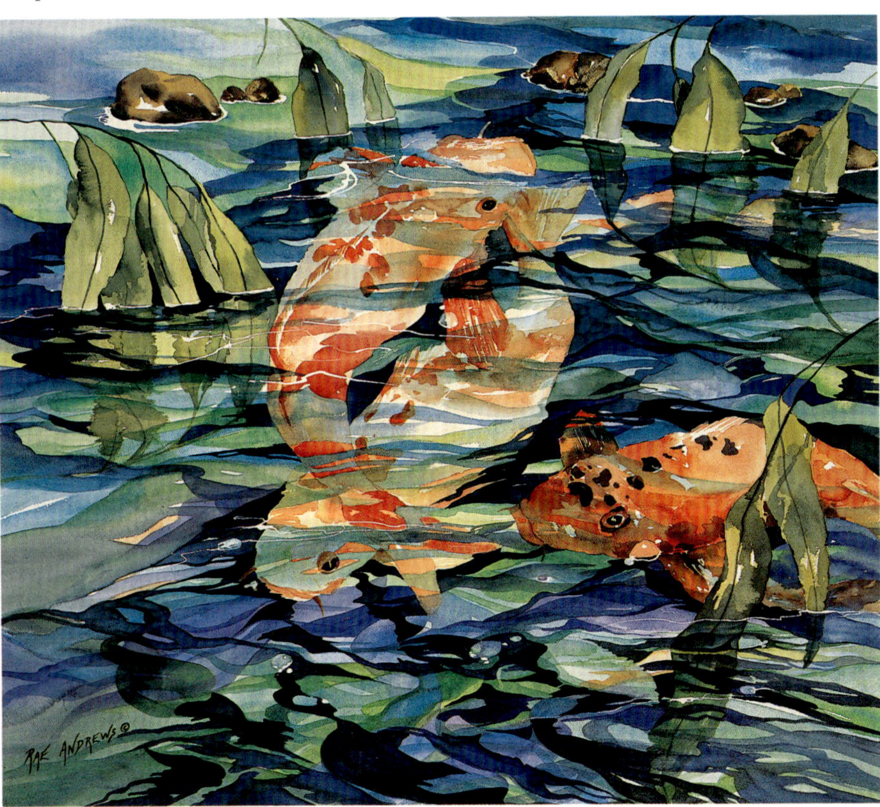

"Wailea Koi" 26" x 25" Original Watercolor Painting

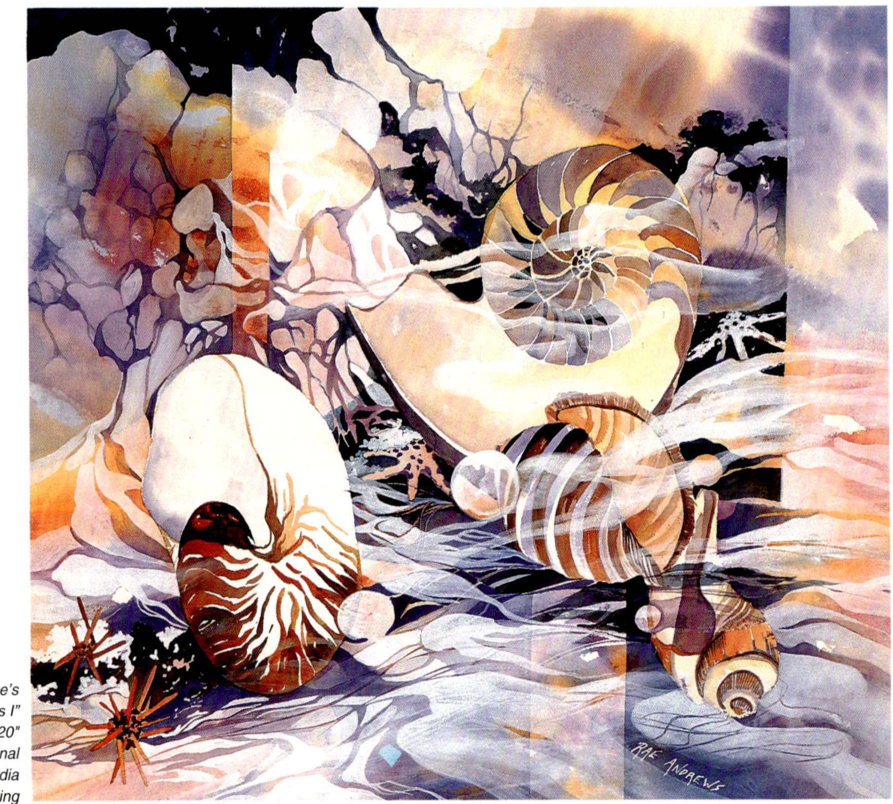

"Neptune's Nautilus I" 23" x 20" Original Watermedia Painting

"Echoes Of Iao" 41" x 28" Original Watermedia Painting

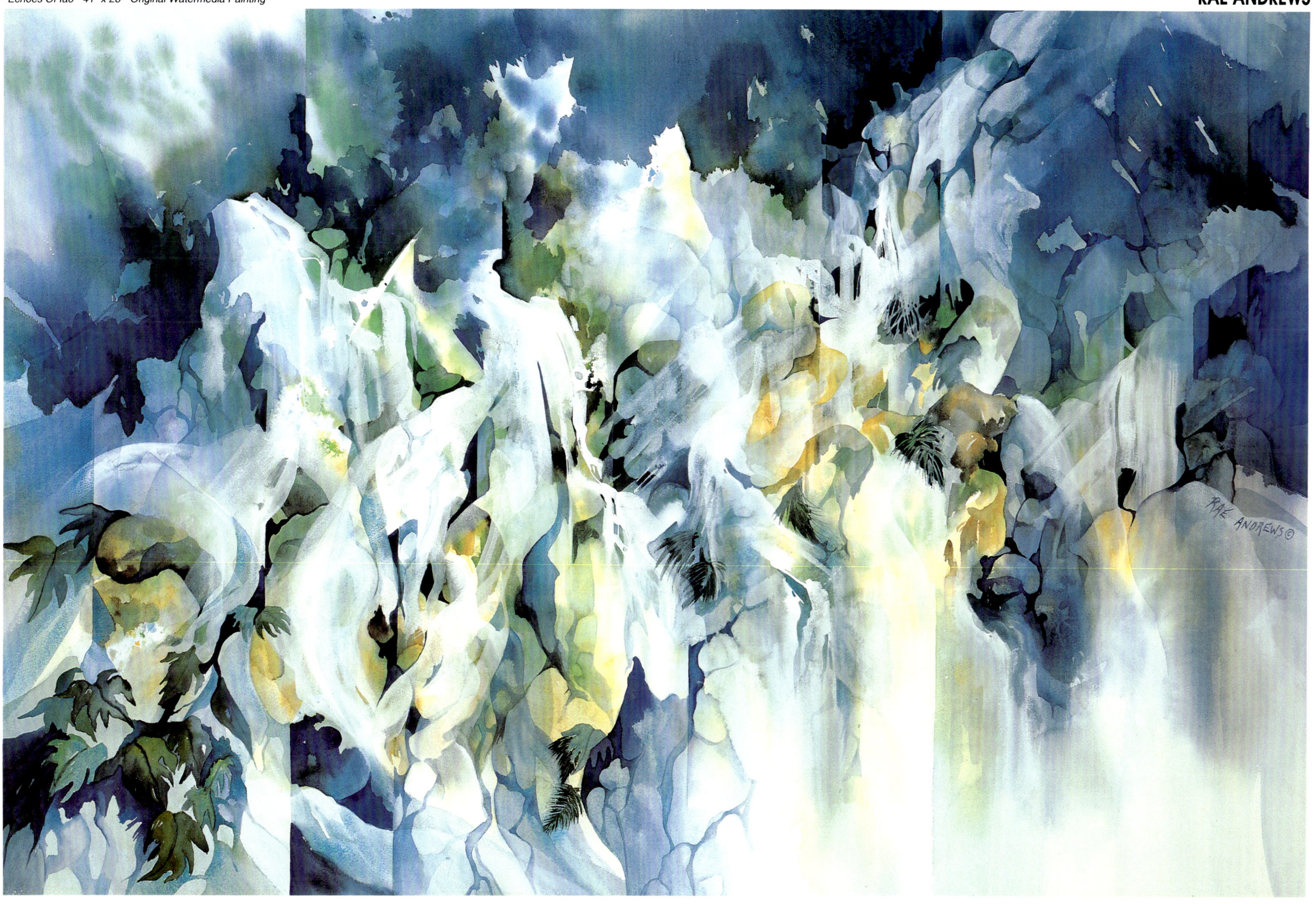

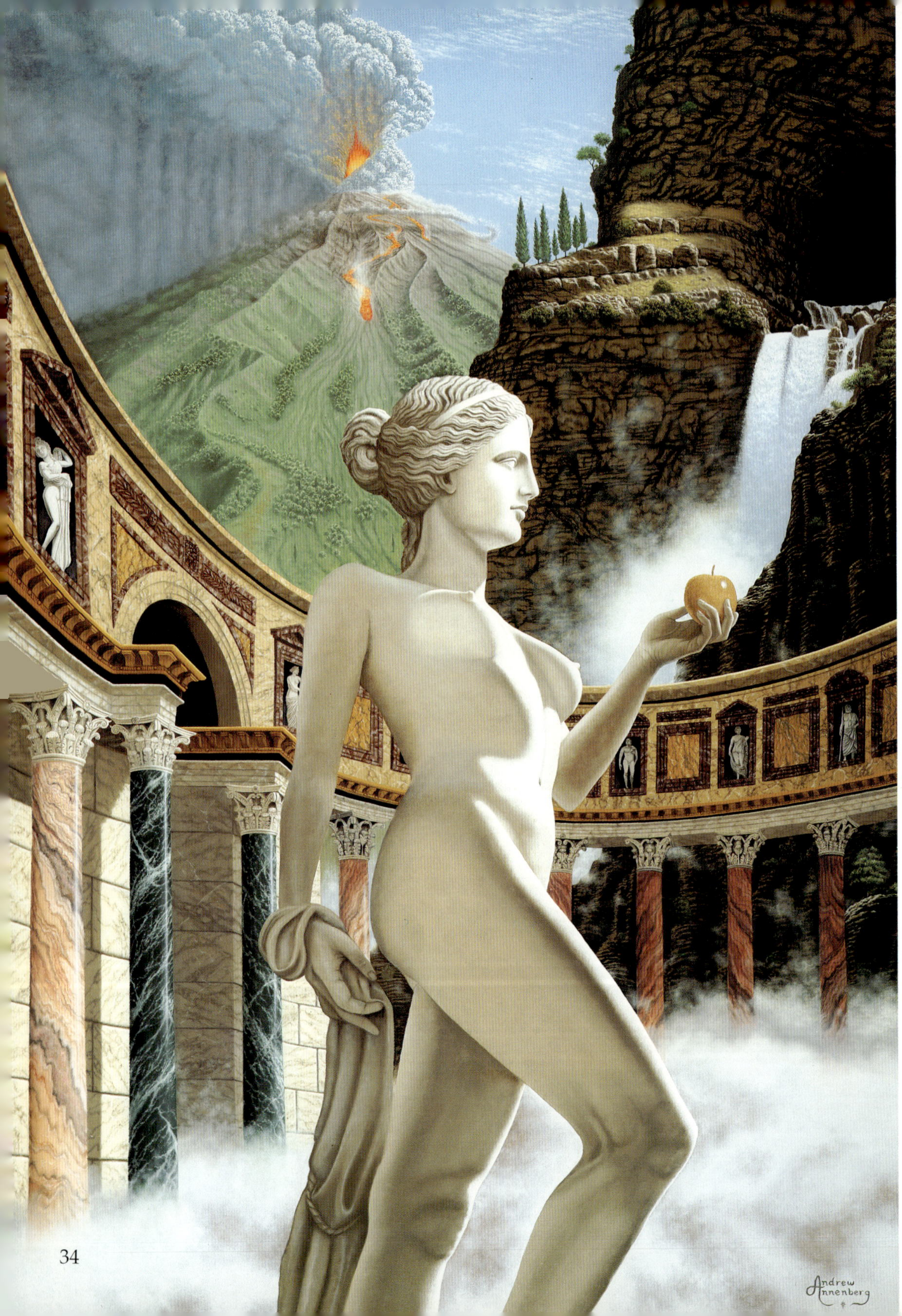

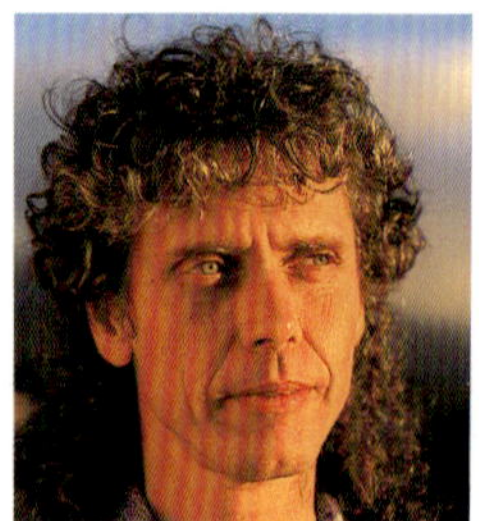

ANDREW ANNENBERG

Andrew Annenberg is recognized as one of today's foremost visionary artists, acclaimed for his meticulous detail, imagination and wit. His works-original oils and limited editions-have been collected and published throughout the world.

Born in Santa Monica, California, on September 25, 1945, Andrew spent his youth in Washington, D.C., where he frequently visited the nation's prime repositories of art treasure: the Smithsonian Institute, the National Museum of Art and the Natural Museum of History.

Stirred by these masterpieces and encouraged by his mother, he began to draw. Andrew recalls his early years. "I was always drawing or painting. Everything else was something I had to do so I could return to my art."

Since 1974, Andrew has resided on the idyllic Hawaiian island of Maui, where his sense of wonder and awe flourish. Themes from ancient Egypt, classical Greece and England and the lost civilizations of Atlantis and Lemuria are powerful focal points in much of his work.

Now Andrew unveils his latest master-work entitled, "Guardians of the Grail", the fourth in the series of his "Suite of Lost Worlds". The subject of the four by six foot oil painting is the medieval legend of King Arthur and the Quest of the Holy Grail. Like the other paintings in the series, this work uncovers yet another historical civilization. Andrew turns our minds within to the fantastic realms where consciousness is unconfined, and brings us to a meditation on that which lies beyond.

Andrew is interested in what he calls the "environment of the mind". He believes that his provocative paintings move people to ponder their surroundings by making the viewer aware of the viewer's own participation in the rise and fall of civilizations. Witness the classical Greek-inspired beauty and dynamic earth forces of "Venus Triumphant".

The primal, the Archetypal, the Mythological, the Ancient-it is their timelessness and the enduring nature of the spirit that Andrew captures with his art.

Welcome to Andrew's world.

""Venus Triumphant" oil on canvas 25" x 38"
Original and Limited Edition of 50 Cibachromes Available "24 x 36"

ANNENBERG MASTERWORKS
P.O. Box 778
Kula, Maui, HI 96790
Tel: (808) 878-3010
Fax: (808) 878-1662

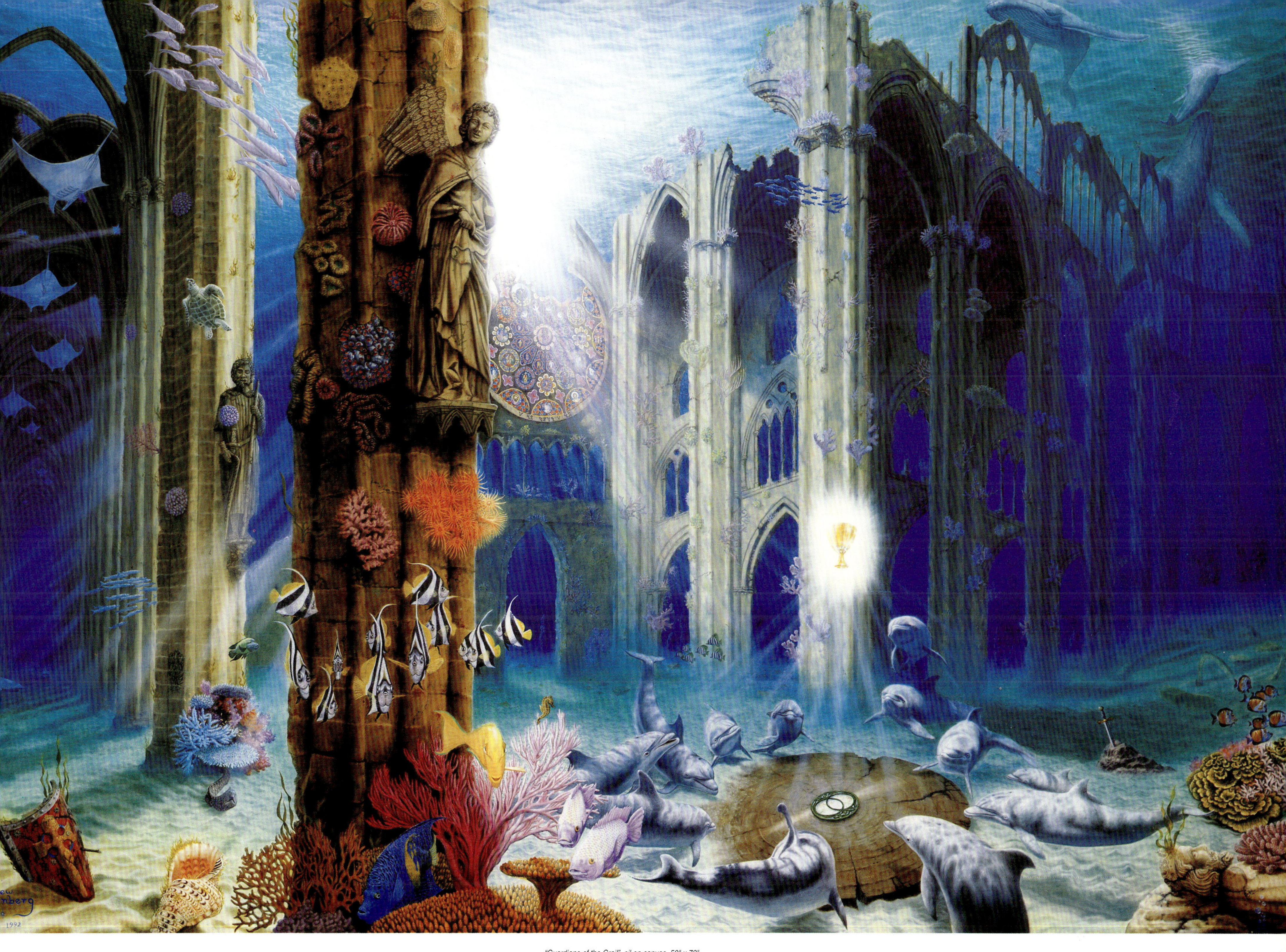

"Guardians of the Grail" oil on canvas 50" x 72"
Original and Limited Edition Seri-Lithographs "24 x 36"
Limited Edition Cibachromes 36" x 48"

ANDREW ANNENBERG

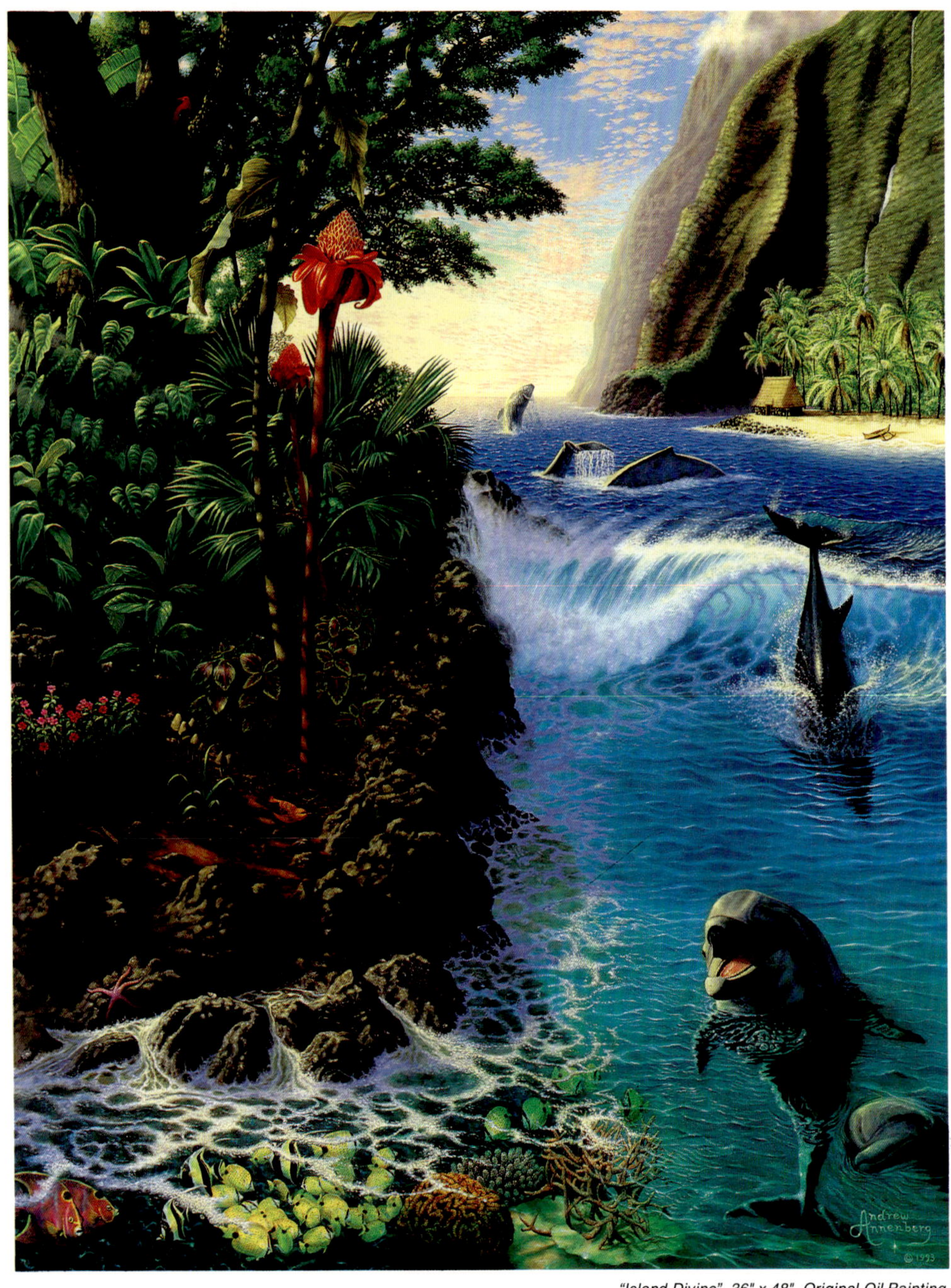

"Island Divine" 36" x 48" Original Oil Painting and Limited Edition Prints - Offset S/N & Proofs

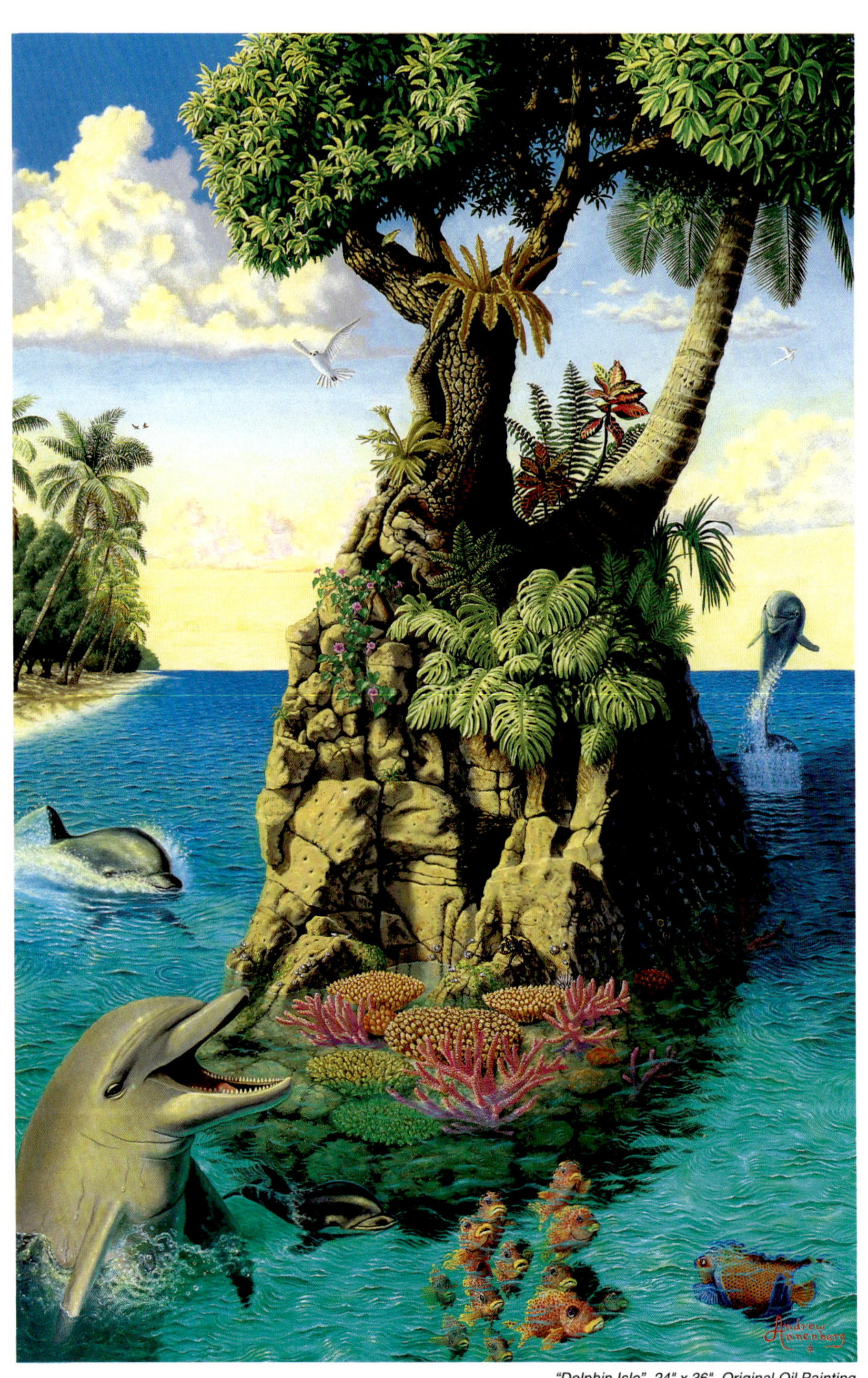

"Dolphin Isle" 24" x 36" Original Oil Painting and Limited Edition Prints - Offset S/N & Proofs

ANDREW ANNENBERG

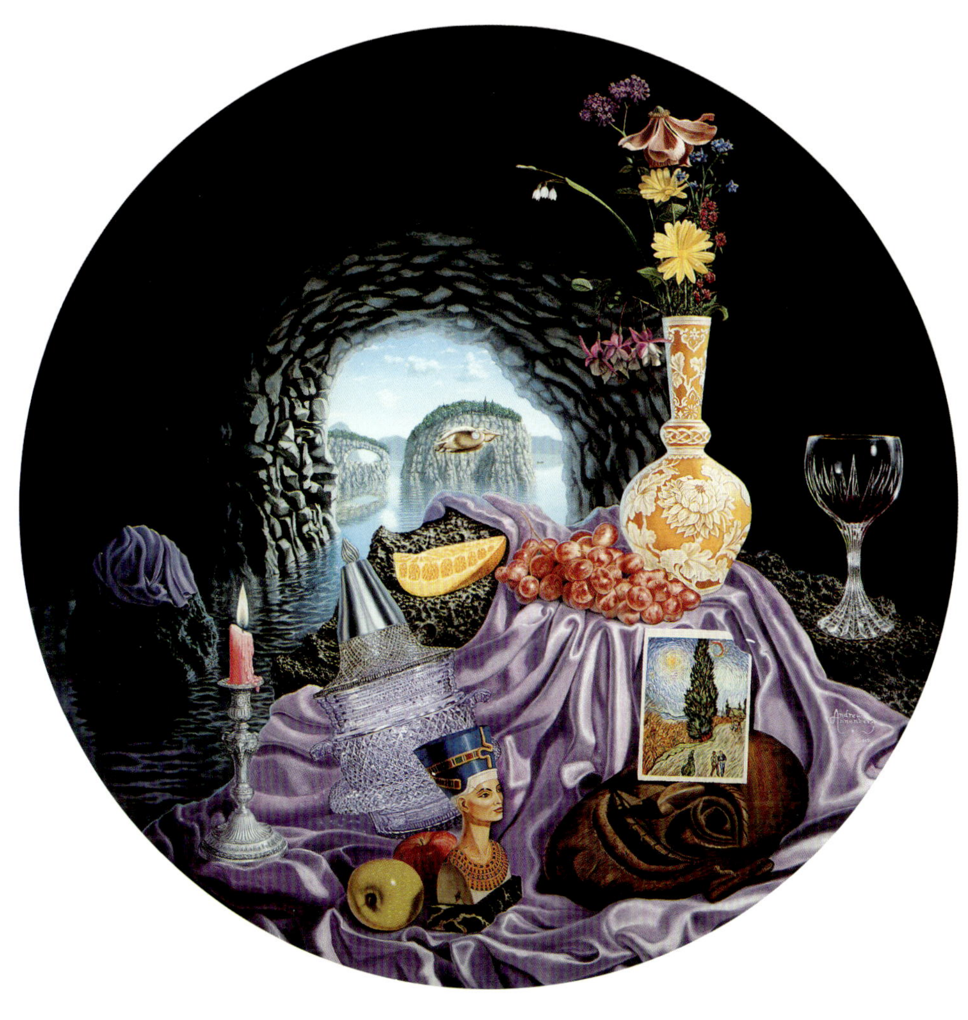

"Thou Art That" oil on canvas 36" Diameter

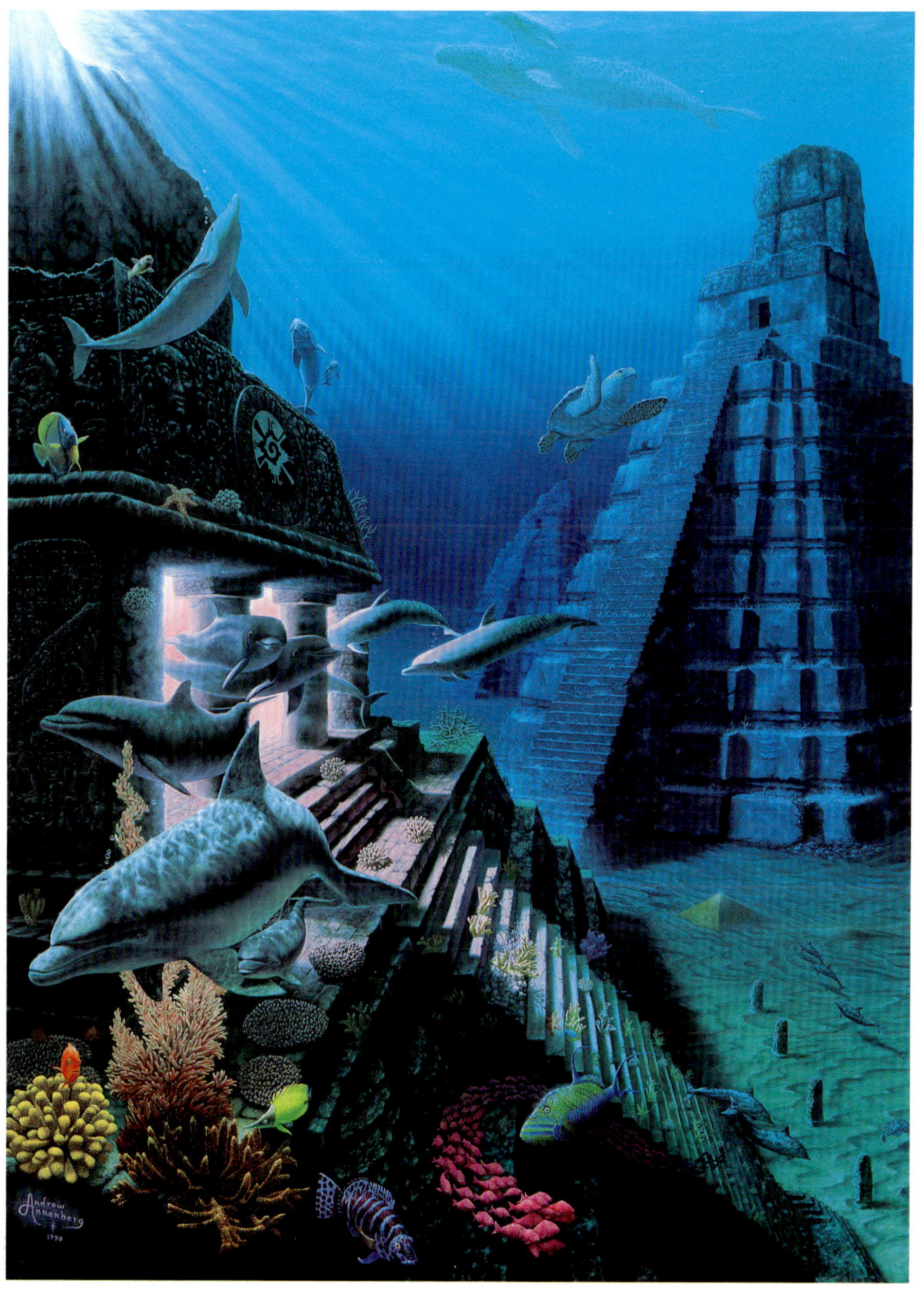

"Portal of Hunab Ku" oil on canvas 36" x 50"

ANDREW ANNENBERG

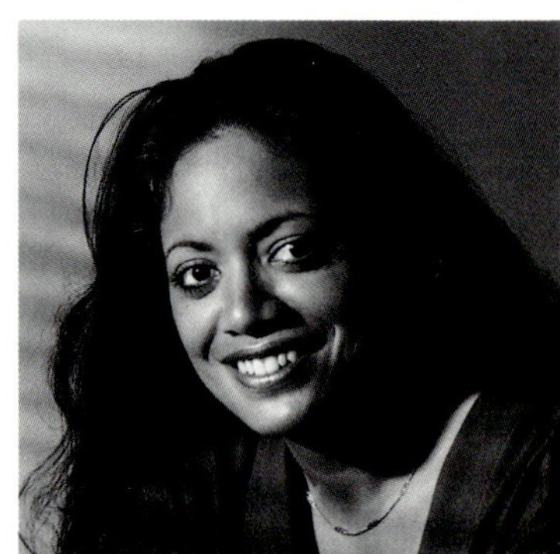

ARNA JOHNSON
P.O. Box 4277
Kaneohe, Oahu, HI 96744
(808) 236-0009
(800) 439-9612
FAX (808) 236-0009

Arna grew up on a flower farm in Hakipu'u on the windward side of the island of Oahu where she and her brothers spent much of their time helping their mother with the family business of flower farming and floral design.

In 1980 she received a Bachelor of Arts degree in commercial photography from Brooks Institute of Photography in Santa Barbara, California. Since then she has been operating her own professional photography and fine art business on Oahu.

This award-winning photographer and artist has been commissioned by Bank of America, Bank of Hawaii, Bishop Estates, and Kapiolani Medical Center to name a few.

These images are originally black and white photographs that are enlarged onto fiber based paper. Transparent photo oils and pencils are then applied to create a certain mood and a quality of timelessness.

Being of Hawaiian ancestry and having lived in Hawaii all but four years of her life and seeing the changes that are forced upon these islands daily, it has become a personal interest to try to preserve a fragment of the romantic lore that is not lost but just harder to see through all of the layers of things new, exciting, and different.

"It is through my work that I am trying to express the spirit of these islands and the intangible qualities these islands possess. Though my work does not demand a lot of attention, it is there for the subconscious. It evokes emotions, an appreciation and perhaps an understanding one only finds here in Hawaii. I hope that my work can help to instill a subconscious awareness to protect and administer these qualities in our daily lives."

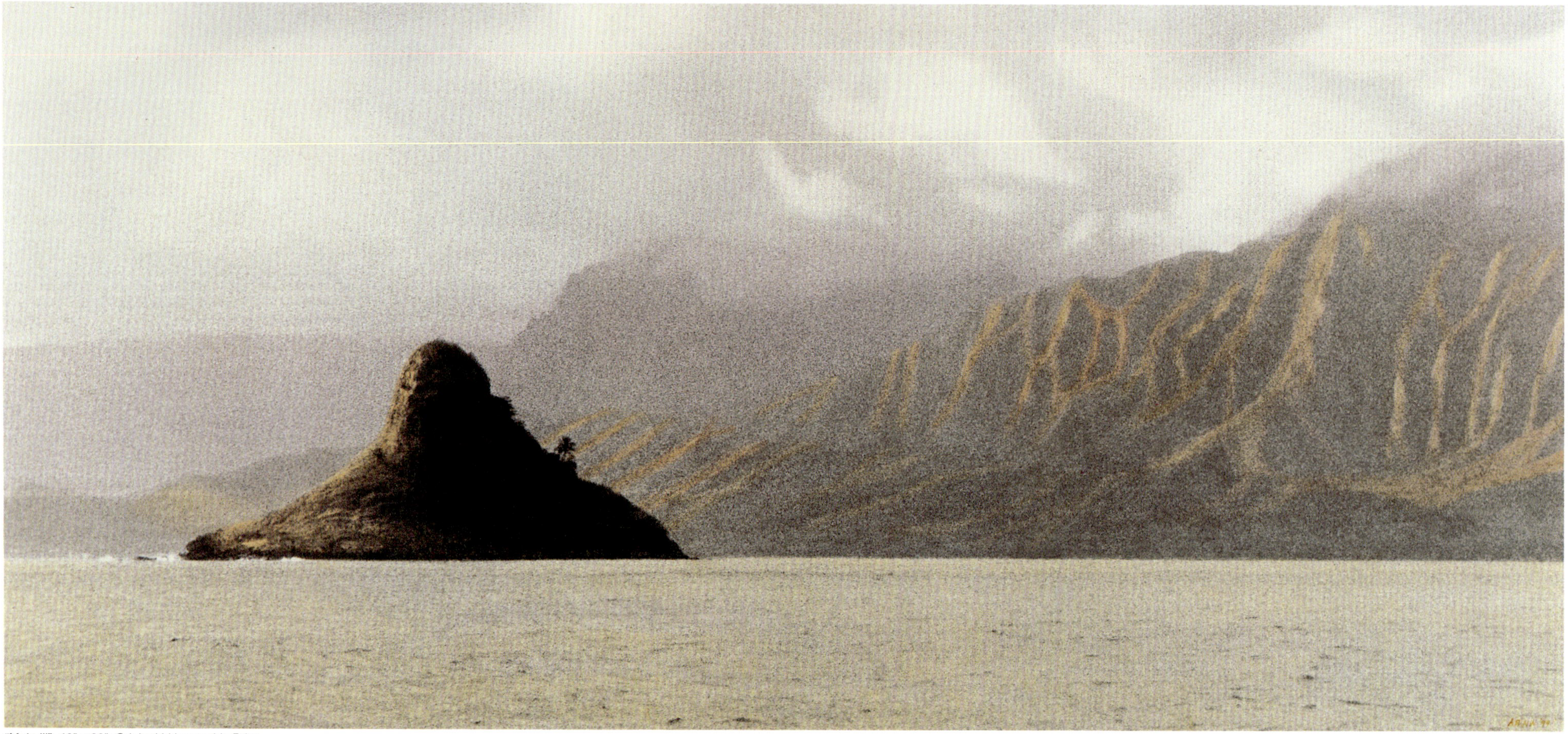

"Mokolii" 40" x 20" Original Lithographic Print

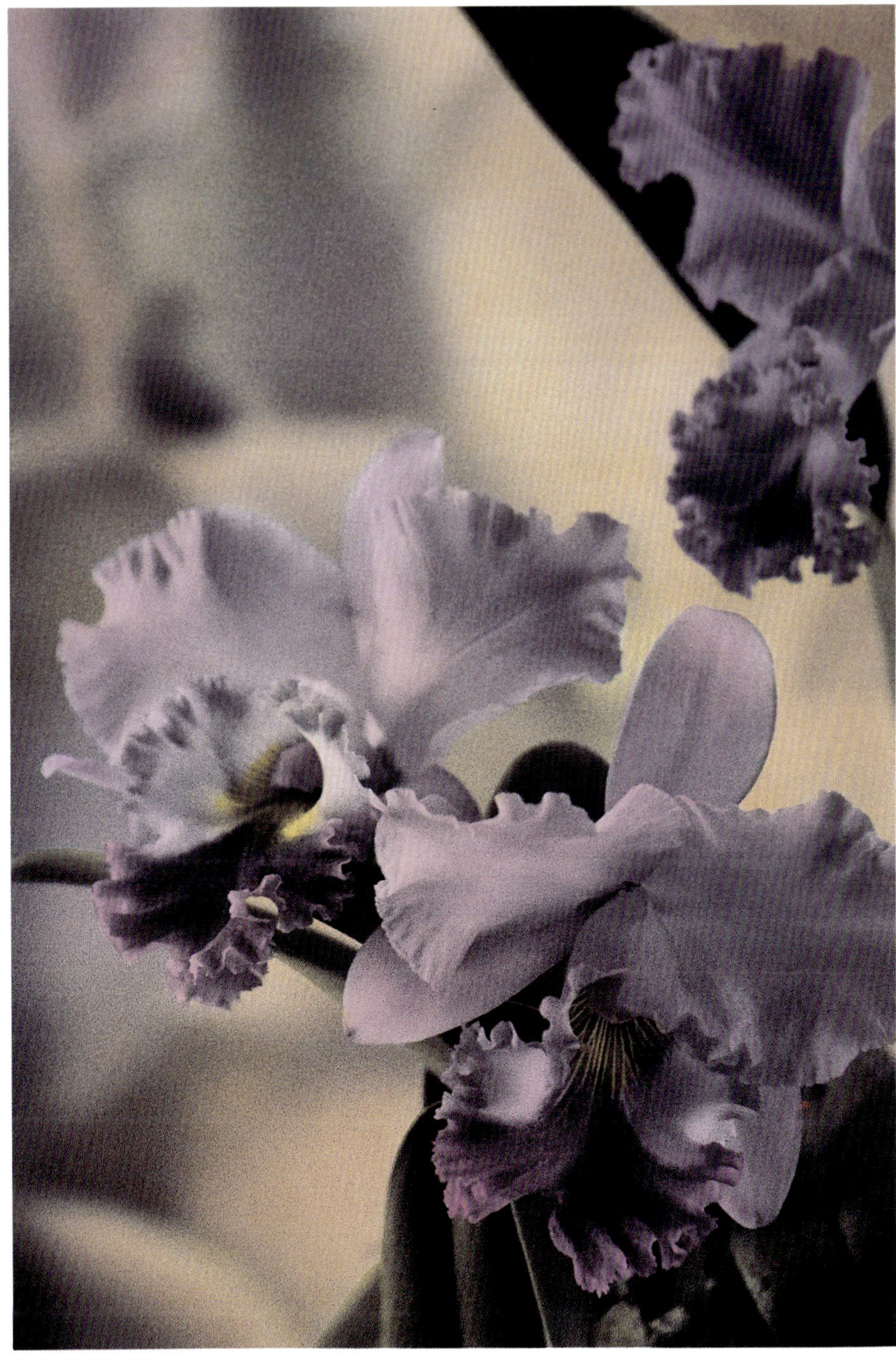

"Cattleya" 30" x 48"
Original Photo Print

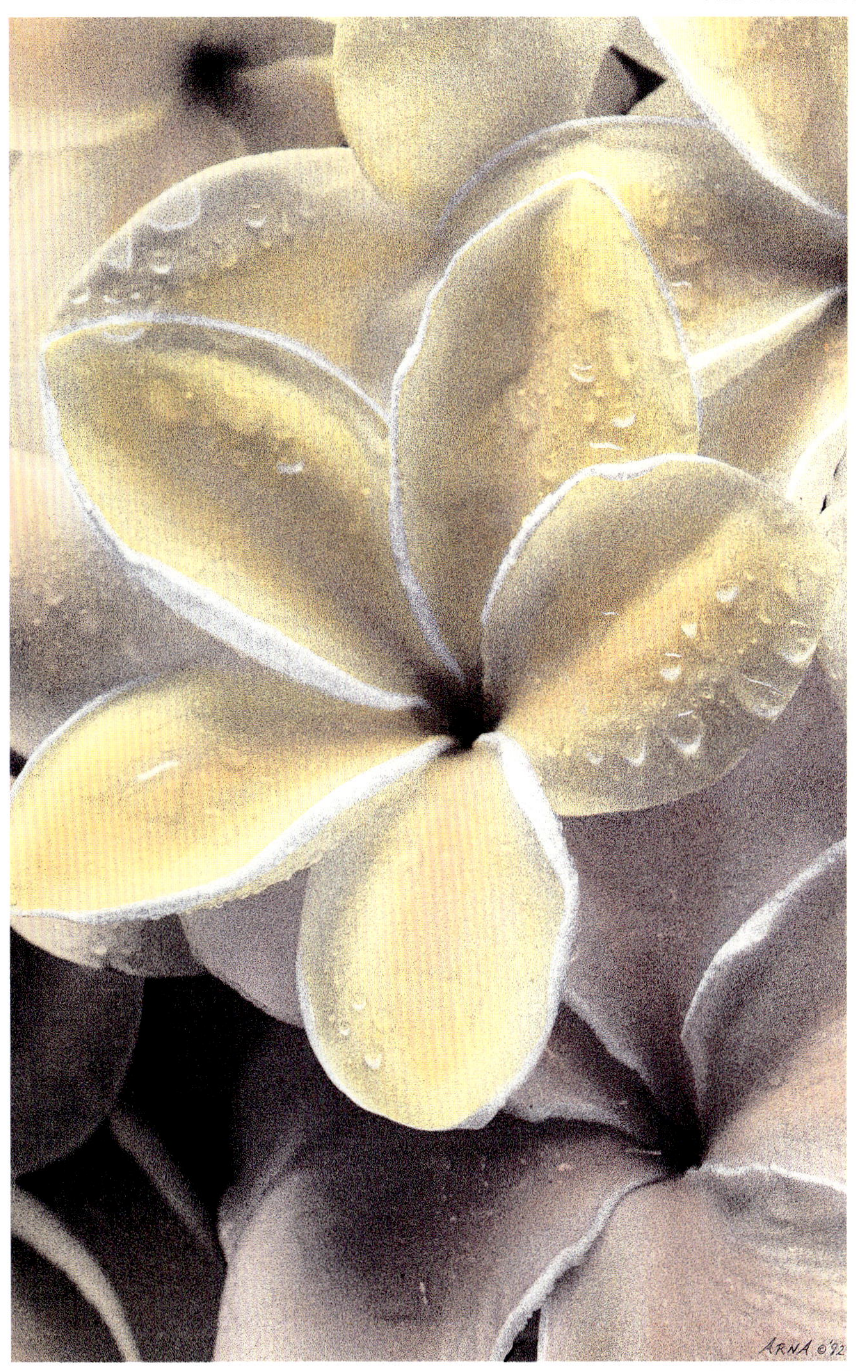

"Plumeria" 30" x 48"
Original Photo Print

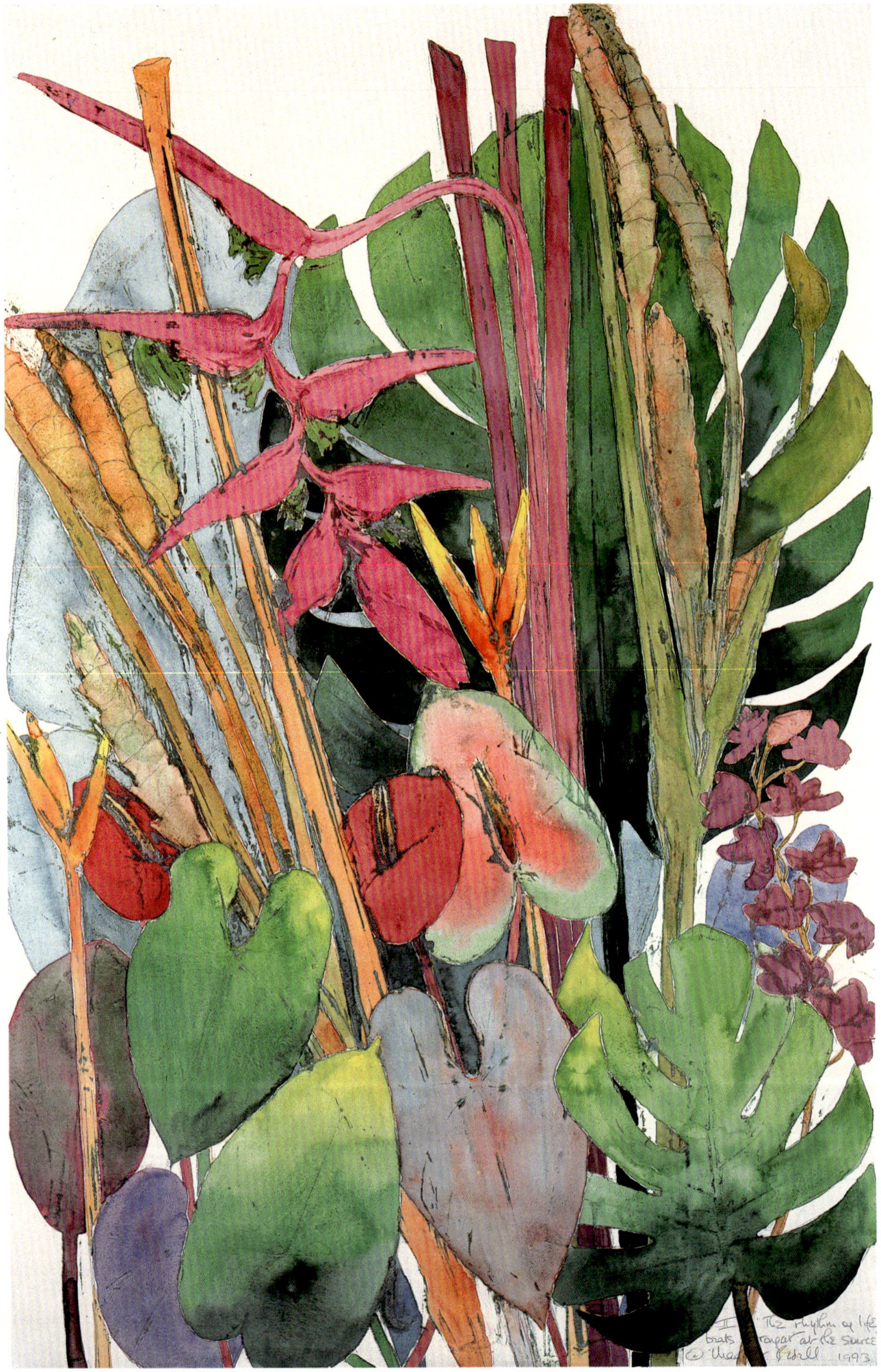

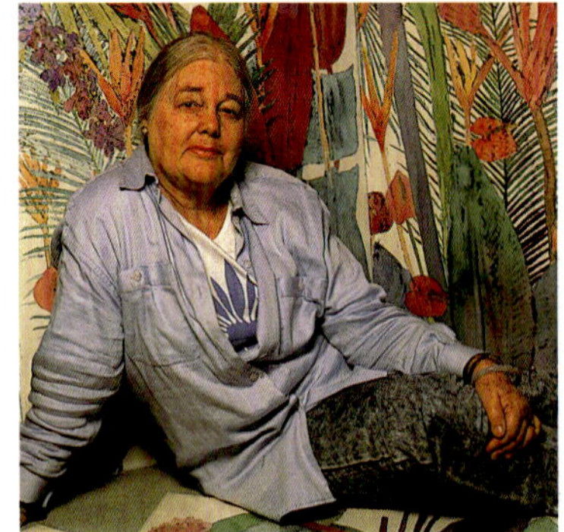

MARGARET BEDELL

Kihei, Maui, HI 96793
(808) 879-9911
Fax: (808) 875-4115

Known for her use of saturated color, Margaret Bedell is both a printmaker and painter. Born in Toronto, educated in Canada and England, she graduated from the University of Toronto in 1944 in English Language and Literature. Two years later, she and her former U.S. Navy husband migrated to southern California where they remained until the early seventies. Says Bedell, "We started drifting towards Hawaii - six weeks, six months - whatever we could afford. Now we live here full time near the ocean in a combined house and studio."

Sometime in the sixties, Bedell became a professional artist. Her training included private study with Alex Brandt, Joan Irving, George Post and Roger Armstrong, all watercolorists from the "California Light" tradition, and culminated in a Master's degree in Art (Printmaking) from California State University at Long Beach. At that time, Bedell also took workshops in monotype from Nathan Oliveira, eventually incorporating monotype techniques into her Master's thesis.

Meanwhile, in 1976 Bedell established a studio and gallery in Corona Del Mar, where she evolved her unique method of making a printing plate from actual plant material.

Bedell says, "Thousands of original prints emanated from that studio, finding their way to the walls of corporate offices, banks, hotels, hospitals and most of all to private collectors. During those years, I actively participated in the Los Angeles Printmaking Society. For ten consecutive summers I exhibited at the Laguna Beach Festival of Arts.

"For the past twenty years, I have also been a

"Ala 'aka IV" 22" x 30" Original Mixed Media

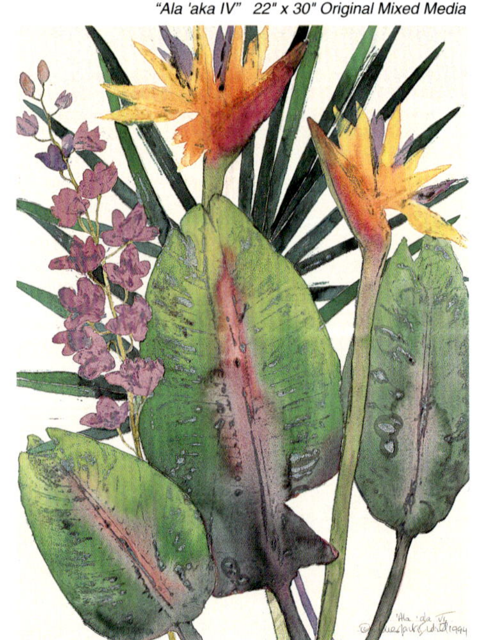

"Rhythm of Life II" 32" x 48" Original Mixed Media

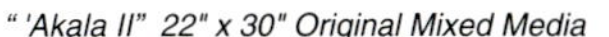
" 'Akala II" 22" x 30" Original Mixed Media

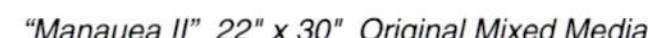
"Manauea II" 22" x 30" Original Mixed Media

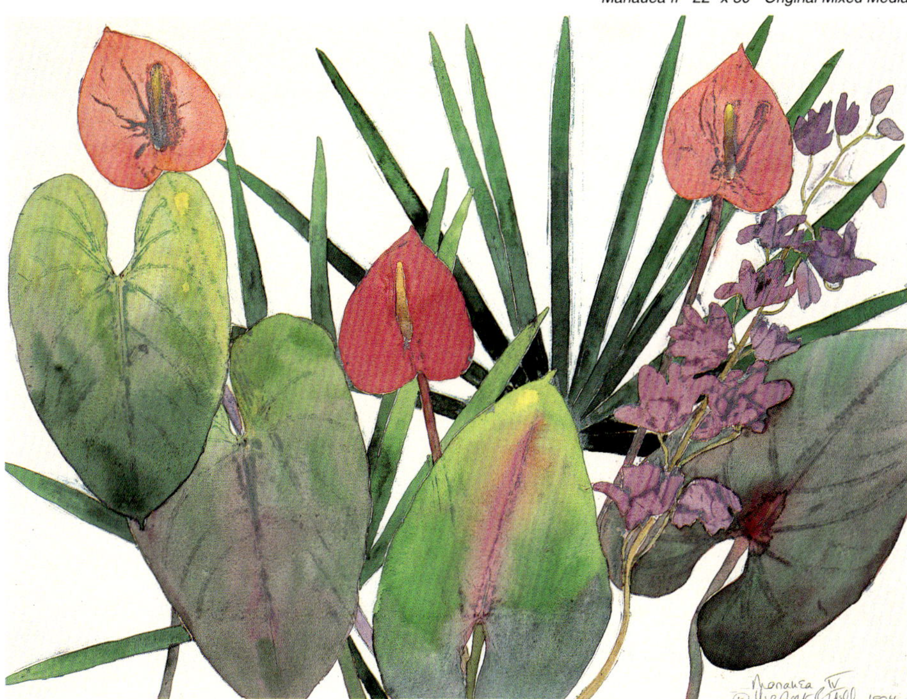

member of the art community here on Maui, and have been represented by Village Galleries, where I have had many solo shows. Presently, I also exhibit at Coast Gallery Wailea, where I had a solo show in 1994. I have also exhibited at Coast Gallery Hana for several years."

A longtime exhibiting member of Volcano Art Center, Ms. Bedell also has other connections to the Big Island, since several grandchildren and other family members live in Kona. The artist also belongs to Hui No'eau, where in the past she has worked and taught, Art Maui and Kihei Arts Council. She also took an active part in "Art On The Green" in 1993 and "Celebration Of The Arts" in 1994, both held at the Ritz-Carlton Hotel, Kapalua. In 1993, she exhibited in the Hawaiian Art Expo at the Coast Gallery, Hyatt Regency Hotel, Kaanapali.

Margaret is also a member of Lama Ho'ike, the overall purpose of which is "... to bring insight into the best qualities of the Hawaiian culture." In "Maui: Earth, Sea Sky" at Hui No'eau in September/October 1994, she exhibited new paintings, continuing a series launched two years ago, when the artist began to paint the environment on location, using the intense colors of her large-scale mixed media works to create small scale watercolors and monotypes.

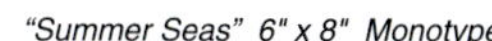
"Summer Seas" 6" x 8" Monotype

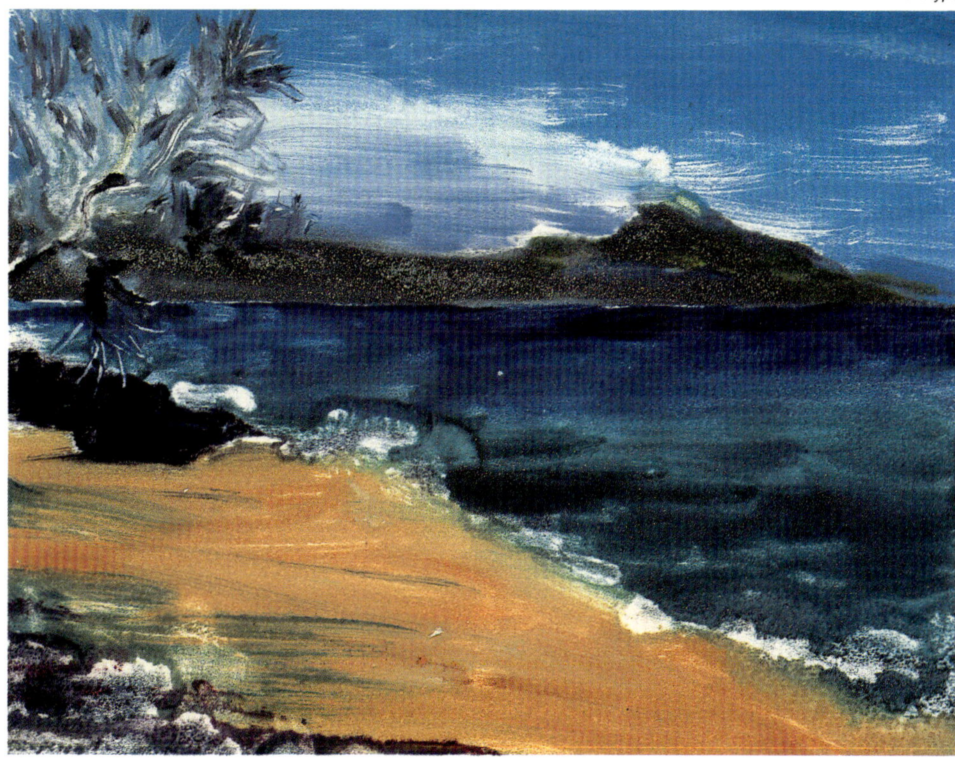

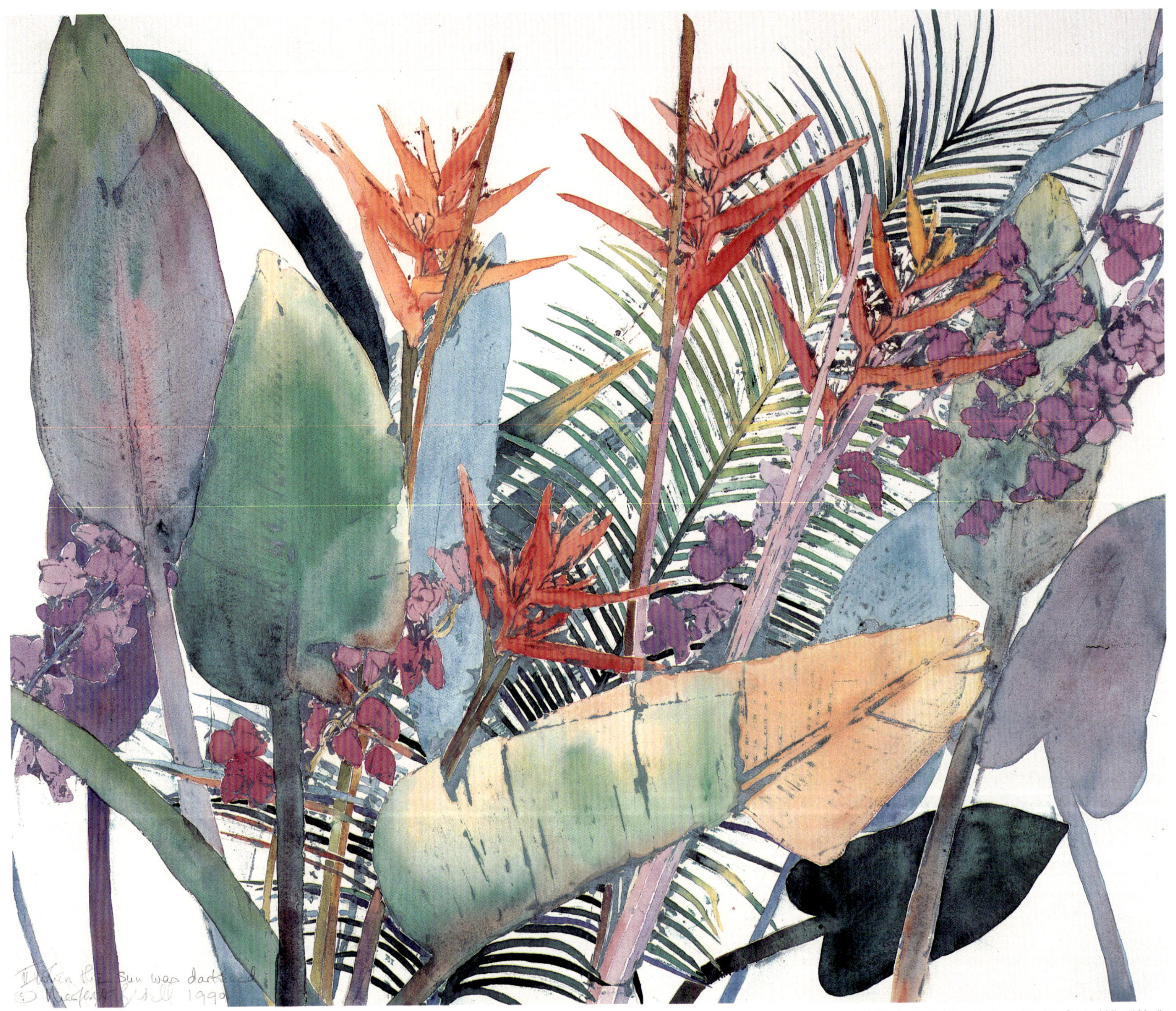

MARGARET BEDELL

"When The Sun Was Darkened" 36"x42" Original Mixed Media

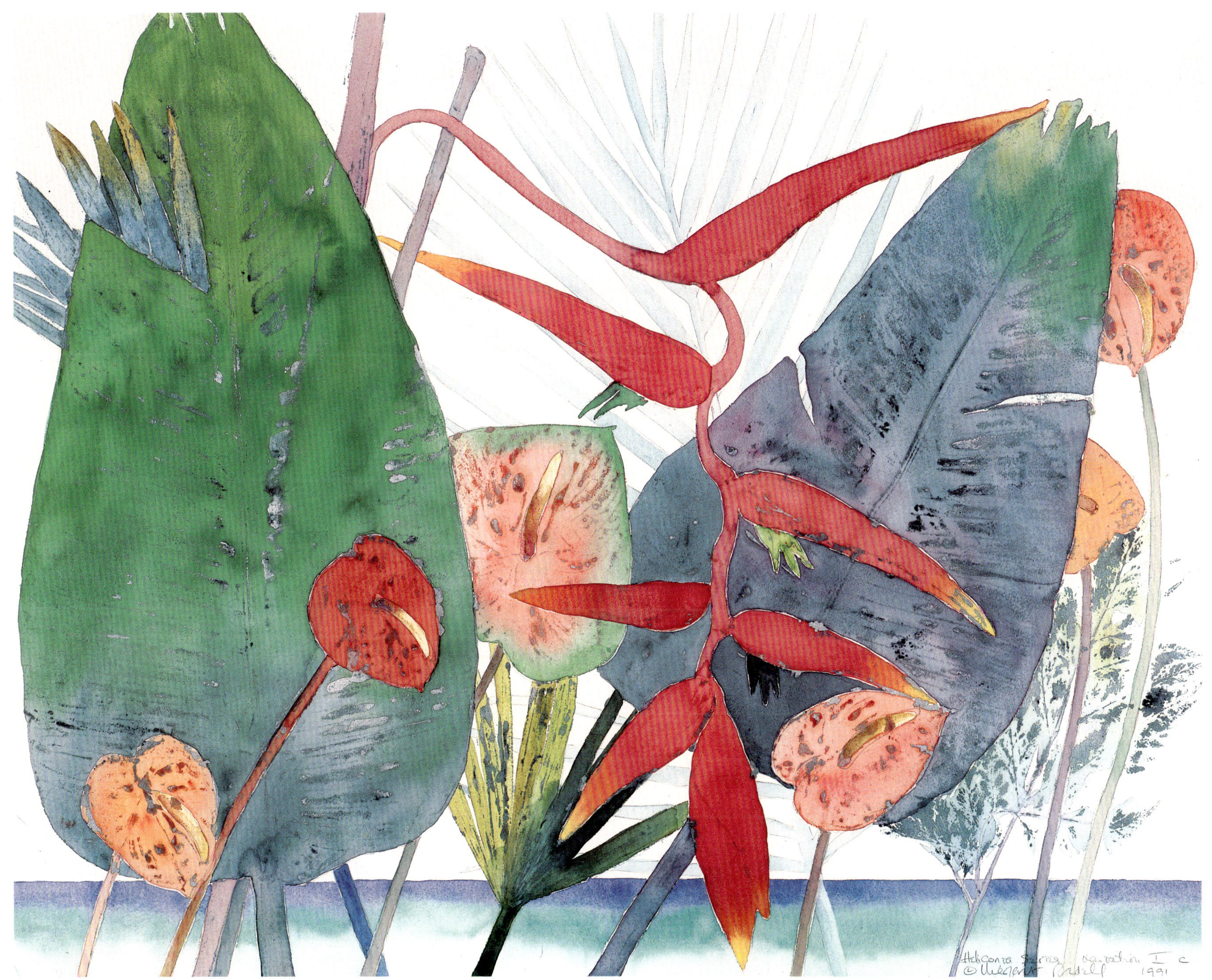

"Heliconia I" 30"x38" Original Mixed Media

MARGARET BEDELL

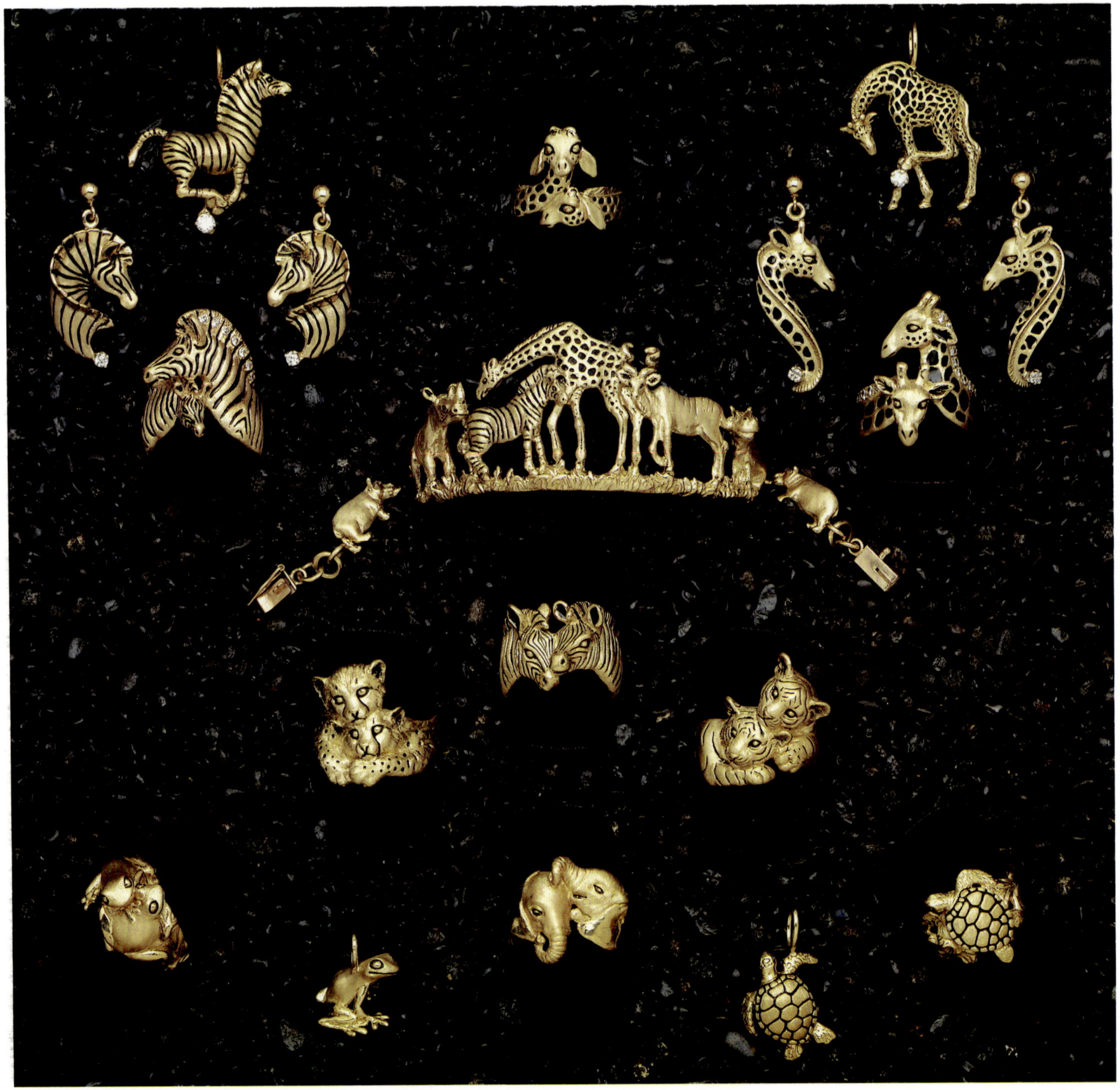

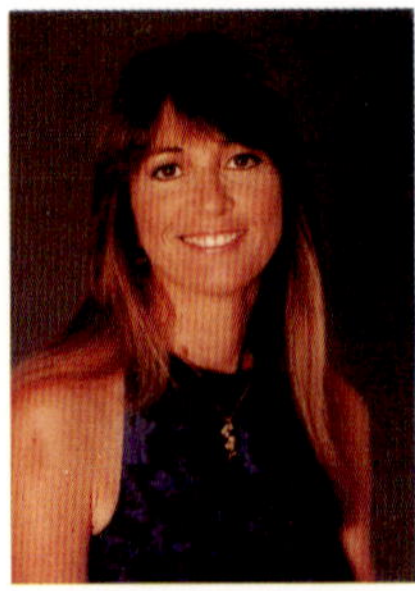

GAYLE BRIGHT

Soft brushed textures contrast with the gleam of polished gold and the brilliance of fine diamonds. The detail is superb. The proportion is precise. The lines are graceful and elegant.

Since 1969 Gayle Bright has been designing and sculpting exquisite miniatures. She offers an extraordinary collection of over 350 animal bracelets, pendants, rings, and earrings in gold, as well as vessels and small sculpture in bronze. Most are available in signed, limited editions.

Gayle supports the World Wildlife Fund, ASPCA, PETA, HSUS, Cousteau Society, Wilderness Society, GREENPEACE, National Wildlife Federation, San Diego Zoological Society, and the East Maui Animal Refuge (among others) in their efforts to preserve and protect animals and their environments.

By Appointment
Kihei, Maui, HI 96753
(808) 879-4212
(800) 392-4419

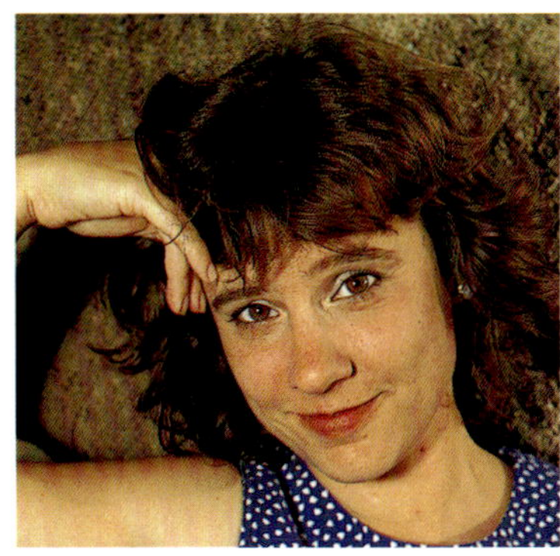

MARY BRONG

738 Menehune Lane, Suite 4
Honolulu, HI 96826
(808) 942-0156
800 287-0998

Mary Brong began her career as an environmental artist 15 years ago. While attaining a Fine Arts Degree from the University of Illinois, her lifelong love of nature blossomed into a keen interest in endangered animals and their habitats.

Currently living on Oahu, she has come to know the fragility and beauty of Hawaii and its native flora and fauna. Creating an awareness of that fragility is the focus of her latest artistic efforts in Mary's recent painting, "Hawaiian Monk Seal".

Also trained as a landscape architect, Mary serves as a design consultant for zoological parks, creating animal environments, including the African Savanna and the design of the Honolulu Zoo Master Plan. The artist's design capabilities have allowed her to take a direct hands-on approach in creating a greater awareness of nature through her projects at zoos and other public locations.

Mary's love of painting and wildlife combined with her unique experiences in working with rare and endangered species allows her to reflect each animal's distinctive personality in her art. Brong's painting of animals are truly "portraits", for she looks at each animal as a unique individual. Her landscapes are "naturescapes", depicting a strong sense of global ecology. Mary Brong's commitment to saving our natural world shines through in her art.

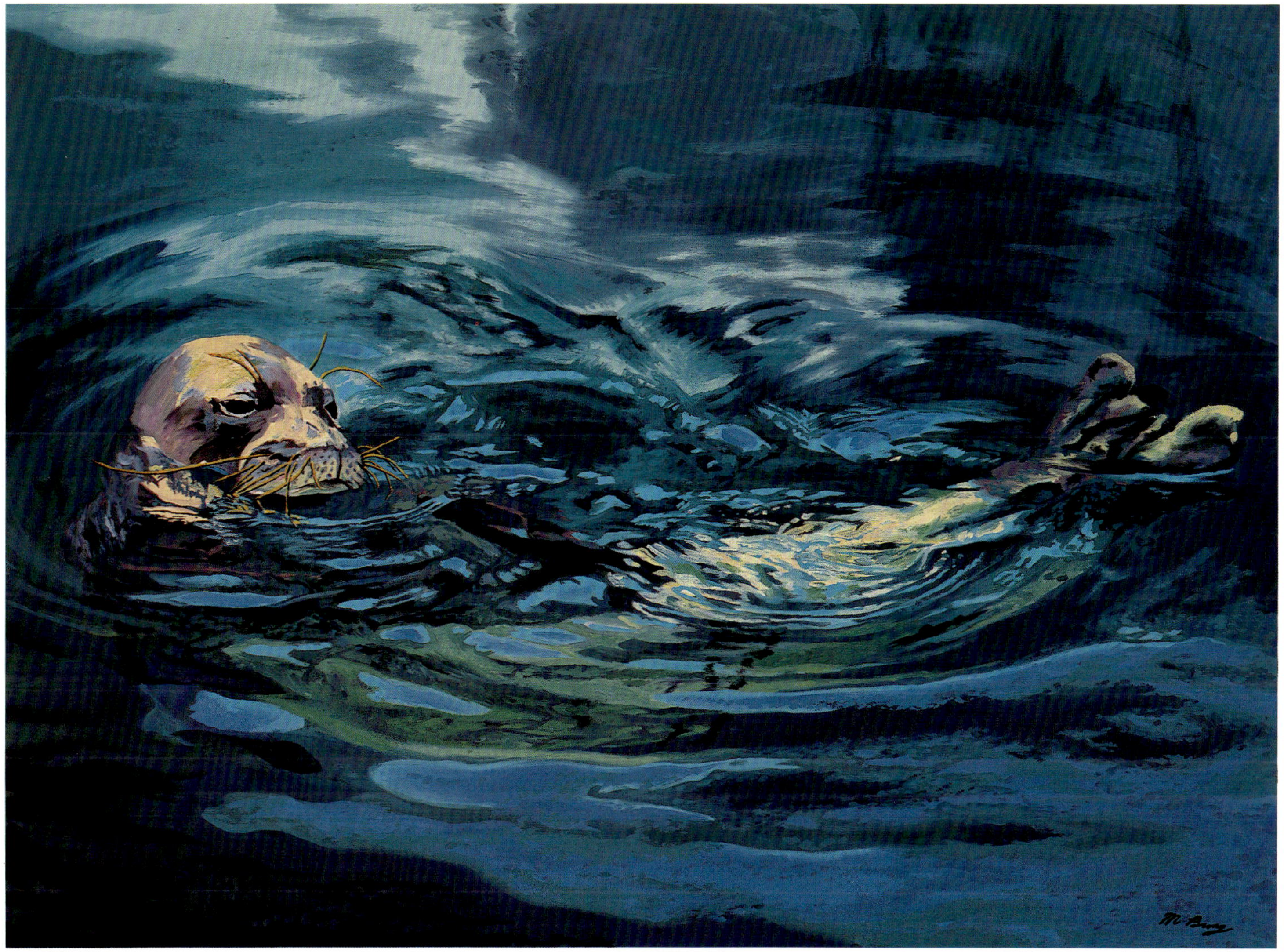

"Hawaiian Monk Seal" 30" x 24" Original Oil Painting

"Tembo" 40" x 30" Original Oil Painting

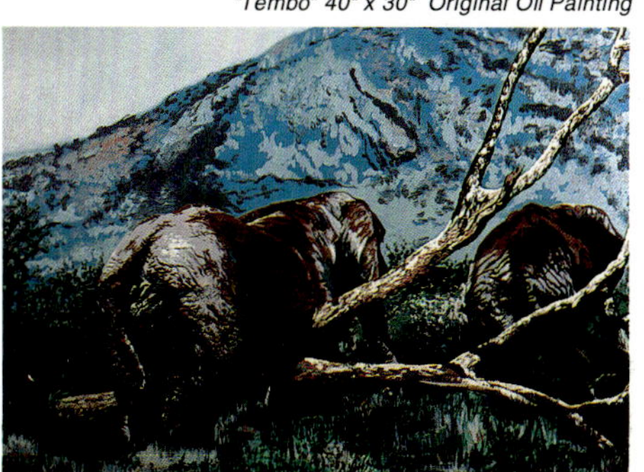

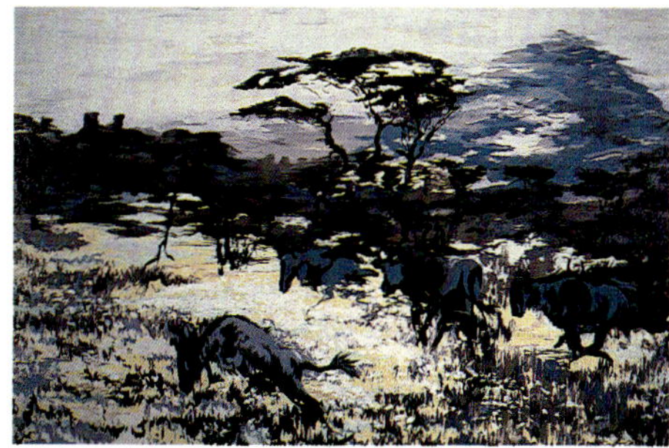

"Wildebeast" 36" x 24" Original Oil Painting

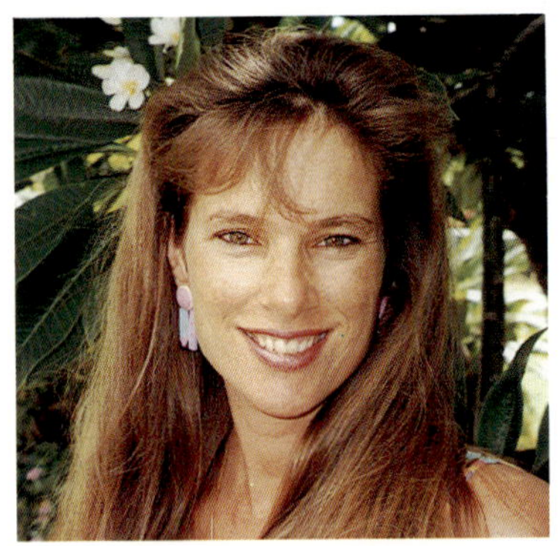

KIRSTEN BUNNEY

Australian artist Kirsten Bunney came to the Islands in 1987 from Bali where she had been painting and working as a designer. Her background in art includes book illustrator, record cover and logo designer, commissioned artist for large scale interior projects, as well as some experience in stage design for concert production.

In 1981 Kirsten first travelled to Bali, Indonesia. This vibrant, mystical culture transformed her art and instilled in her a deep desire to live and work in a tropical environment. She answered this dream in 1986 moving first to Bali and then to Hawaii.

Using the fine pen and ink technique of cross-hatch, the picture is gradually woven together under and over layers of watercolor producing a rich tapestry of organic form and dream imagery. Alternatively she uses large areas of gouache or water color, applying detail with shapes and patterns to create an effect of dynamic color and design.

Intricate detail, bold, provocative use of color and a strong sense of balanced composition exemplify the work of Kirsten Bunney. She is constantly experimenting and developing her styles and medium, exploring the dynamics of form, composition and color. Her work is stimulating, reflecting a unique vision of cross-cultural influences, unhindered by preconceived ideas about how art *should* look.

Kirsten's work has been purchased by the Hawaii State Foundation for Culture and the Arts and hangs in select private collections in the United States, Guam and Australia. She is represented in several galleries on the island of Maui where she lives. They include Viewpoints Gallery in Makawao, Foundation Gallery in Lahaina, Studio Blue Gallery in Lahaina and Kihei, Olde Wailuku Gallery in Wailuku and Hana Hou Gallery in Paia. Since 1986 Kirsten has been the exclusive designer for Manali Trading Company creating their very popular, whimsical collection of sealife statues, clocks and jewelry. Her designs can be found in gift galleries throughout the Islands, the Mainland and as far away as the Jacque Cousteau Foundation in Paris.

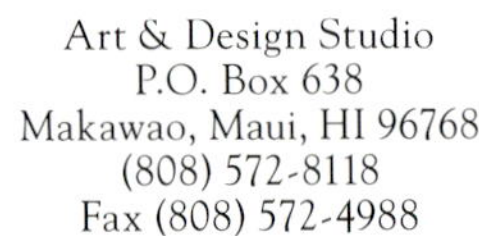

Art & Design Studio
P.O. Box 638
Makawao, Maui, HI 96768
(808) 572-8118
Fax (808) 572-4988

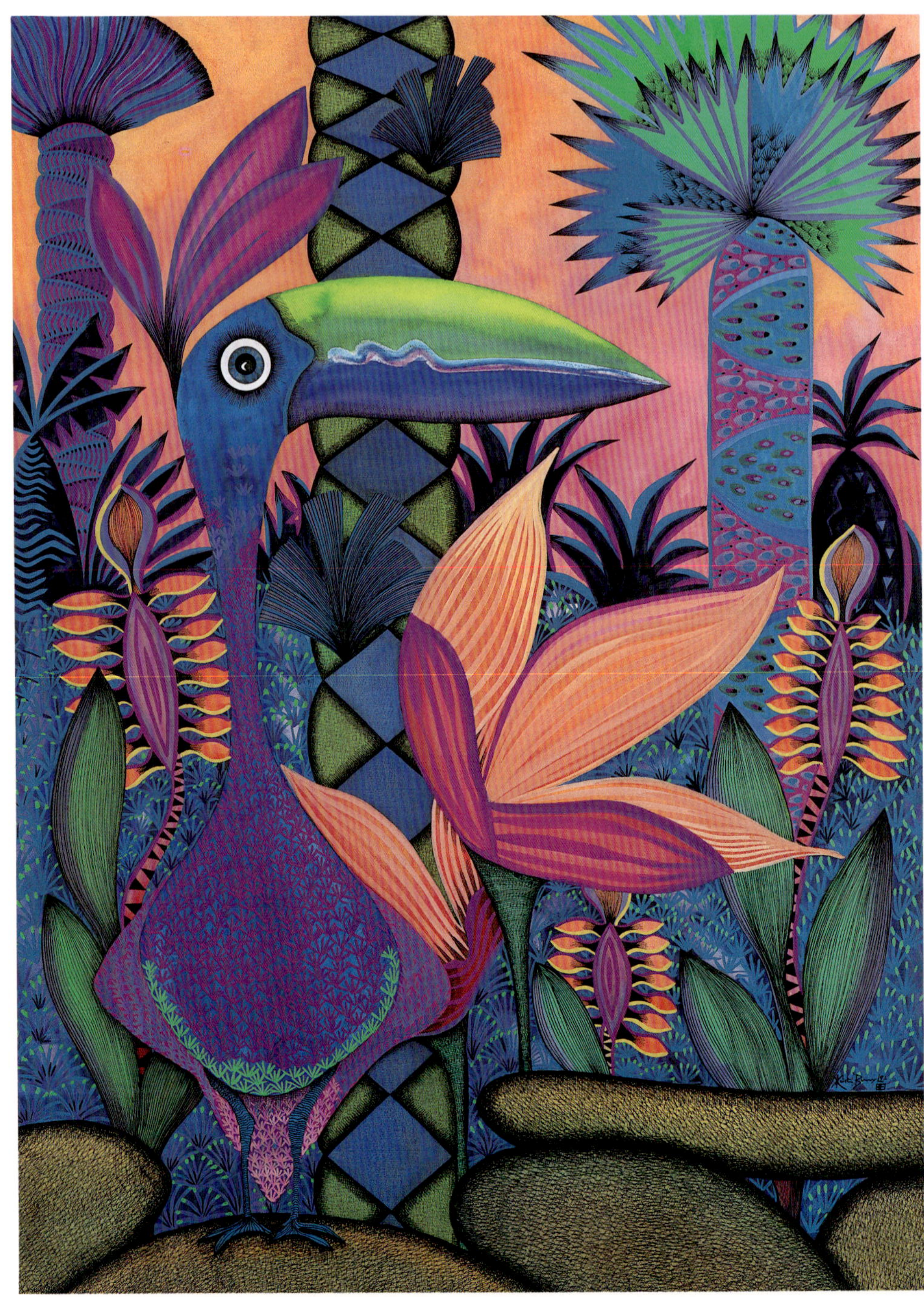

"Rocking Bird" 22" x 30" Original Pen, Ink, Watercolor and Gouache

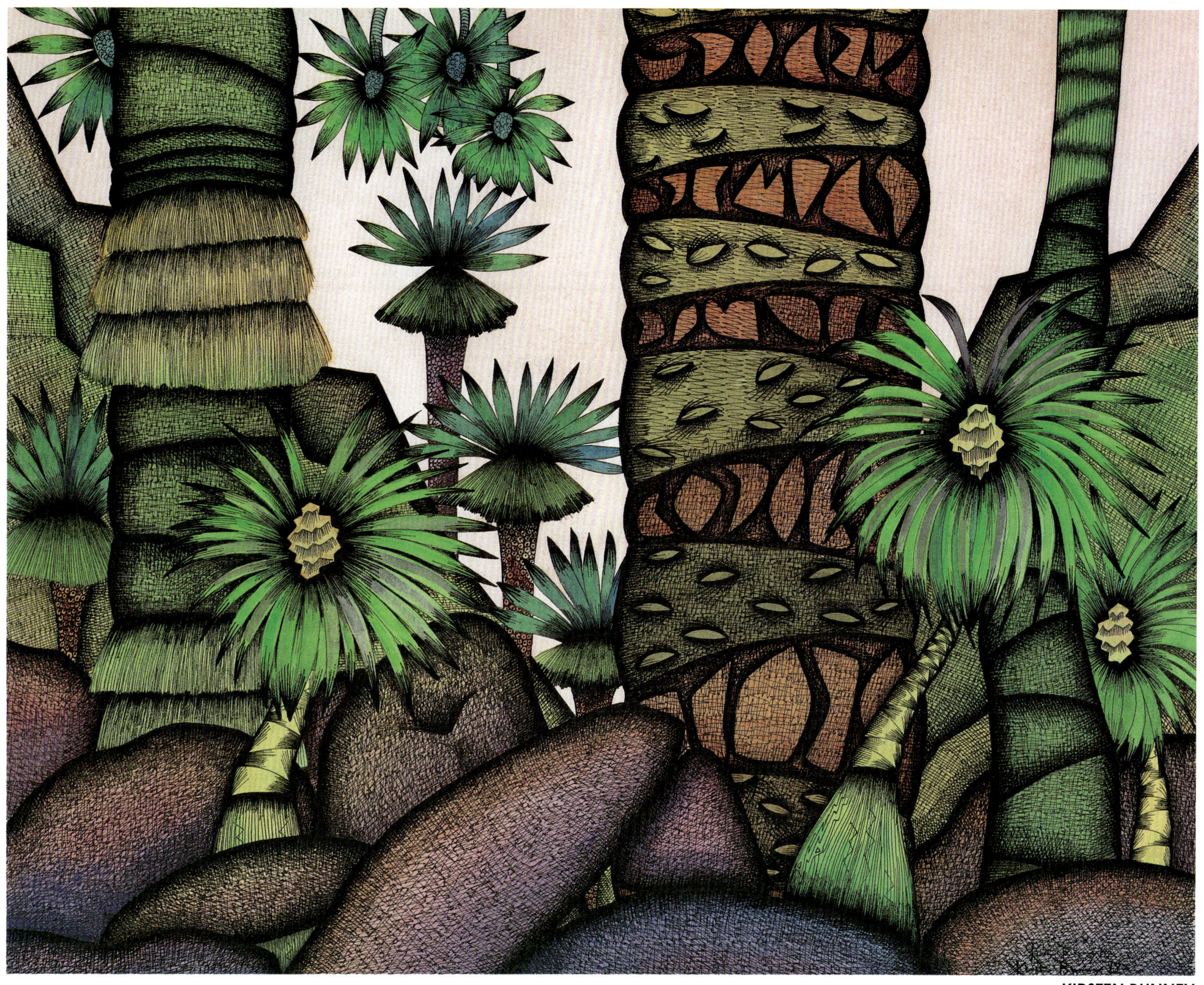

"Jungle Forms" 14" x 11" Original Pen, Ink, Watercolor and Gouache

KIRSTEN BUNNEY

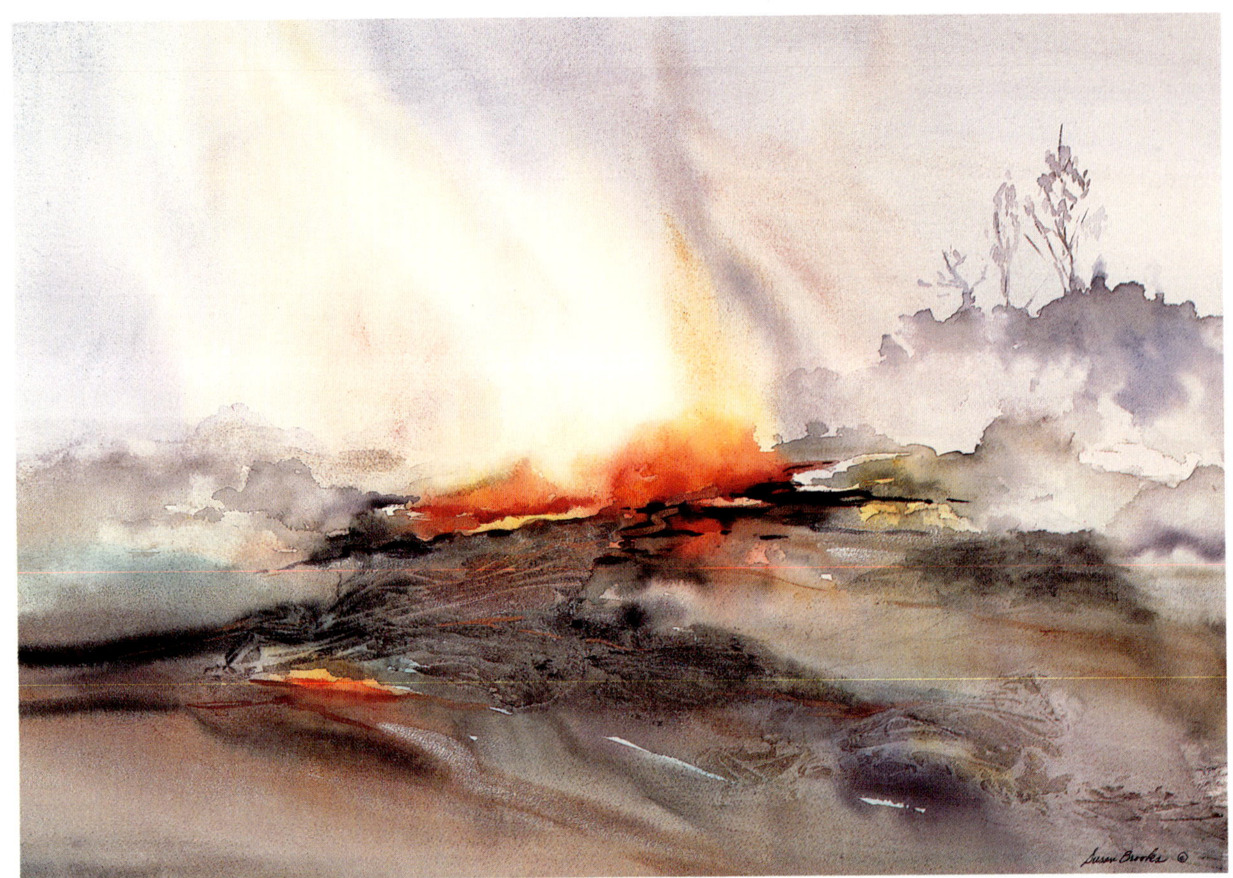

"Lavascape" 32" X 23" Original Watercolor Painting and Limited Edition Prints - Offset S/N 500 & Artists Proofs 50

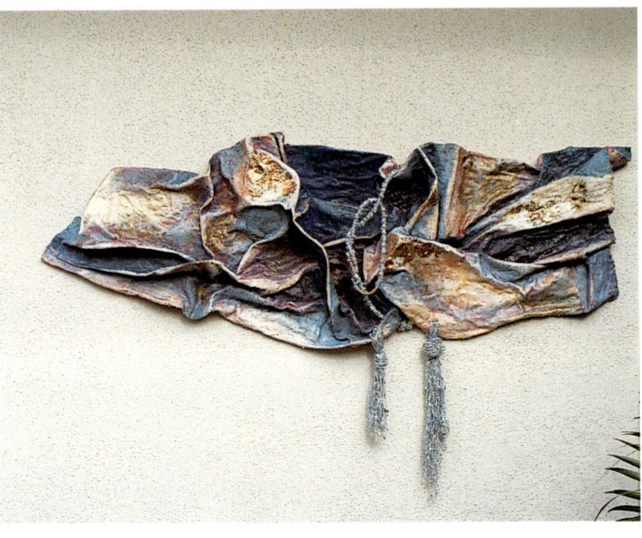

"Ocean Fantasy"
30" x 53" Wall Sculpture

Formed Canvas Cloth with Acrylic & Mixed Media

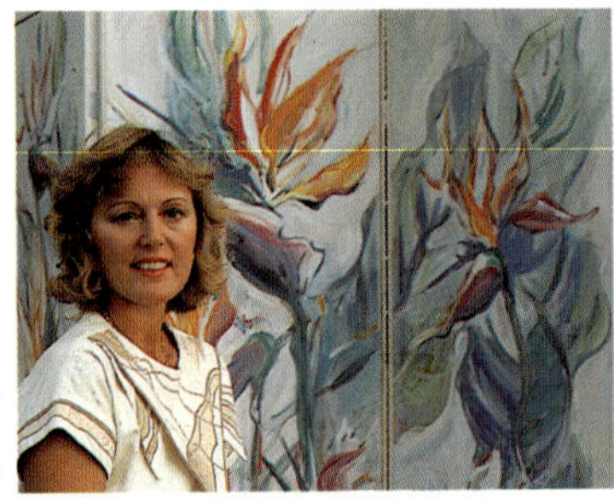

Three Panel Floor Screen 96" x 62"

SUSAN BROOKS

Susan Brooks, an American artist for many years, lives in Hawaii where she paints the beauty of the islands. Her current work leans more toward abstract and non–objective styles than realism.

Susan has spent many hours hiking the trails around Kilauea volcano in awe of the magic and mystery of this wonder of nature. 'Lavascape' is her impressionistic interpretation of the beauty and construction of Hawaii's dramatic landscape. Molten rock still pours forth from deep beneath the Pacific and Hawaii continues to grow, while Madame Pele, the fire goddess is the Hawaiian deity most feared and respected in the islands.

"I find abstract art more interesting than realism, more challenging to me, and more challenging to the viewer," Susan says.

"I like to leave much to the imagination. The way different forms and shapes, color and value go together presents a new experience each time you look at an abstract piece. Each time, there is a new interest."

Susan Brooks' experience includes her early studies in realism and the glazing techniques of the Old Masters, portraiture, impressionism, and abstract expressionism.

She has traveled widely, visiting the major galleries and museums of the world and compiling numerous sketches and photographs to use as resource material for her art.

Art by Susan Brooks is on display at Arts of Paradise gallery at the International Market Place in Waikiki, where she has been co–owner since 1988. Artful Framer, Interior Accents and Volcano Art Center also exhibit her work.

For studio appointments, telephone 395-7365 in Honolulu.

Arts of Paradise Gallery
International Market Place
2330 Kalakaua Avenue
Waikiki, Oahu, HI 96815
(808) 924-2787

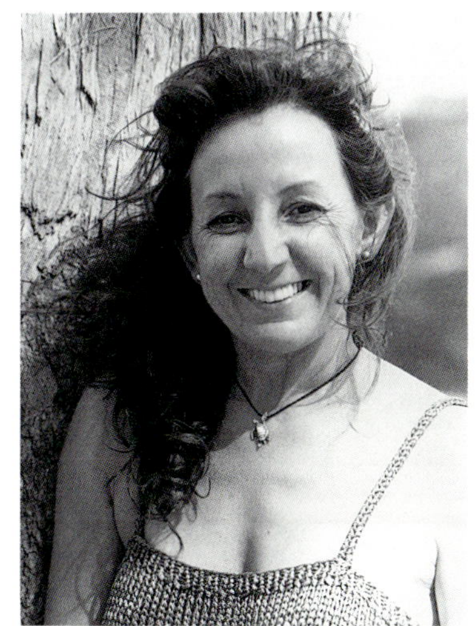

JOELLE CHICHEPORTICHE PERZ

Born and raised in Paris, France Joelle Chicheportiche studied at the University of Aix-en Province on an art history and fine art scholarship.

Her interest in various art forms took her through Mexico and San Francisco. She won her first major award in 1975 for the "international year of the woman" and has since been shown, awarded and greatly collected throughout the world.

After many travels and studies Joelle Chicheportiche arrived in Hawaii in 1982. In making Maui her home, Joelle has found a true fit to her creativity and deepest love and understanding of nature. Through the years, she has developed a great interest for printing techniques such as etchings, linoleum cuts and monotypes, which she combines in a very unique way with hand-made papers and mixed media.

Joelle Chicheportiche's work is available at both her studio's, Viewpoints Gallery, the Maui Crafts Guild and the Lahaina Arts Society.

Joelle C. Studio's
3620 Baldwin Avenue, Suite 104
Makawao, Maui, HI 96768
(808) 572-3479
Fax (808) 572-3479

256 B Front Street
Lahaina, Maui, HI 96761
(808) 667-5561

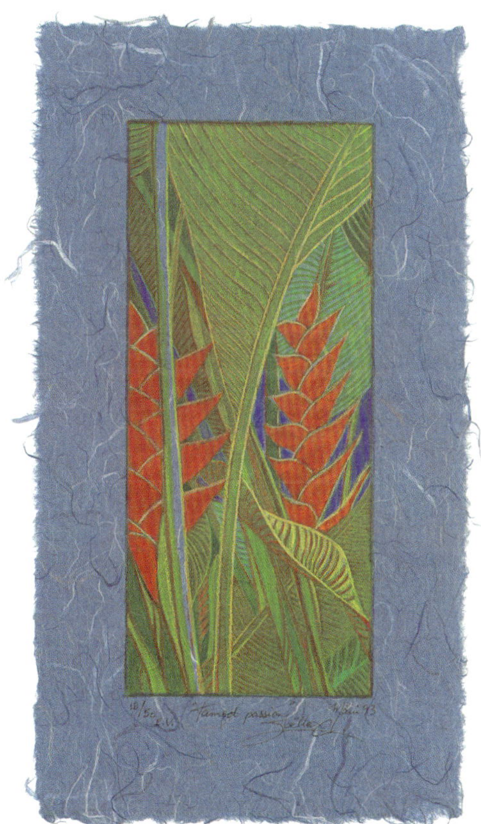

"Tamed Passion"
4.25" x 9.75" Linoleum Block Prints with Mixed Media
on Japanese Handmade Paper- S/N 50

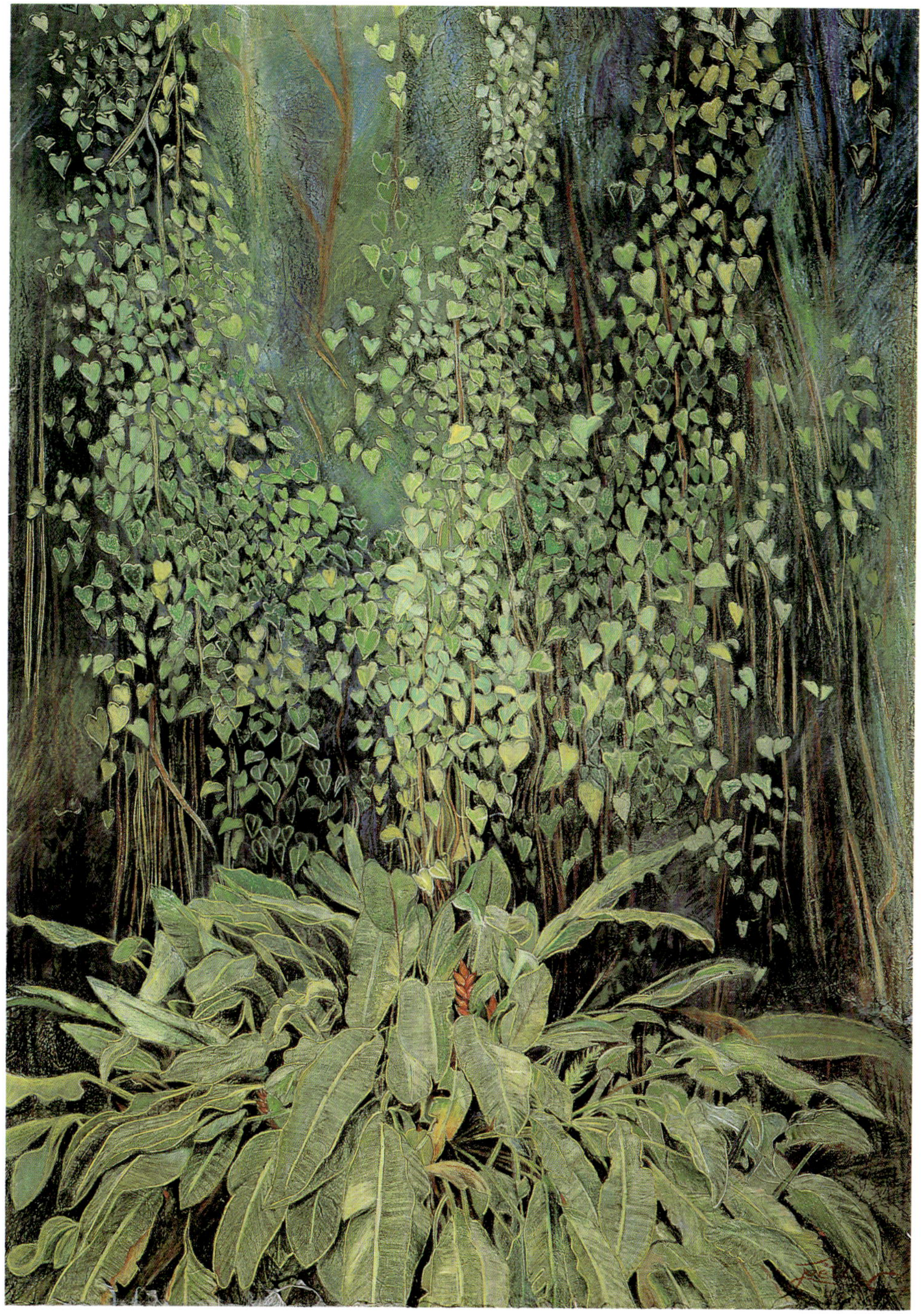

"Showers of Love"
30" x 40" Original Monotype with Mixed Media
on Japanese Handmade Paper. Prints Available in Various Sizes

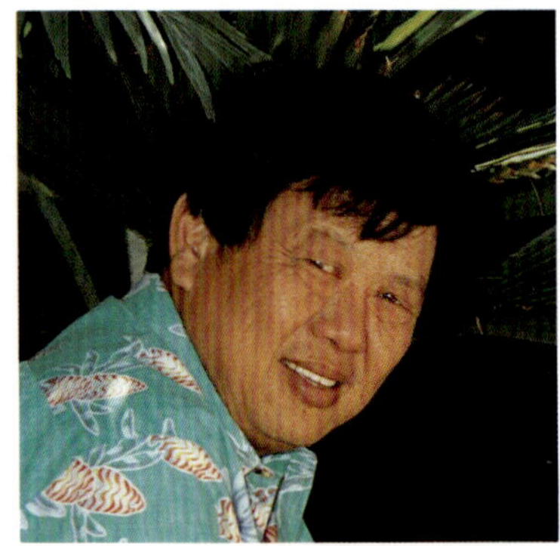

LAU CHUN

2259 Kalakaua Avenue
Honolulu, Oahu, HI 96815
(808) 922-8818
Fax (808) 396-0922

Hawaii's visionary master of impressionist art, Lau Chun has been a resident since 1971. Born in Kiangsi, China in 1942, his interest in art began to emerge at age 10. After completing high school, he studied for two years at the Canton School of Fine Arts.

In 1962, while living in Hong Kong, he was hired by Francis Bobo, the noted Mexican artist, to paint mosaics and murals. Through a grant with the Revox Corporation in Switzerland, Lau's work began to receive exposure and recognition in Europe as well as Asia. Since moving to Hawaii, his paintings have been shown at major exhibitions from Honolulu to New York.

Lau's superb impressionist landscapes seem to cast a spell of pleasant remembrance. His paintings are like panoramas of the mind. Like favorite reveries, they reveal moments almost suspended in time. Serenity blends with romance, becoming a mood of idyllic imagination

Painting exclusively in oils, each canvas is a personal celebration of color. They are alive with a natural movement that beckons to our eyes, inviting us to dream. There is freedom yet control in his brush strokes. Passion combines with peacefulness. Over each design, an ambiance of harmony prevails.

Lau's style of painting is constantly evolving. Early in his career he was known for his abstract motifs which were executed with a bold energetic brush. The subtle colors he used then were earth tone. In the mid-seventies he began to paint landscapes and his palette became alive with dabbles of green and blue hues. Today, the colors burst upon the canvas... brilliant reds, oranges, yellows and pinks.

Lau continues to epitomize inventiveness in balance with discipline. Because he paints what he feels, his mood may find expression in a human form, or it may seek the style of abstraction, or it may be immersed in impressionism. But in every painting there is the powerful instinct for composition and color.

Since January of 1988, Lau Chun has displayed his paintings in his own gallery in the Royal Hawaiian Hotel. His brilliant canvases adorn the walls of Waikiki's most popular hotels including the Moana Surfrider, the Parc Hotel and the Sheraton Waikiki where one of the largest collections may be viewed in the Hano Hano Restaurant.

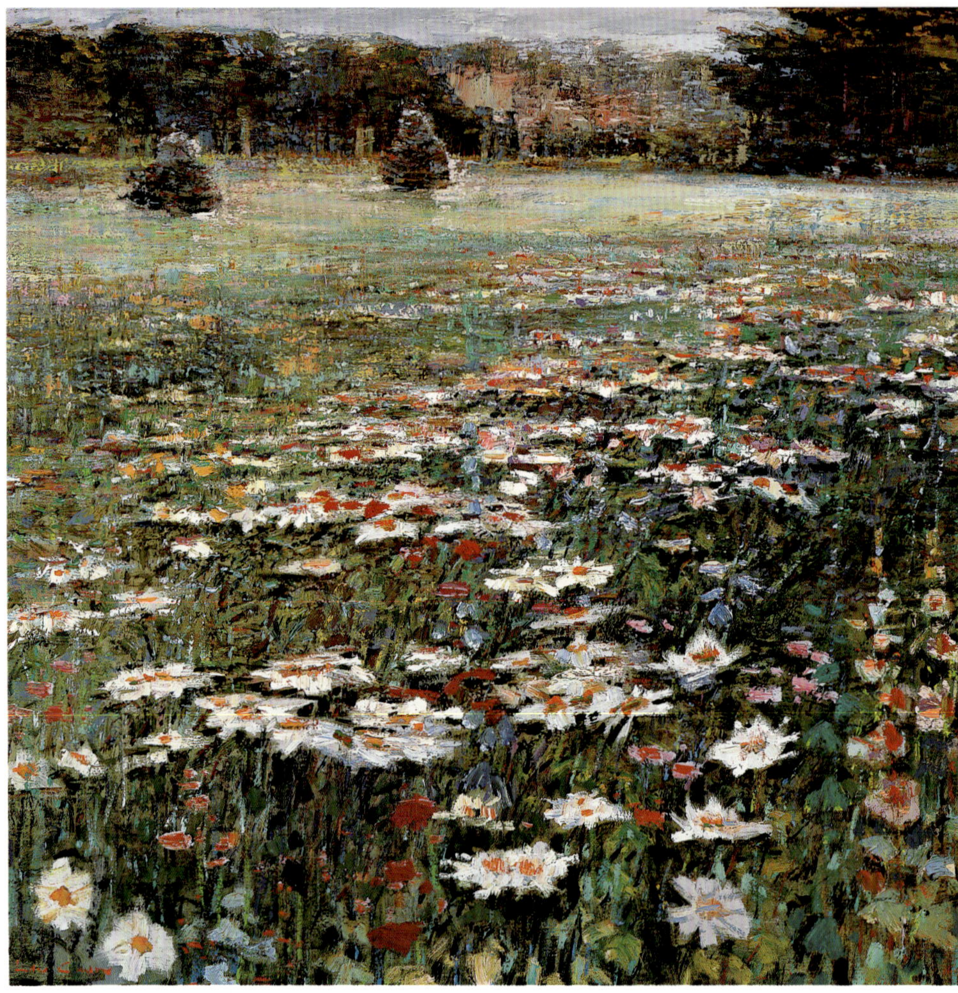

"Daisies" 40" x 40" Original Oil Painting

National and international clients and collectors include the Hawaii State Foundation on Culture and the Arts; Alexander and Baldwin, Inc.; JTB Hawaii, Inc.; Marshall Field and Company, Chicago; Nelson Rockefeller Collection, New York; Queen Elizabeth II/ Cunard Cruise Line; Rocks and Gems, Canada; Pharma-Verlags Publishing Company, Germany and the Dun and Bradstreet Corporation, Connecticut.

Lau's paintings can be found at Lahaina Galleries in Hawaii and California; Sierra Galleries in Lake Tahoe, California; Sybill/Dawson Fine Art, Carmel, California.

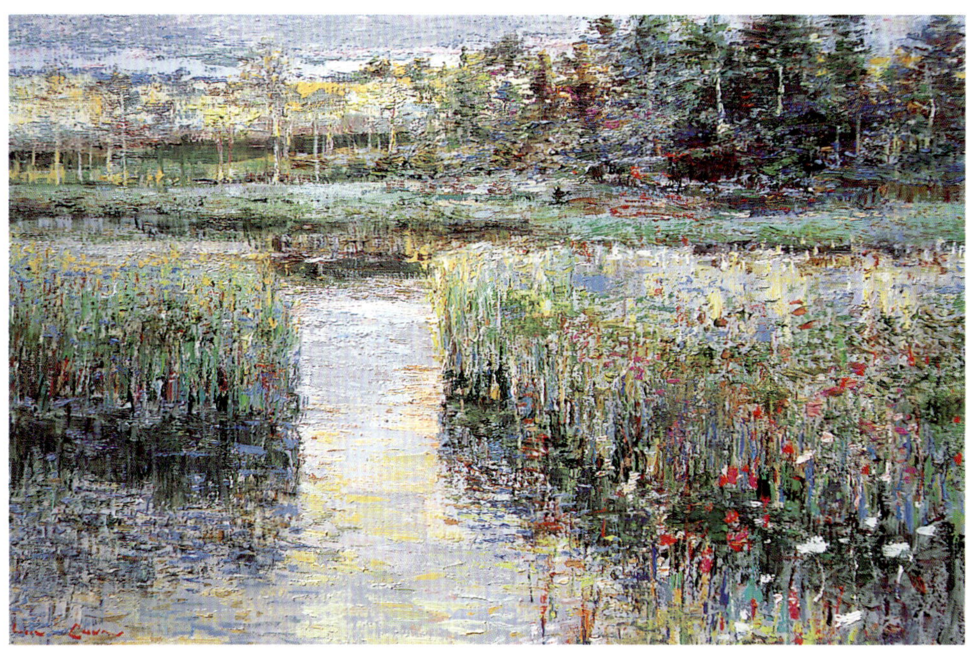

"Peaceful Lake" 36" x 24" Original Oil Painting

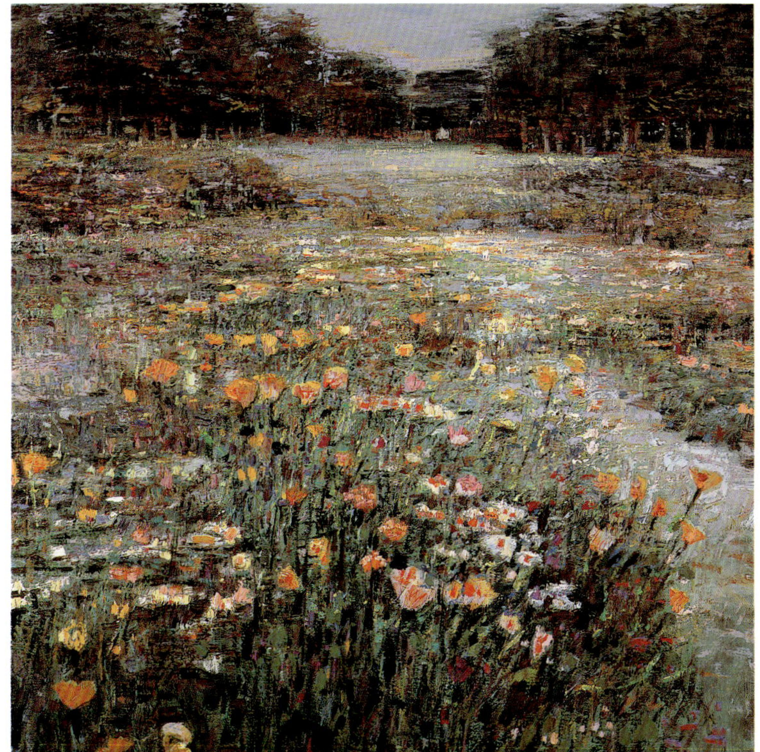

"Springtime" 40" x 40"
Original Oil Painting

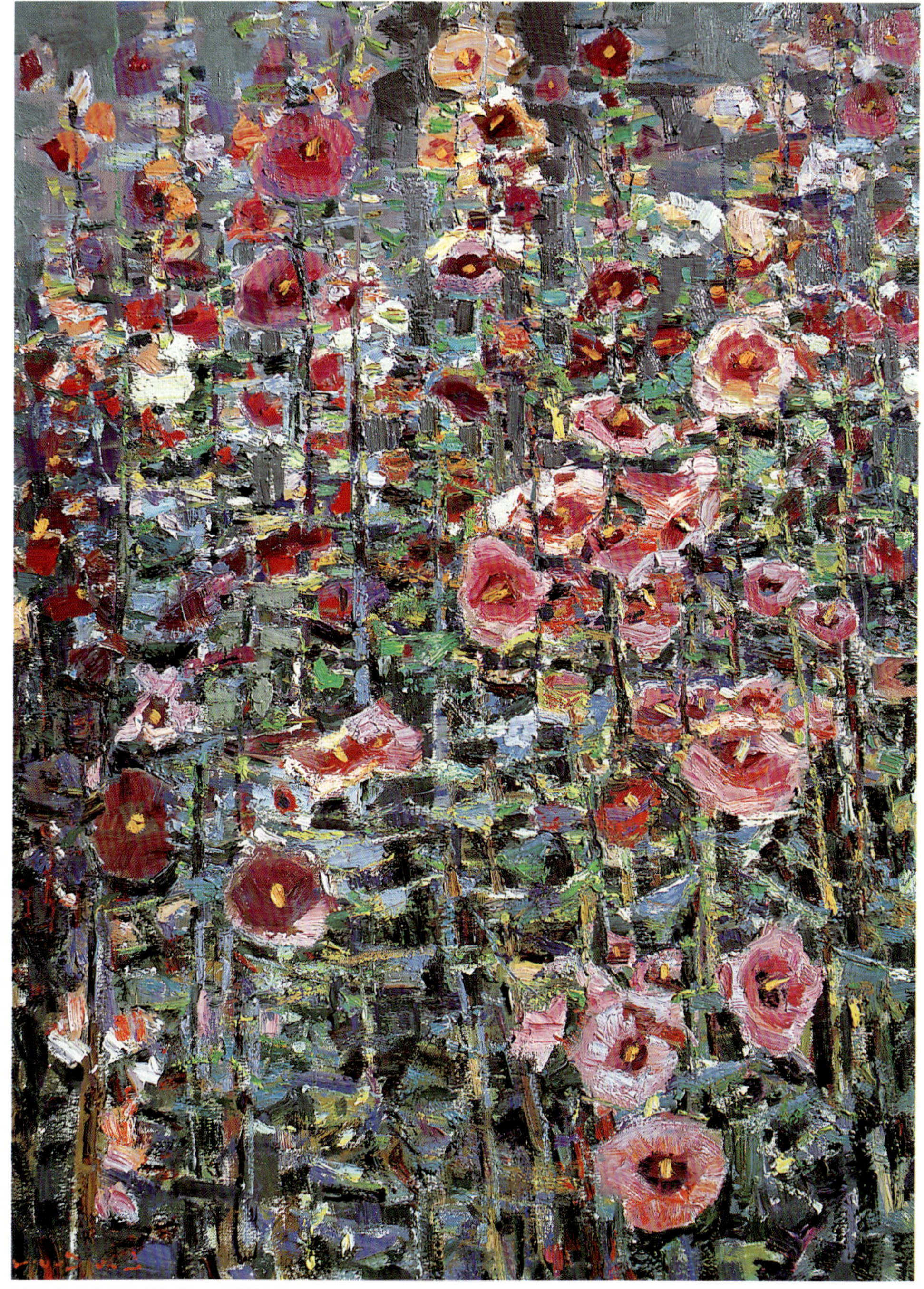

"Holly Hocks" 30" x 40" Original Oil Painting

LAU CHUN

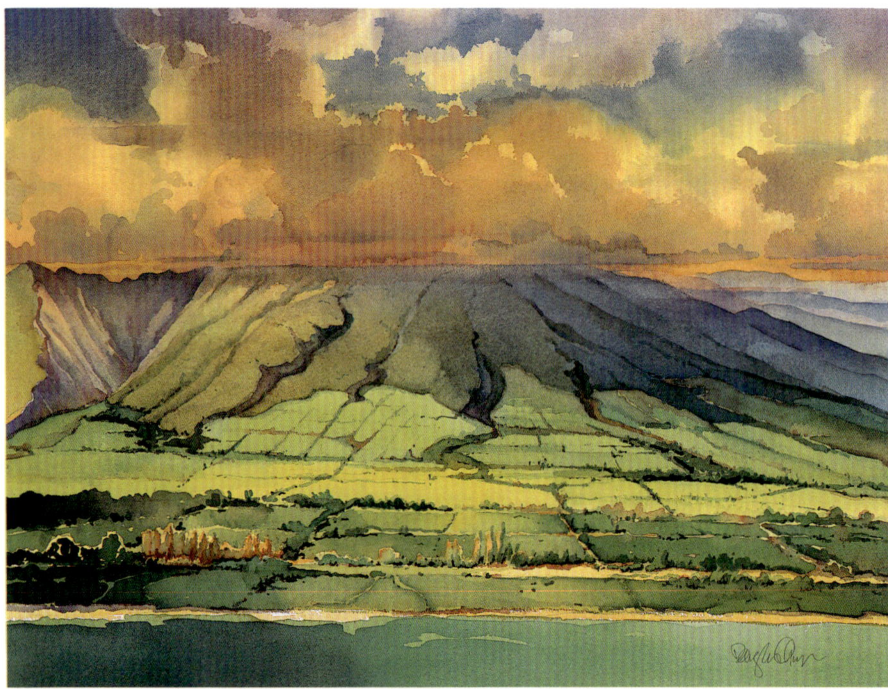

"Cloud-Covered" 18" x 24"
Original Watercolor and Limited Edition Prints

DOUGLAS CHUN

The goal of Douglas Chun's work is to portray the natural beauty surrounding us and to increase public awareness of our fragile land and our vanishing landscape. Honoring the alignment between sky, earth and water, his work reflects his Chinese heritage which manifests a deep reverence for the forces of nature.

"Sensing the spirit of a place is an experience that I want to convey in my paintings. My intent is to capture the essence of each place, hoping to inspire the public to revere and care for what nature has given us and to ultimately preserve what is left".

Douglas Chun was born in Canton, China and attended the Honolulu Academy of Arts and the San Francisco Art Institute. In 1958 he established Chun/Ishimaru in San Francisco, specializing in architectural illustrations.
He returned to the islands after the devastating loss of his home/studio and all of his work in the Berkeley/Oakland fire of 1991. His watercolors have recorded a variety of subject matters from Italy, France, California and other locations. Chun's work is represented in many collections throughout the United States and abroad.

Douglas Chun Studio
116 Holopuni Road
Kula, Maui, HI 96790
(808) 876-0142

"The Old Church" 18" x 24"
Original Watercolor and Limited Edition Prints

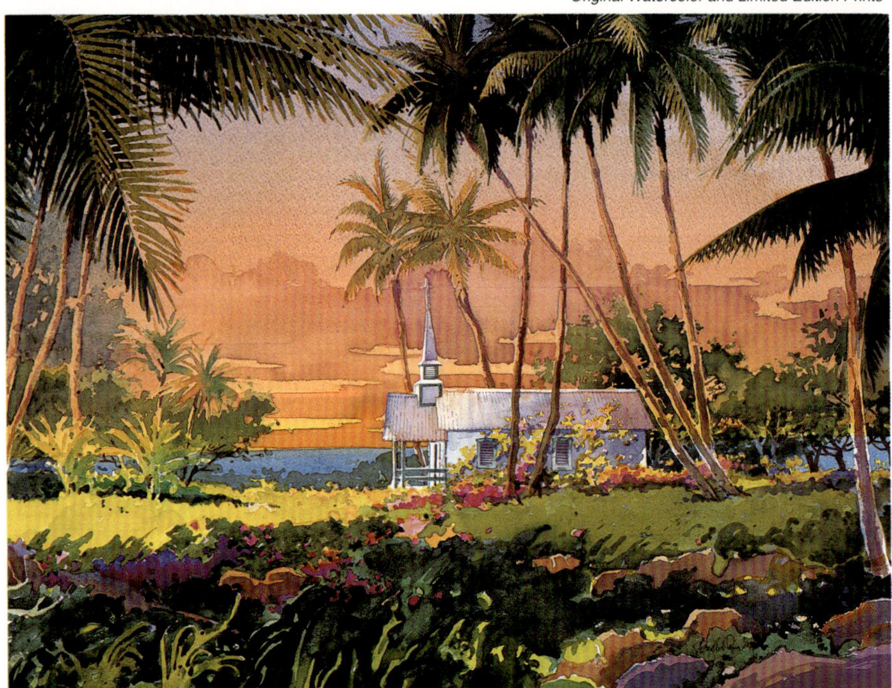

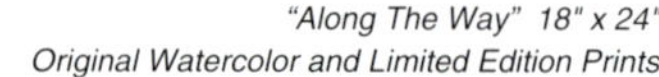

"Along The Way" 18" x 24"
Original Watercolor and Limited Edition Prints

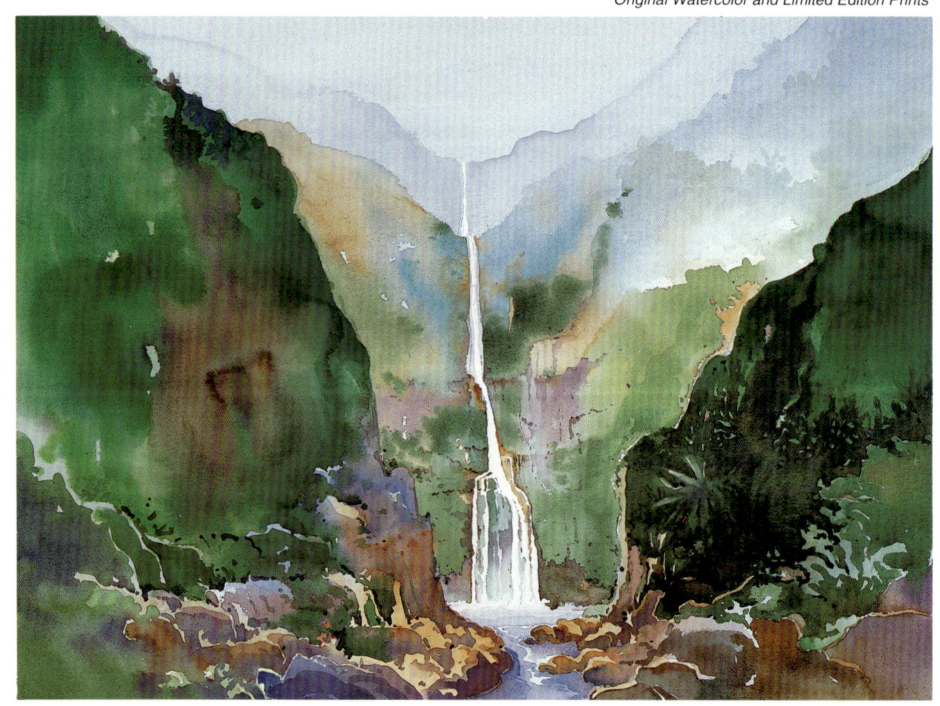

"By the Sea" 21" x 28" Original Watercolor and Limited Edition Prints

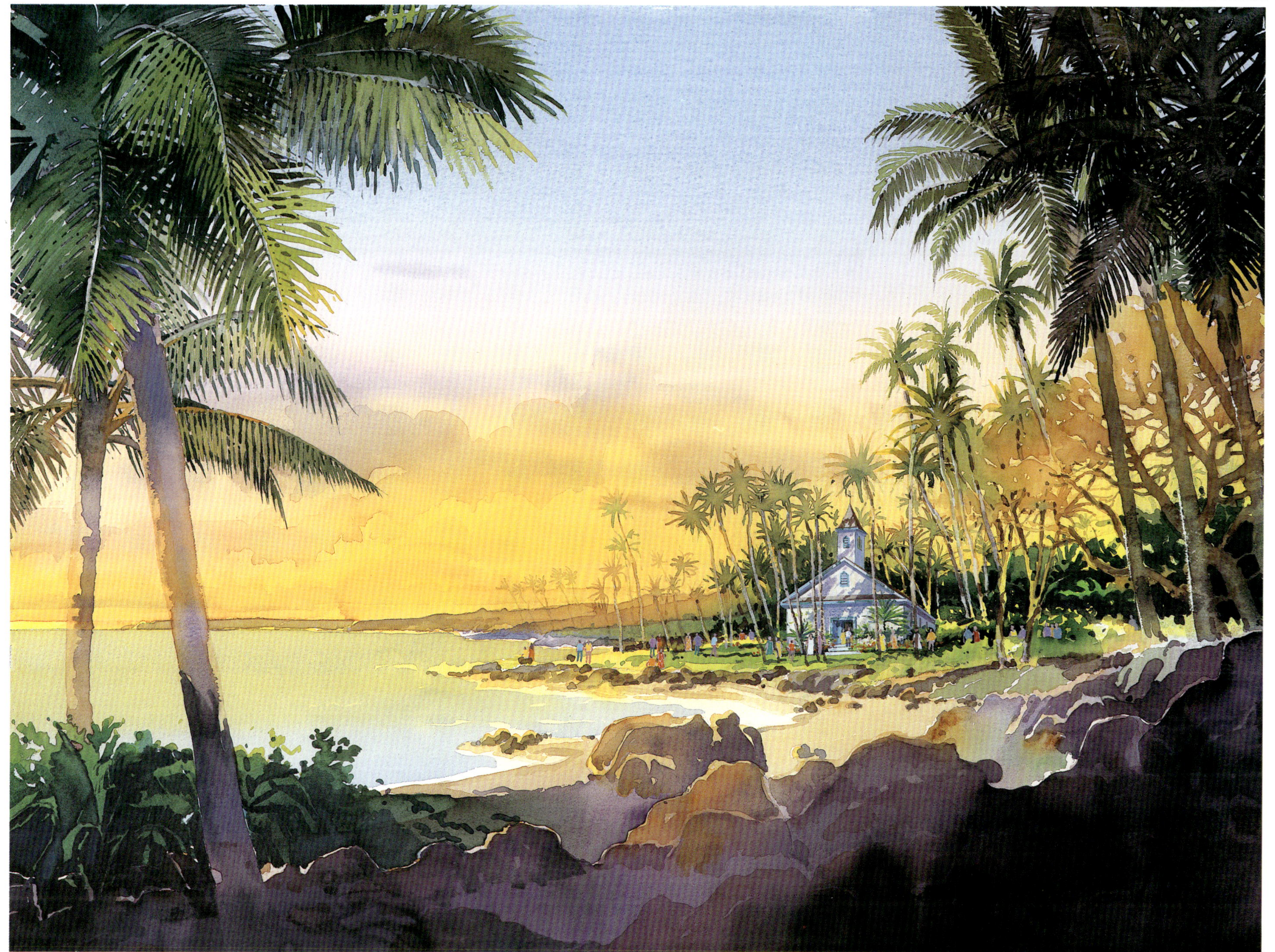

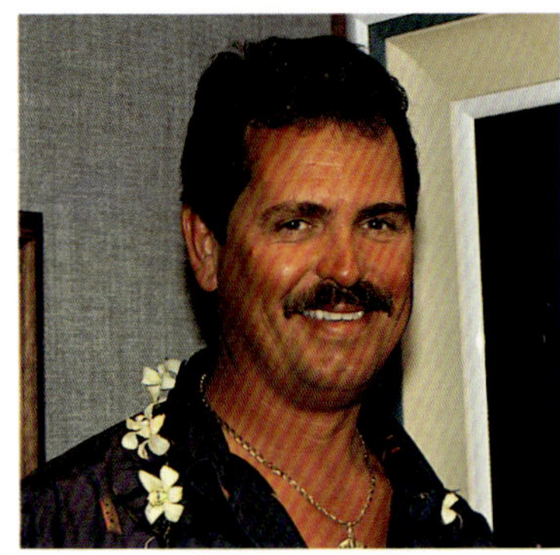

JAMES COLEMAN

James Coleman is a name synonymous with sweeping skies, tropical rain forests, rich deep woods and silent deserts. The images created by this talented man continue to delight all who view them.

James Coleman was born in Hollywood, California in 1949. As a youth his creative abilities seemed to dominate his world. Though he lacked the athletic skills of his young friends, he more than made up for it with imagination and ingenuity. As a young man his interest in film making and fine art would be the genesis for a long successful career in animated films.

In 1969, Coleman found his creative energies welcomed by Walt Disney Productions. As an animation background designer, Coleman styled and worked on nine feature films and over 30 short subjects. Twenty-two years with Disney found him ready to develop all of his time and talent to the love of his life, fine art.

Today he continues to illuminate the art world with vibrant colors, gentle moods, powerful design and exquisite detail.

Coleman works in oil, watercolor, gouache and pastel. His work is impressionistic and luminous. His pieces intrigue the eye and touch the heart. His paintings are warm inviting and unique.

Coleman began doing paintings of the Islands in the early 1980's. "Originally Hawaii was an escape for me, a place to recharge my batteries and enjoy the peace and tranquility of heaven on earth. The land, its history and its people were my secret to serenity and relaxation. Soon my love for these beautiful islands and its people began to translate into paintings. My desire has been to connect those who view my work with the past, present and future of the Hawaiian experience".

Though traditional in technique and medium, Coleman's tropical pieces are anything but traditional. They are a fresh and unique personal view of Hawaii.

His mastery of color, light and design has in recent years made Coleman one of the most collected and sought after artists in Hawaii and around the world.

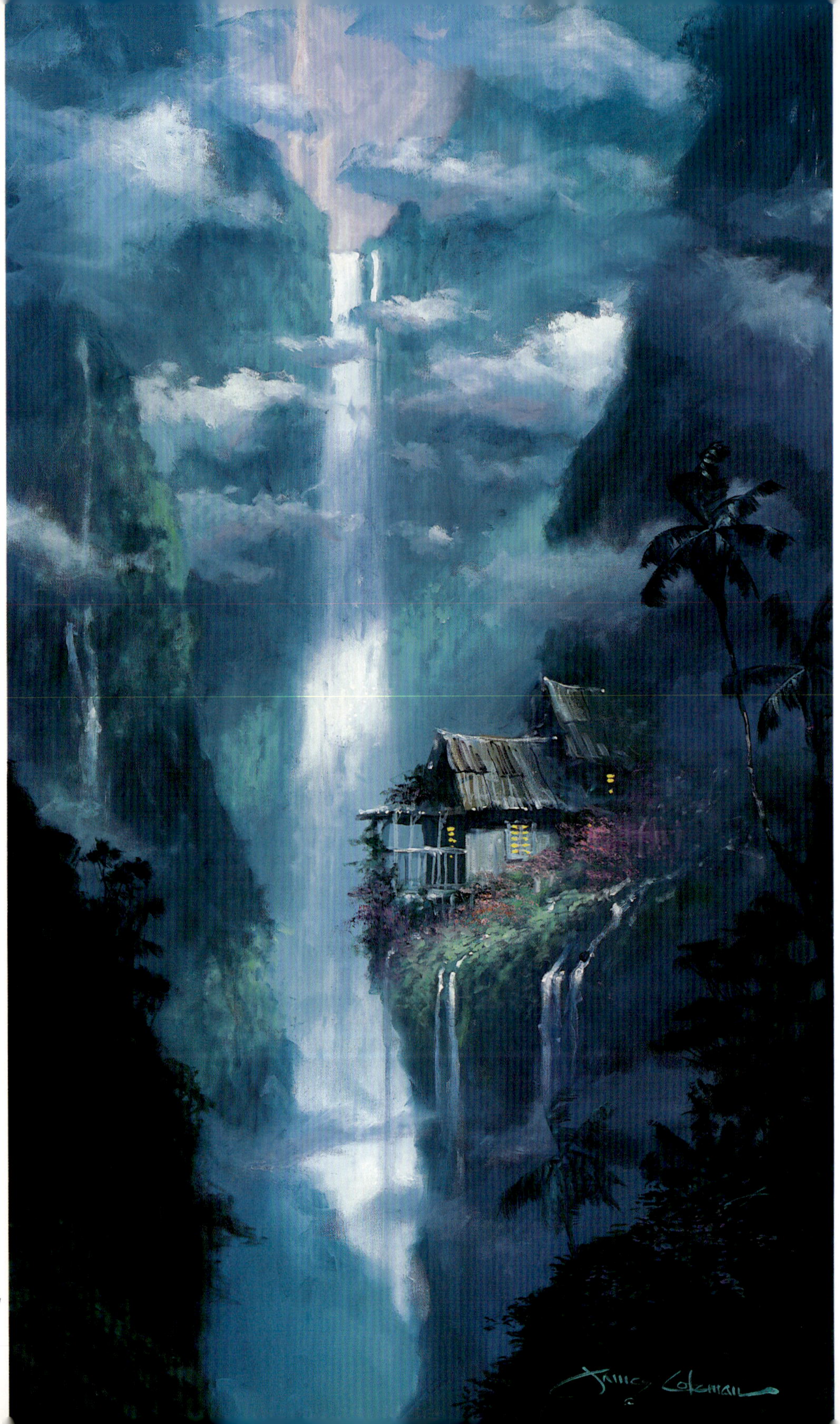

"Never Ending Spirit" 48" x 60" Original Oil Painting

"Impressions of Paradise" 72" x 48" Original Oil Painting

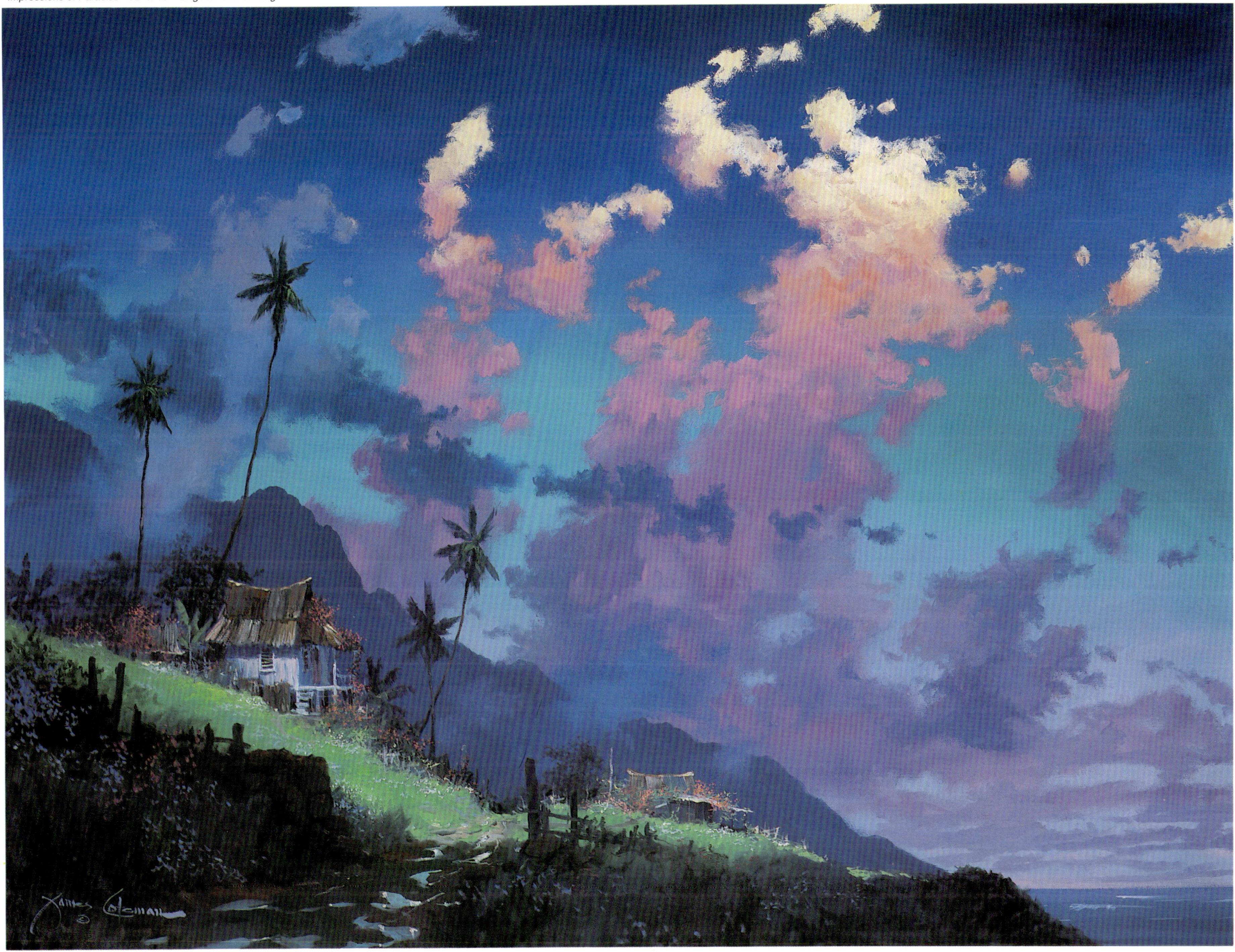

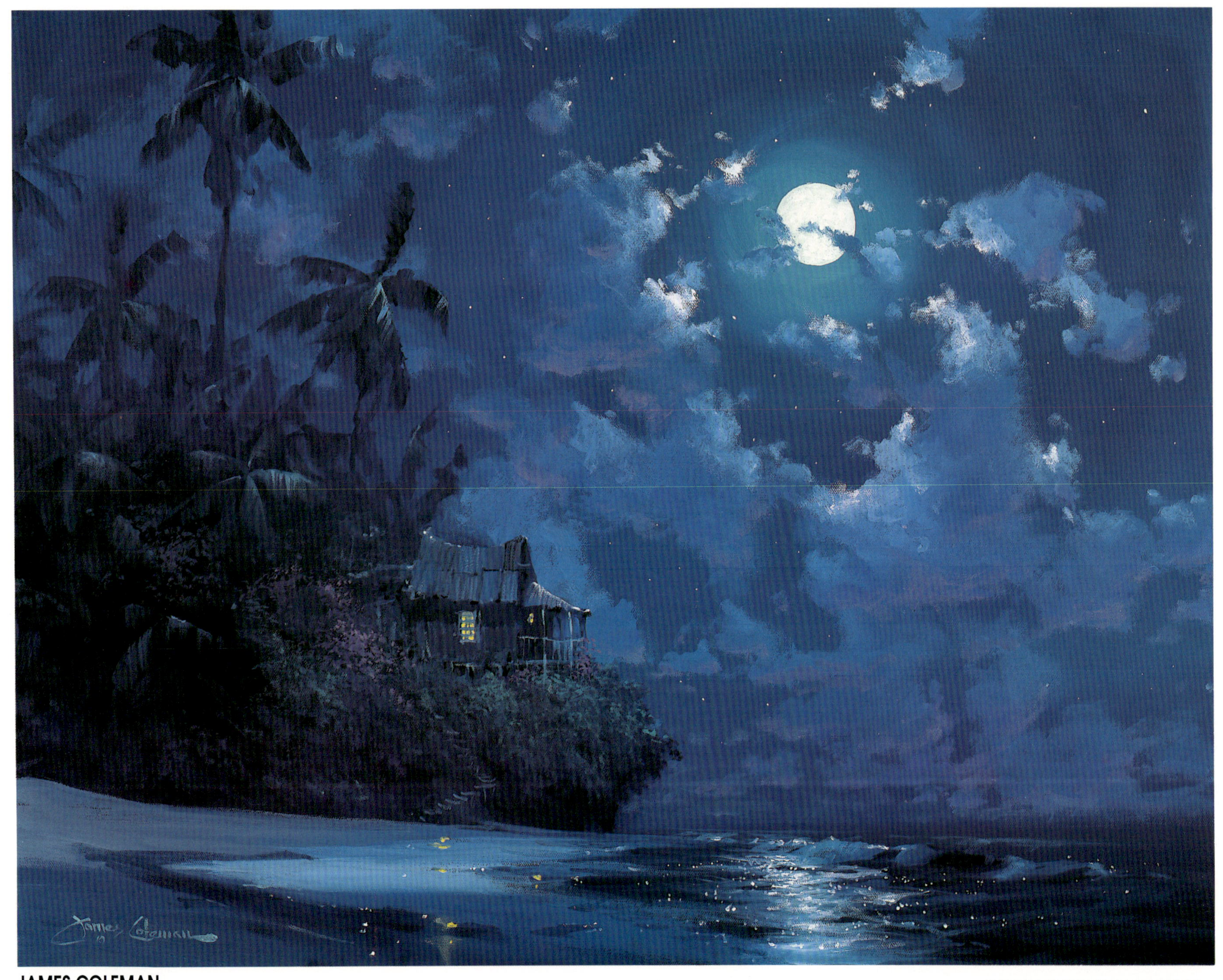

JAMES COLEMAN

"Midnight Surf" 72" x 48" Original Oil Painting

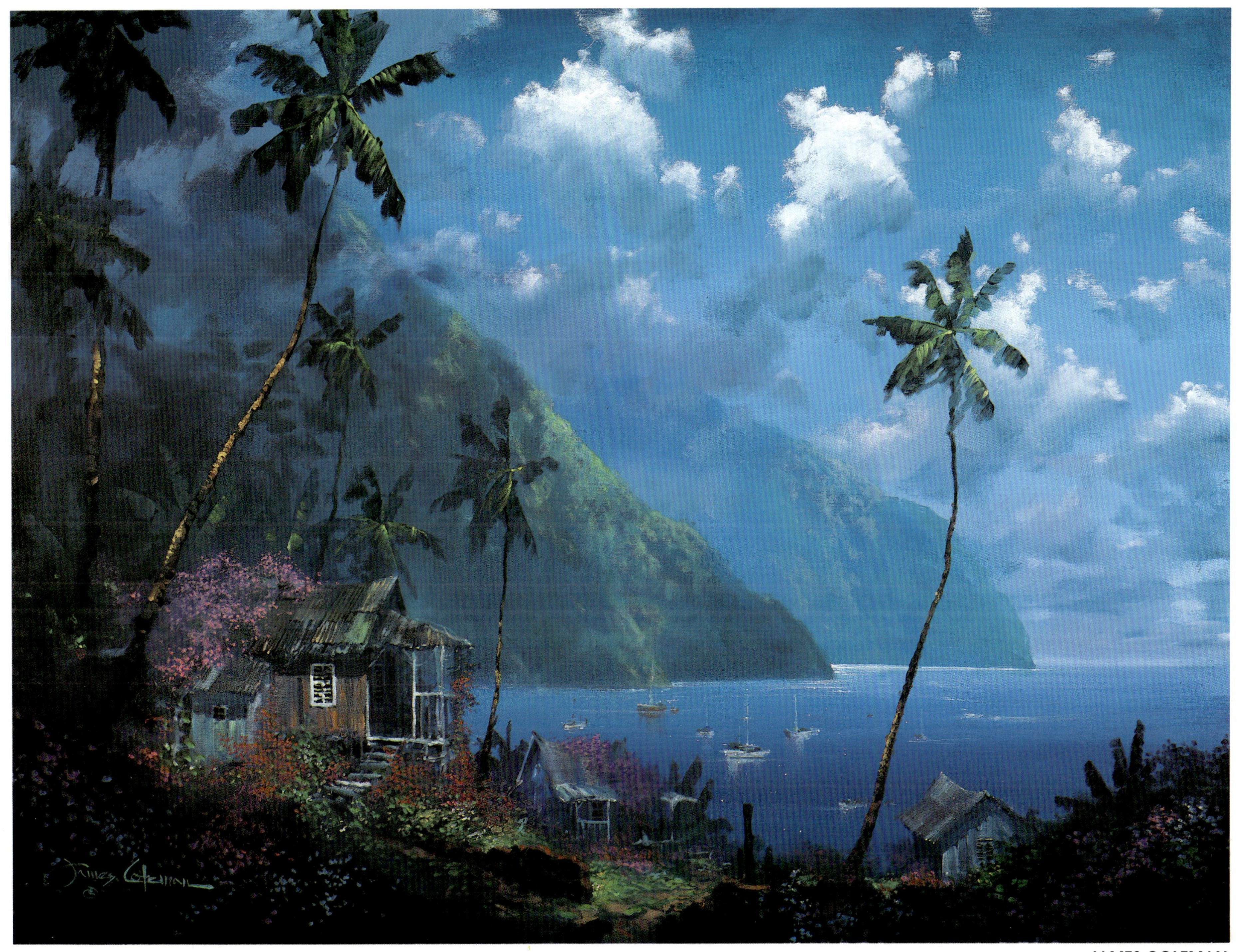

"Memories of Paradise" 72" x 48" Original Oil Painting

JAMES COLEMAN

JAMES COLEMAN

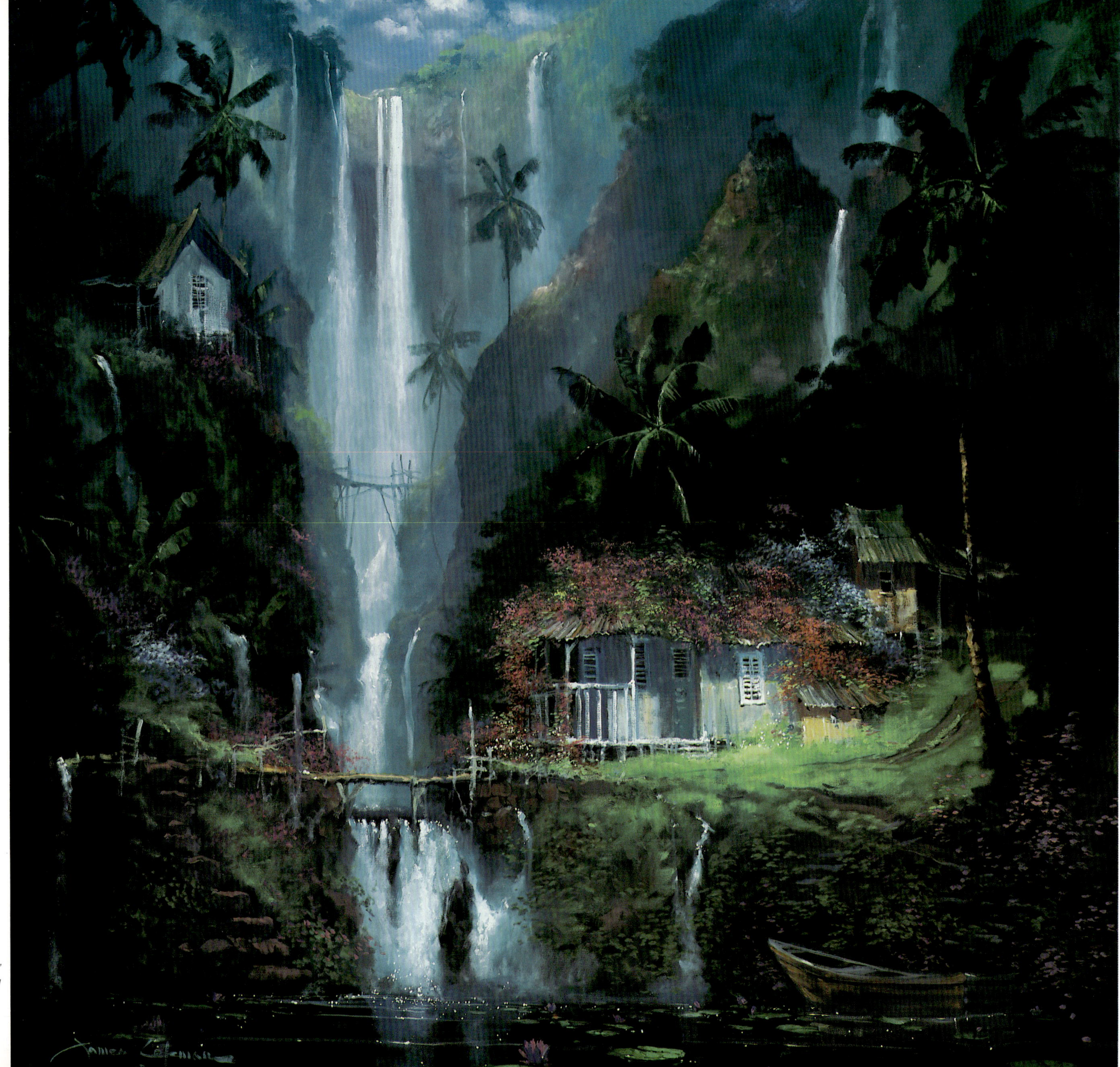

"Peaceful Rythms"
72" x 48" Original Oil Painting

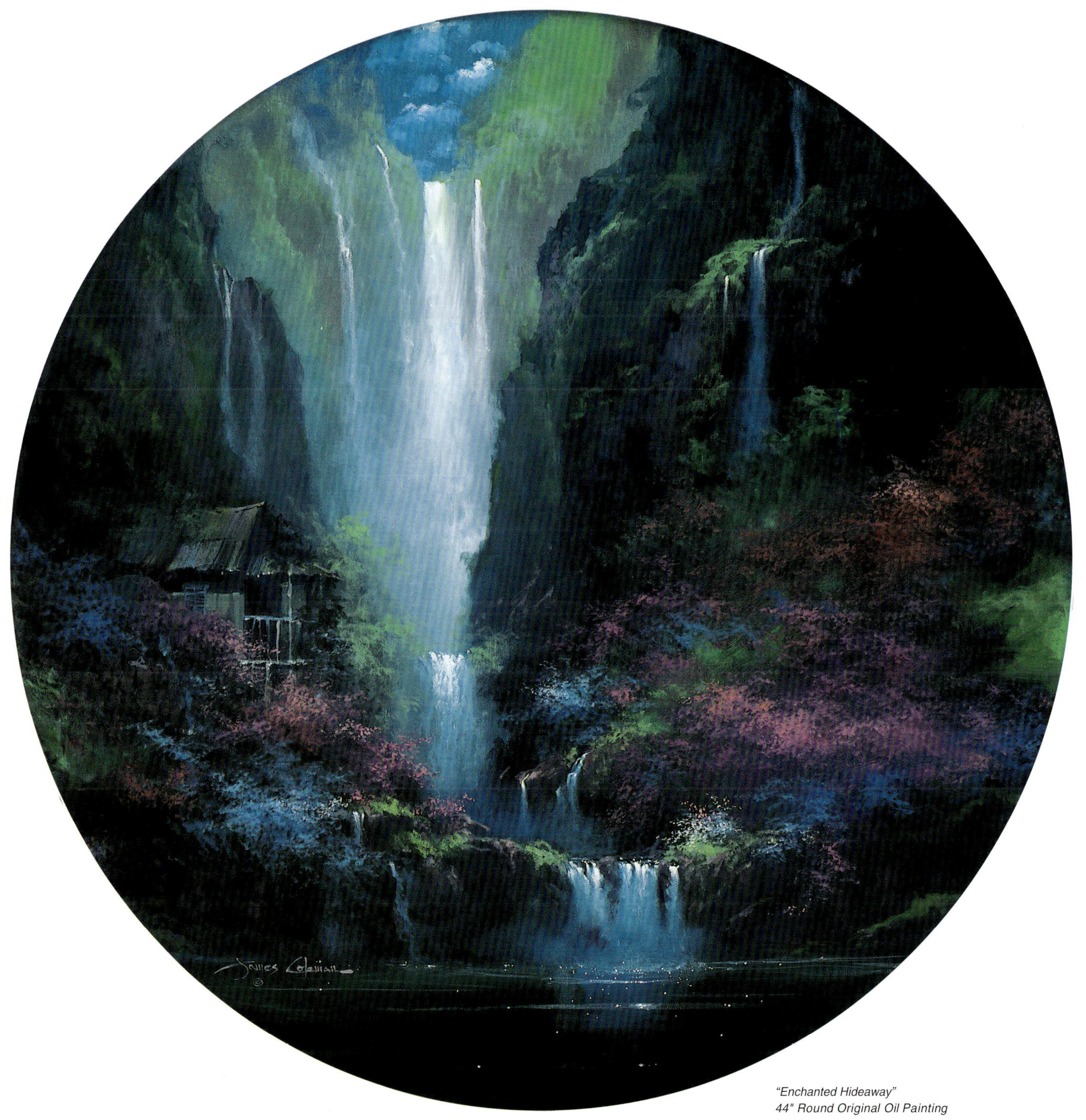

"Enchanted Hideaway"
44" Round Original Oil Painting

JAMES COLEMAN

James Coleman pieces can be found in many fine, personal, and corporate collections, including the Disney family.

His collaborative work with the artist Wyland has drawn interest worldwide.

Coleman is a naturalist and environmentalist who involves himself with the National Parks and other environmental organizations. He has been a finalist 5 years in the Arts for Parks competition.

The contribution made by Coleman to the world of art over the last 26 years, both in film and fine art, makes him one of the most collected artists in contemporary art. His work is represented by some of the most prominent and respected galleries in North America, the Orient and the Hawaiian Islands.

James Coleman Studio
1297 Lamont Avenue
Thousand Oaks, California 91360
(805) 373-2990
Fax (805) 373-2991

"Whale of a Time" 6' x 7' Copper and steel gate

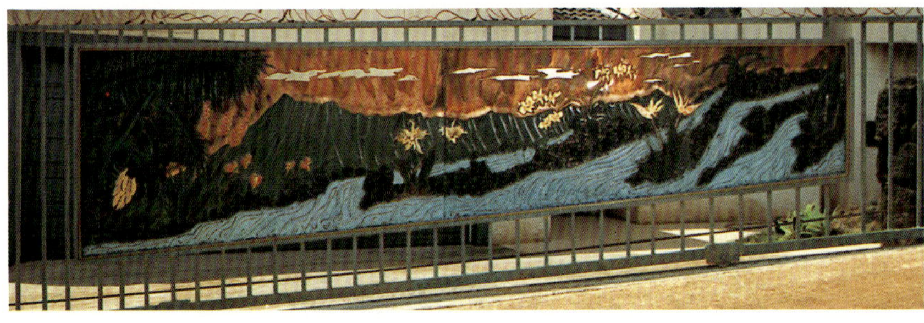

"Diamond Head" 28' x 6' Copper and Steel gate

GREGORY CRAFT

Gregory Charles Craft has been creating master artworks on metal for over 25 years.

Craft moved to Hawaii at the age of 12 as his brother's protege and his natural talent for spatial-relationships quickly began to show itself. He opened his first gallery at the age of 18 in Aspen, Colorado, and began to shift his direction from the non-functioning medium to an aesthetic, kinetic and operable format.

Thus, after 10 years of transformation, Craft's "Art as Gates" made their first appearance in the late '80s. In the early '90s his gates exploded onto the new architectural scene; his sculpture and sculptured paintings followed a parallel growth, topped off by a sold-out show in Osaka, Japan.

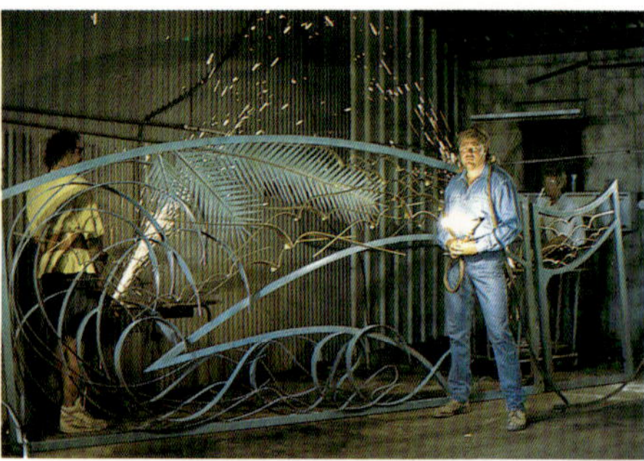

Left to Right: Andrew Smith-Artist's protégé, Gregory Craft-Artist, David Helwig-Assisting on the commissioned piece "Stenella Longirostris" for James K. Schuler

Craft's works are exceptional in their devotion to quality. He states, "When art endures the elements and time, a master 'Craftsman' is involved!"

For Gregory Craft, attention to integrity is as important as motif and design. This philosophy is a powerful force behind the creation of the most extraordinary aesthetic art works in metals.

THE ART OF GREGORY CRAFT
148-E Mokauea Street
Honolulu, HI 96819
Pager (808) 525-1884

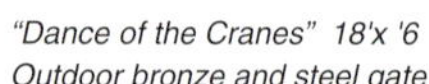

"Dance of the Cranes" 18'x '6
Outdoor bronze and steel gate

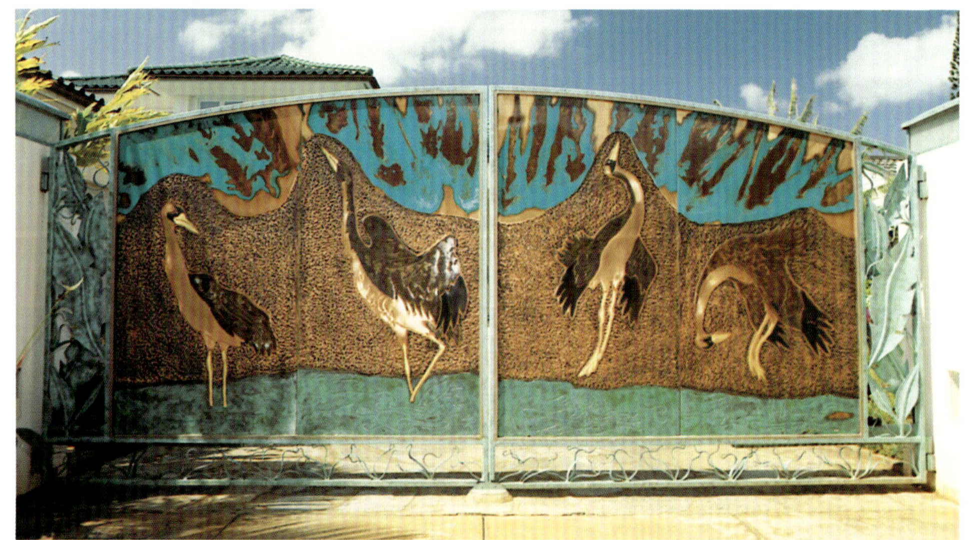

GREGORY CRAFT

"Two Sides of the Buddha"
4' x 4' Brass and Stainless Steel
Sculptured Painting

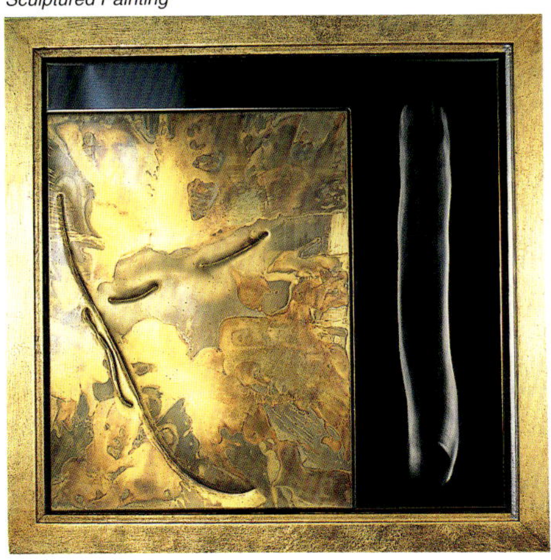

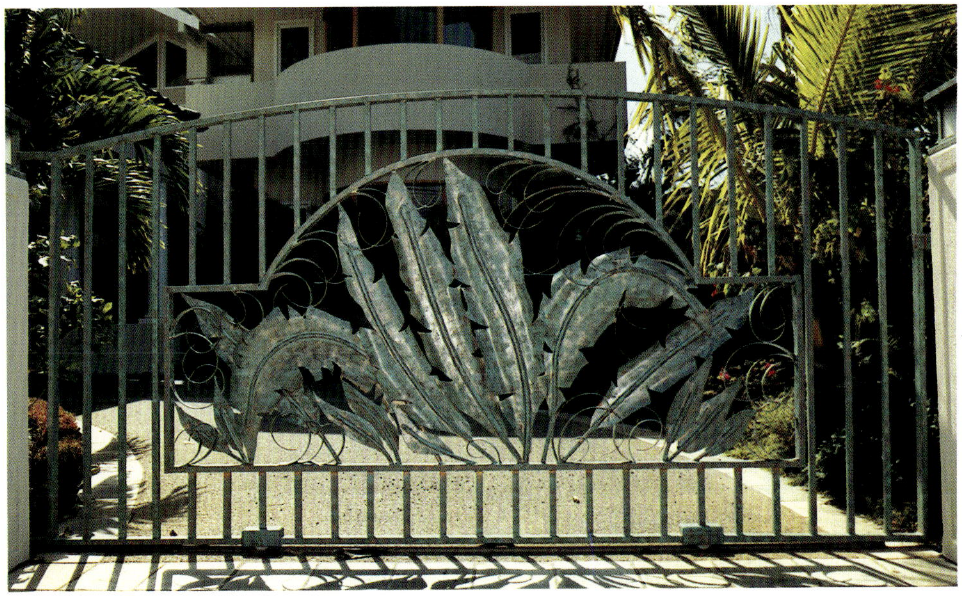

"Banana Leaves"
20' x 8' Steel and Copper
Colored Patino

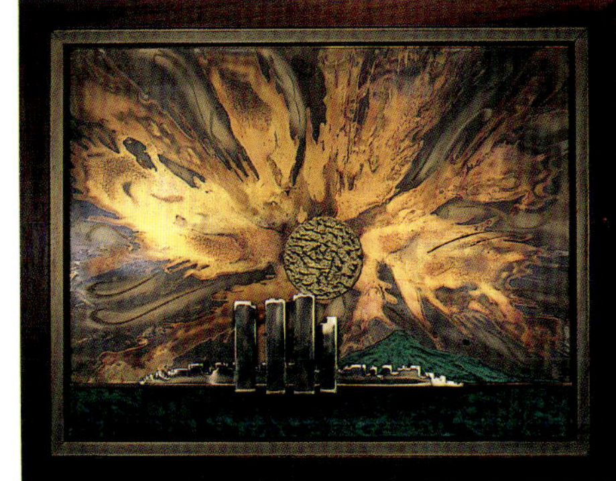

"The City Scapes"
4' x 3' Brass Bronze and Copper
Sculptured Painting

"Cactus in Bloom" 24' x 6' Copper 23kt. Gold Leaf

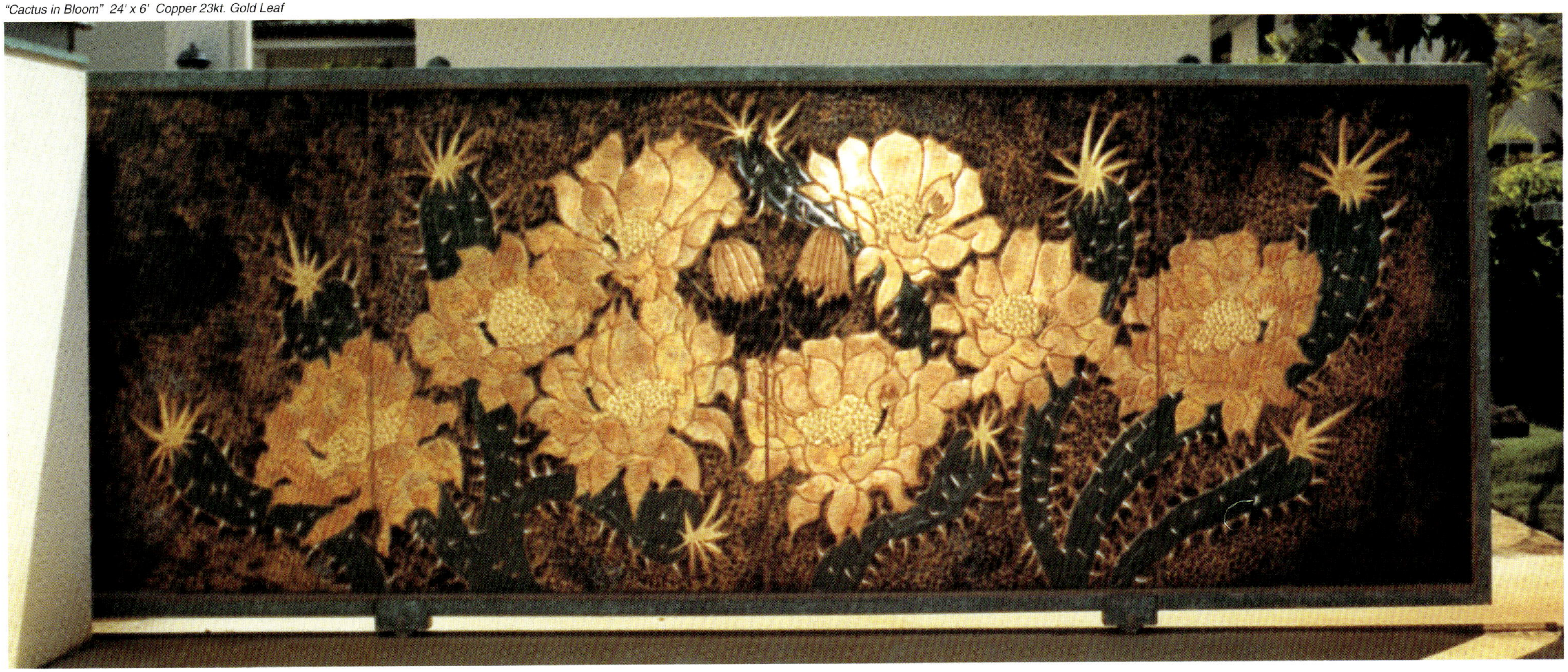

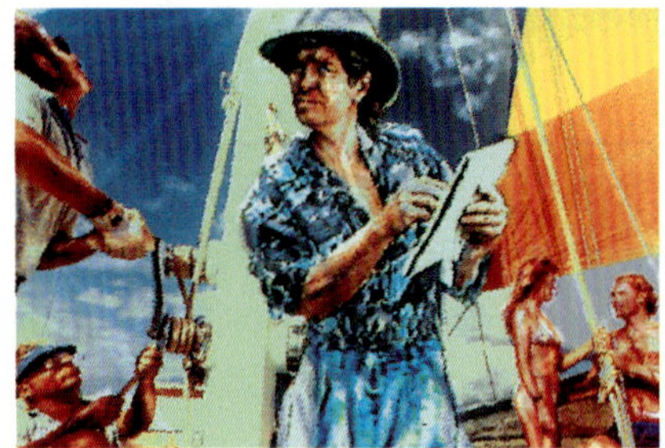

"Self Portrait" 30" x 20" Acrylic on Canvas

MICHAEL DAVID

Upon viewing his paintings, it becomes immediately apparent why many regard Michael David as one of the fastest rising stars in the marine and environmental art fields. He has been an artist for 20 years but it has only been in the last few years that he has focused solely on painting and printmaking.

After graduating from the University of Illinois College of Art with highest honors and distinction, he set off for adventure in the tropics. "I felt I had to live the life of sailing and diving before I could honestly paint it." In 1980 he finished building his 42' catamaran and sailed it to Hawaii.

While building a successful dive and sail business he had the incredible opportunity to dive with sharks and "gators", turtles and manatees, dolphin and whales. "For 18 years I have been fortunate enough to spend my life sharing my adventures with tens of thousands of people."

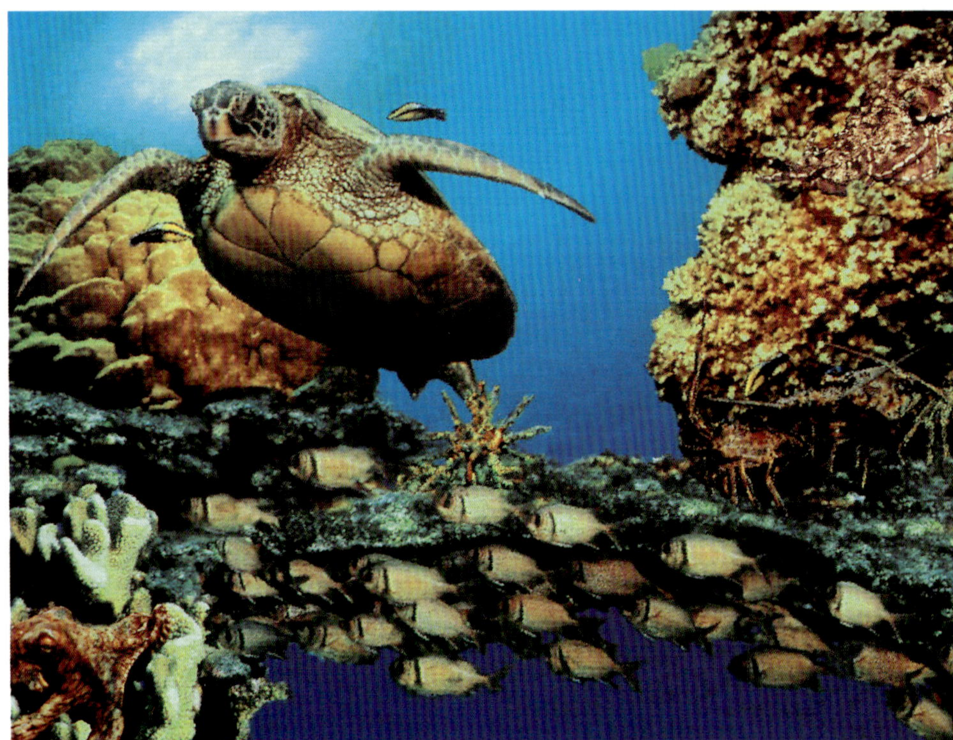

"Cleaning Station" 40" x 30" Acrylic Multi-Media On Canvas

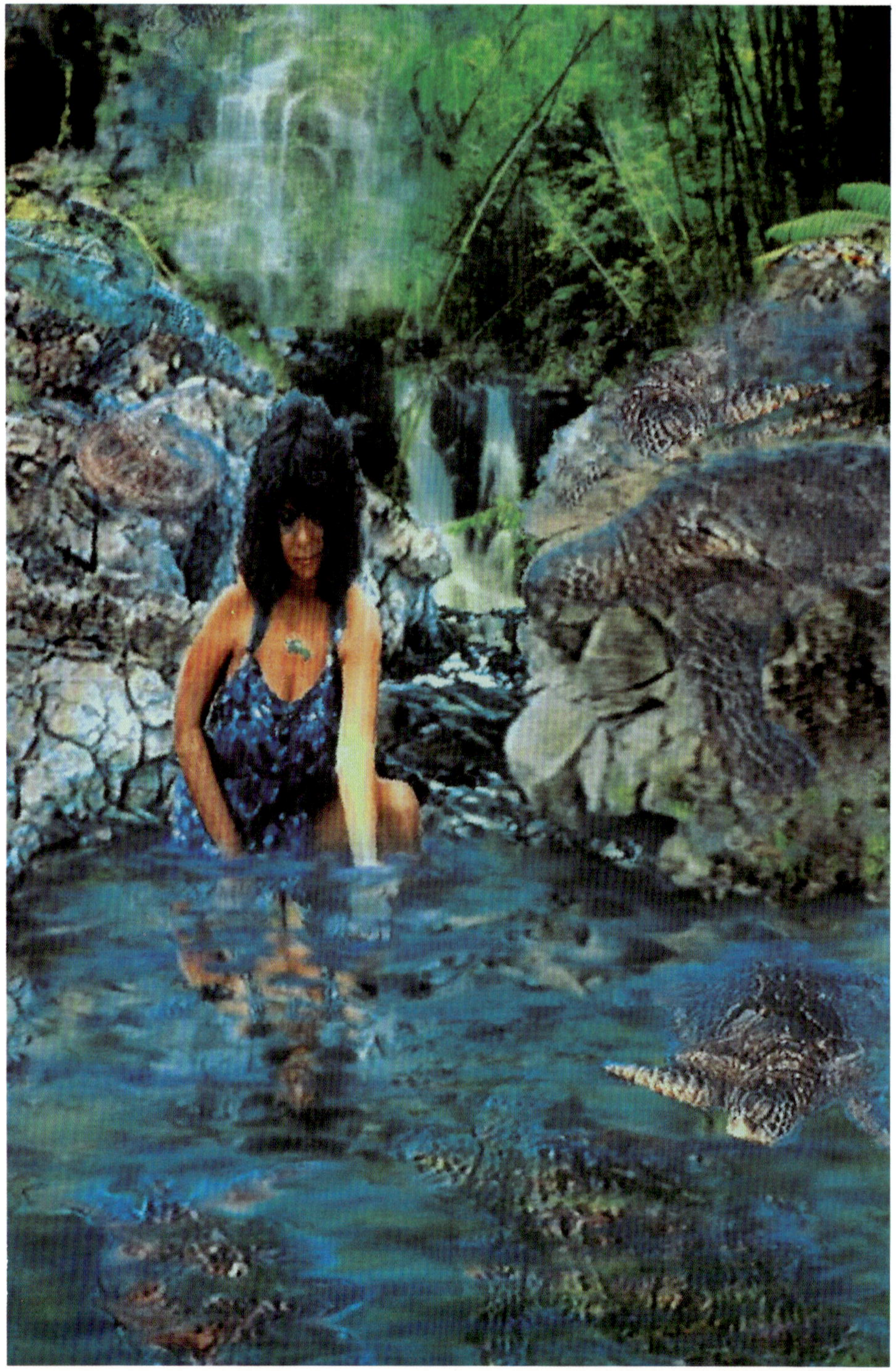

"Turtle Haven" 24" x 36" Limited Edition Print

MICHAEL DAVID

When Michael David paints nature we can trust his research of the subject. He often incorporates fantasy, but never uses it as an excuse for inaccuracy.

More importantly, he is an incurable romantic. Within his themes are subtle threads of humor, mystery, romance and adventure. His brush strokes can be powerful enough to capture the surge of the ocean or subtle enough to caress the cheek of a woman.

Michael's client list reads like a "Who's Who" and attests to his expertise: Ann-Margaret, Kenny Rodgers, Richard Dreyfuss, The Gatlin Brothers, just to name a few.

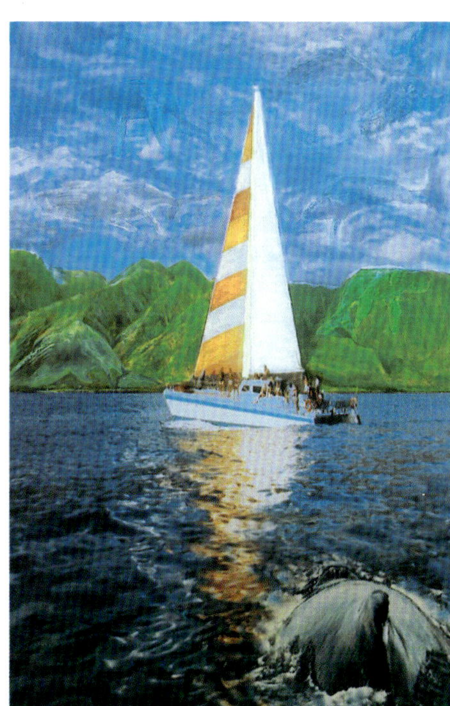

"Whales Watching" 20" x 30" Acrylic On Canvas

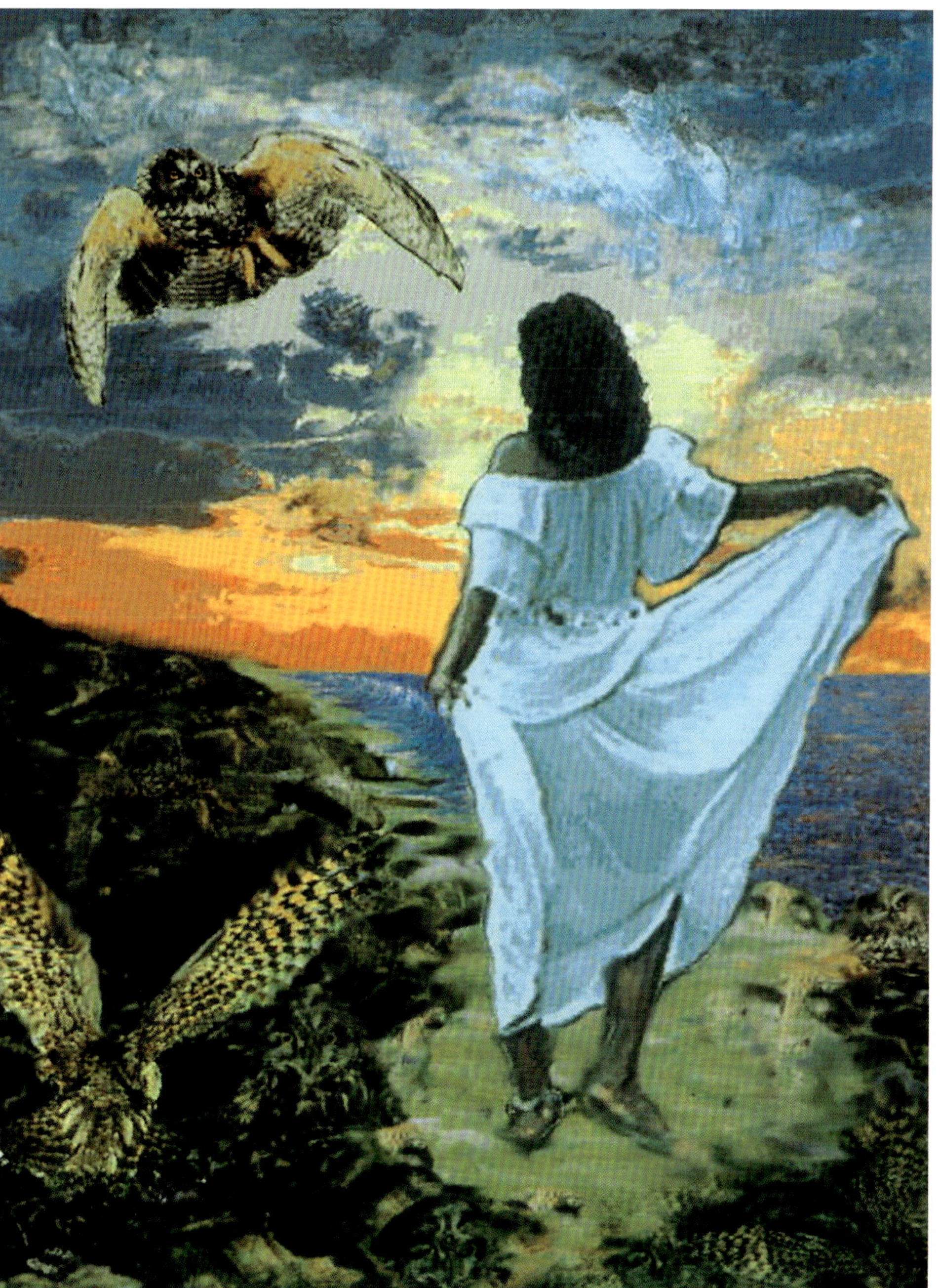

"Cloud Dancer" 24" x 32" Limited Edition Print

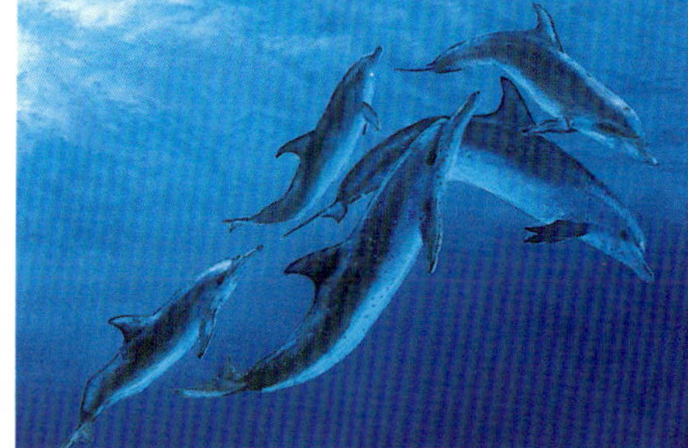

"Fluid Friendship" 30" x 22" Acrylic on Canvas

There always seems to be something more to discover in his art, like subliminal themes and camouflaged characters. The more you see his art, the more you see in his art. His work needs to be viewed full size to see all the nuances and hidden images.

Michael's ocean and environmental paintings are unlike any other Hawaiian artist. Uniquely his art often explores how his human characters relate to nature. The women in his paintings seem beautiful yet strong, independent but still caring. "I'm trying to paint even more than light and color, I'm reaching for the passion, the emotion."

Michael still finds time to do privately commissioned paintings and portraits. "Although painting people is very challenging, it is very rewarding personally."

Spectrum Fine Art
75-909 Hiona Street
Holualoa, Hawaii, HI 96725
(808) 329-9999
FAX (808) 326-5444

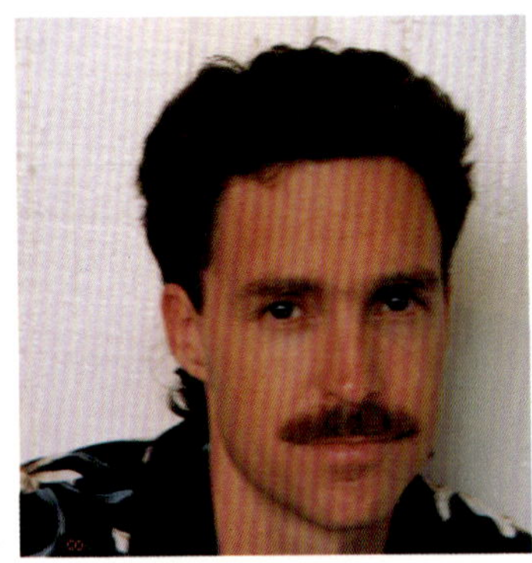

LANCE FAIRLY

Lance's work on metal represents a new dimension in artistic expression. By combining actual light with his original paintings, he achieves effects impossible by traditional means.

Through continuous experimentation, Lance has developed the process he calls LUMIFLō™ meaning "Flowing Light". "LUMIFLō™ has given me the ability to literally paint with light," explains the artist. When used expertly by an artist of Lance's caliber, the results can be stunning; treating the viewer to a fantastic new visual experience. Objects appear to float free from the surface, creating an illusion of space and depth extending beyond the confines of ordinary painting. However, this effect can only be experienced from the original or special prints that are hand-made individually.

Lance was born in Florida where he grew up in and around the ocean. Largely self-taught, he showed tremendous natural ability for art at an early age, often illustrating the ocean images around him. After attending the Ringling School of Art in Sarasota, Florida, he moved to St. Thomas in the Virgin Islands where he lived in the "Dolphin House". This was the site of early research into dolphin intelligence. Its secluded location and inspirational past had a strong influence on Lance's work.

Ultimately, Lance was lured to Hawaii by its natural beauty and colorful ocean environment. He now lives with his family in his oceanfront home and studio on Oahu's North Shore, where the spectacular view of the ocean and mountains continue to inspire him.

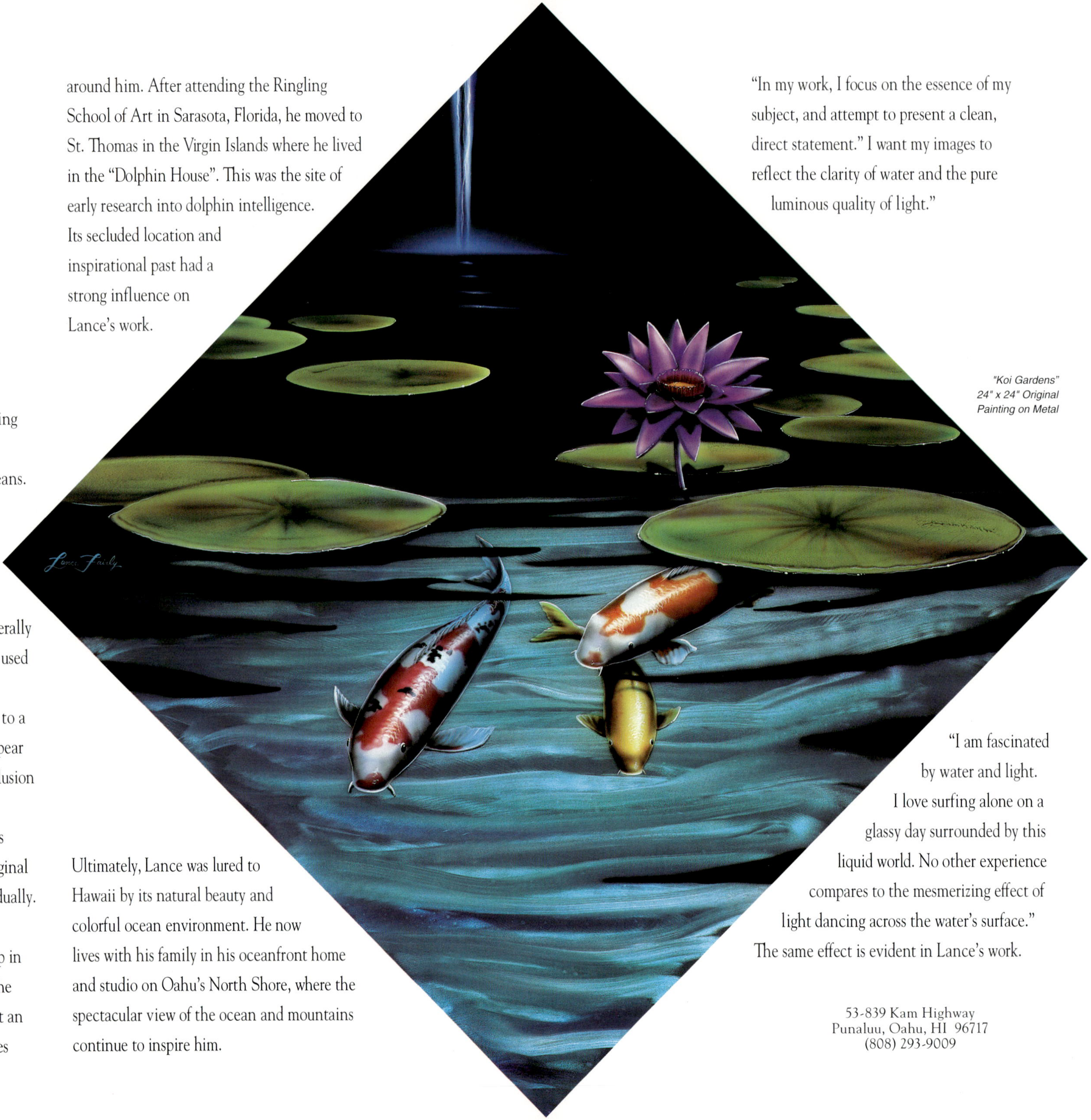

"In my work, I focus on the essence of my subject, and attempt to present a clean, direct statement." I want my images to reflect the clarity of water and the pure luminous quality of light."

"Koi Gardens"
24" x 24" Original
Painting on Metal

"I am fascinated by water and light. I love surfing alone on a glassy day surrounded by this liquid world. No other experience compares to the mesmerizing effect of light dancing across the water's surface." The same effect is evident in Lance's work.

53-839 Kam Highway
Punaluu, Oahu, HI 96717
(808) 293-9009

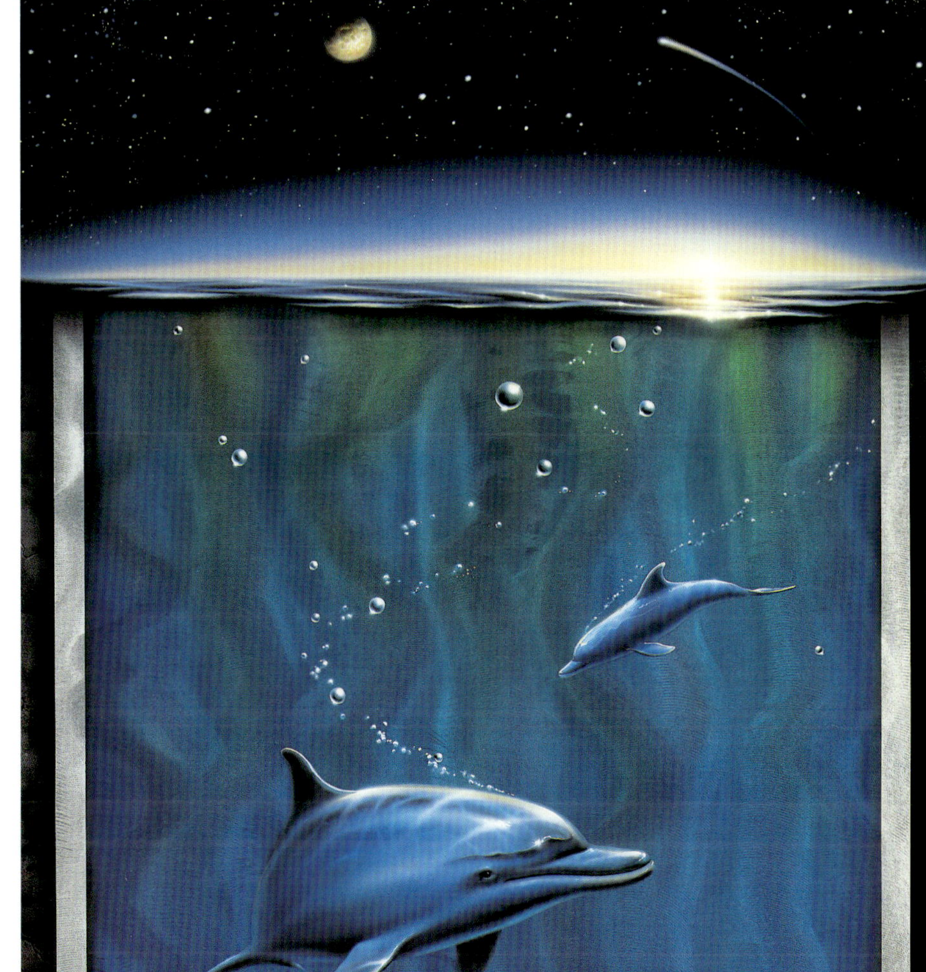

"Dolphin Day" 24" x 36" Original Painting on Metal

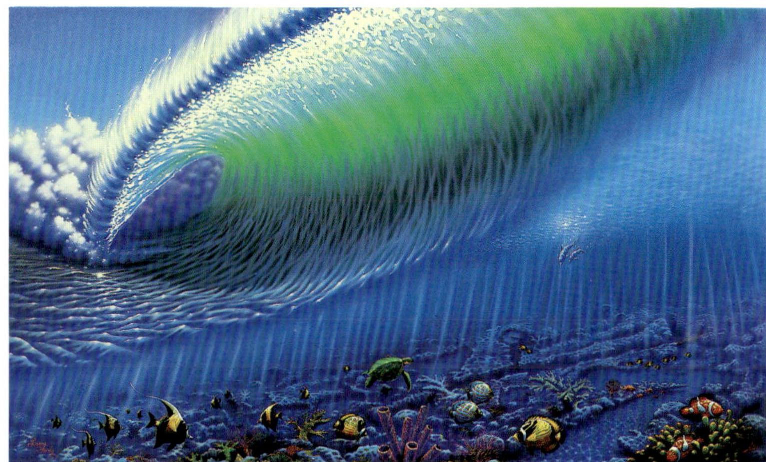

"Reef Break" 72" x 36"
Original Acrylic Painting

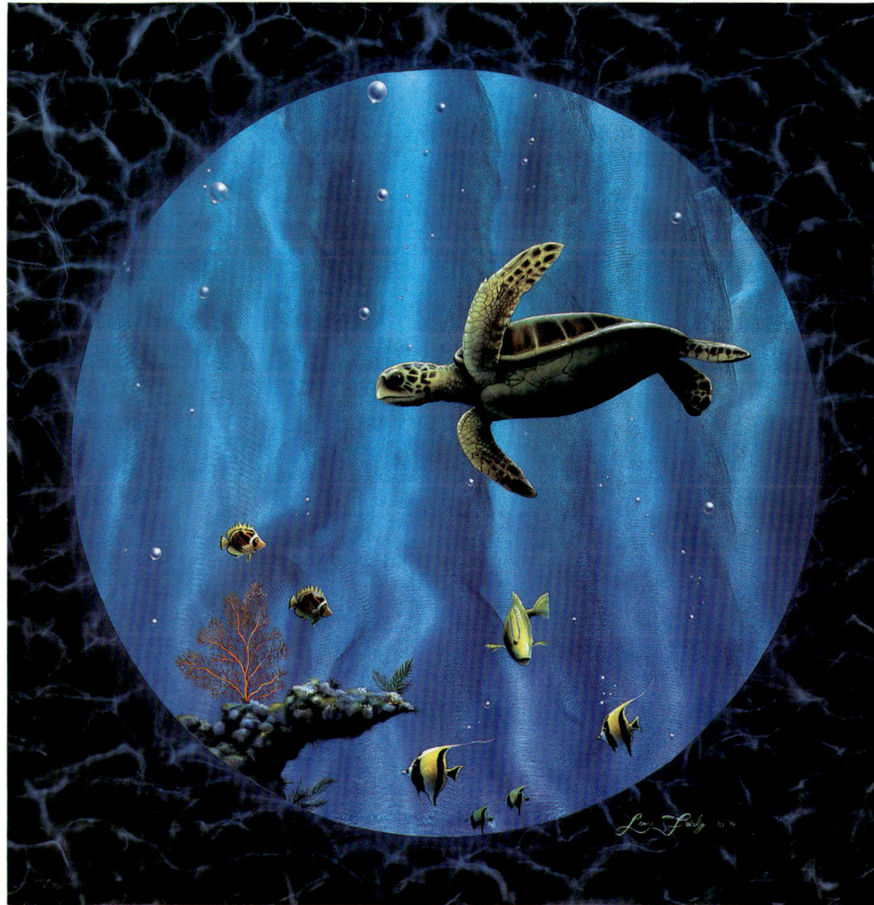

"Turtle Canyon"
24" x 24" Original
Painting on Metal

TOM FAUGHT

Born in 1946, Tom Faught was educated at Orange Coast College and Long Beach State College, both in California. He established the Russian River Studio in 1968, and in 1973, the current studio location in Maui. Faught has been greatly influenced by Japanese masters working in the medium of pottery, admiring their elegant forms and the quiet integrity of expression. The exciting Raku style of high luster glazing so prevalent in Japanese works has long been inspirational to the artist's own creations.

He has taken an experimental approach, pushing the leading edge in both design and materials for more than 25 years. Perhaps the most innovative development is the artist's unique metalizing technique. Donning protective mask and clothing, he works with 6,000 degree Fahrenheit temperatures, surfacing his decorative works with bronze, copper and aluminum. Often combined with shimmering color glazes, the burnished metal adds a new dimension to big pots, bronze doors, panels, tiles, murals and other custom installations. His big pots in solid 6' by 4' dimensions and weighing in at a half of a ton are so perfectly balanced, that they somehow give the impression of being fluid and lightweight, even delicate.

Tom's works are in numerous public and private collections including that of the Emperor of Japan.

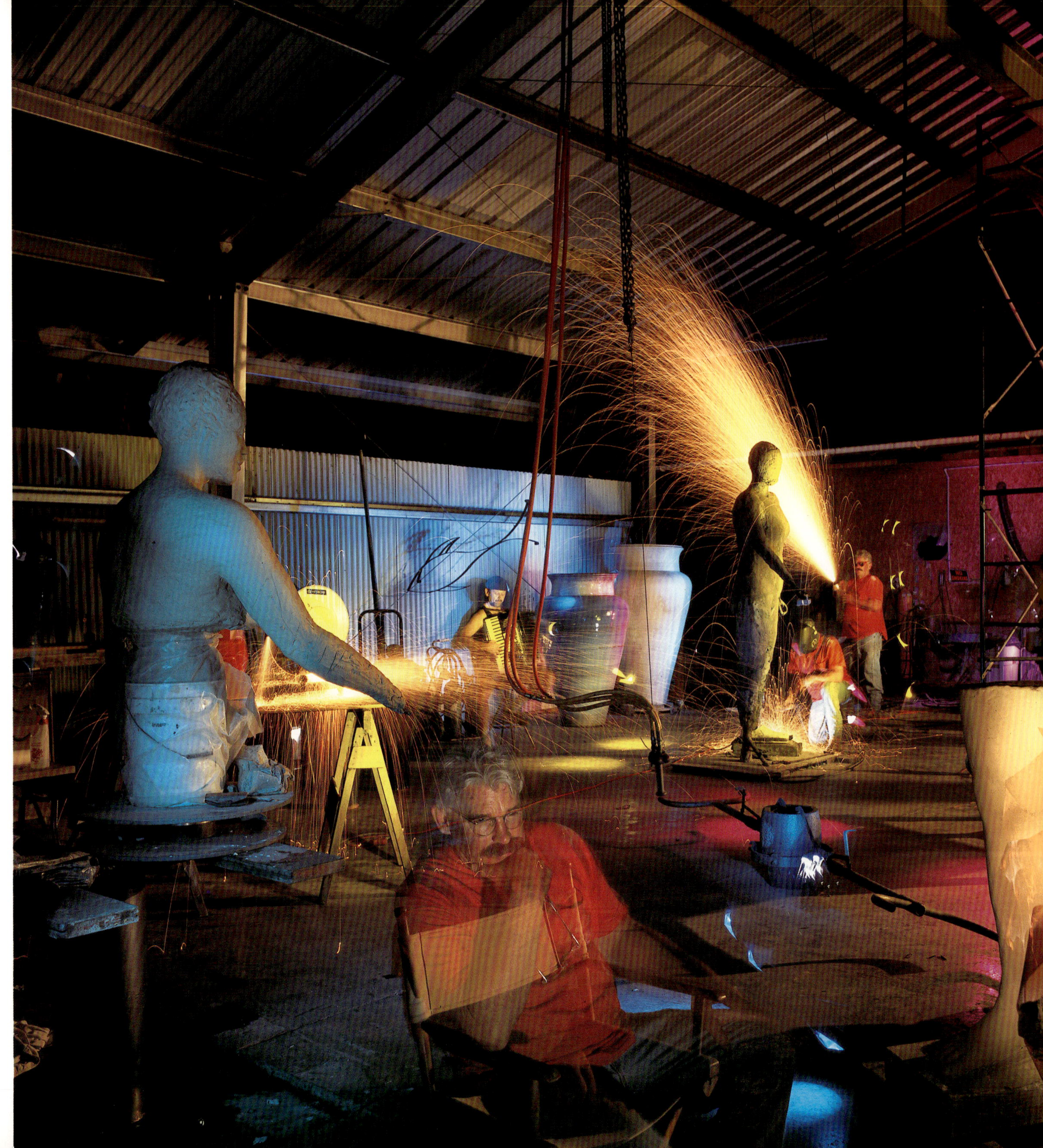

TOM FAUGHT

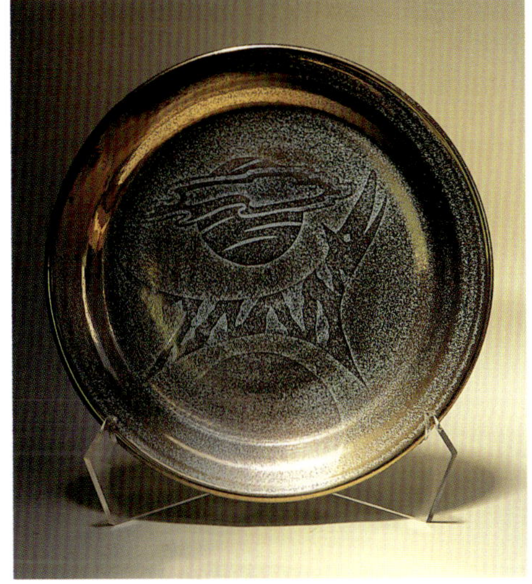
October Moon
28" diameter clay and metal

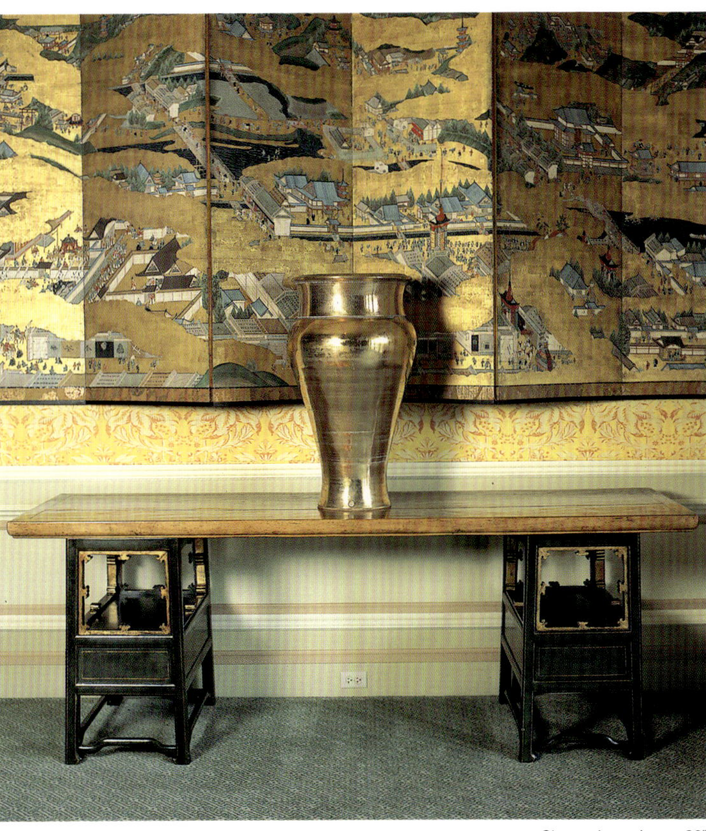
Clay and metal vase 36"

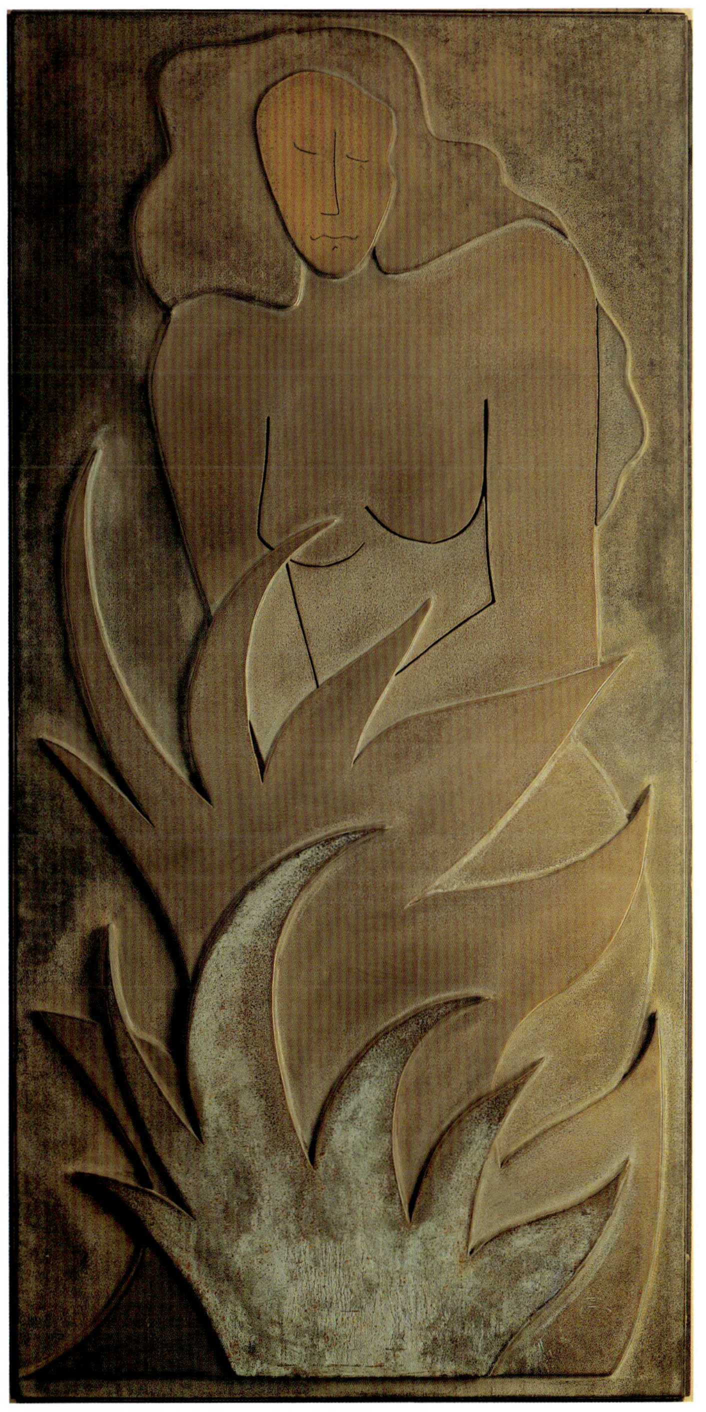
The Lady
8' x 4' bronze over wood

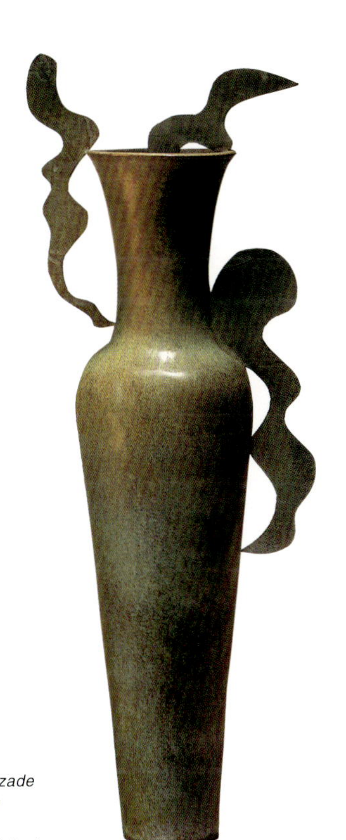
Scheherazade
Dreaming
48" cast
bronze original

Tom Faught Studio & Foundry
2927 Kaluanui Road
Makawao, Maui, HI 96768
(808) 572-8904
FAX (808) 572-2642

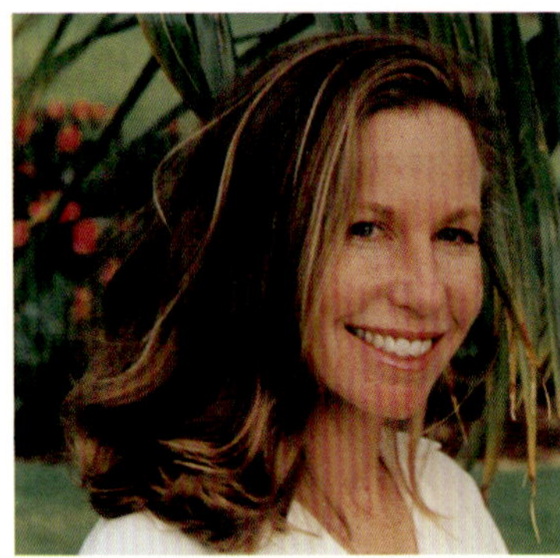

MARY LUCAS FAUSTINE

The talented and delightful artist, Mary Lucas Faustine, brings a love of paradise and an acute eye for detail to the world of art. Mary's interest in art started at a very young age and was nurtured and refined throughout her school years. Amongst her credits, she studied at the Maryland Institute, College of Art, in Baltimore, Maryland and received her Bachelor's degree in Fine Art from the San Francisco Art Institute.

While raising three daughters, her desire to create beautiful visions of lush scenes never abandoned her. She now devotes full-time to her passion, showing artistic versatility by being accomplished in both oils and watercolor.

Exciting coloration and exacting attention to detail mark her style as she executes varied scenes in either medium. The results of this enhance our lives in a meaningful way. Her artwork is in collections worldwide and she has a growing and enthusiastic following. Many of Mary's paintings are available in limited edition prints. Her works can be viewed in some of Maui's finest galleries and are available unframed or elegantly framed by her husband Joe who is one of Maui's top picture framers.

P.O. Box 831
Paia, Maui, HI 96779
(808) 572-3718

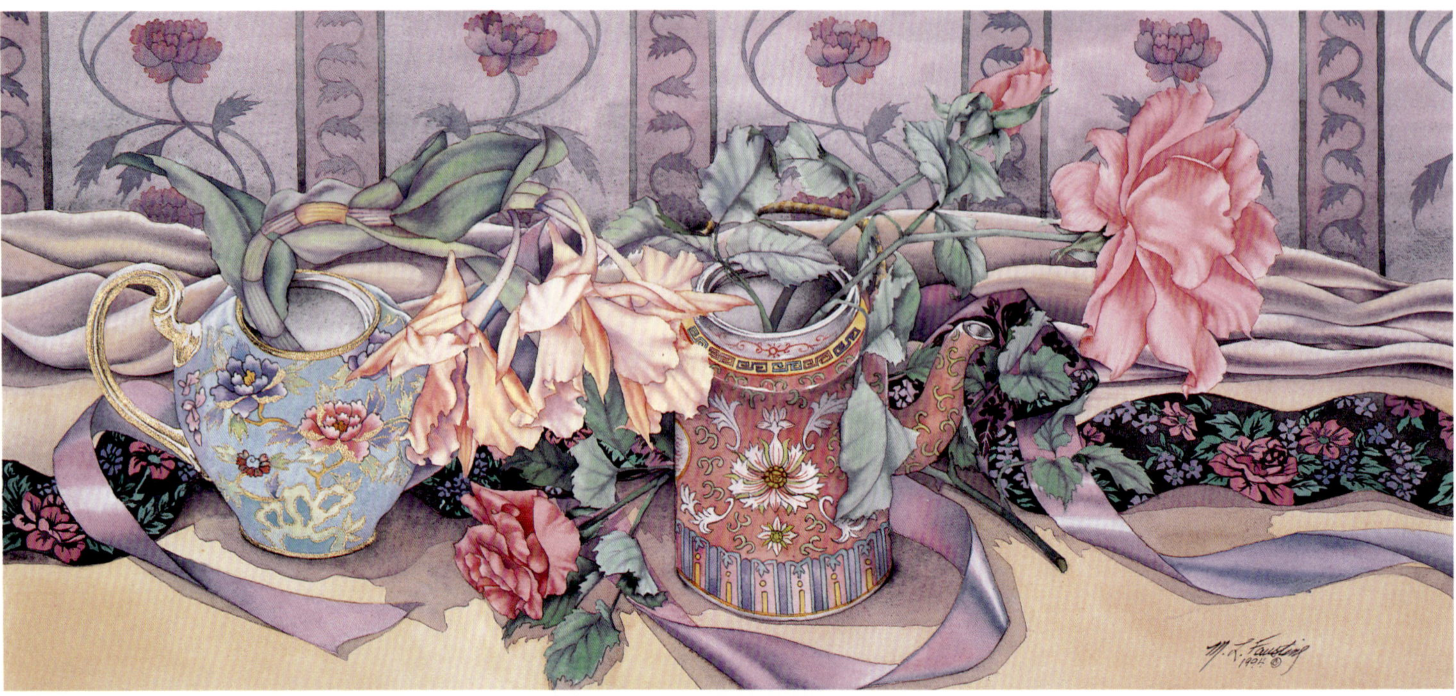

"Orchids and Roses" 30" x 15" Original Watercolor Painting

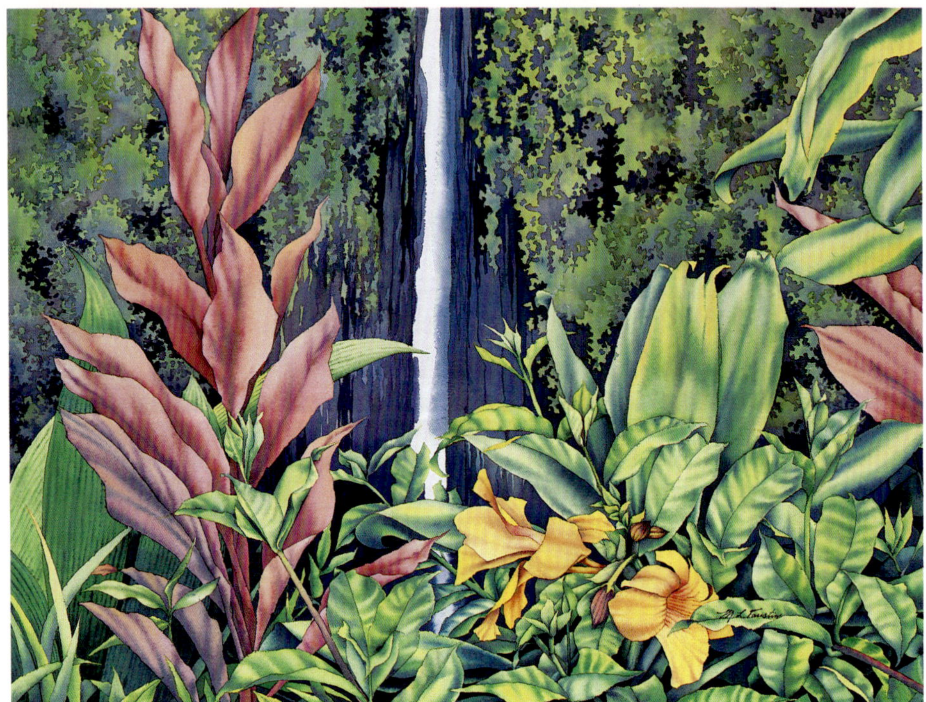

*"A Secret Place" 30" x 22"
Original Watercolor Painting*

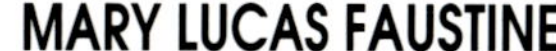

MARY LUCAS FAUSTINE

"Stripes and Polkadots I" 22" x 9" Original Watercolor Painting

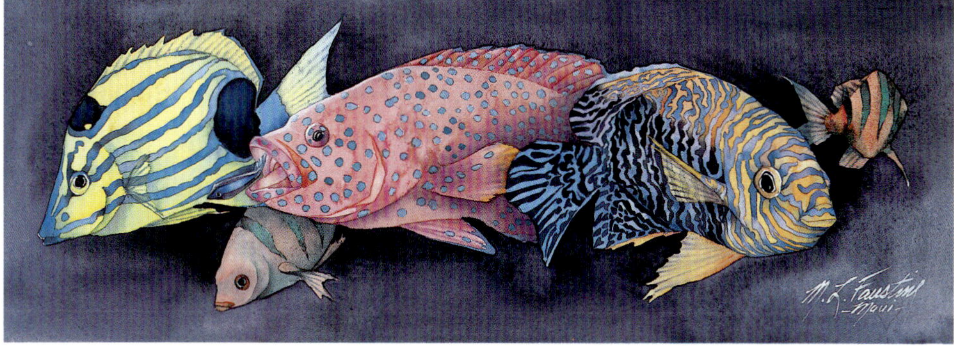

"Stripes and Polkadots II" 22" x 9" Original Watercolor Painting

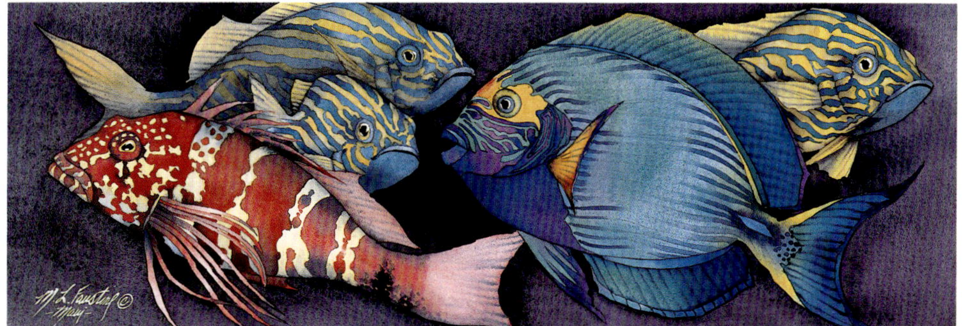

"Haleakala Dairy Delight" 17" x 14" Original Watercolor Painting

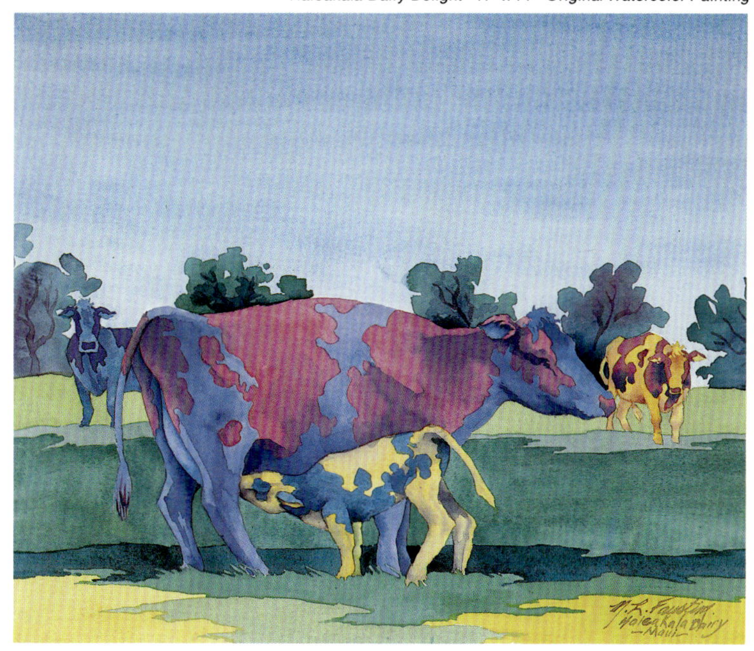

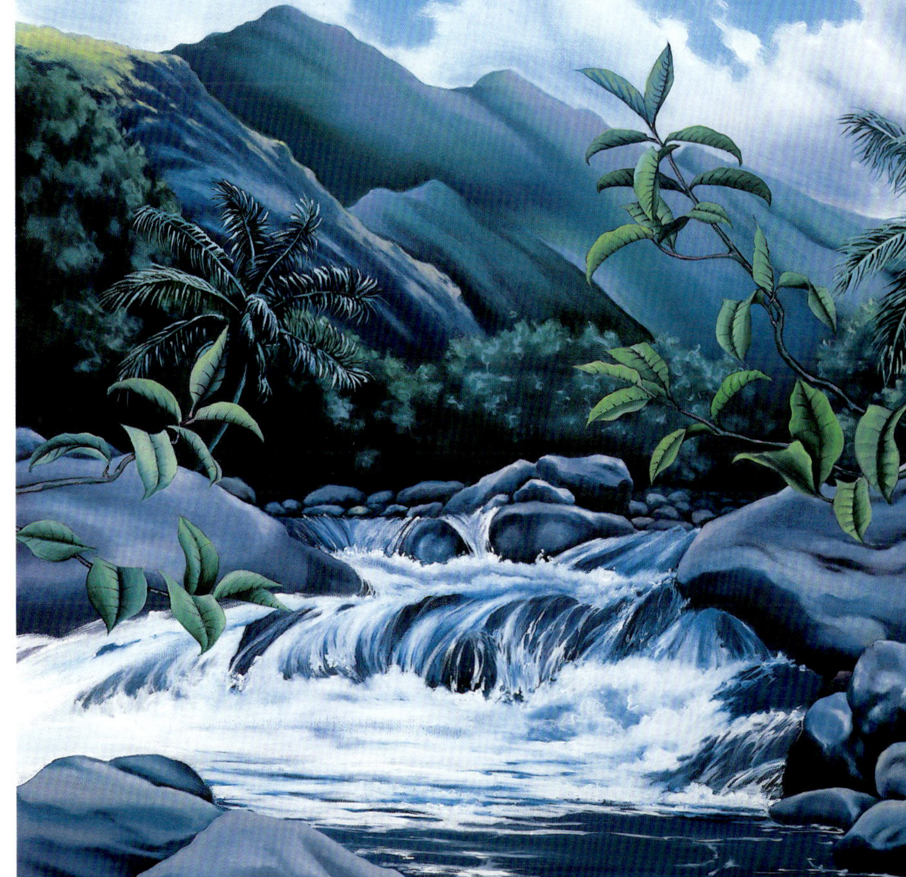

"Iao River, Maui" 24" x 36"
Original Oil Painting

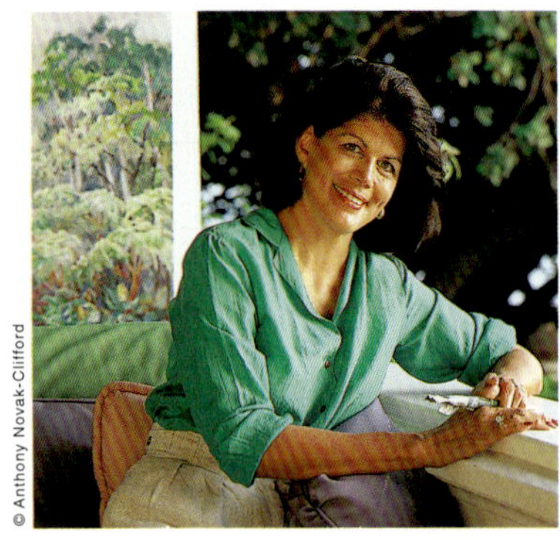
© Anthony Novak-Clifford

BETTY HAY FREELAND

Paintings are, in a sense, a portrait of the artist. Regardless of subject matter, the artist emerges through the conscious and intuitive choices made throughout the painting process. Betty Hay Freeland's landscapes are no exception.

Her paintings reveal a portrait of one who shares her Hawaii with us through a visual language requiring no interpreter.

Land meets water and sky in an array of vibrant hues, illuminated in bright warm sunshine and modified by atmospheric transitions. This artist neither sermonizes nor psychoanalyzes - she paints with a soul founded in her Hawaiian ancestry and nutured by a devotion to her craft. Her paintings, like the land, are an invitation to share an environment of unequalled beauty in the tradition of Hawaiian Aloha.

Betty Hay Freeland
439 Front Street
Lahaina, Maui, HI 96761
(808) 661-5766

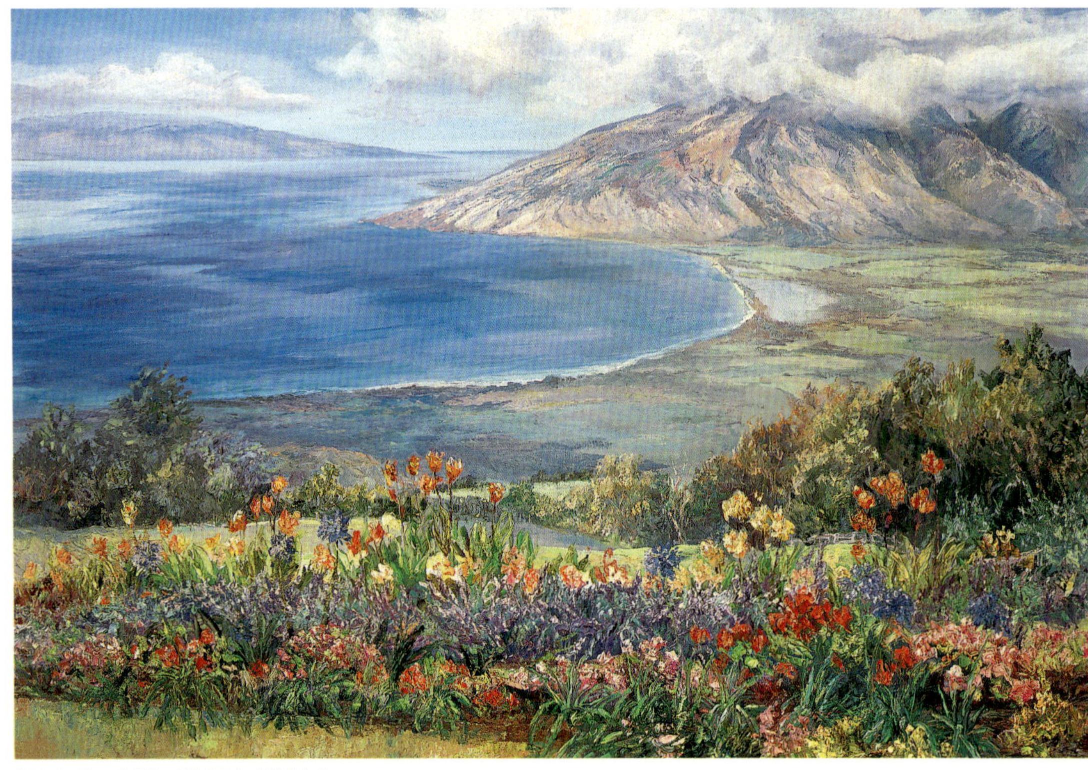

"Kula In Bloom" 28" x 40" Original Oil Painting

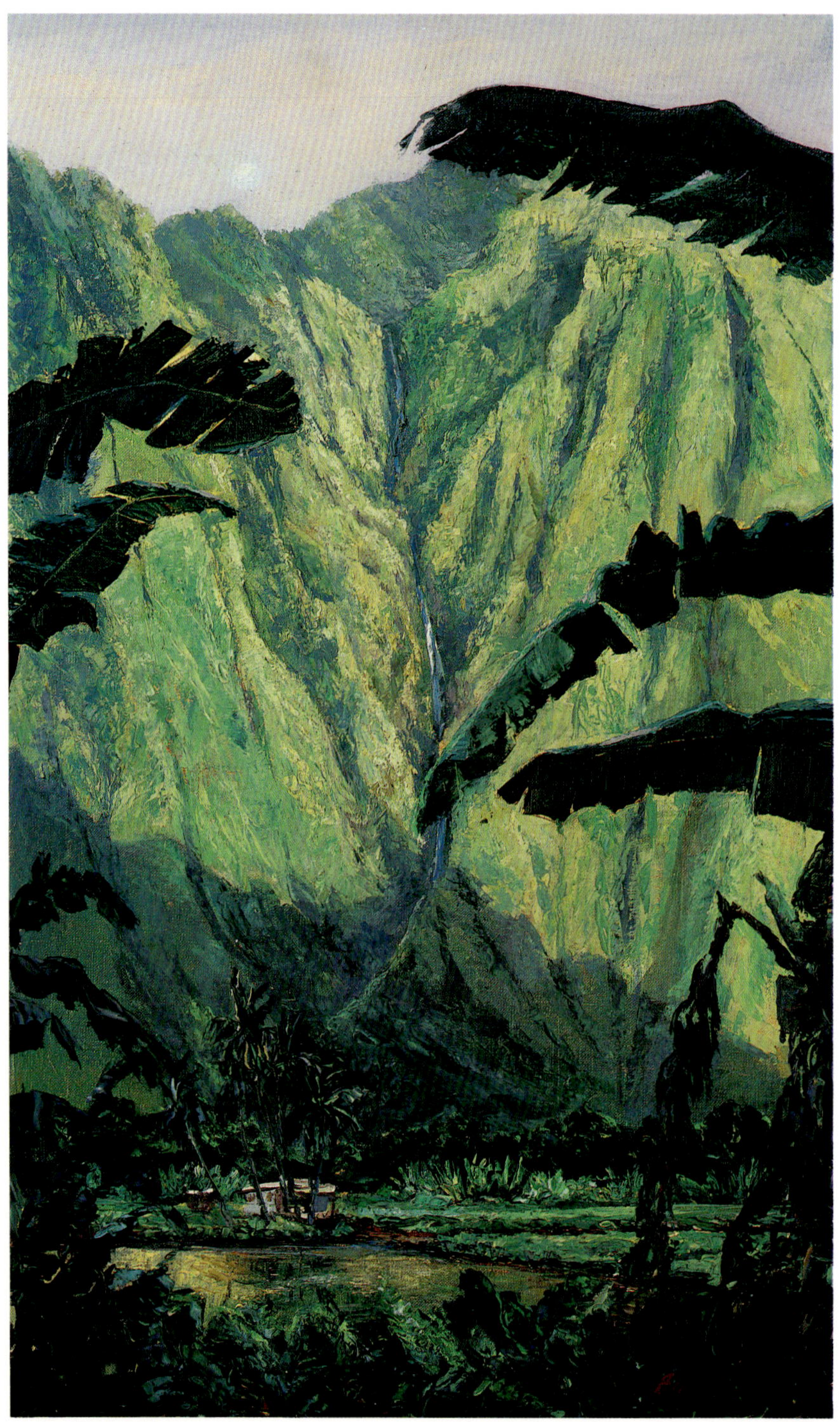

"Banana Moon" Waipio, Hawaii 18" x 30" Original Oil Painting

"Napili Point" 24" x 36" Original Oil Painting

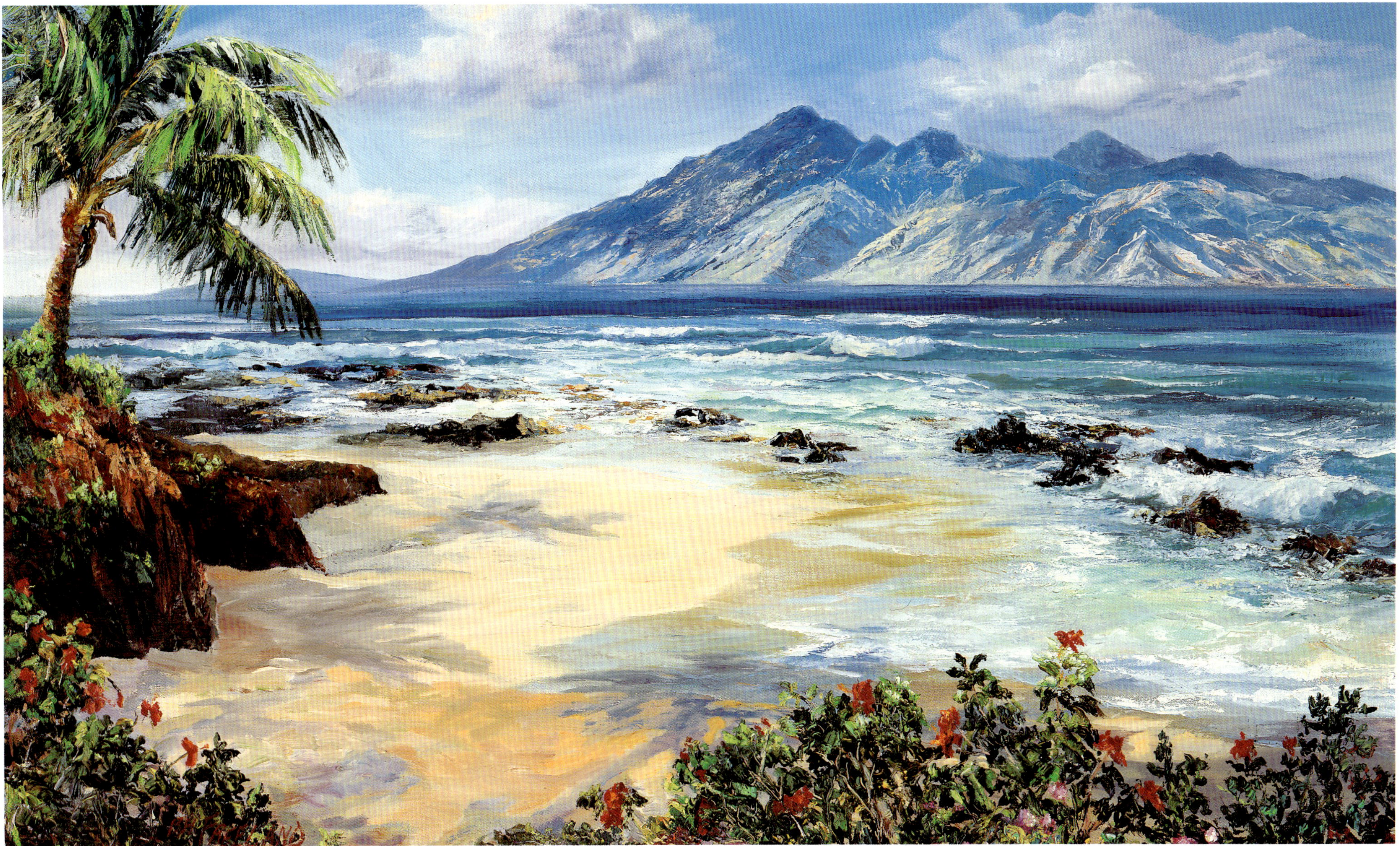

Born Betty Hay Wodehouse, in Kohala, Hawaii, she graduated from Punahou School, the University of Colorado, and continued studies in New York City. She returned to the islands, and in 1963, she married George (Keoki) Freeland of Lahaina, Maui.

She has a family history which dates to the days of the Monarchy. Her great-grandfather was the first Governor of the islands. Her Grandmother was half-sister to Princess Kaiulani. One hundred years of Hawaiian heritage suffuse the relationship she shares with her three children as well as her art. Betty Hay and Keoki currently reside in Lahaina, Maui.

Betty Hay's original oils can be viewed at Village Galleries, Lahaina; Coast Galleries, Hana and Wailea; Kahn Galleries, Kauai; and Fine Art Associates at the Art Loft, Honolulu.

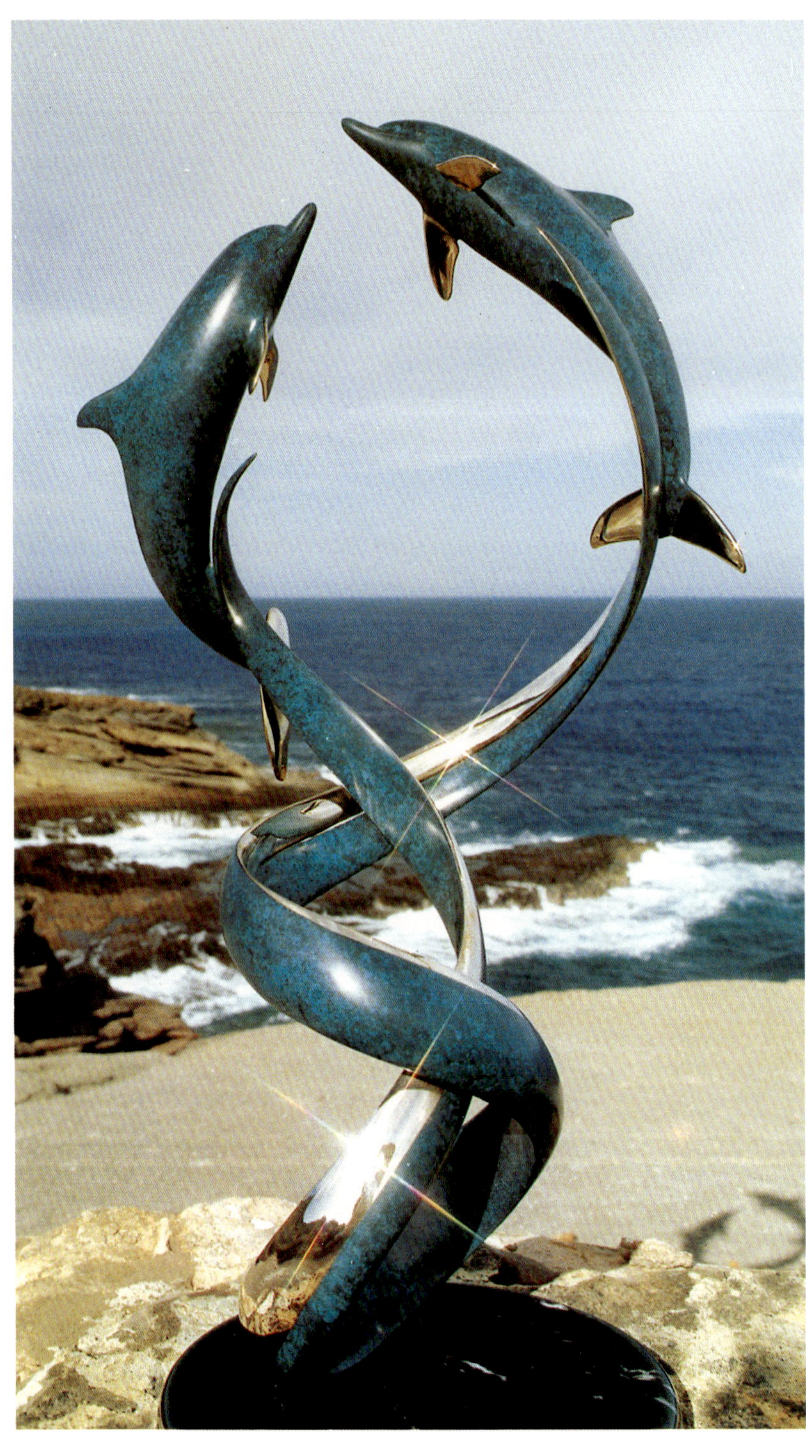

Ka Mele O Ke Kau Wela "Summers' Song" 32" x 14" Limited Edition Bronze Sculpture

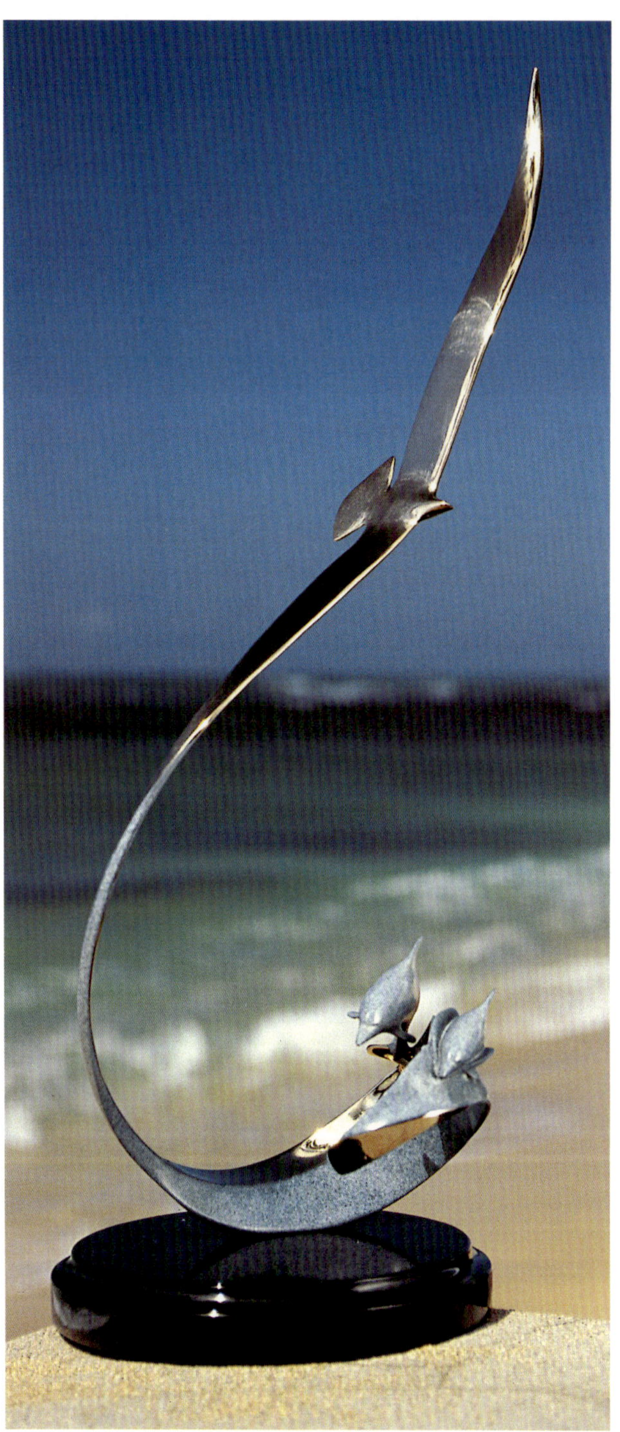

Makani Kai "Wind and Sea" 18" x 24" Limited Edition Bronze Sculpture

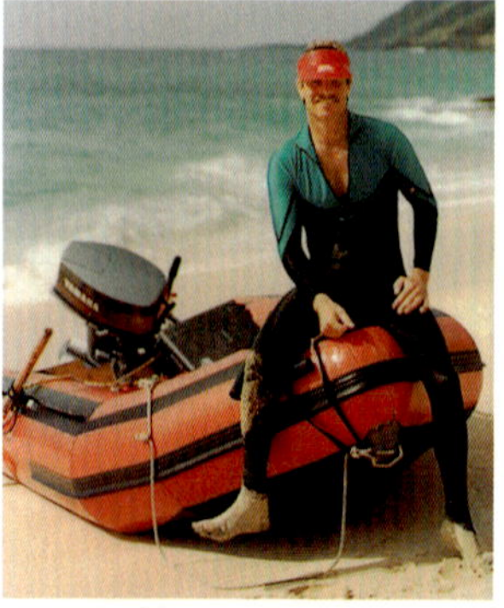

SCOTT HANSON

Hanson Studios
4962-1 Kilauea Avenue
Honolulu, Oahu, HI 96816

Originally from La Jolla, California with a life style centered around the sea, Scott Hanson was first drawn to Hawaii twenty years ago by the prospect of clear tropical waters and abundant marine life. He has called the islands home ever since.

An avid dive traveler and underwater photographer/videographer, Scott has logged countless hours of first-hand observation and interaction with his subjects, particularly dolphins in their natural habitat. This extensive familiarity with his subjects allows him to impart to his sculptures a real sense of the gregarious fun-loving nature of these magnificent animals. His bronze dolphins are often described as conveying a feeling of "warmth and personality".

Hanson's artistic mentor as well as dive buddy is the renowned artist and fellow waterman John Pitre. "We've swam together with schools of sharks in Palau and were both nearly run over by three Humpback Whales while diving off Oahu." These diving

Lokahi "Harmony" 10" x 14" Limited Edition Bronze Sculpture

experiences and ocean life-style provide Scott with abundant inspiration for his art

Whether it be free diving solo with the Manta Rays off the Kona Coast at 3:00 am, dodging whales, or simply enjoying with friends the

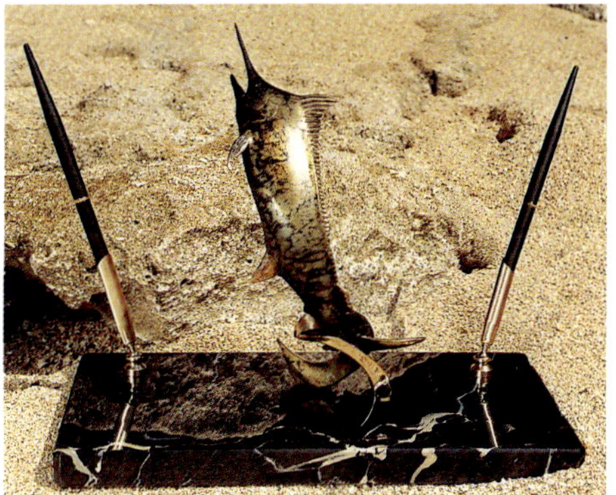

"Touché!" Limited Edition Bronze Sculpture - Pen Set

exuberance of a wild dolphin encounter, Scott Hanson endeavors through his sculpture to enthusiastically share with us these personal visions from the sea. He is represented throughout Hawaii by Wyland Galleries, 800-992-7498.

"Free & Easy" Limited Edition Bronze Sculpture - Pen Set

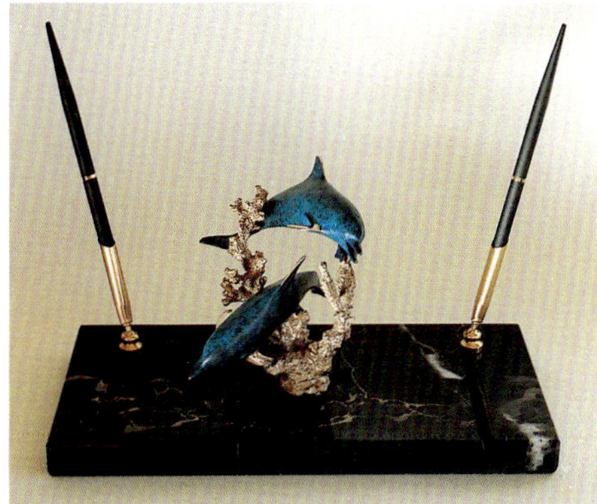

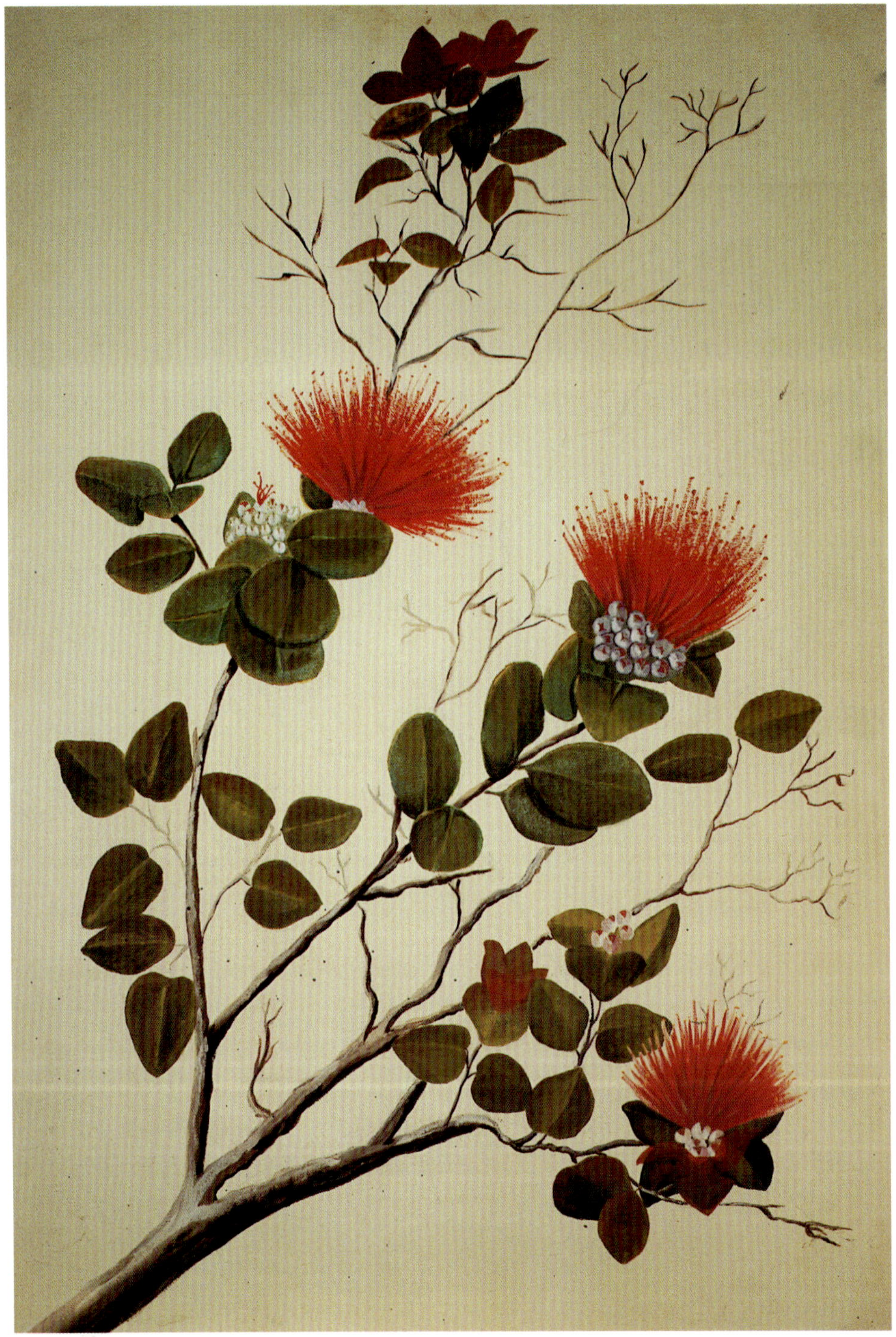

"Ohi'a Lehua" 18" x 26" Original Oil Painting on Canvas

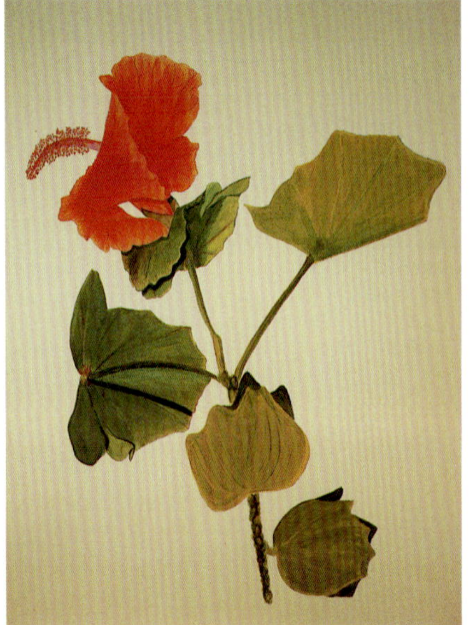

"Ka Pua Nani O Hau Hele Ula" 18" x 24"
Original Acrylic Painting

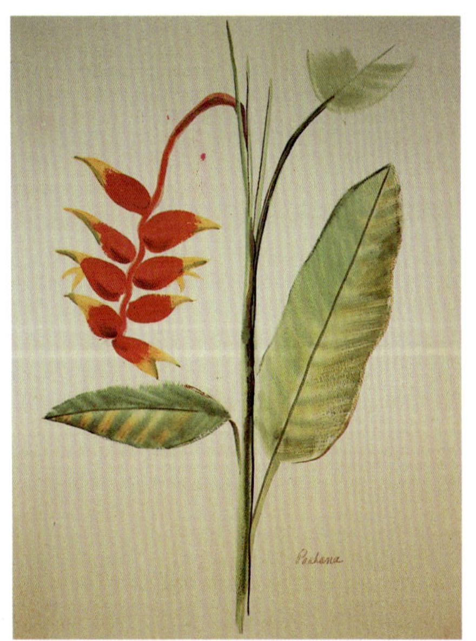

"Na Pua O Heliconia" 22.5" x 30" Original Acrylic Painting

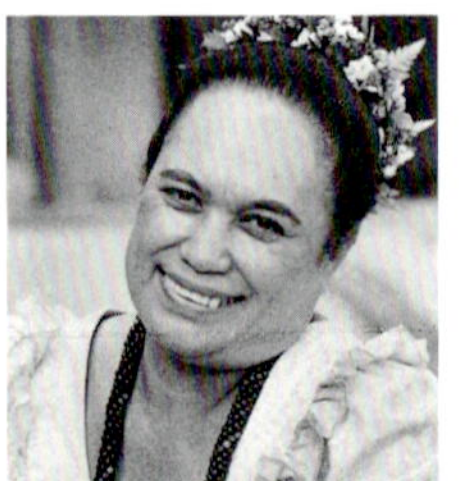

LORETTA PAAHANA HERA

Lorrie has been a resident of Lanai for more than twenty years. You can find her artworks at three locations on this island. At the Lodge at Koele, native Hawaiian flowers were painted in oil on each guest room door. Large paintings of tropical flowers hangs in some of the suites.

At the Manele Bay Hotel, a collection of crests and coat of arms representing Pacific island countries were painted on wooden panels, and flushed into the ceiling of the library. In the Polihua room of the Conference Center hangs large oil paintings of the Hawaiian reef fishes, and the green sea turtles. More Hawaiian fishes shares a place in the Naha room.

Lorrie treasures the natural and native beauty of Lanai and hopes it will never change.

P.O. Box 794
Lana'i City, Lana'i, HI 96763
(808) 565-6115

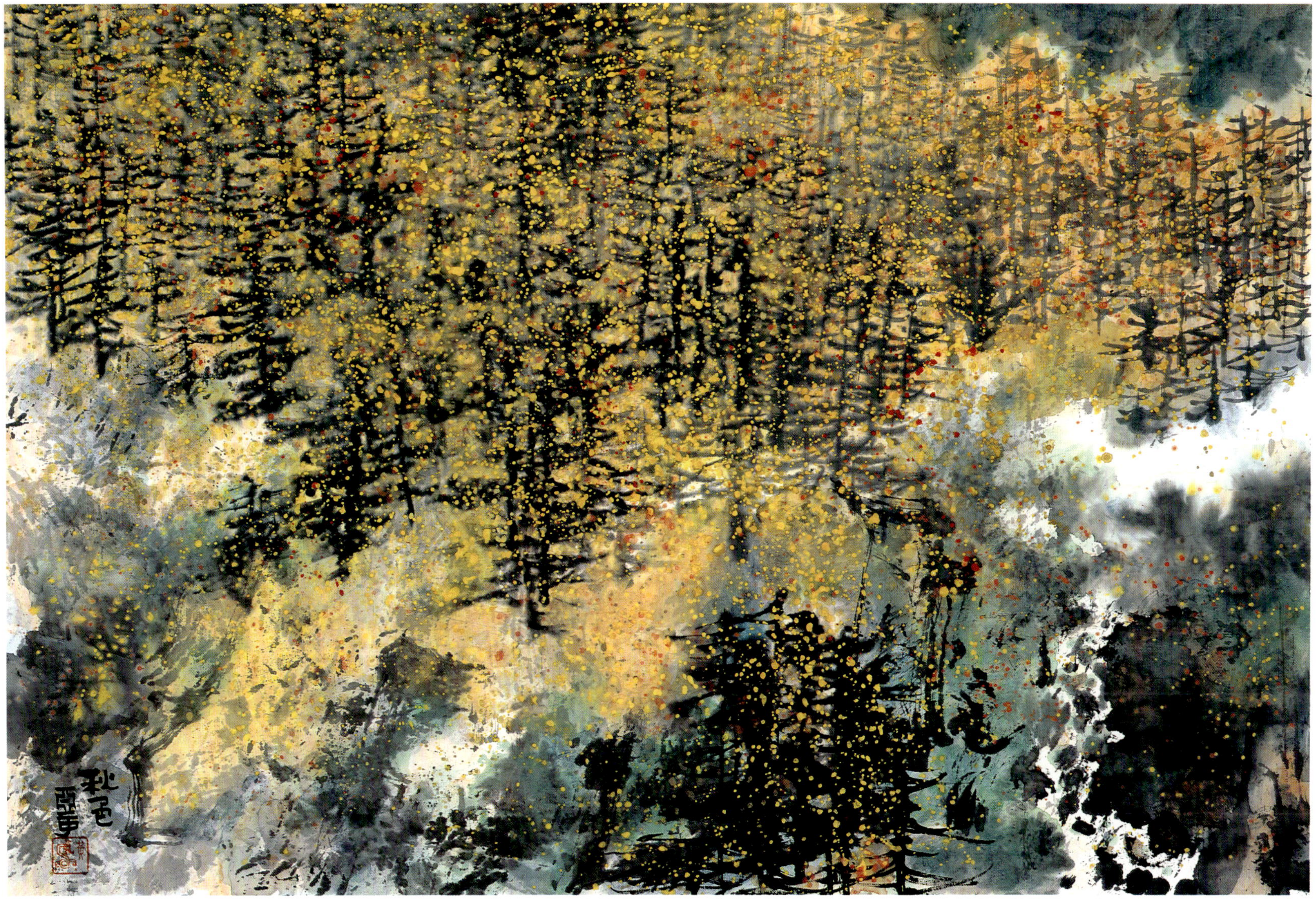

"Autumn Colors" 30" x 44" Original Watercolor Painting

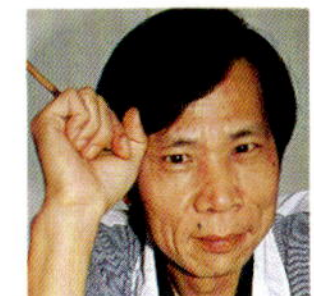

HO HUNG WONG

Ho Hung Wong, grandson of famed Chinese artist Yi Ru Yang, is a product of China's diverse history. He was introduced at an early age to the world of letters and arts in his home province of Guang Dong. At the age of 10 he began his formal study of calligraphy and later studied with the Cantonese master Ren Ding Fang and then apprenticed to the scholar-artist Zai Qing Pan.

Now a resident of Honolulu, he has had numerous exhibitions and commissions in his adopted home. His "dancing brush" is deeply influenced by the traditions of his homeland. He feels that the world is in a time of great artistic vitality; all the great civilizations are drawing strength from each other.

The vibrance of his colors, the confidence and force of his brush and the romance and cheer of his images attest to his place at the forefront of Contemporary Chinese art.

Robyn Buntin of Honolulu
900-A Maunakea Street
Honolulu, HI 96817
(808) 523-5913

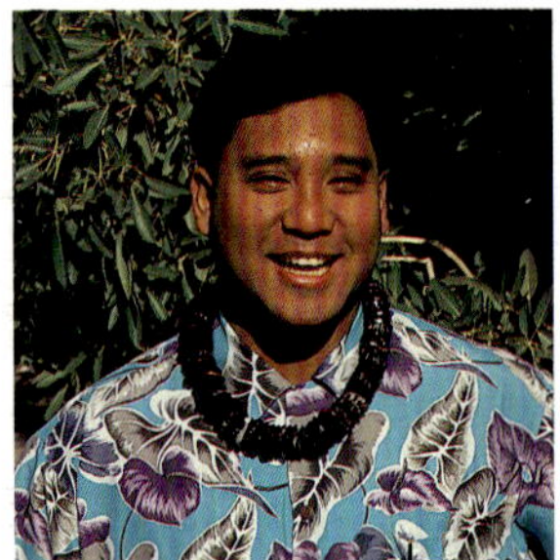

BRIAN IBAAN

Island-born and raised, the works of Brian Ibaan reflect the deep affection and pride of his island heritage and local culture. Many of his artworks depict the fond memories of his early childhood: climbing and swinging on Banyan trees in the parks, playing hide and seek in the lush green forests, and exploring the many streams and tidal pools around the islands.

By combining twentieth century realism and abstract expressionism in his paintings, Brian is able to capture the "mana" (the essence or spirit) of his subject matter. This mana is manifested by the graceful yet powerful hula dancers portrayed on canvas, by the bold, energetic brushstrokes that flow through his nature works, and by utilizing a vibrant and colorful palette that permeates the "aina" (land) of Hawaii.

"My work directly reflects my personal experience in these Islands. I'm very capable of painting the usual landscapes and

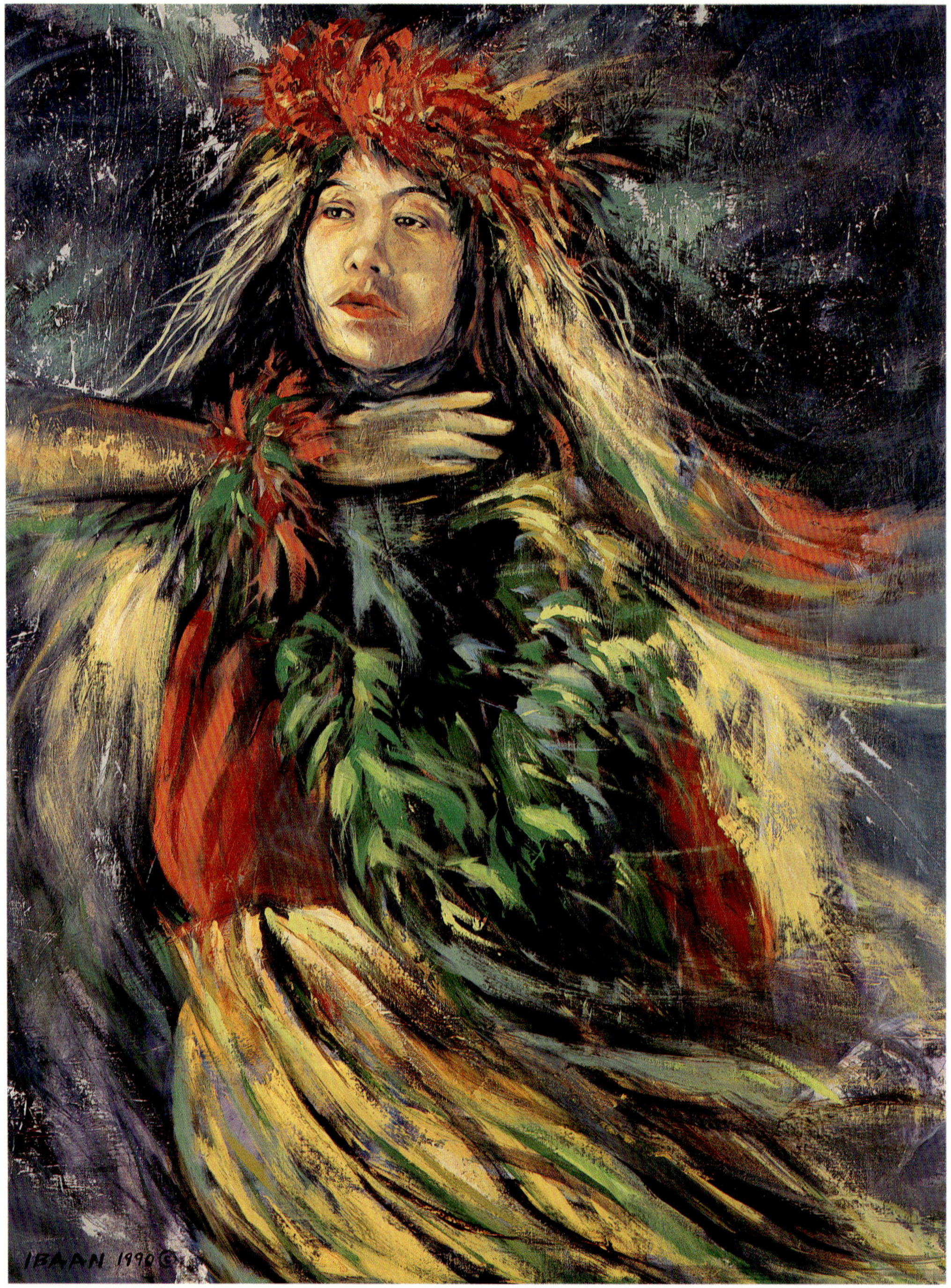

"I Ke Alo O Ke Akua Malihini"
(In the Presence of the Foreign Goddess), Oil on canvas 36" x 48"

seascapes. I find that so distant, so impersonal. My work provides a "closer" look at life. When you purchase one of my paintings, you not only gain an artwork produced with great passion, but you now possess a part of me… A part of my past and personal experience. It is then that I receive the greatest joy and honor in sharing my mana and love of the islands with you."

The works of this local boy have been exhibited in Honolulu, Los Angeles, and Manila, and have been purchased by Bank of Hawaii, private foundations, state and federal government agencies, and select private collections in the United States and the Philippines. He is represented on Oahu by the Robyn Buntin Galleries and the Fine Art Associates at the Art Loft.

Presently, Brian teaches art in the Hawaii Public School system. Drawing, painting, portraiture, comicbook and fashion illustration are just a few of the classes this island artist and instructor teaches on a private level. His aspiring students range from second graders to grandparents.

You may contact the artist at his studio for commissioned works, portraiture, and graphic design.

BRIAN IBAAN

94-167 Kiaka Loop
Millilani, Oahu, HI 96789
(808) 623-3365

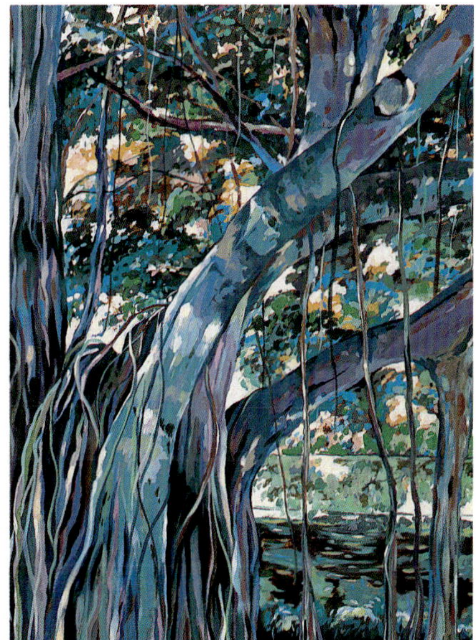

"Zoo Banyan"
Acrylic on canvas 36" x 48"

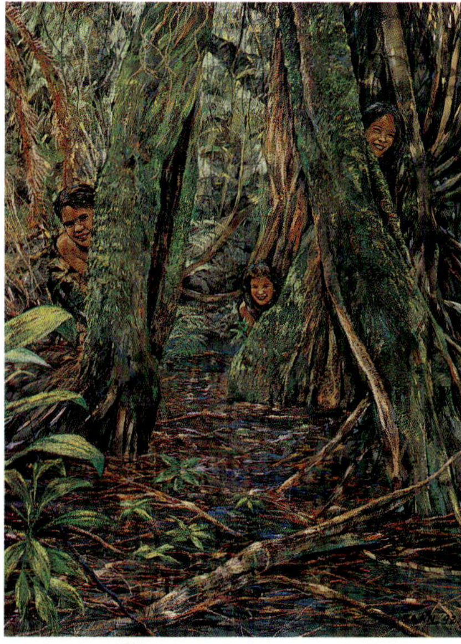

"Na Keiki O Ka La'au"
(Children of the forest), Watercolor/ Pastel on paper 36" x 48"

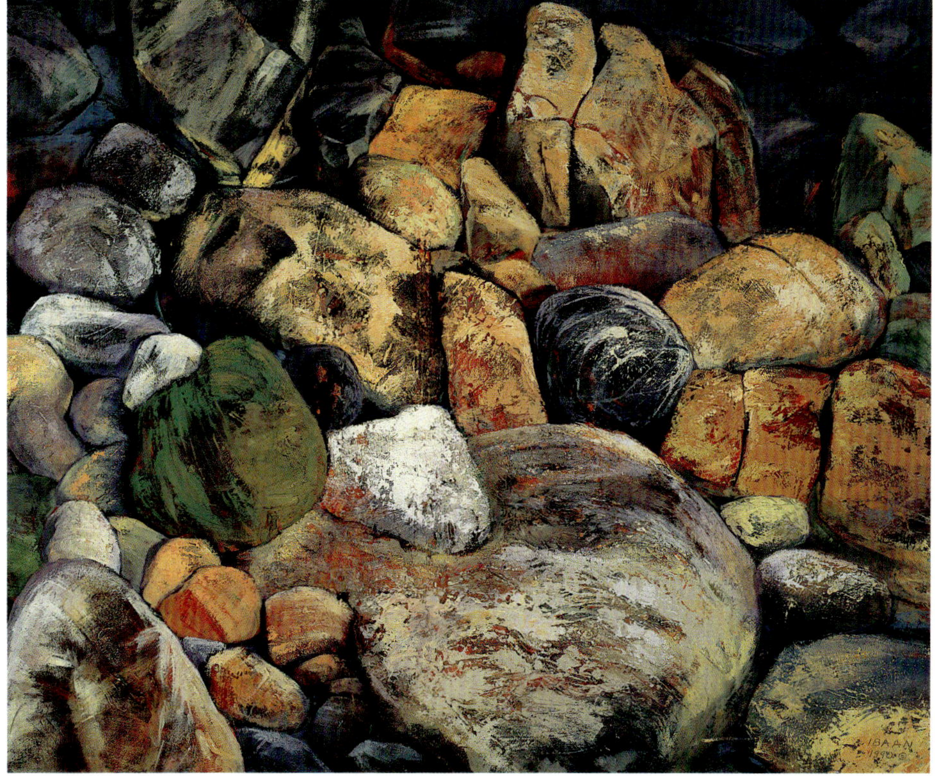

Na Pohaku, Helu 'Elua
(Rocks, #2) Oil on canvas 48" x 60"

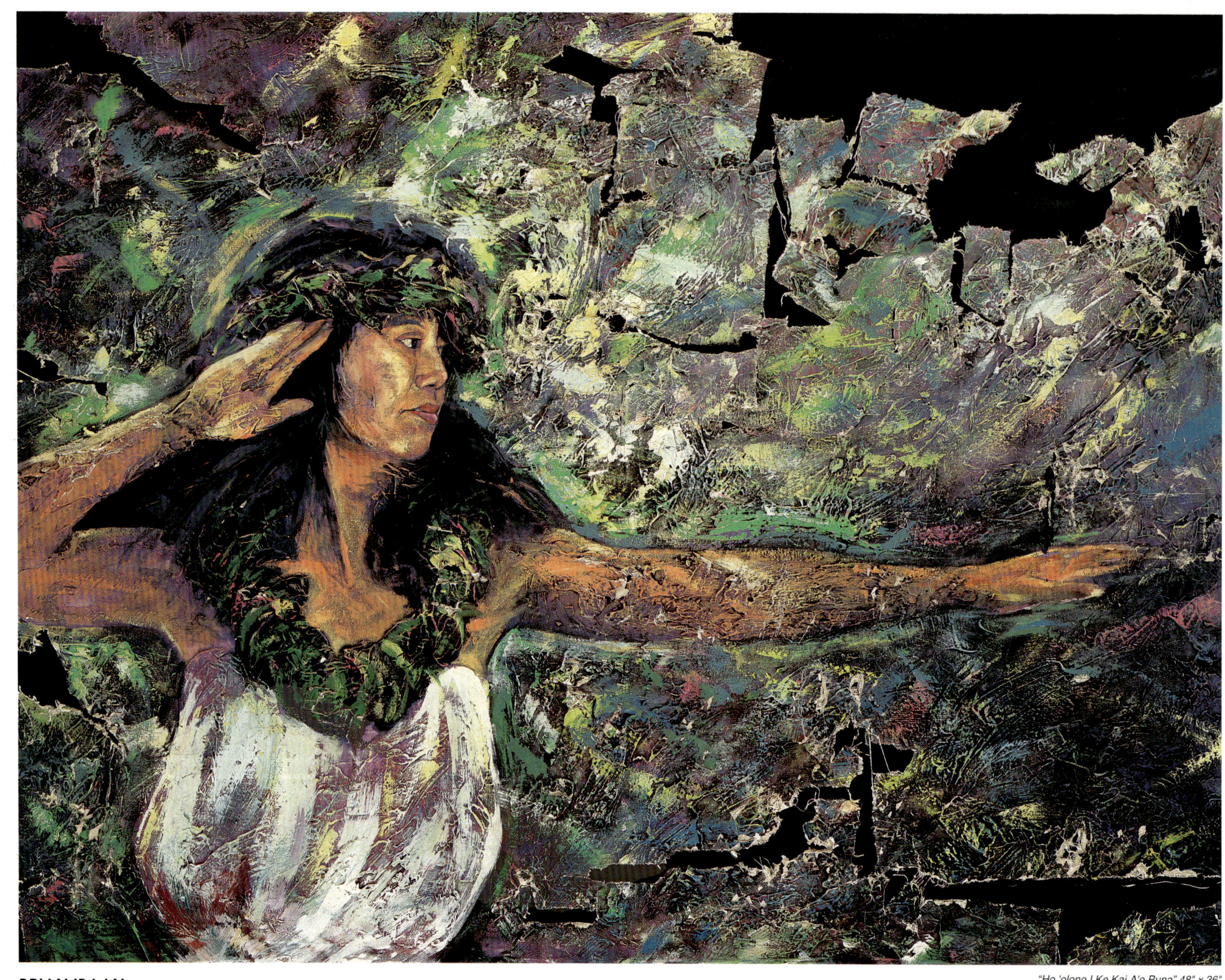

BRIAN IBAAN

"Ho 'olono I Ke Kai A'o Puna" 48" x 36"
(Listen to the sea at Puna) Oil, Acrylic and Pastel

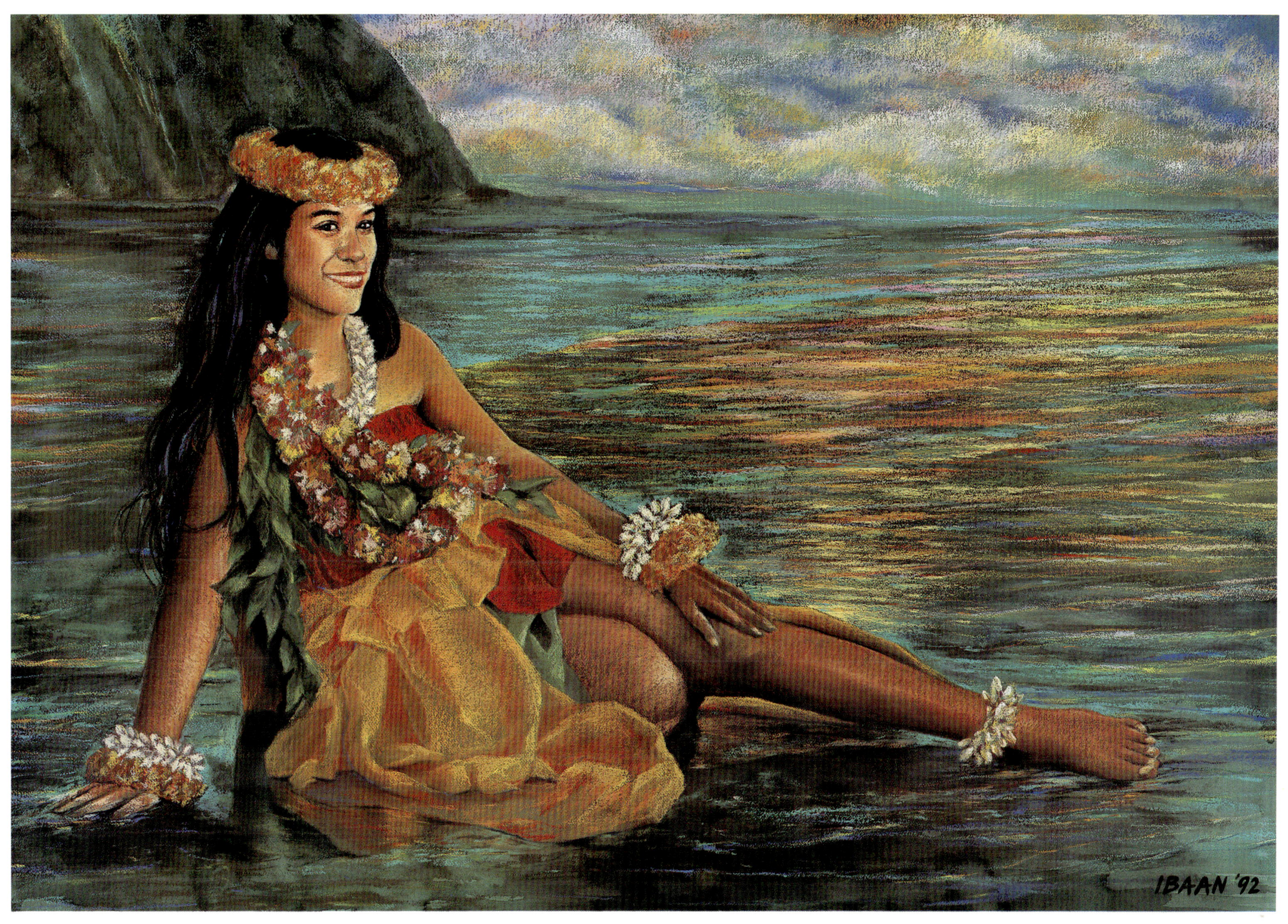

"Noho Malie Ka Wahine I Ke Kai" 36" x 51"
(The woman sitting calmly by the sea), Watercolor and Pastel

BRIAN IBAAN

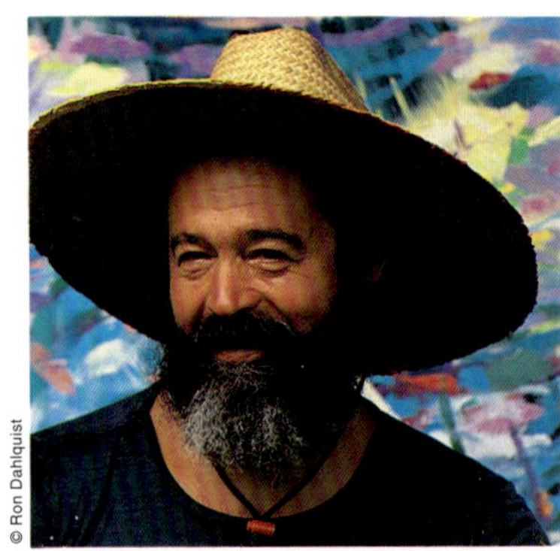

JAN KASPRZYCKI

Maui artist, Jan Kasprzycki, has lived and painted high on the slopes of Haleakala for twenty years. A passionate man, in love with color and awed by the beauty that surrounds him, Jan has constructed an inspiring studio environment made up of spectacular vistas, clean, cool air and thousands of flowers. It is impossible to overlook his natural exuberance when meeting him in person, and this powerful energy can be felt through his paintings as well.

We know an artist often "sees" things in a different way than the rest of us. The world through Kasprsycki's eyes is throbbing with color and in constant motion. Life and light emanate from his paintings which bring an unmistakable energy and joy to the spaces they inhabit. With a style that is broad in scope, Kasprzycki captures sweeping landscapes, intimate portraits, vibrant city scenes and, of course, his trademark floral extravaganzas. In addition to his original oils, gouaches and pastels, he expresses himself in sculpture, the making of fine art prints, and architecturally scaled projects.

Kasprzycki has attracted the attention of private and corporate collectors from all over the world. His work is offered at Coast Gallery at the Hotel Hana Maui, and his originals are displayed in the permanent collections of the Kapalua Bay Hotel, Mama's Fish House, Haliimaile General Store, David Paul's Lahaina Grill, and The Chart House Restaurants (which have collected over 100 of Jan's paintings). Together with his wife and business manager, Kathy, Kasprzycki often entertains clients by appointment, individually. They have discovered that serious patrons of Jan's work appreciate personal service and direct involvement with the artist. The studio experience they offer allows collectors to "feel and smell the paint", as Kasprzycki puts it.

The nature of the man and the impact of his work inspire unconventional expressions and bold projects. For example, Jan has collaborated with his brother and fine woodworking artist, Paul, to create large Oriental-style screens framed in exotic Koa wood. His brilliant designs will soon be featured in high-end fabrics manufactured by Ametex Fabrics of New York and offered as custom upholstery in designer showrooms via Robert Allen Fabrics. In 1995, Kasprzycki plans to unveil a line of exquisite, hand-knotted, Oriental-style rugs featuring his dramatic designs. In perhaps his most ambitious project to date, Kasprzycki has conceived of a comprehensive body of paintings that will portray his experience of the great cities of the world. The two year research and production plan for the *NightScapes* ™ collection will give us Jan's international view of people and places from dusk to dawn.

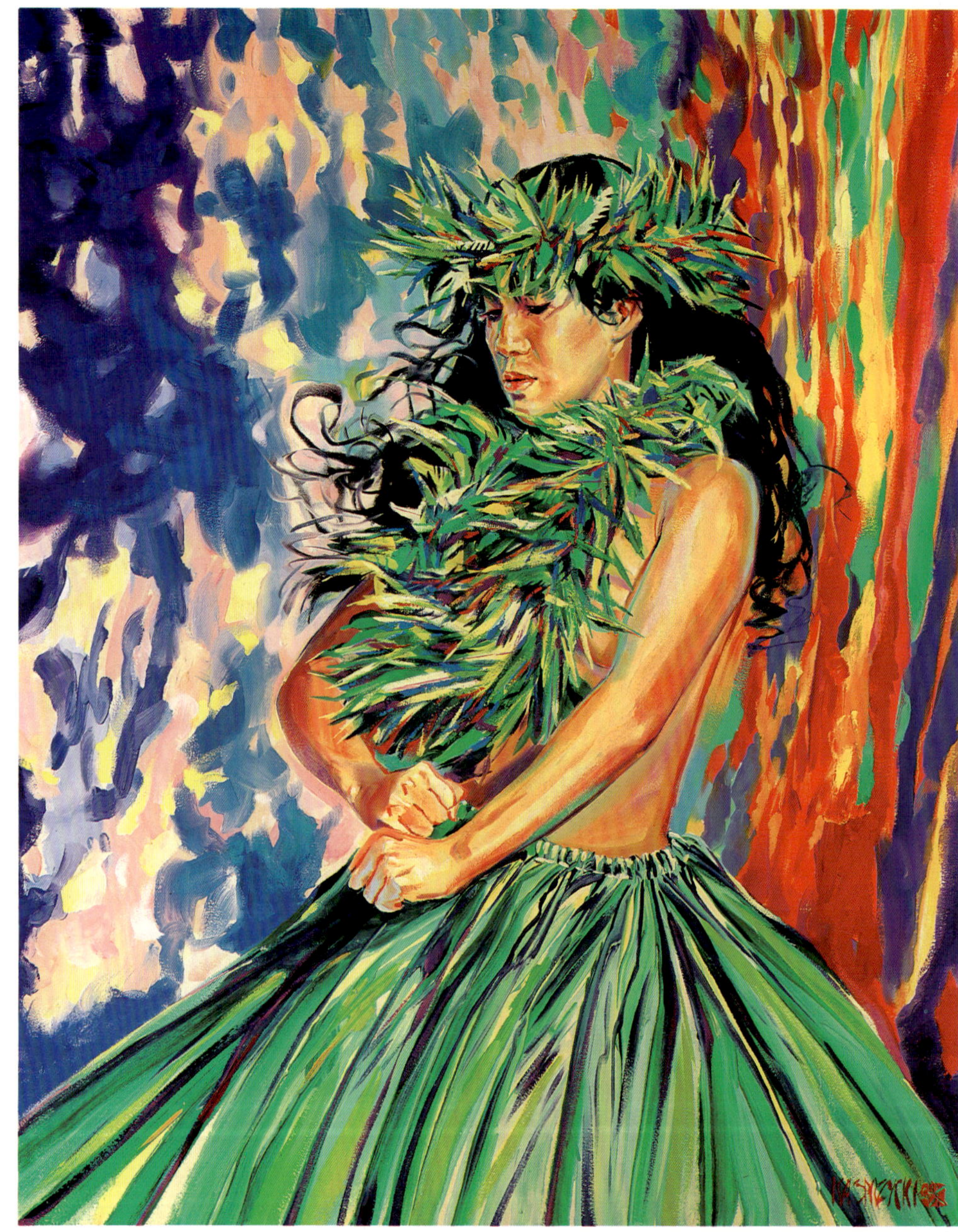

"Pele's Appeal" 48" x 60" Original Oil / Alkyds Painting

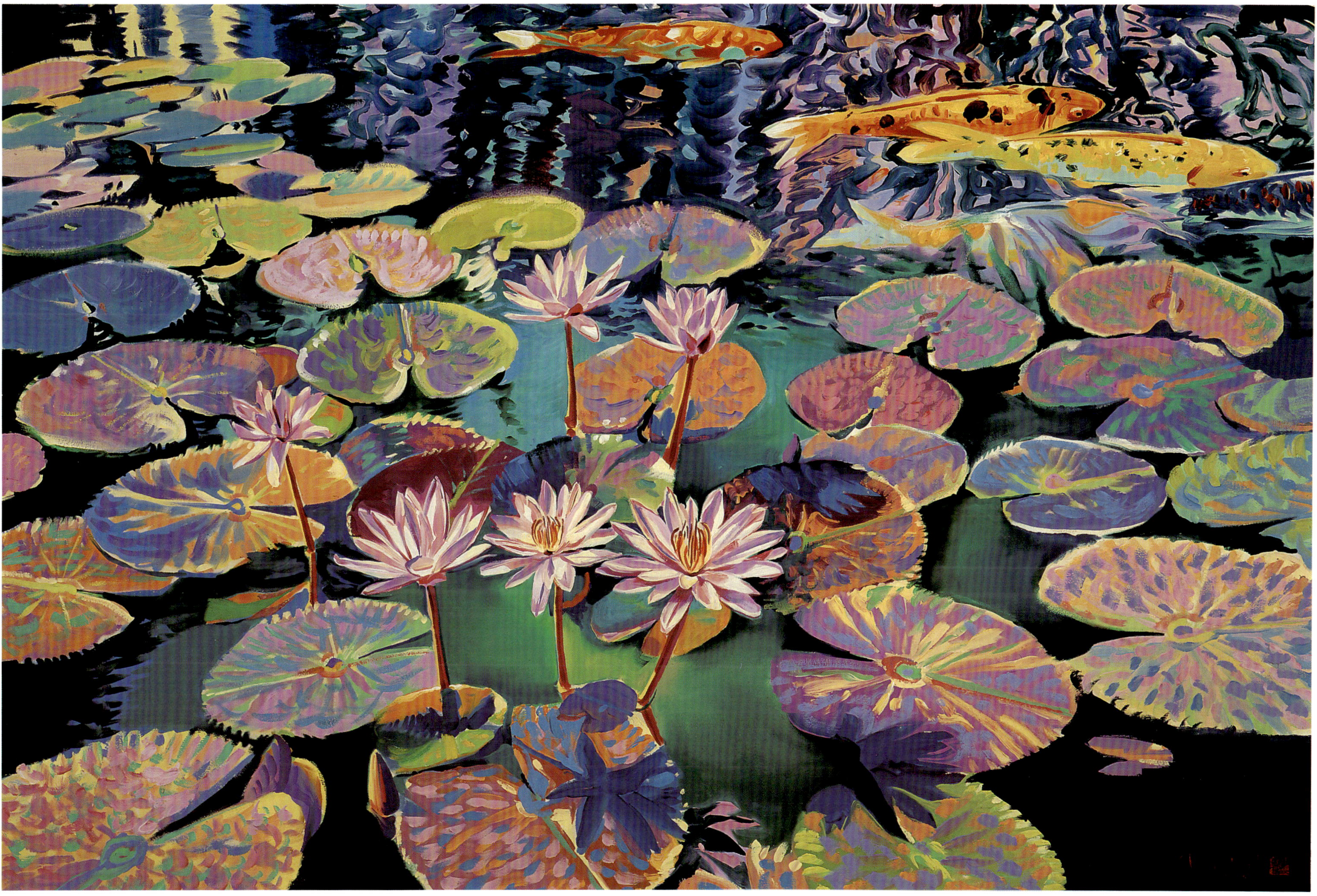

"Waterlilies in Teal" 72" x 48" Original Oil Painting

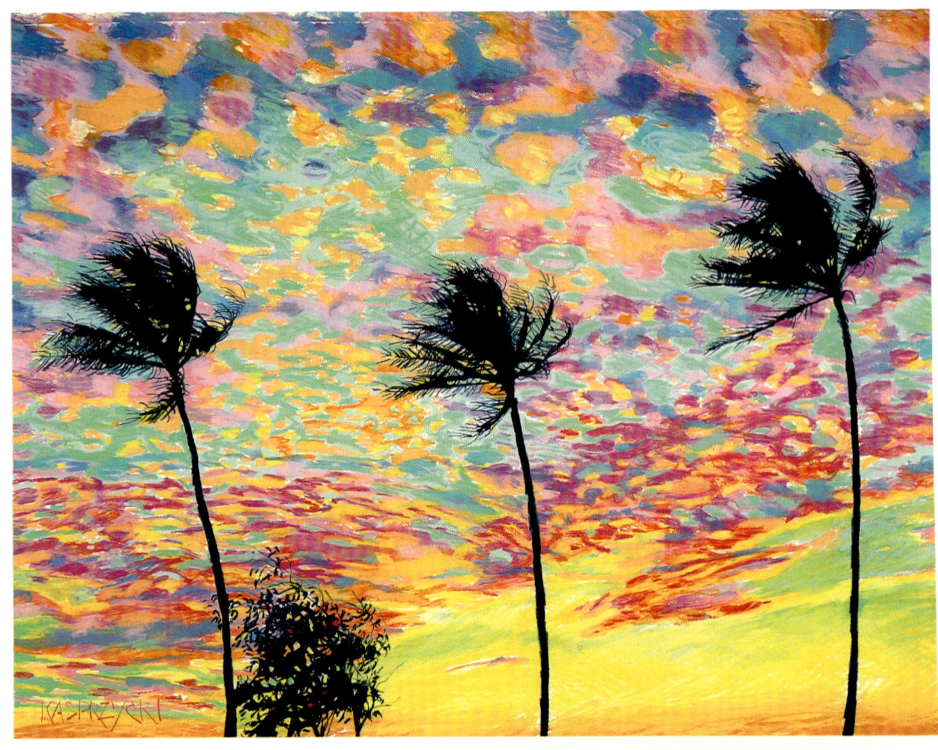

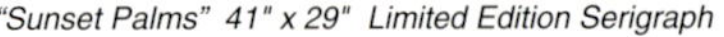

"Sunset Palms" 41" x 29" Limited Edition Serigraph

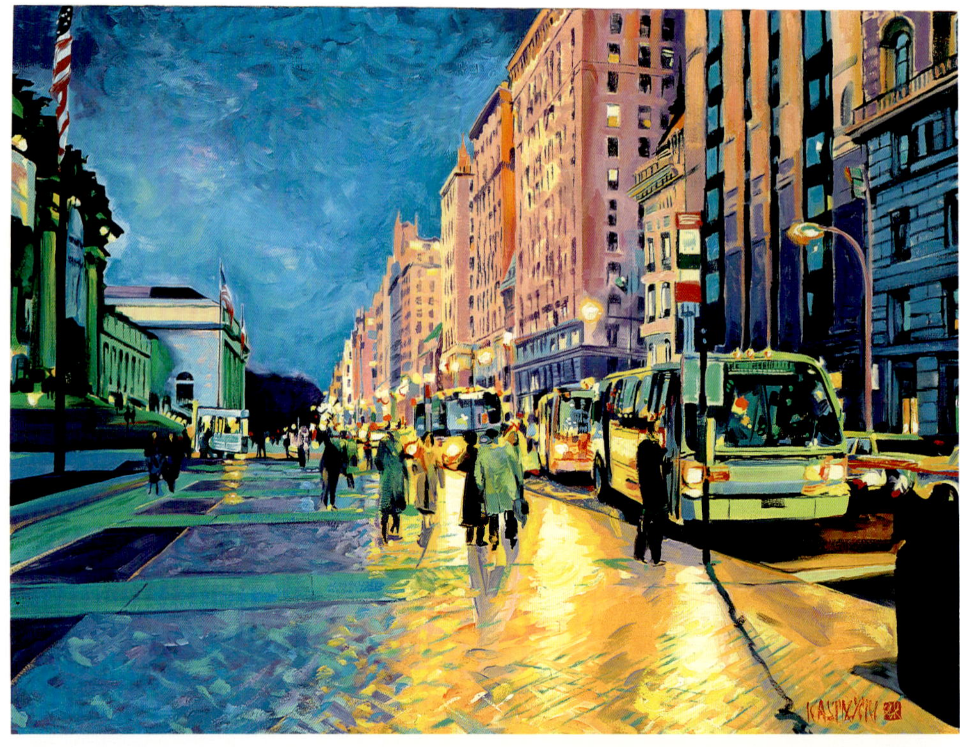

"After A Day at the Met" 51" x 38" Original Oil Painting

"Feed Me" 60" x 26" Original Oil Painting

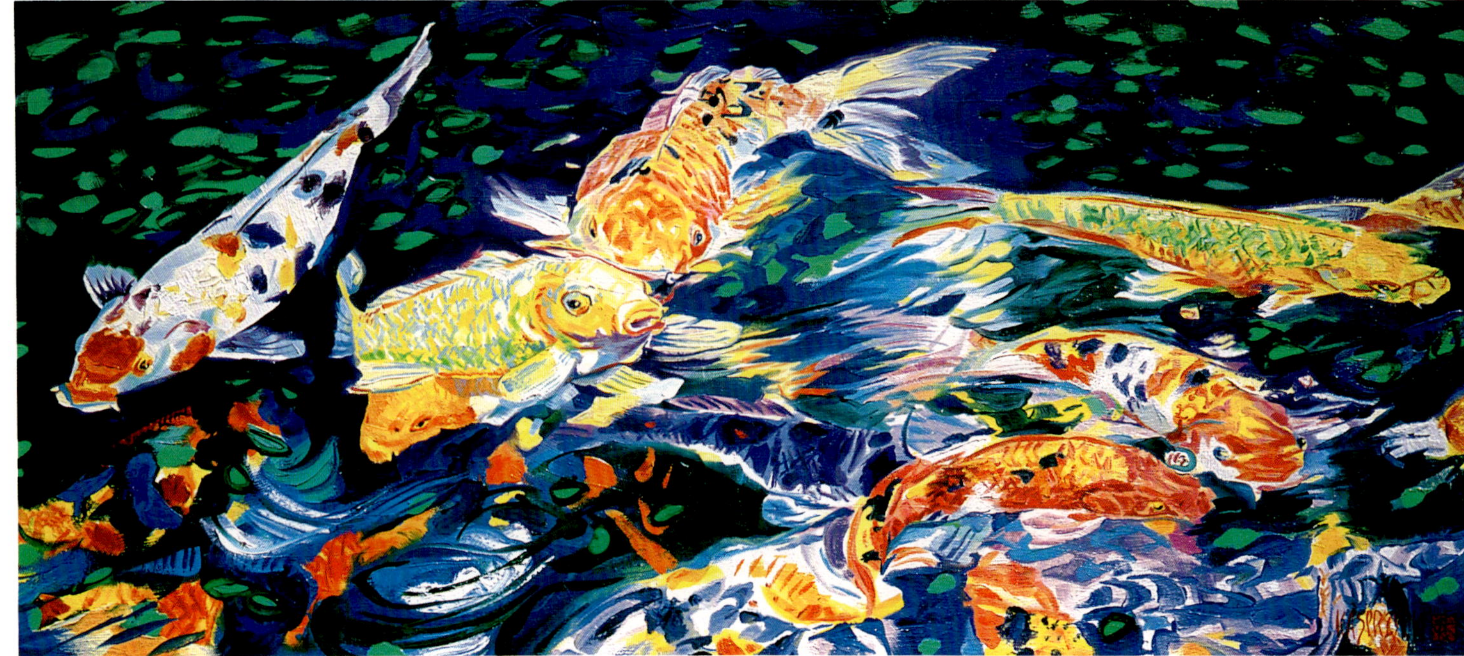

Artists possessing an active social conscience often feel the need to portray the turmoil and adversity they observe or experience in life. Jan has certainly been moved to do this, but after repeated attempts throughout his career, he reports: "I can't paint grim — my hand won't let me!" He has found that his hand is led by his heart, and his heart by beauty. He has embraced the enviable task of giving beauty back to the world, secure in the belief that beauty heals the mind. Residents of Maui know how true this is. Collectors of Jan Kasprzycki's paintings take a part of that healing beauty with them to wherever they call home.

JAN KASPRZYCKI

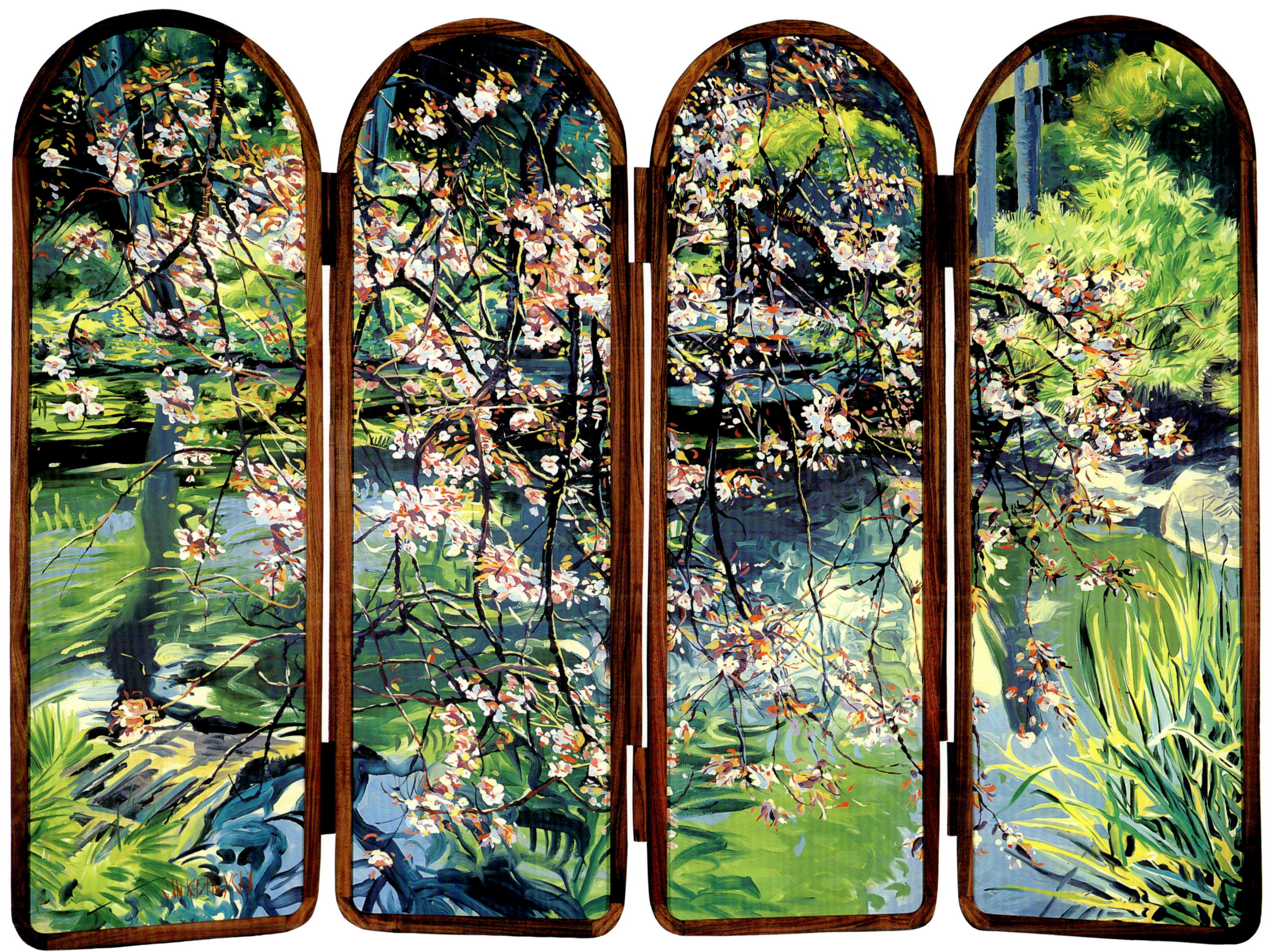

"Kyoto Gardens" 104" x 78" Original Oil Painting - Four Panel Screen, Koa Hardwood Frames

JAN KASPRZYCKI

JAN KASPRZYCKI

"High Tide" 30" x 19" Limited Edition Prints - Iris S/N & Proofs

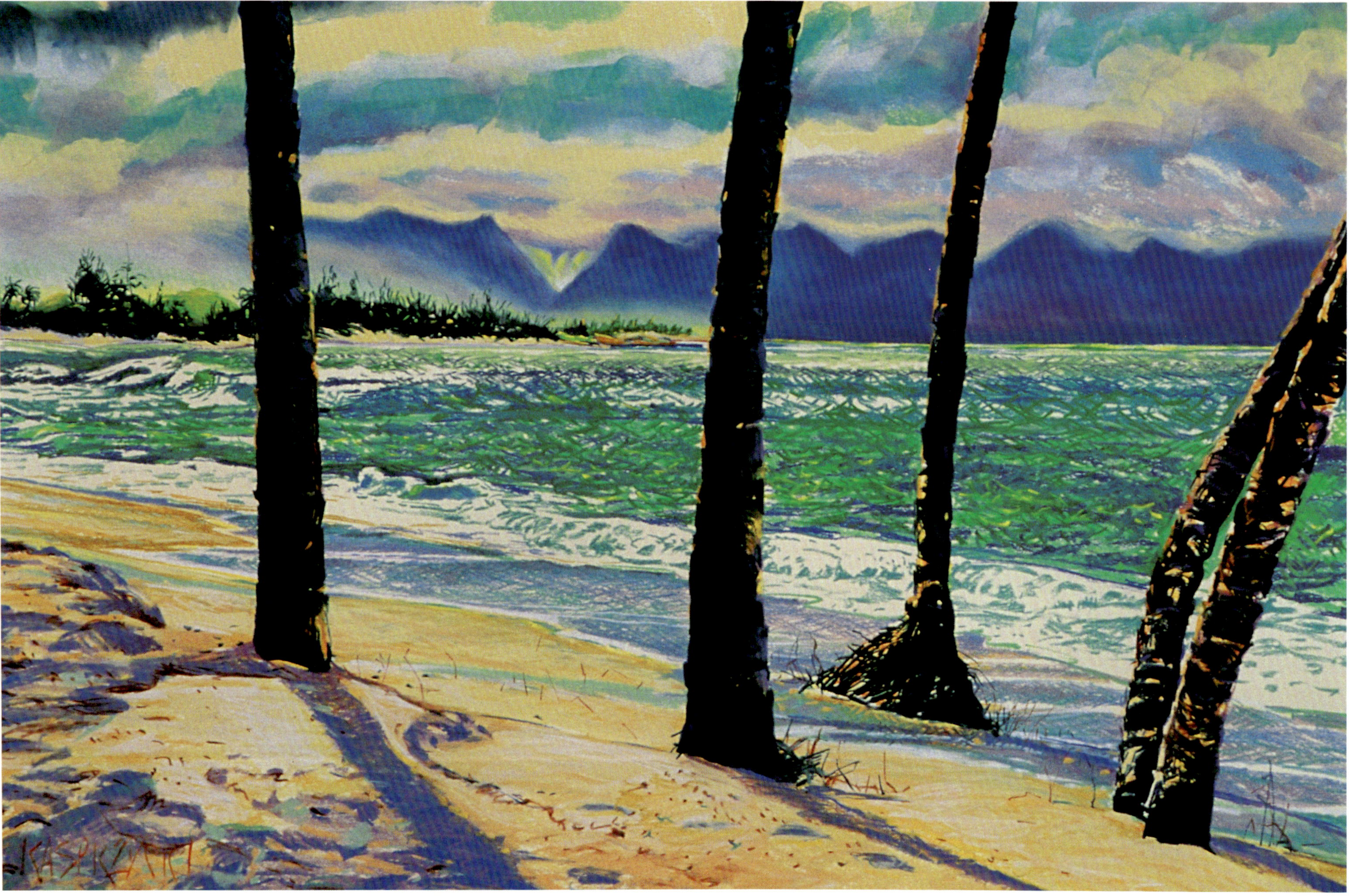

JAN KASPRZYCKI

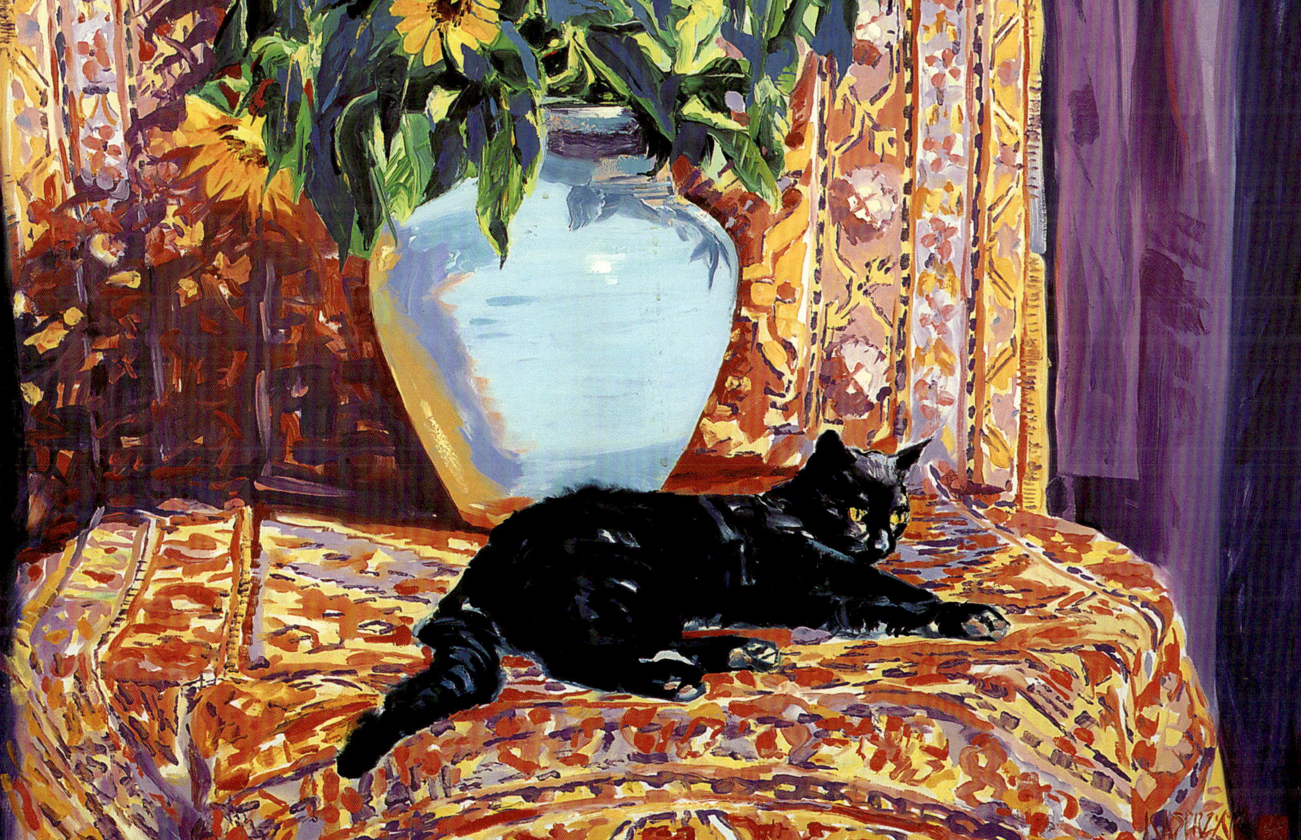

"Gauguin and Sunflowers" 29" x 30" Original Oil Painting

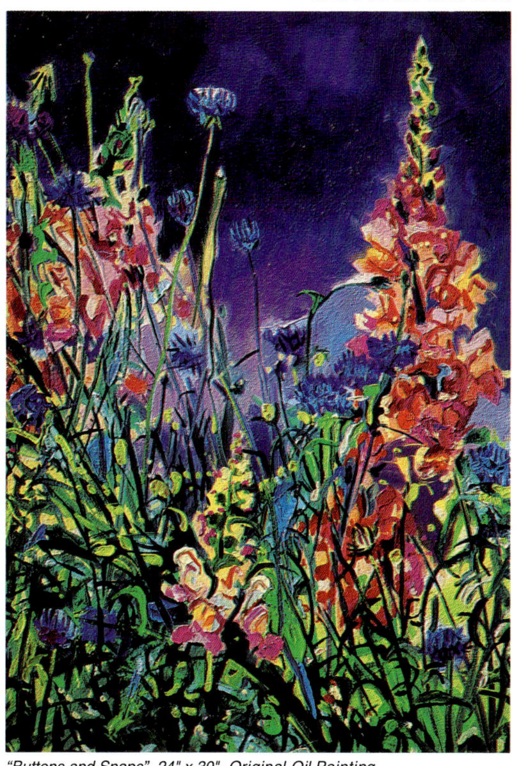

"Buttons and Snaps" 24" x 30" Original Oil Painting

For more information, or to inquire about a visit to the studio, contact Kasprzycki fine art at:

Kasprzycki Fine Art
P.O. Box 277
Makawao, Maui, HI 96768
(808) 876-0259 (808) 572-0585
Fax (808) 876-0077

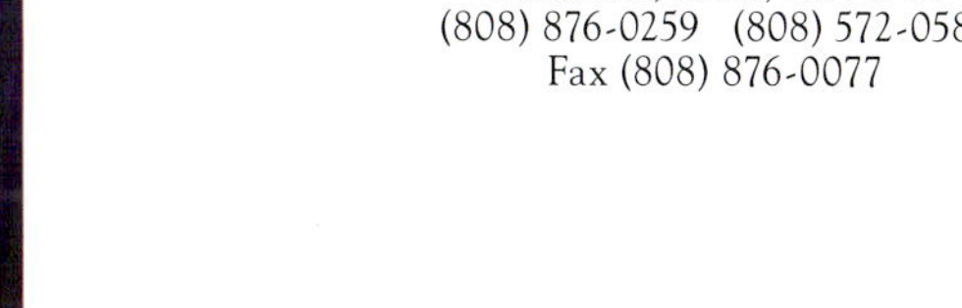

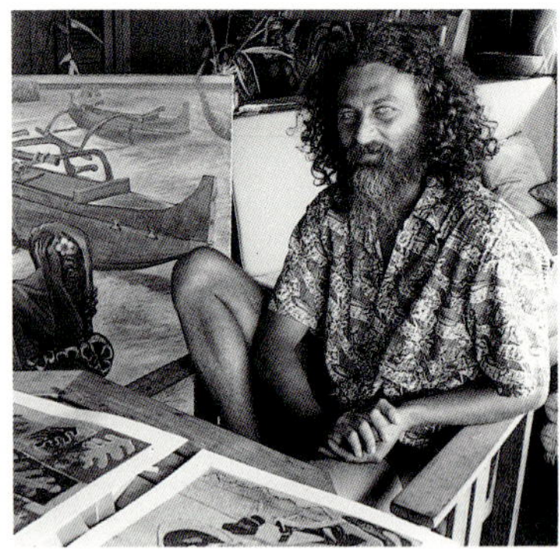

AVI KIRIATY

Pacific Prints
P.O. Box 37
Honomu, Hawaii, HI 96728
(808) 963-6706

Avi Kiriaty, the son of an artist, grew up in the world of art. Born in Israel, his journey through life has taken him from the Israeli army, to a Greek island, to a winter cottage in New Hampshire. Following the birth of his first child, Katie, Avi moved from New Hampshire to Hawaii. His first year was spent in Kauai, where he experimented for the first time with oil painting. From there he moved to the Hamakua side of the Big Island to live "Kaimaaina;" with the land, farming, and fishing. His son, Jazz, was born here in an old Hawaiian homestead. Avi then moved to the Puna rainforest and began to live the life of an artist.

Avi has worked in many media: oil painting, linoleum block printing, lava and wood sculpturing, pencil, pen, ink drawings, watercolors, and silk screening. His works are a feast of lush colors and bold lines, often depicting the Polynesian lifestyle in everyday events.

His artwork can be found in several places on the Hawaiian Islands. On the Big Island, at Volcano Art Center, in the Volcano National Park and also at Kohala Kollection in Kawaihae; on the island of Maui, at the Village Galleries, on Oahu through Dale Hope (at 737-1117).

His hot lava sculpture was featured several times on the PBS show, "Spectrum Hawaii." These works are created of molten lava from run off tributaries on the slopes of Kilauea. Lava artists dig into the lava and shape it either by shoveling the red hot lava into molds, or pounding it with tools. Avi is fascinated with the beauty of lava art, and does not produce these pieces for sale.

Using his hands with a carver and linoleum block, Avi creates a unique colored and textured linoleum block print. Each piece is composed of a series of overlaid printing done with the same block. The design is carved on a block and printed in stages, with a new color added for each stage. Each block is destroyed through the cutting and printing process, making each print an original and one of a very limited series.

In the textile field, he has been working with Kahala, one of the oldest "Aloha" shirt manufacturers. Together they have created an Avi line of "Aloha" shirts which is having great success throughout Hawaii and the United States. In May of 1994 Kahala had 52 Nordstrom stores promoting Avi's designs of wearable art. Crazy Shirts of Hawaii has also created a new Hawaiian line of Avi's designs.

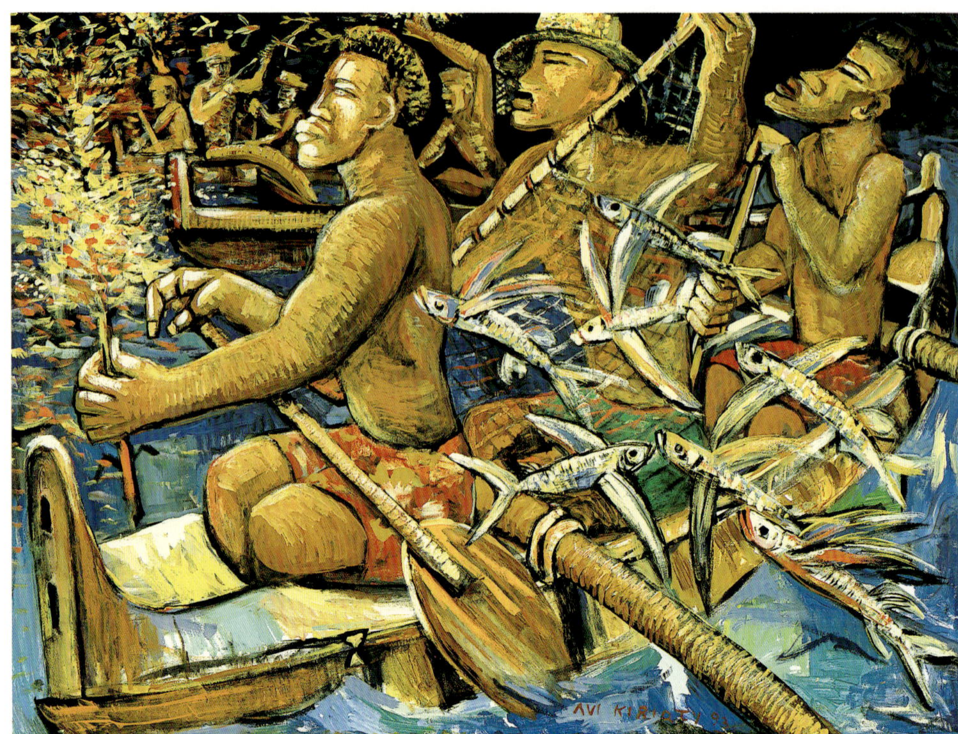

"Malolo" 40" x 30" Original Oil Painting

Canoe Makers" 40" x 30" Original Oil Painting

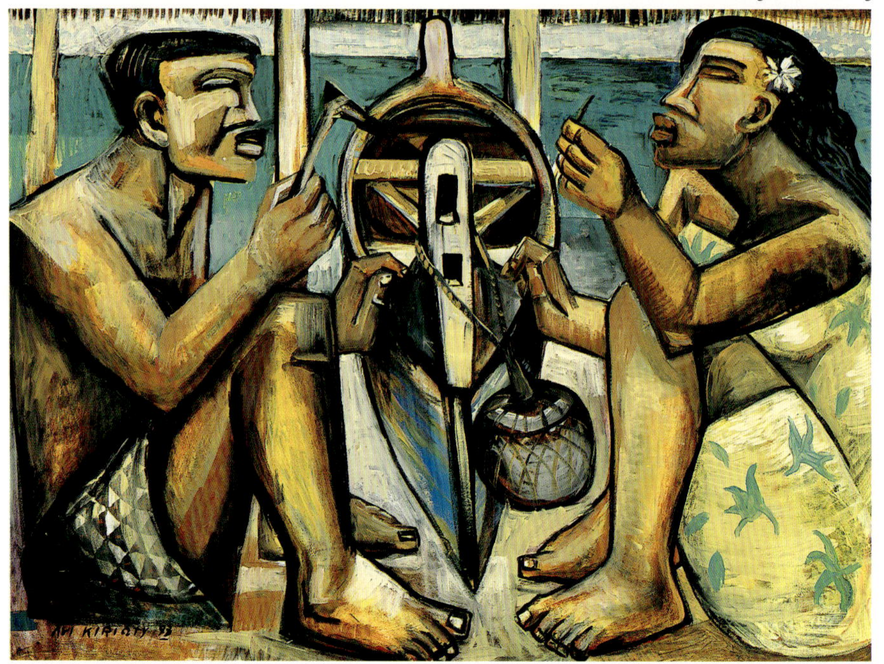

"Kava" 30" x 40" Original Oil Painting

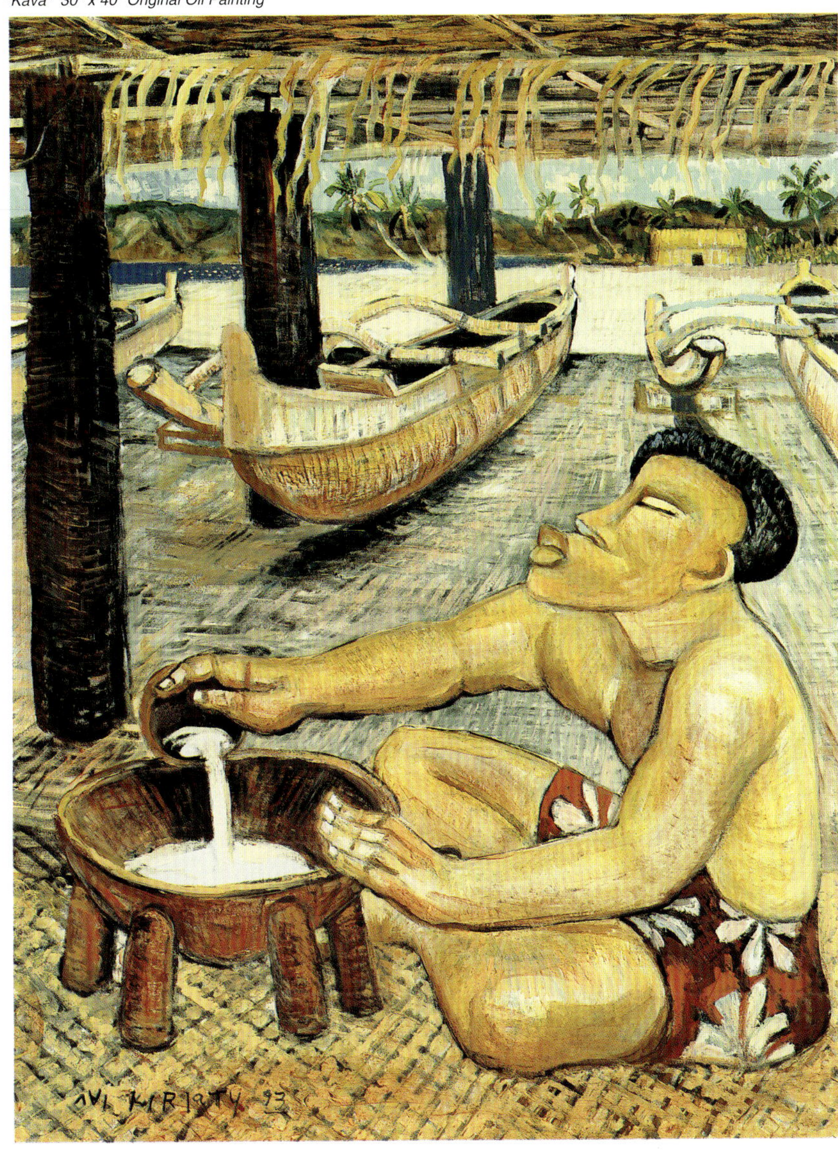

"Rapa Nui" 44" x 55" Original Oil Painting

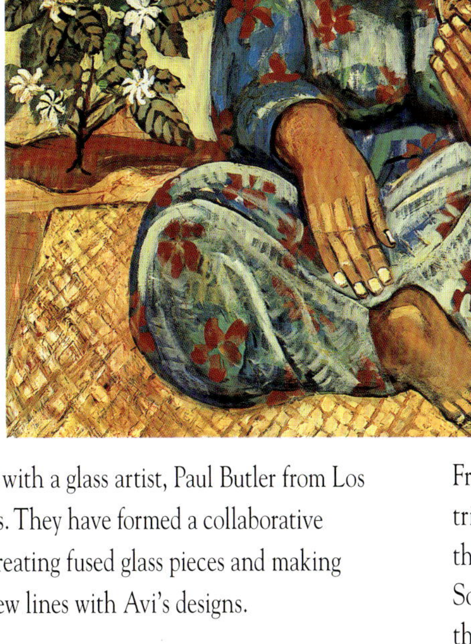

The shirts are enjoying great success while at the same time promoting art, Avi, and Hawaii. Pacifica Arts and Graphics in Makawao is printing some of Avi's designs on greeting cards.

Avi has representatives in Europe, Ute and Halmut Hajek from Munich, Germany. Avi had his first one-man show, "Kai'ma'aina," in July of 1993 at "Beckhaus" in Munich. Some of Avi's prints will be in the 1994 international show in Portugal.

The Thomas T. Thron Gallery of San Francisco represents Avi on the West Coast. Thomas has also merged with a glass artist, Paul Butler from Los Angeles. They have formed a collaborative effort creating fused glass pieces and making some new lines with Avi's designs.

Recently, Avi and his family went on a three month excursion to 19 different islands in French Polynesia and the Cook Islands. This trip was for the purpose of further studying the Polynesian culture. After researching the Society Group in French Polynesia, he sailed through the Tuamotu Islands and then visited the islands of the Marquesas. Avi resides on the island of Maui.

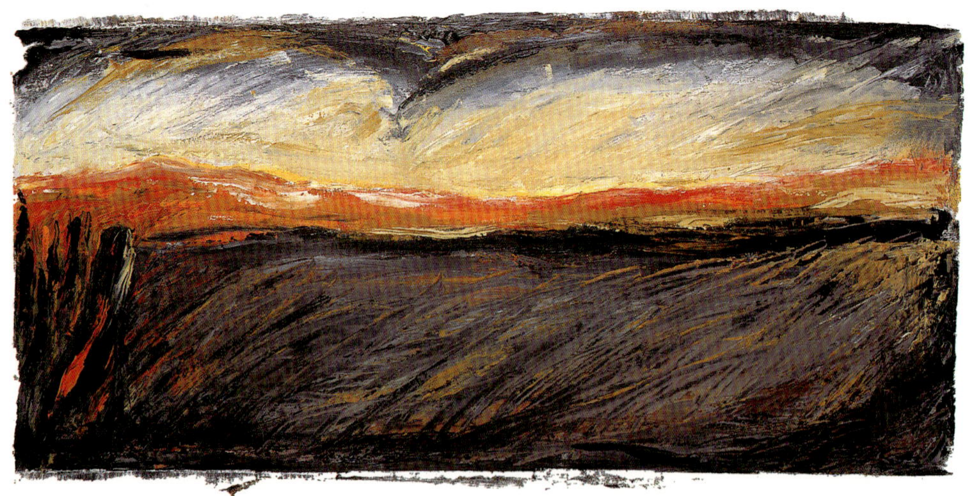

"Many Lands" 37" x 18" Original Oil Painting

Elisabeth K, a visual artist and writer, moved from Hamburg, Germany to Honolulu, Hawaii in 1981. Her international formal and informal fine arts training has brought her work to numerous art collections throughout Hawaii, the Continental U.S., and Germany. Some of her poetry, written while on a retreat in Mexico, is currently in the process of being published, with her own artwork serving as the book's cover.

"I am the result of a free-spirited academic mother, and generations of professional artists from my father's side. For the last 20 years, I have explored in my work not only the inherited talents of my ancestors, but also my most intimate feelings and expressions. As my life took its ever-changing course, my work changed with it. Uprooting myself by choice, and now living in Hawaii as a foreigner, I have gathered a deep respect and empathy for the indigenous people of this nation. My frequent journeys to New Mexico have opened me to the Native American's sensitivity of nature, and to the awesome freedom of the flight of birds. My recent work is, therefore, about a conglomerate experience of the many lands I walk... and my place in them."

Elisabeth holds dear a poem given to her by a fellow artist during a Master's Program in Santa Fe with the renowned Nathan Oliveira. This poem mirrors her artistic and personal journey:

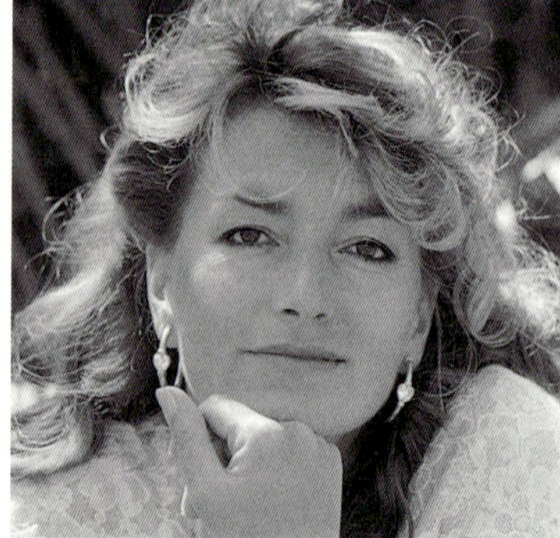

ELISABETH K
ATELIER EK
2999 Kalakaua Avenue, Suite 601
Honolulu, HI 96815
(808) 923-1711

I live my life in growing orbits which move
out over the things of the world...
Perhaps I can never achieve the last but that
will be my attempt.
I am moving around God, around the
ancient tower, and I have been
circling for a thousand years.
And I still don't know if I am a falcon,
or a storm, or a great song.
--Rainer Maria Rilke.

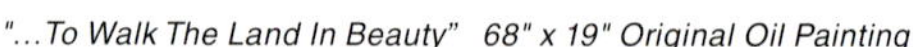

"...To Walk The Land In Beauty" 68" x 19" Original Oil Painting

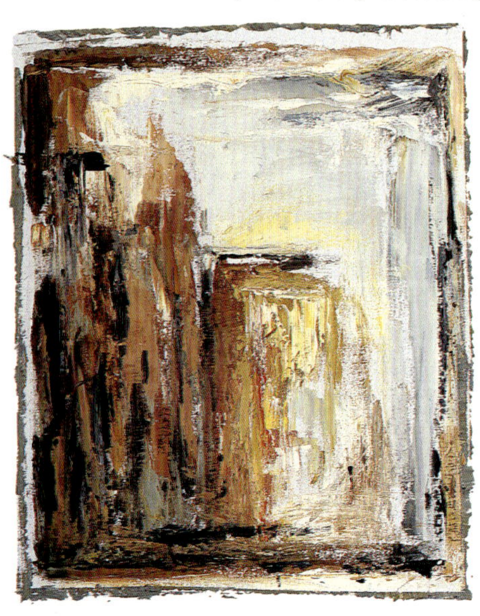

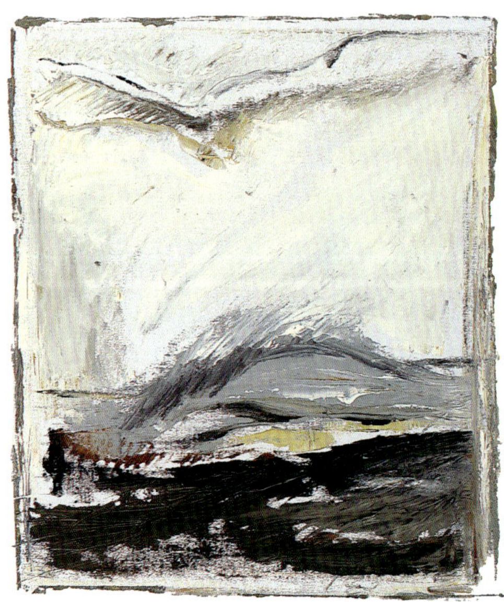

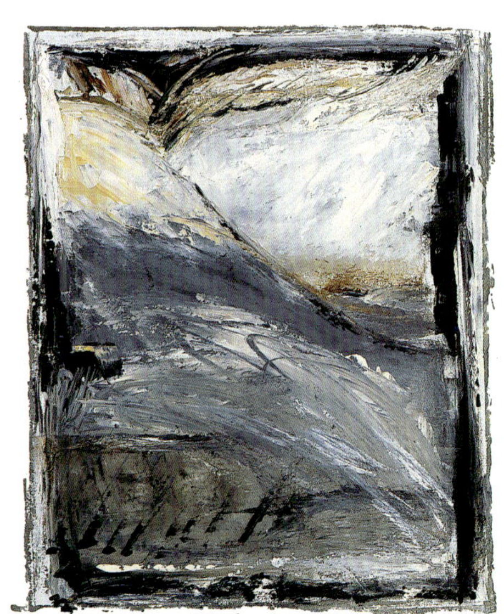

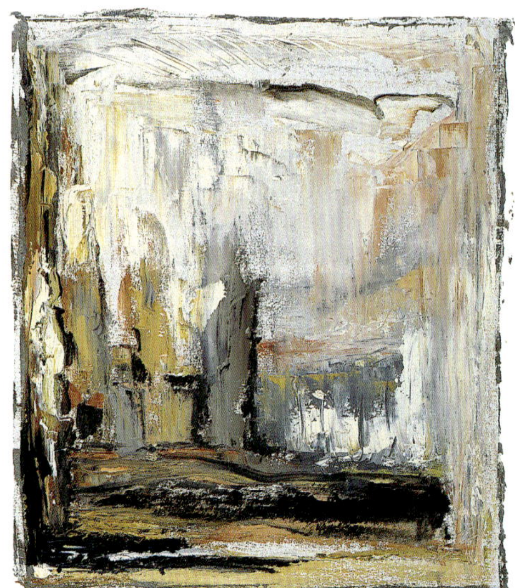

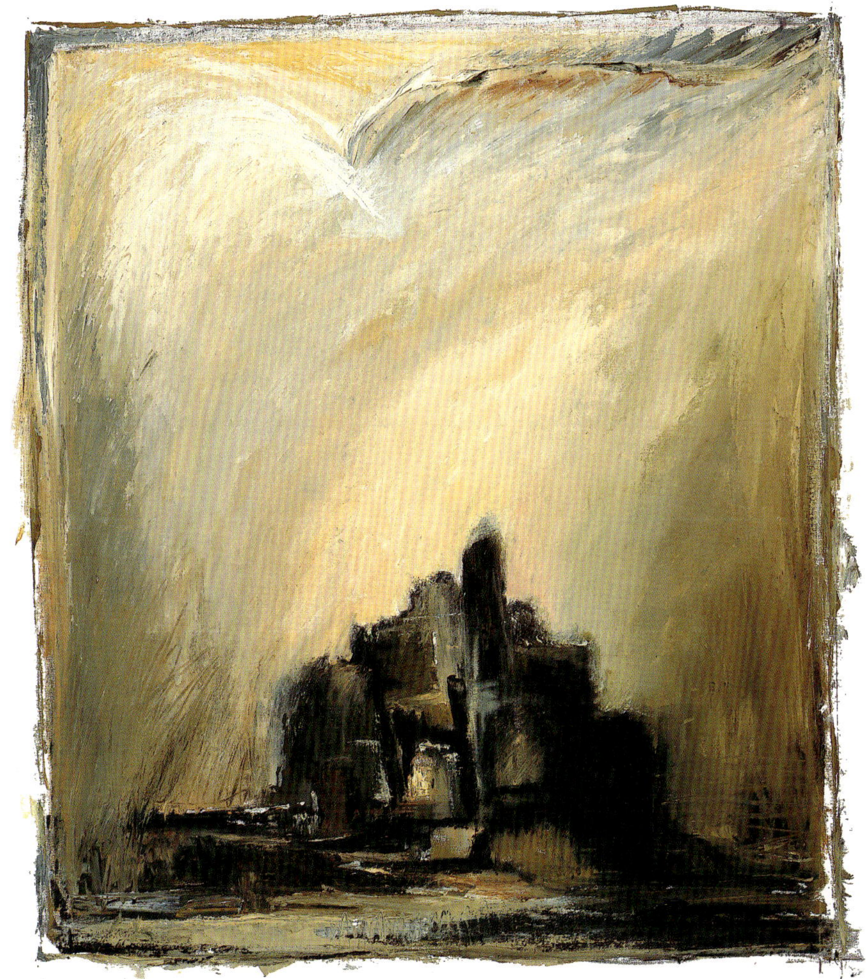

"Circling The Ancient Tower" 32" x 37" Original Oil Painting

"In Black There Are Colors" 46" x 20" Original Oil Painting

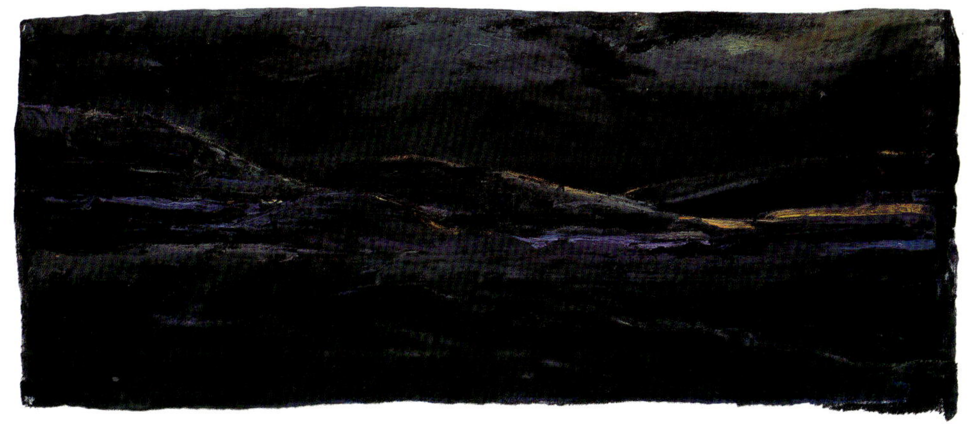

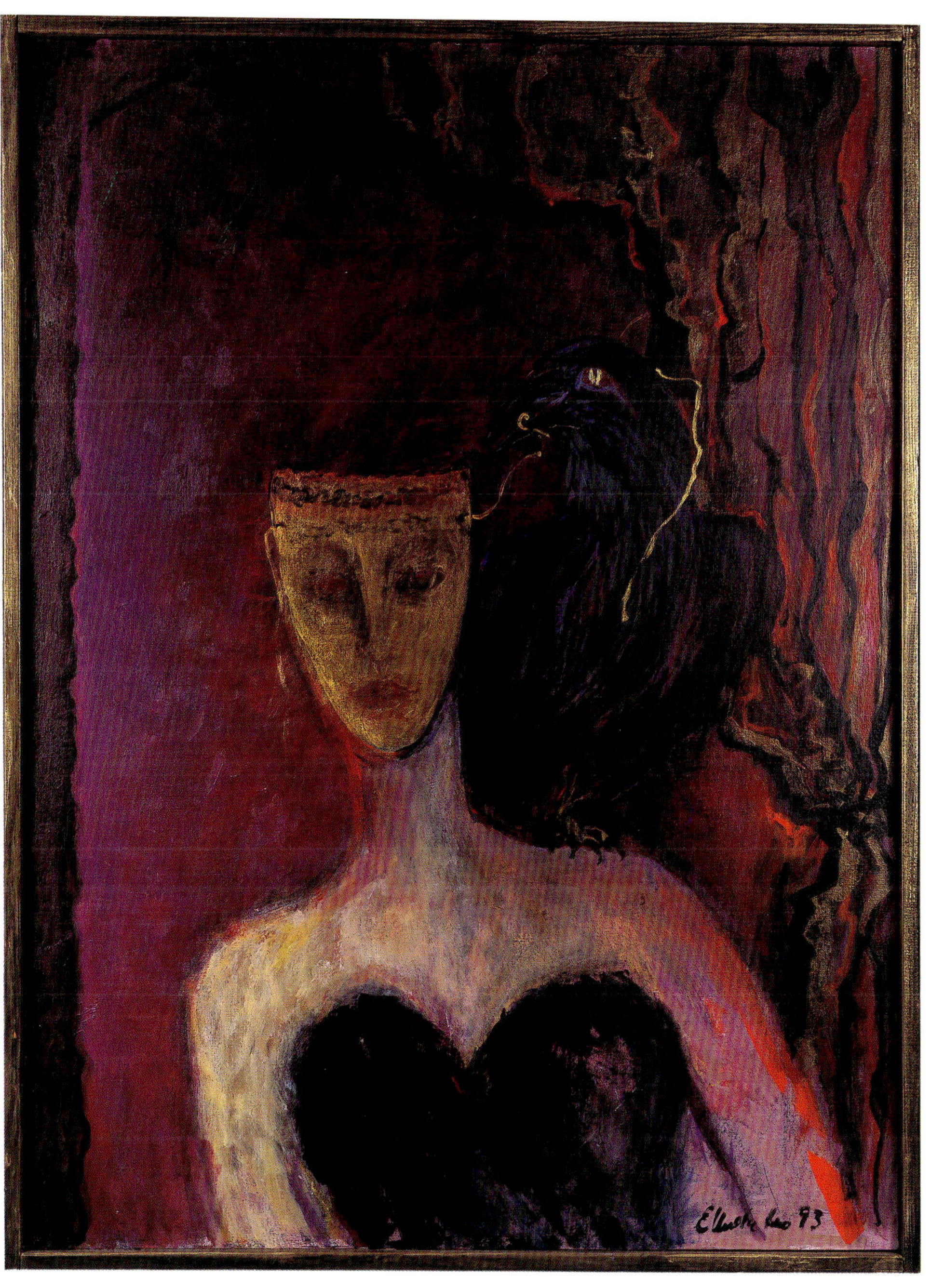

"Alzbeta-Unveiling The Golden Mask" 36" x 48"
Original Oil Painting

ELISABETH K

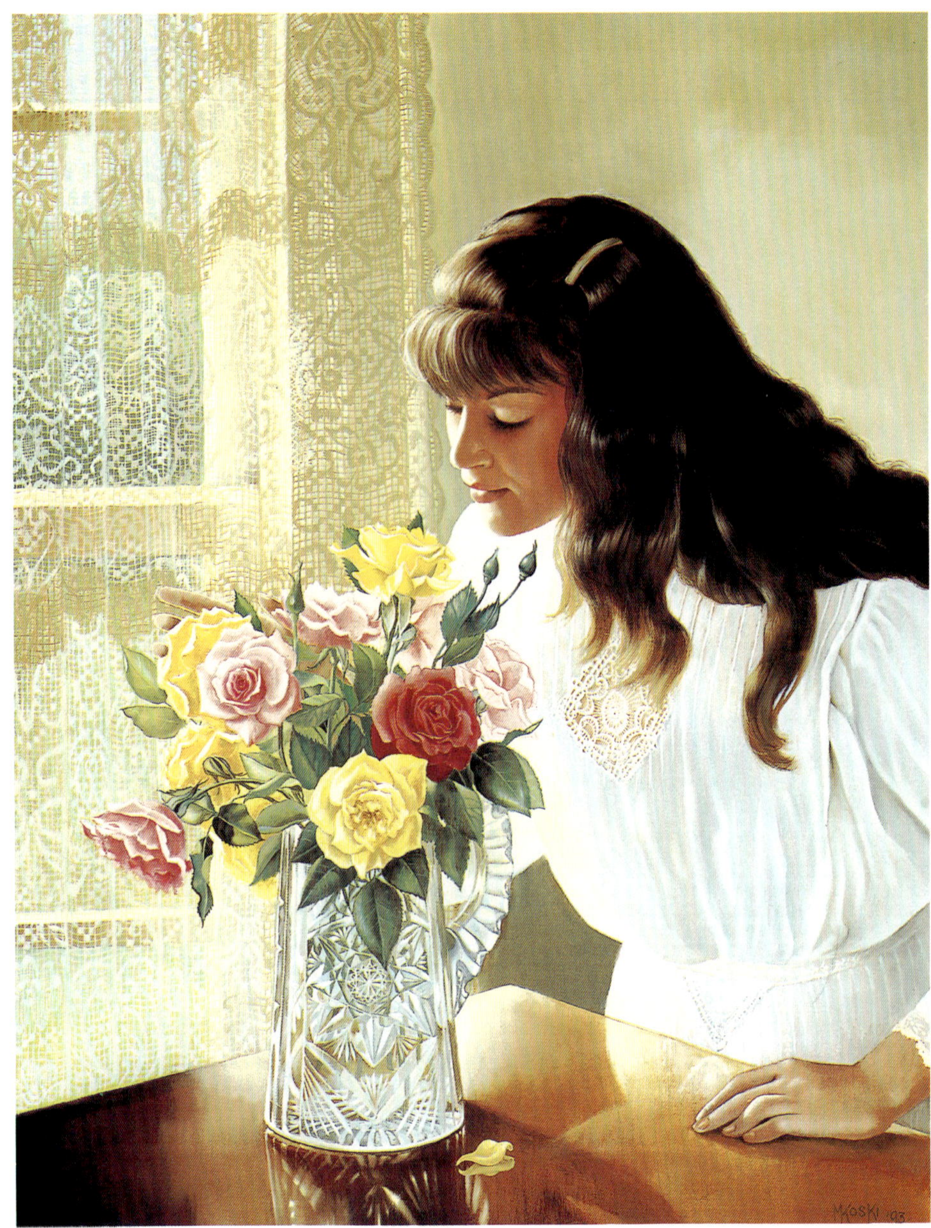

"Waimea Roses"
Limited Edition Print
20" x 26"

Represented by:

Coast Galleries - Hotel Intercontinental - Maui
Livingstons Gallery - Oahu
Collectors Gallery - Kailua-Kona, Hawaii
Gallery of Great Things - Waimea, Hawaii
Montage Gallery - Princeville, Kauai
Island Heritage Publishing

Born in San Diego, Mary Koski began her career as a professional artist at the age of seventeen. Talented in art, ballet, and music, she majored in art at the University of California at Santa Barbara and at Mexico City college in Mexico City.

In 1970 she began an extended painting tour of Europe with commissions and exhibitions in Germany, Austria, Switzerland, Liechtenstein and Finland.

In 1983 she moved to Hawaii with her husband, Oiva, mother, Sheri, and daughter, Kathy Long, and her family. There they live in an idyllic setting, nestled in the green foothills of the Kohala mountains. She now creates images of the best of Hawaii, past and present.

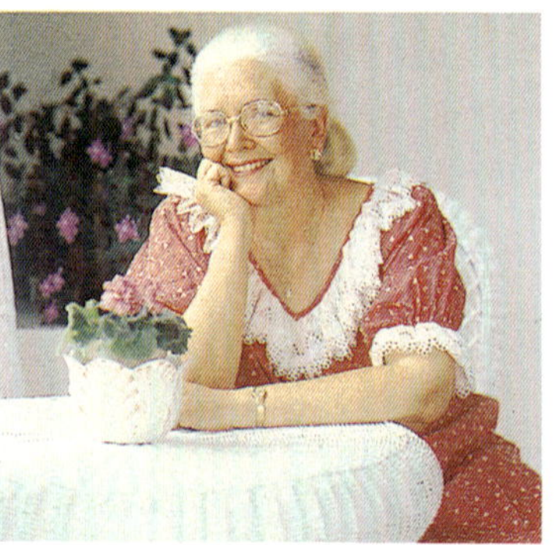

MARY KOSKI

P.O. Box 1349
Kamuela, Hawaii, HI 96743
(808) 885-6912

Her depictions of Hawaii speak of her love for the Hawaiian people and their heritage. Her images of them, and especially their children, have brought her acclaim throughout the Islands and around the world. Her original oil paintings, pastels and her many limited edition prints are widely sought after.

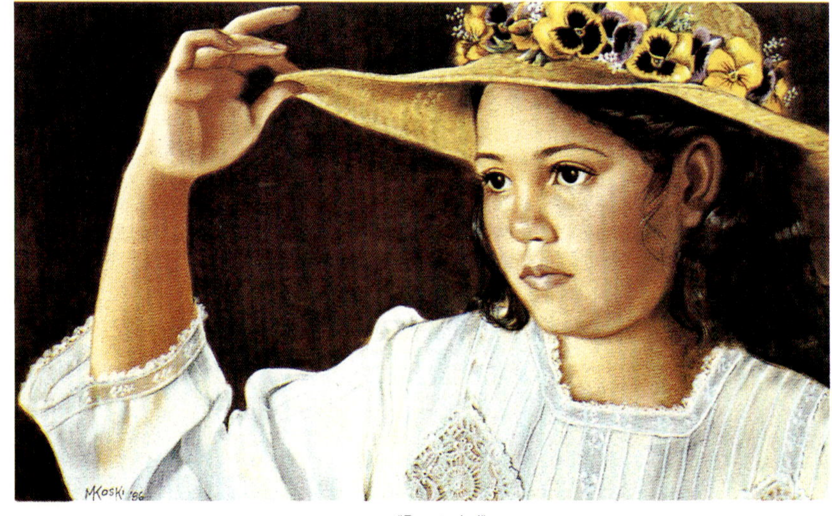

"Pansey Lei"
Limited Edition Print
20" x 12"

MARY KOSKI

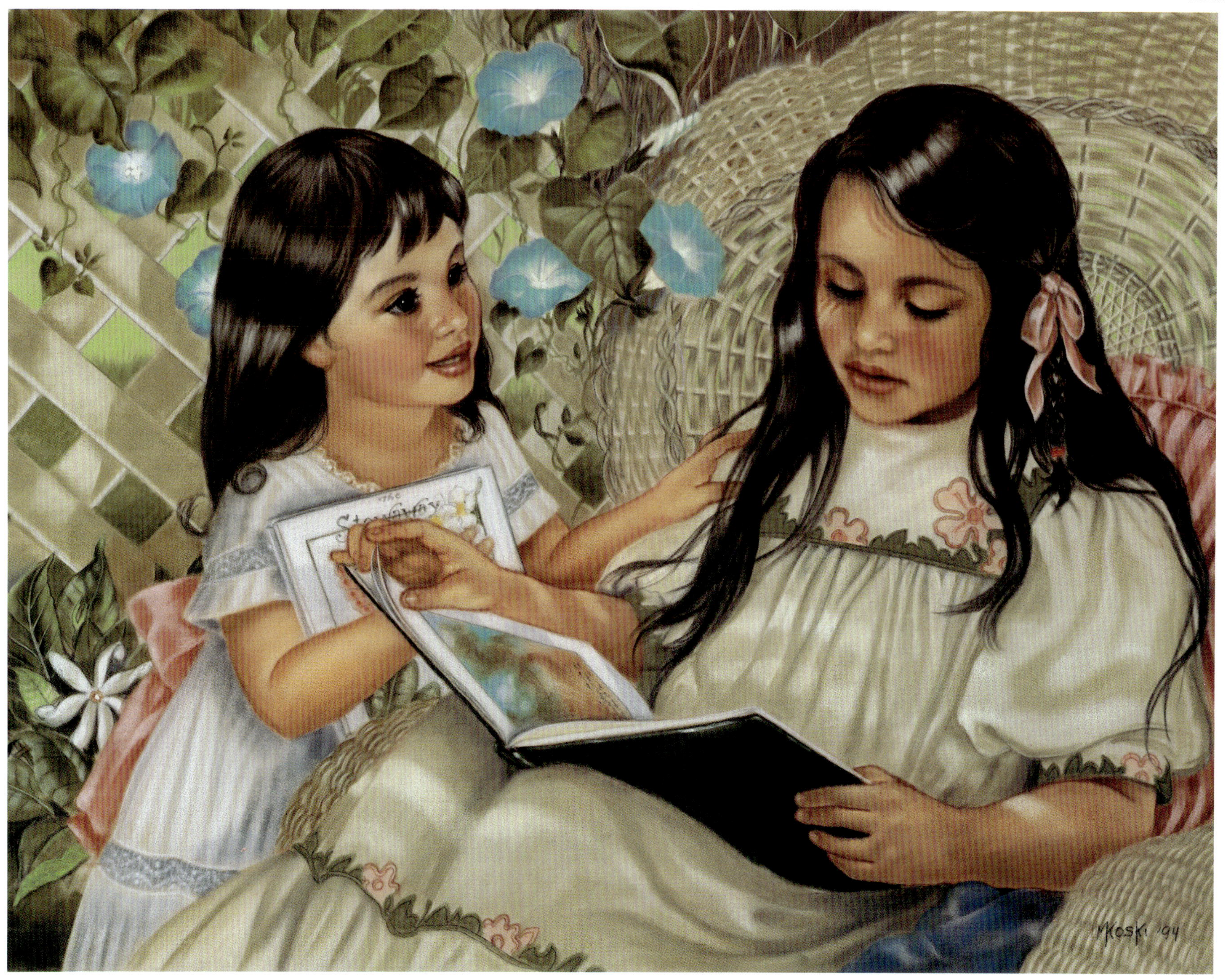

"Read to Me" 20" x 26" Original Pastel

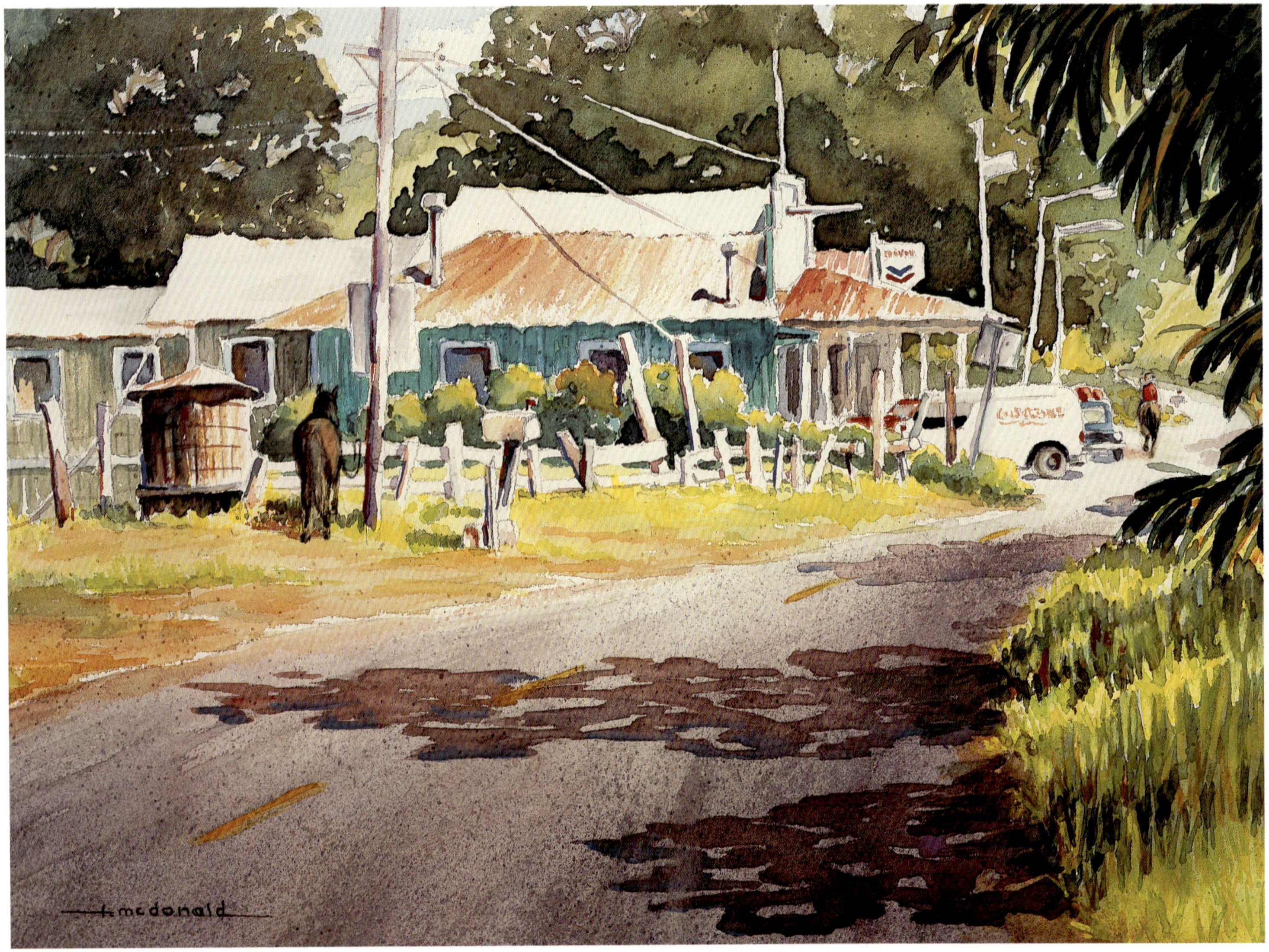

"Downtown Keokea" 9.5" x 7.3" Limited Edition Prints

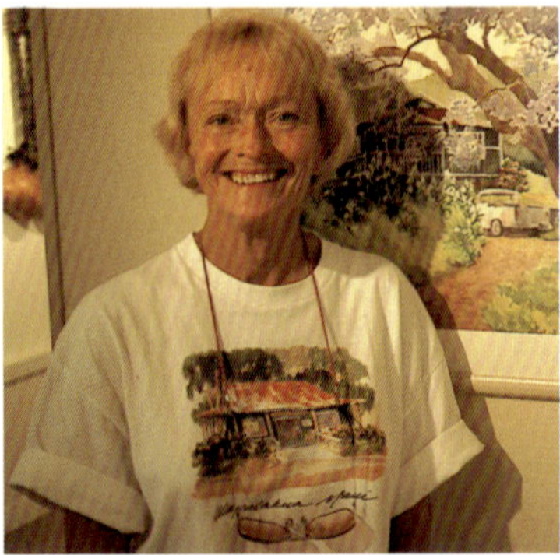

TERRY MCDONALD
R.R. 2 Box 230C, Kula Highway
Kula, Maui, HI 96790
(808) 878-6906

Terry exhibits at:
Viewpoints Gallery - Makawao, Maui
Olde Wailuku Gallery - Wailuku, Maui
Hui No'eau - Makawao, Maui

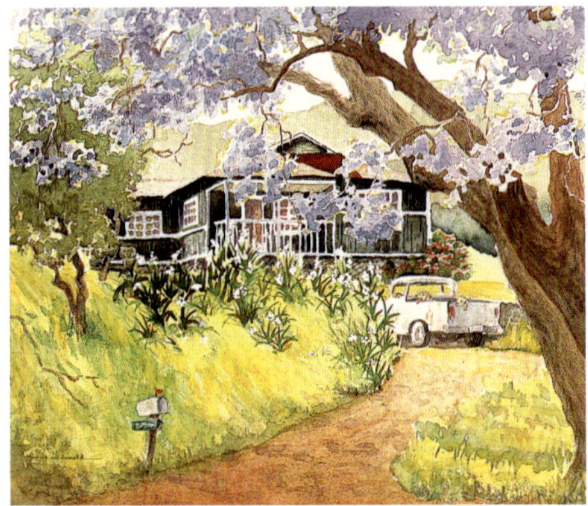

"Lavender and Sunshine" Original Watercolor and Limited Edition Prints

Terry McDonald is recognized as an artist with a true love of Hawaii. Many of her paintings convey a heartfelt message of Hawaii past.

Using watercolors to translate the inspiration and excitement that she feels while witnessing Hawaii's scenic beauty, her painting captures the essence of a timeless dance of color, light and shadows. There is a seemingly effortless quality in her work.

Be it an ocean view, mountain crest, or the charm of an old cane house, Terry reaches inward to express the enchantment of what she sees before her. Combining realism with imagination, she uses darks and lights to portray a drama that brings satisfying pleasure.

Her art studies have taken her to Italy, Greece, the United Kingdom, both Chinas, Russia, Tahiti and the Cook Islands, as well as numerous locations in the United States.

Terry's work glows with her joy for the medium, and her love for old homes and buildings. Her paintings promise, and deliver, a soft touch of Hawaiiana that speaks to the heart.

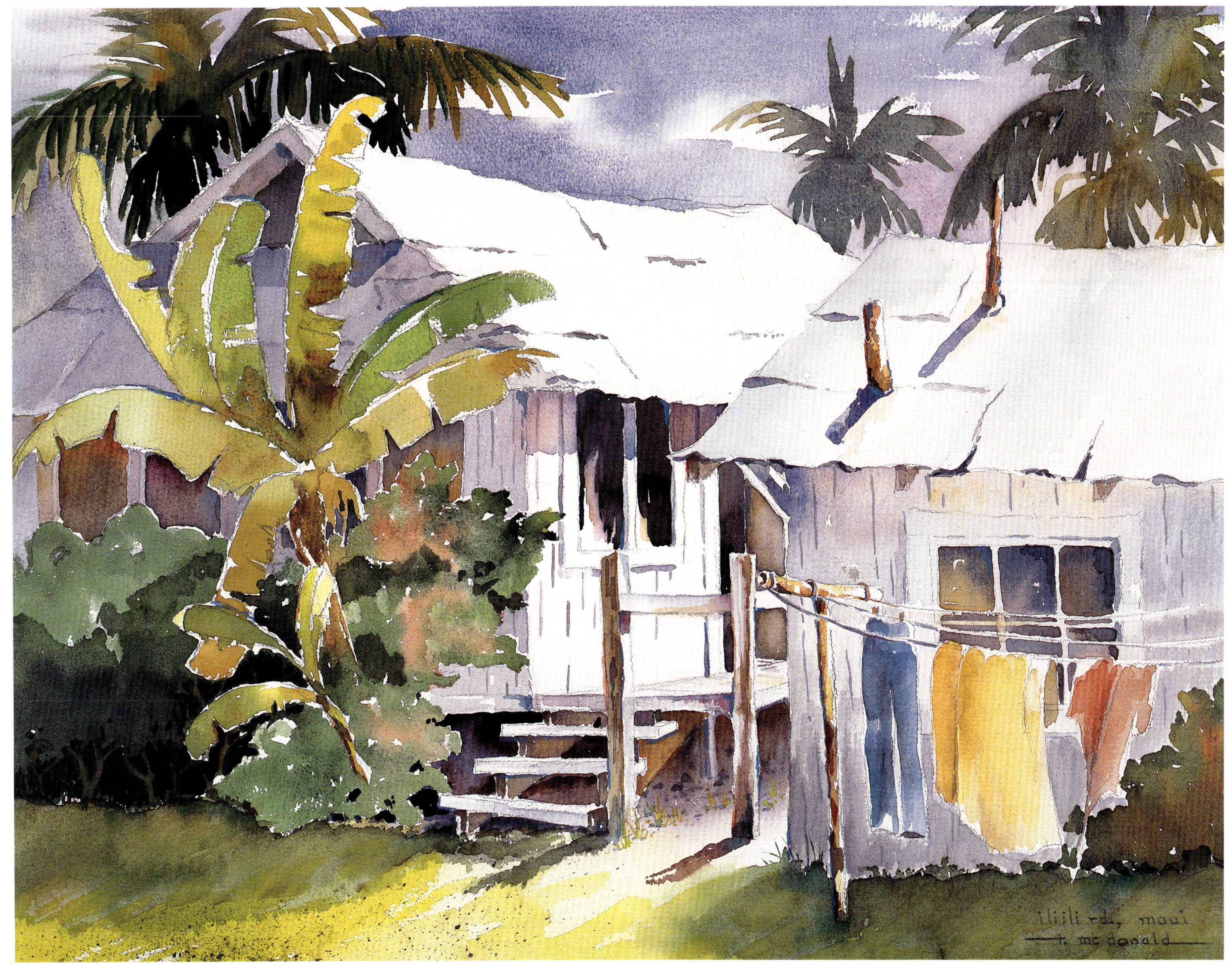

"Ilili Road" 9.5" x 7.3" Limited Edition Prints

TERRY MCDONALD

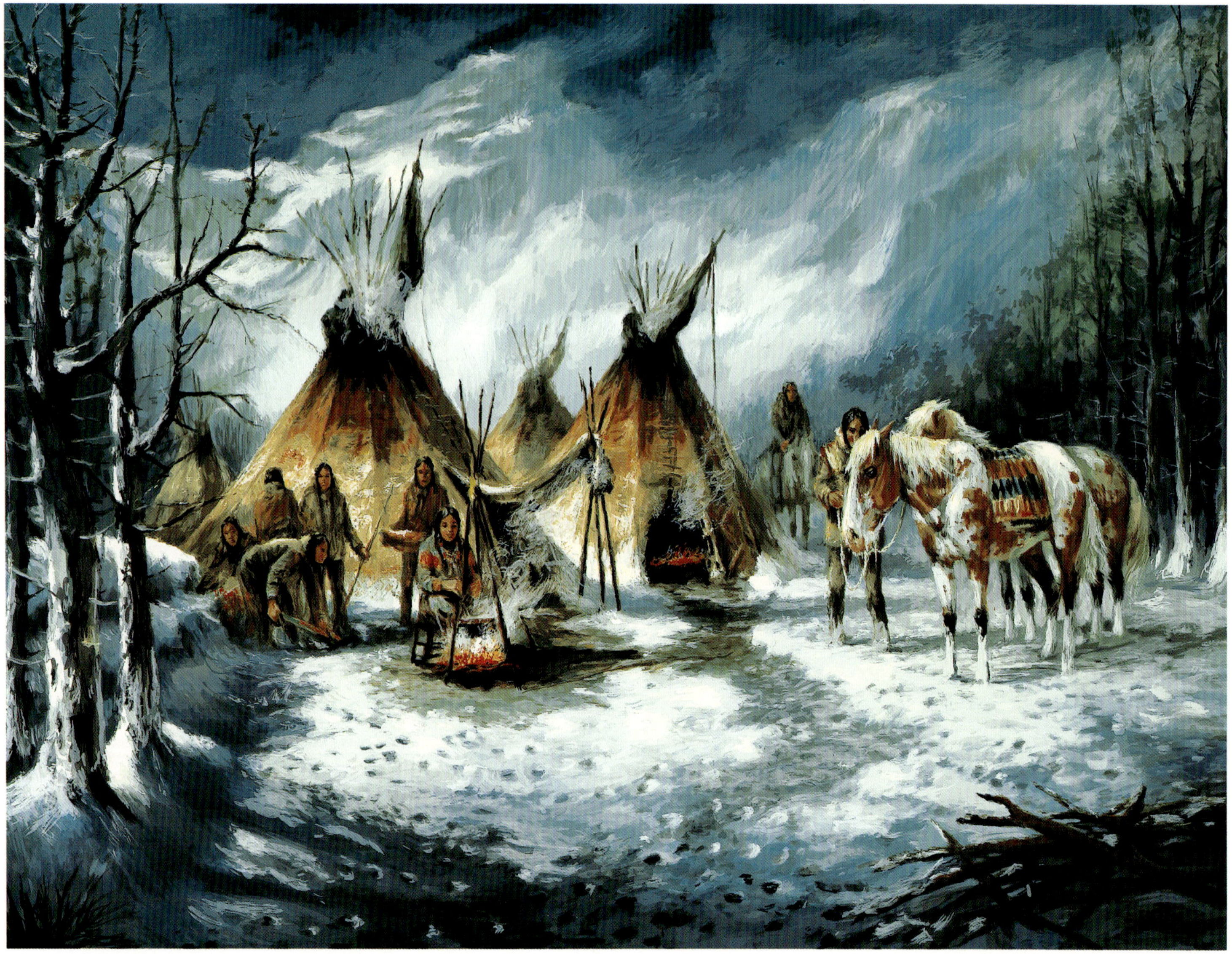

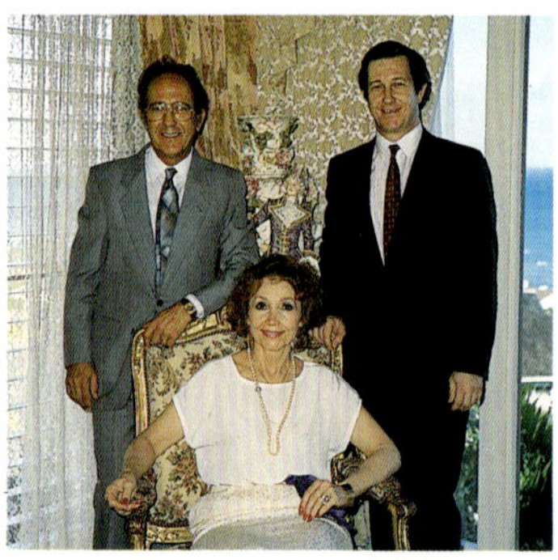

THE MAKK STUDIO

"High Camp" 30" x 40" Limited Edition Serigraph by Americo Makk

Comprised of three individually talented artists, the Makk family shares a closeness that has allowed their artistic expressions to mingle much like a bouquet of fresh flowers. Each lends a separate brightness that easily could stand alone, yet combined, they have enriched serious art collections the world over. Their lifetime of inspired artistic pursuits can be traced, in part, to one of the most passionate and enduring love affairs of this century. While both Americo and Eva had exhibited their respective talents early and pursued their individual artistic training, it was their fateful meeting in 1949 that spawned the synergy they continue to enjoy today.

As a child growing up in the exotic court of Ethiopia, Eva Makk began her keen fascination with the splendid brilliance and muted softness of color and light. She continued her pursuit with formal study in Europe's finest art academies. Although her paintings radiate to fill our sense of sight, we can also feel the warmth of the sun, the cool of a spring morning, which causes us to reflect upon the quiet moments we cherish in our lives.

A native of Hungary, Americo Makk has achieved international fame as a painter who takes ordinary subjects and expresses them with an intimacy that allows us to feel them as if for the first time. His expressions with color tell a story of life gained from living experiences throughout Europe, South America, the U.S. mainland and Hawaii. Americo joined with his wife, Eva, to paint the largest single theme ceiling mural in the world. Located in Brazil, this and fourteen other murals can be seen today as a magnificent achievement of their special skill. Americo Makk tells us, "Talent comes from God; ability from study; and inspiration from the soul." Certainly he speaks to our hearts with every stroke of his brush.

A.B. Makk was born into this talented family during their days in Brazil. His childhood was filled with a profusion of exotic colors, peoples, and events. Experiencing first-hand his parents' complete frescos and paintings, A.B.'s early training as an artist was well under way. Now, after many years of training, he too has taken his place alongside his parents as one of the worlds leading impressionists. His palette, though unmistakably of the Makk style, combines colors in a rhapsody of richness and purity. The full spectrum of colors are manipulated to perpetuate the fleeting moments as they melt into eternal time.

Another bold creation of the Makk family is found nestled in the mountains of Oahu. It is called *Vision Fine Art Press* and it extends the Makk's dedication to excellence into the printing of their award-winning limited edition serigraphs. To achieve the results they longed for, the Makk family decided to open their own serigraph studio not only for their own art, but to offer other artists throughout the world the opportunity to achieve the highest possible integrity and standard when producing their own works.

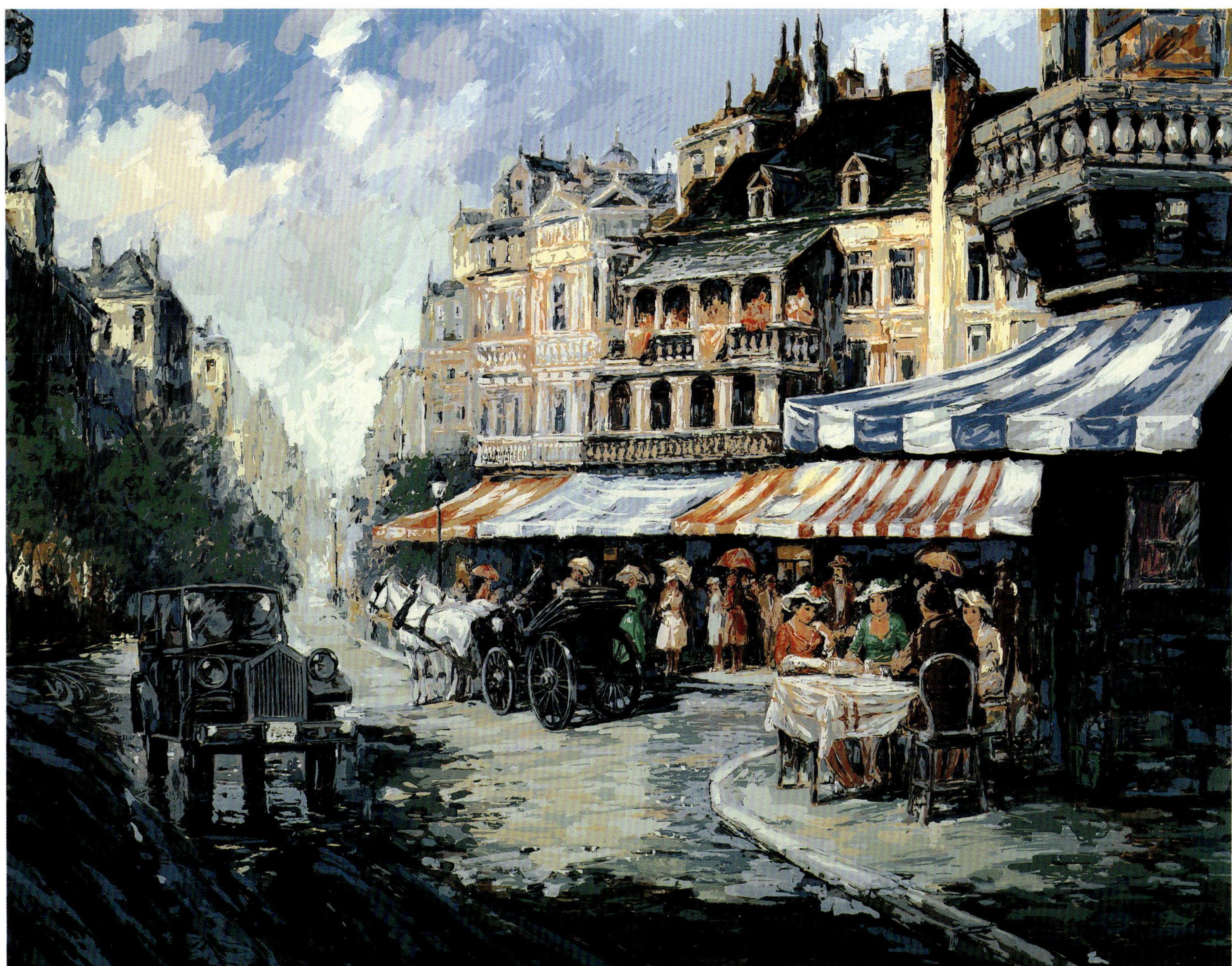

"French Afternoon" 23" x 30" Limited Edition Serigraph by Americo Makk

Vision Fine Art Press has captured the top honors for technical merit in international competition by the Screen Printers Association International for several years. The studio has tackled projects that others said could not be done. Screen printing at *Vision* has developed to such a high degree that the staff feels that they are not printing, but painting using the silk screen process. Each color is custom mixed by hand, and custom created for each screen.

In addition to creating pure serigraphs, the Makk family refined the usage of serigraphic enhancement to lithographs, such as three dimensional varnishing to add surface texture and color enhancements. Artists go to *Vision Fine Art Press* for that something extra for their works.

The goals of the Makk family, their aspirations, and dedication to excellence in art and one's rights to elegance and dignity, are ideals shared by all three artists.

AMERICO MAKK

"Sparkles of Sun" 24" x 32" Limited Edition Serigraph by A.B. Makk

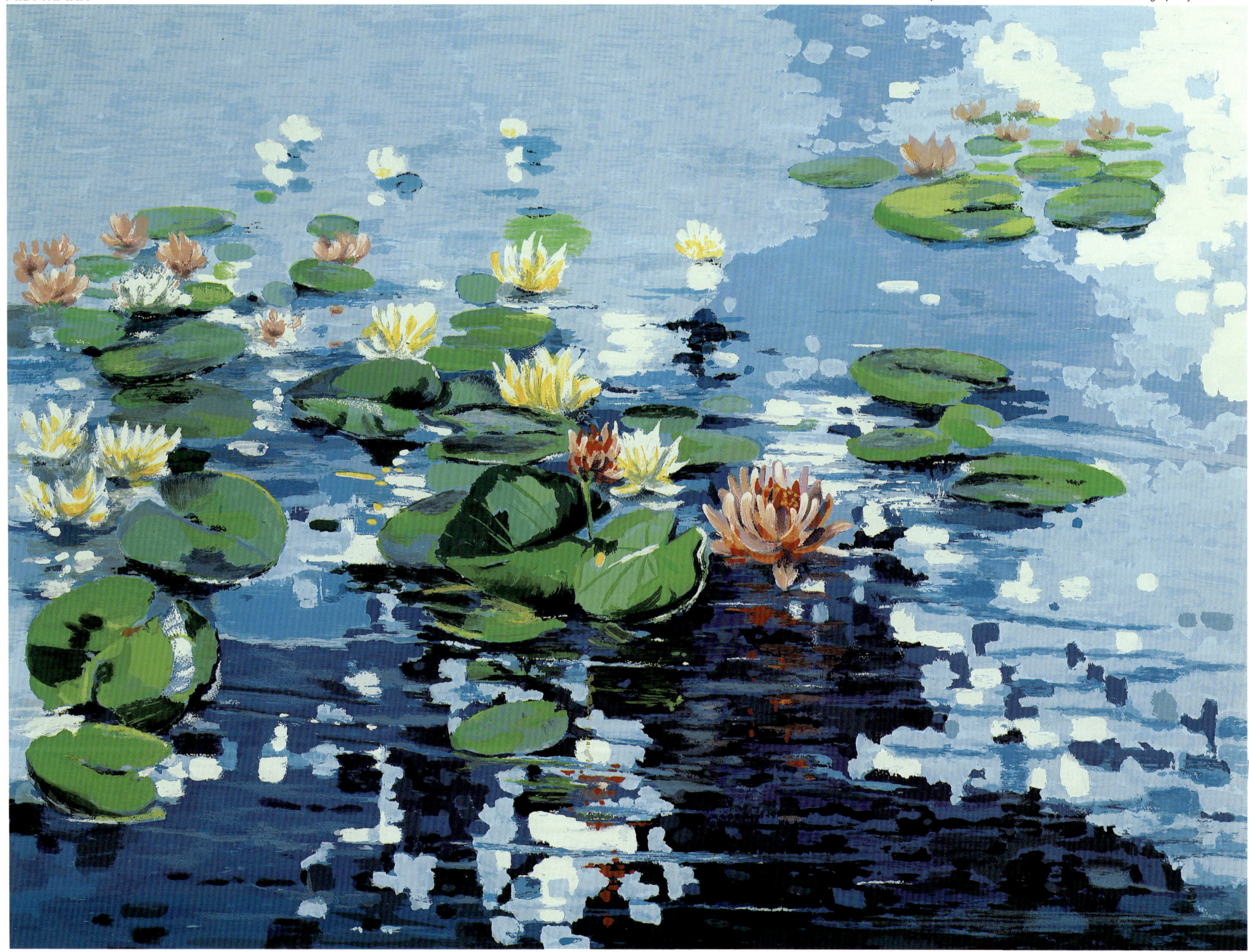

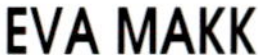

EVA MAKK

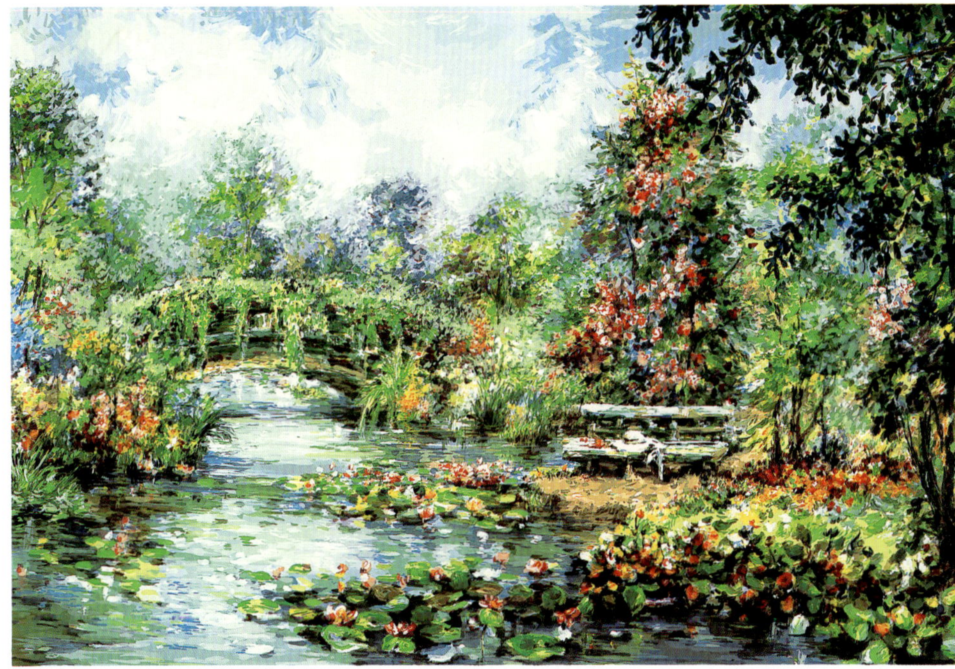

"Profusion" Limited Edition Serigraph by Eva Makk

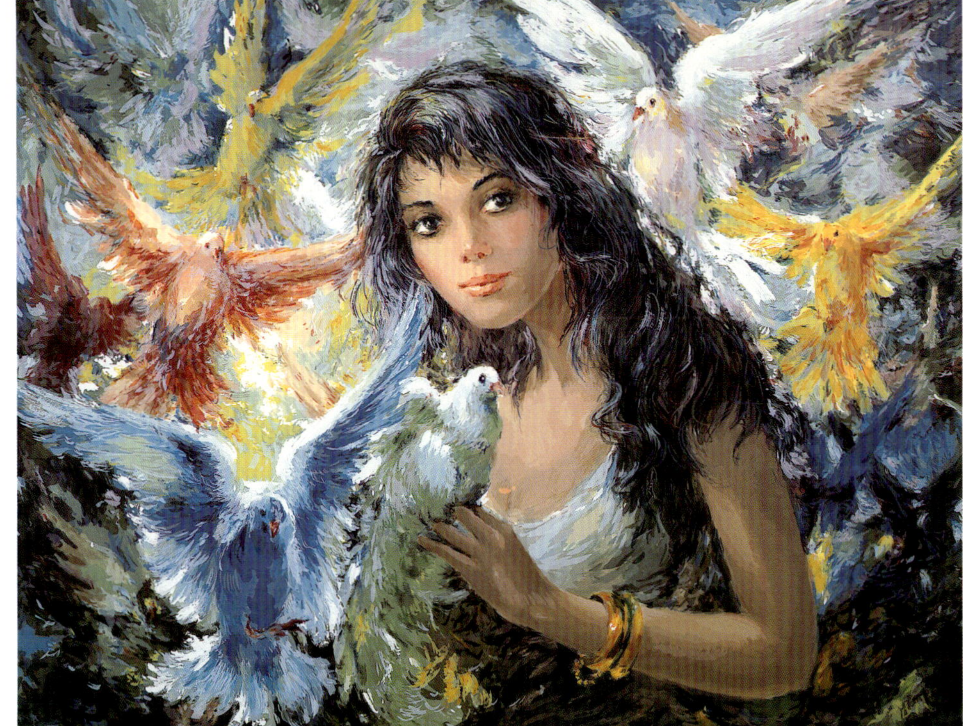

"On Wings" 30" x 40"
Limited Edition Serigraph by Eva Makk

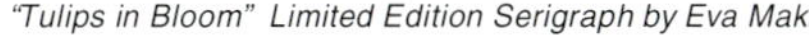

"Tulips in Bloom" Limited Edition Serigraph by Eva Makk

The Makk Studio
By Appointment Only
1515 Laukahi Street
Honolulu, Hawaii 96821
(808) 373-2772 Fax (808) 373-9195 800 654-2787

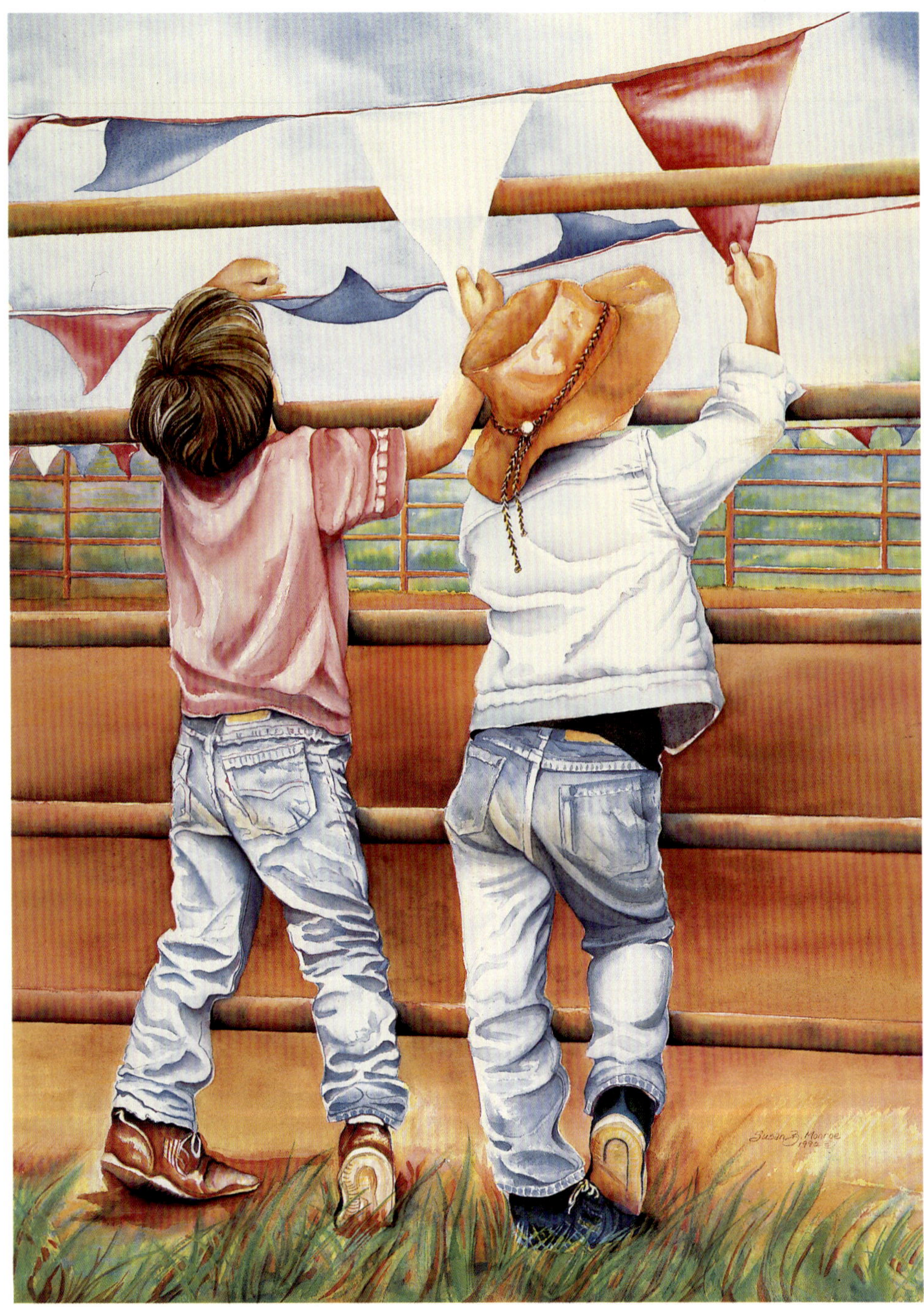

"Ulupalakua Cowboys" 22" x 30"
Original Watercolor Painting

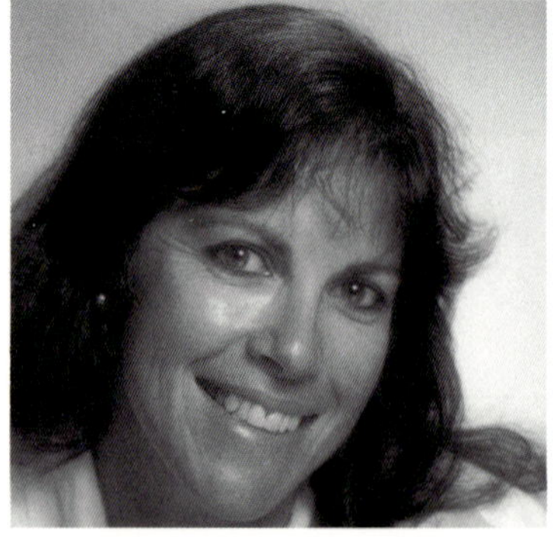

SUSIE BURNSIDE MONROE

Hamakuapoko Studios
P.O. Box 1208
Kula, Maui, HI 96790
(808) 878-3804

The beauty of Maui is a source of creative inspiration for the many artists who have chosen to make Maui their home. It was this beauty that also drew Susie Burnside Monroe back to the islands, and to Maui, after years of international travel.

Originally a native of Australia, Susie spent her adolescence growing up in northern California, near the sea. In 1969, she moved to Hawaii, making her home on the shores of Hanalei Bay, Kauai. From there she traveled extensively throughout the world for many years.

Susie always kept pencil and paints close at hand during these trips, to capture on paper the wonderful diversity of sights she saw at every bend in the road. Although painting was always dearest to her heart, Susie was maintaining her own custom design jewelry business through those traveling years, and was actively collecting wonderful gemstones which she used in her one-of-a-kind creations as well as in pieces commissioned by other jewelers (including Tiffany's) in Laguna Beach, San Francisco and Carmel.

About sixteen years ago, Susie began painting very seriously and has been going strong ever since. Seven years ago, Susie had a run-in with some severe medical problems, which came close to being terminal. While confined to her bed for many months, she took her brush in hand and kept on painting! To this day, Susie must still remain in a reclined position as much as possible, and so has developed a very unique method of painting on her back!

As a single mother with three children to bring up, Susie's lighthearted approach to life seems hard to comprehend. That she can transfer her love of nature and children to paper, is to her eternal credit.

As for her painting goals, she says; *"Now I want to paint the warmth of the sun and the color of the wind."*

Susie's originals are beautifully displayed in two of Maui's most tasteful art galleries... the Hana Coast Gallery in the Hana Hotel, and the Wailea Coast Gallery in the Intercontinental Hotel, Wailea. Several shops on Maui carry her work and the watercolors can be found in numerous private collections in the U.S., Australia, and Europe.

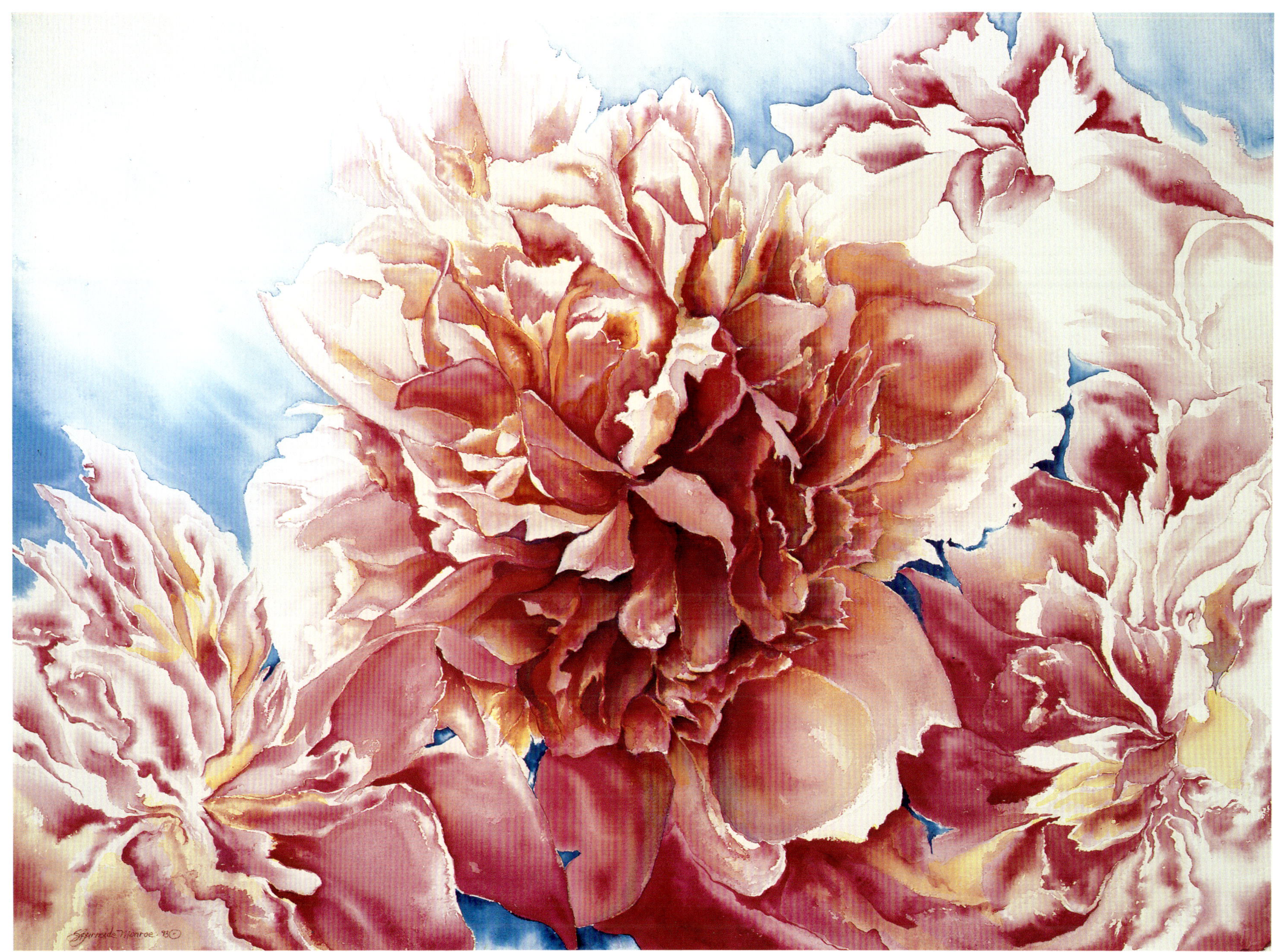

"Wild Peonies" 22" x 30" Original Watercolor Painting - Collection Baron & Baroness Hans Thyssen

SUSIE BURNSIDE MONROE

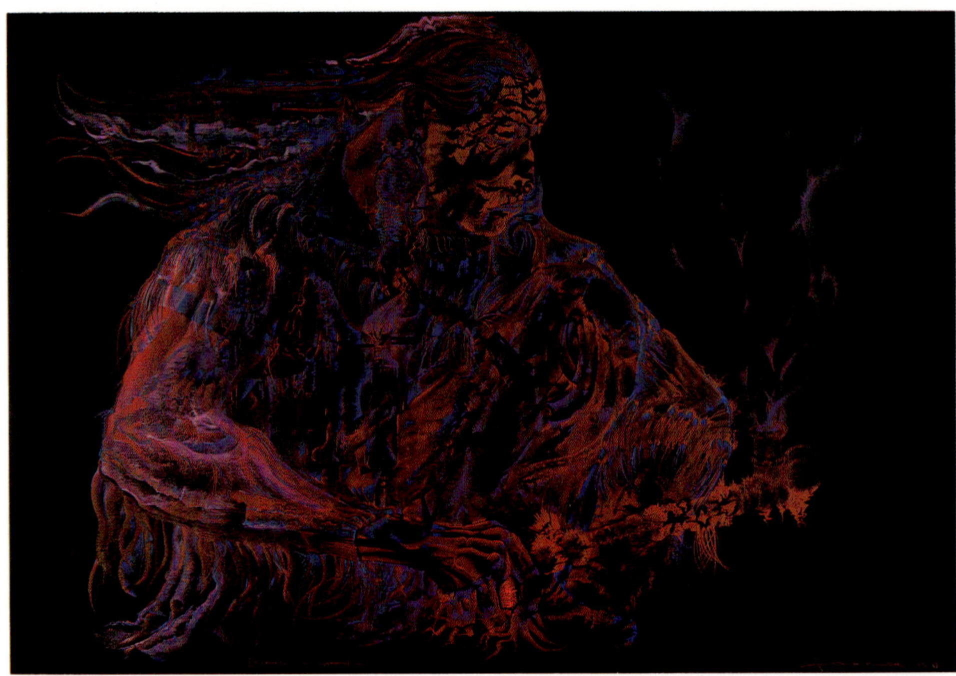

"Dreams of Kanan" 30" x 44"
Original Artwork

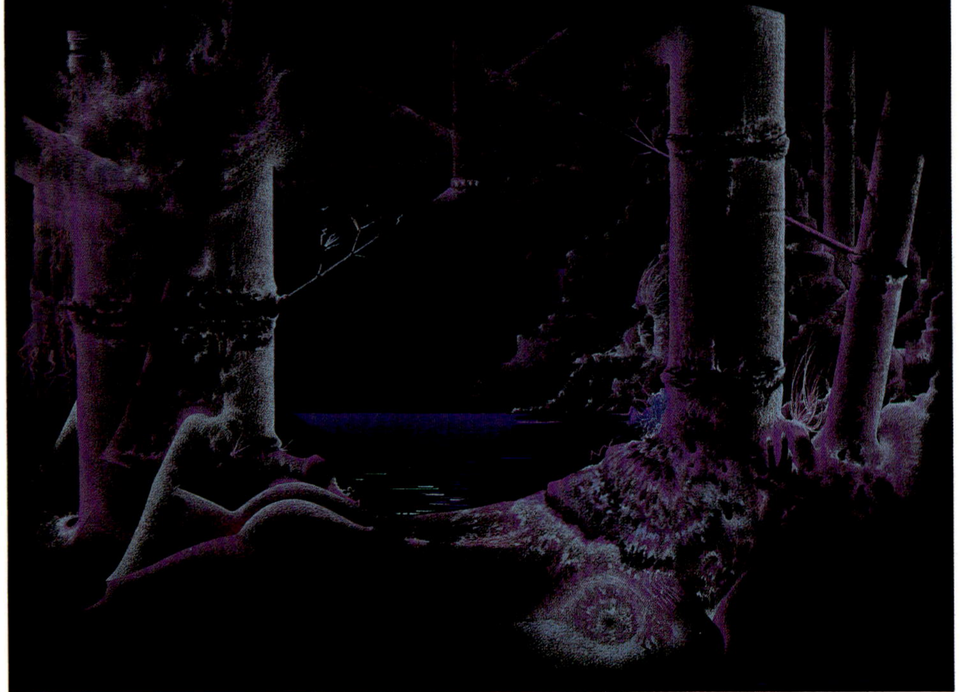

"Bamboo Bondage" 22" x 30"
Original Artwork

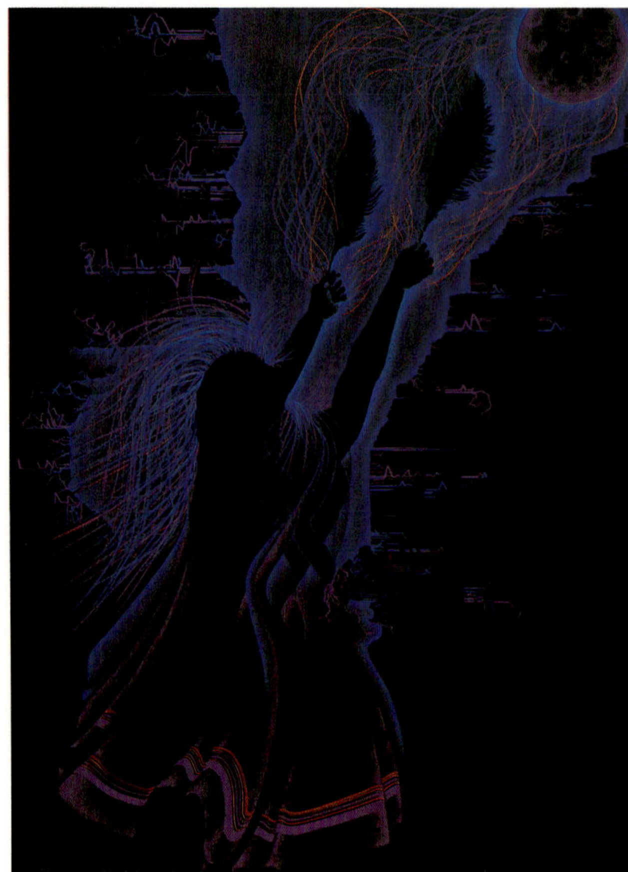

"The Great Mystery" 24" x 36" Trim Size
Limited Edition Print S/N 950 A/P 95

From his home where the lava meets the sea and the sky, Joshua Miller brings his Indian imagery to the fiery shores of Kilauea. His blend of Indian lore and earth symmetry, along with Pele's engulfing "mana" and the islands' intense contrasts, have become a melting pot of experience and technique.

These engaging works can be found on the Big Island of Hawaii at Gallery of Great Things in Parker Square, Kamuela, and Ackerman Gallery in Kapaau, Hawaii. You may contact the artist at "Rolling Fire Studio."

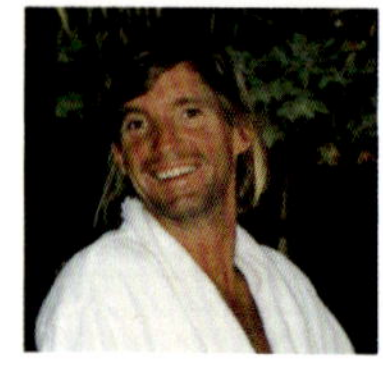

JOSHUA MILLER

Rolling Fire Studio
P.O. Box 1361
Kehena Beach, Hawaii, HI 96778
(808) 965-7345
800 227-0928

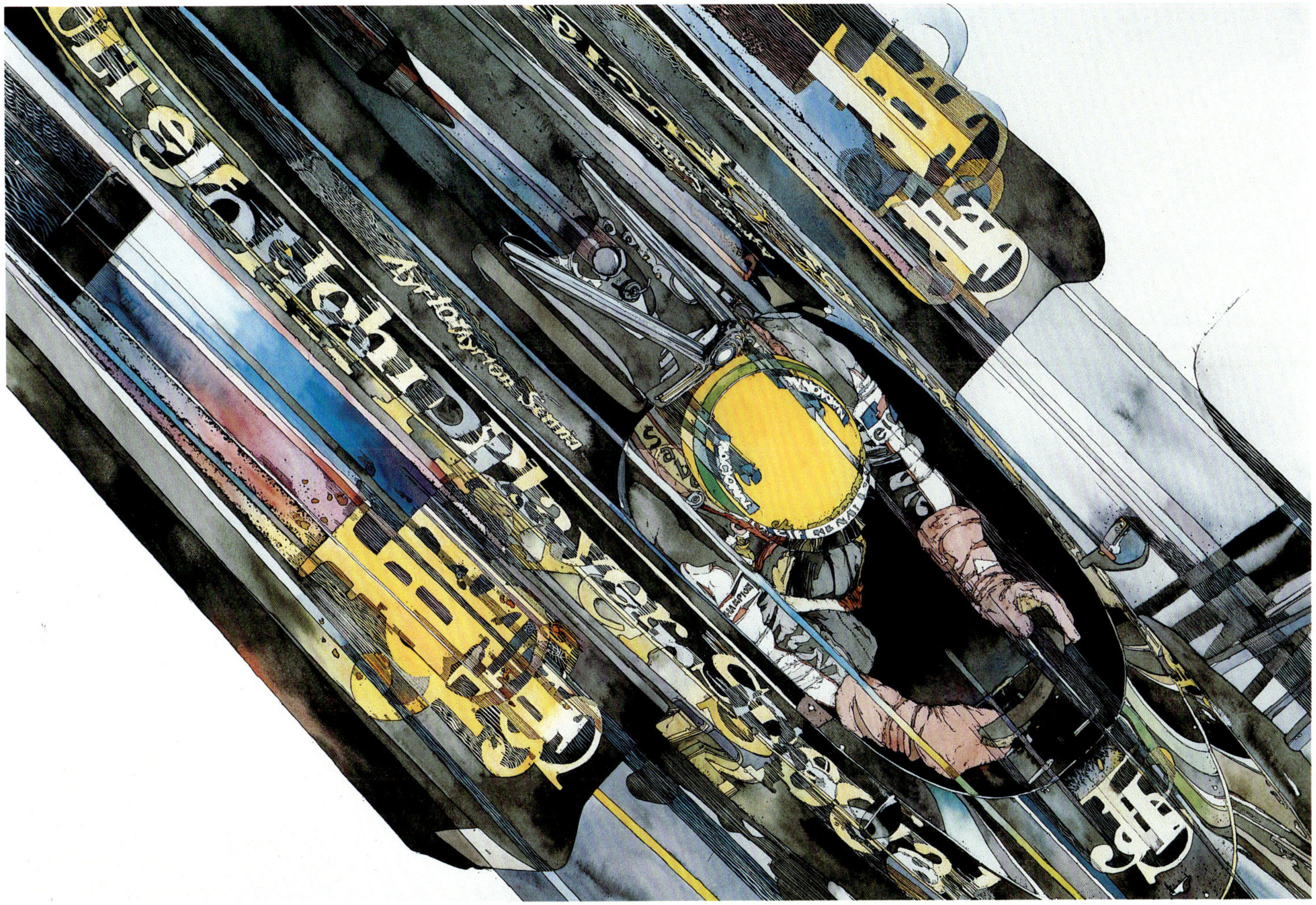

"JPS / Lotus" 20" x 30"
Limited Edition Print

Born and raised in Hawaii, self-taught artist Niles Nakaoka has always had a love for art. Relying solely on his instinctive abilities and a keen eye for color, he produces a wide variety of subjects.

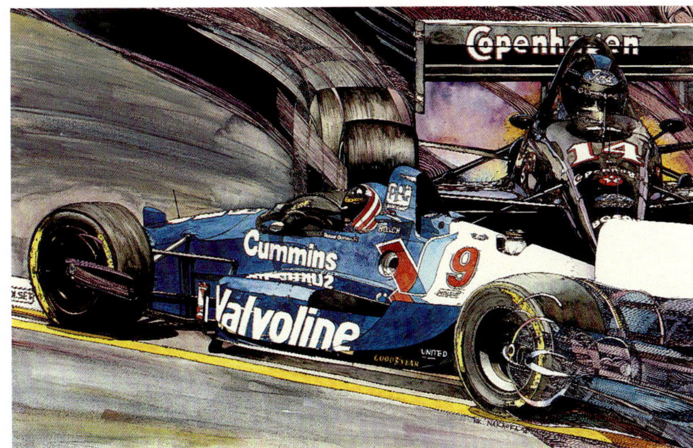

"Rebel Robby Gordon" 24" x 15"
Original Mixed Media

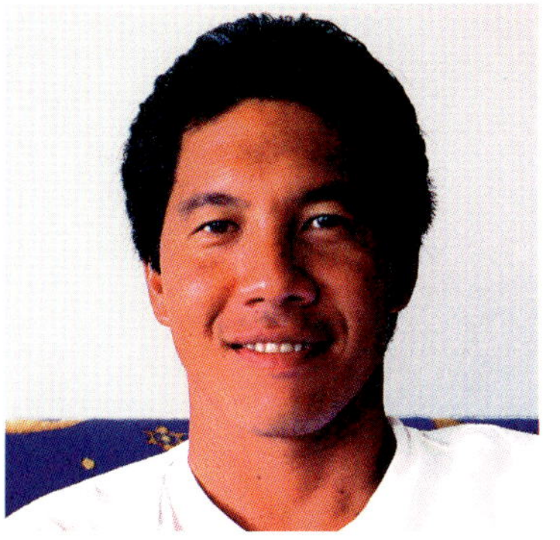

NILES NAKAOKA
284 Mananai Place #R
Honolulu, Oahu, HI 96818
(808) 487-4009

Intrigued by the speed and excitement of auto racing, he began to reveal his passion through his work. His automobile art has been published in "Racer" magazine, and originals are on display throughout the United States and Canada and at New York - Paris Collectible Art in Lahaina, Maui. His talent extends far beyond automobiles. Inspired by his environment, he amazingly captures the beauty of nature as well as the culture of Hawaii in his paintings.

Niles has been an award-winning member of the Hawaii Watercolor Society and a long time exhibitor at the Kaimana Gallery in Honolulu. Working out of a small studio in his home, he has done work for major corporations and small businesses here in the islands. Most of his work is done in watercolors, he also adds inks and acrylics to further enhance each piece of artwork.

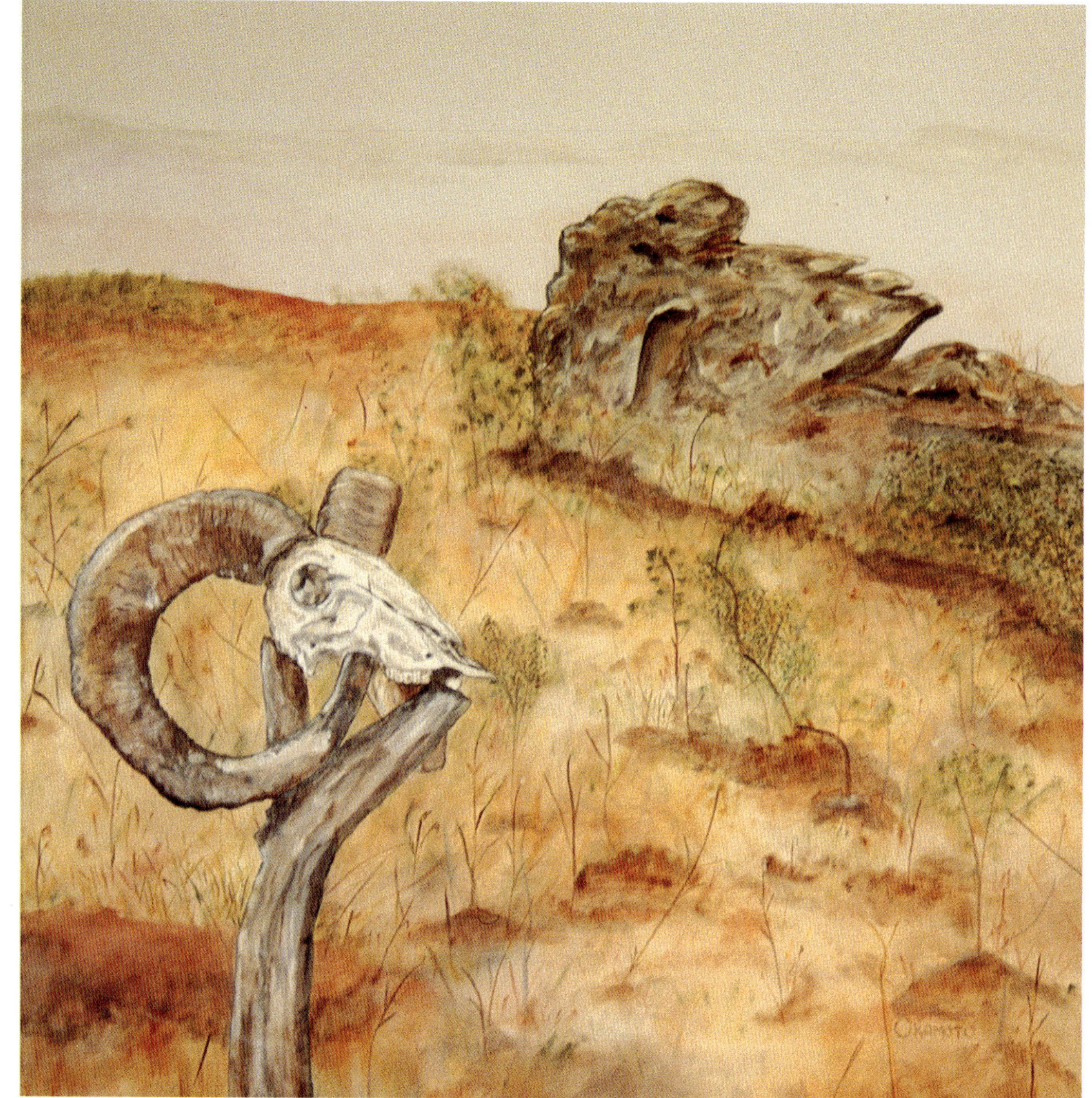

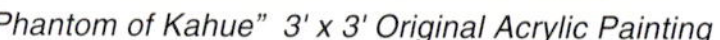

"Phantom of Kahue" 3' x 3' Original Acrylic Painting

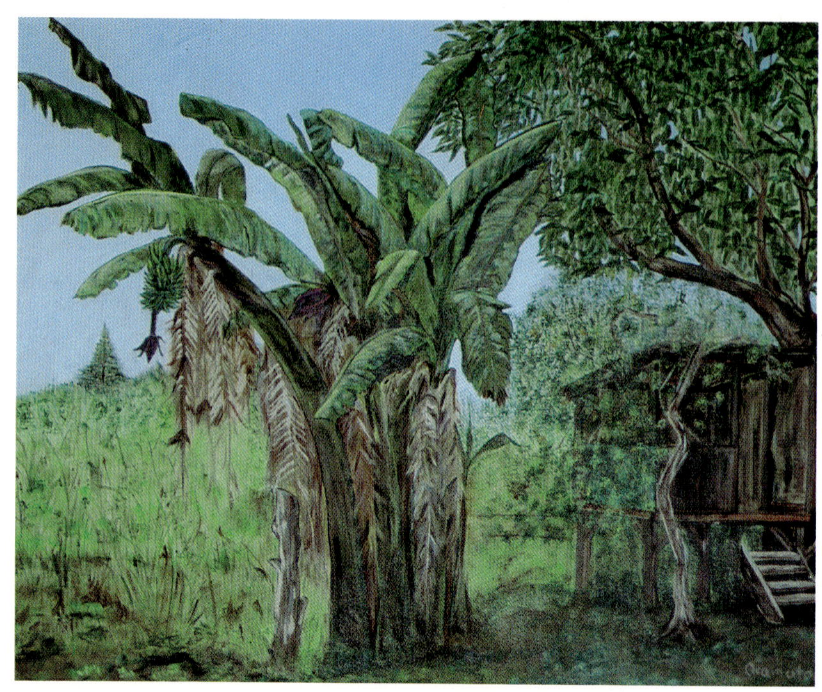

"What Used to Be" 30" x 24" Original Acrylic Painting

P.O. Box 949
Lana'i City, Lana'i, Hawaii 96763
(808) 565-6221

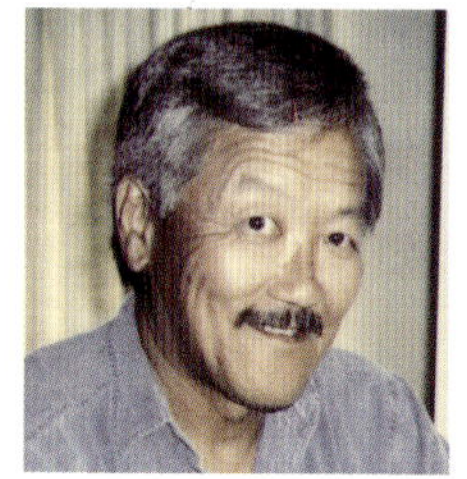

ROY K. OKAMOTO

Roy was born and raised on one of the smallest Hawaiian islands, Lana'i. The least visited island was recently graced by the completion of the Manele Bay Hotel where Roy participated in producing the sweeping murals depicting life on Lana'i. An avid outdoorsman, Roy is constantly inspired by the wildlife that inhabits the pineapple isle. The rare plants, birds and animals that can be found there are his subjects. When not painting or drawing, he works as a fireman for the Lana'i airport. He currently has limited edition prints available of local banyan trees, aweoweo fish, and nene birds. Roy resides in Lana'i City with his wife and three children.

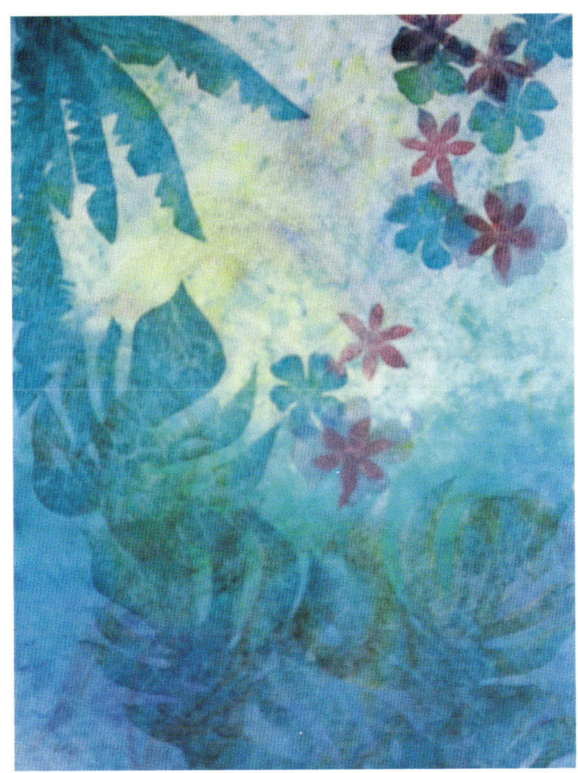

"Floral Fantasy" 4' x 5' Mixed Media on Canvas

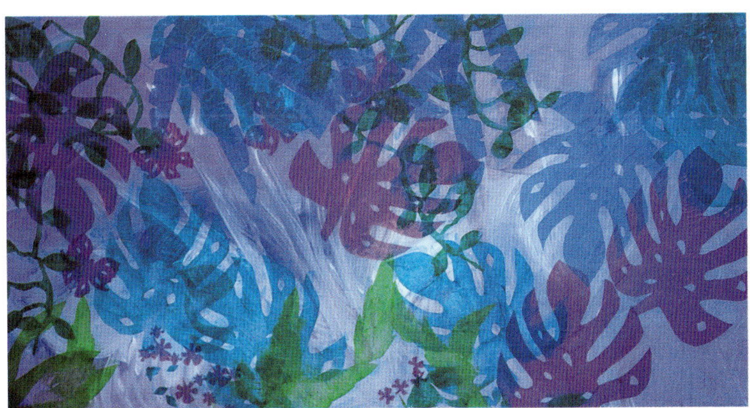

"Rainforest" 4' x 5' Mixed Media on Canvas

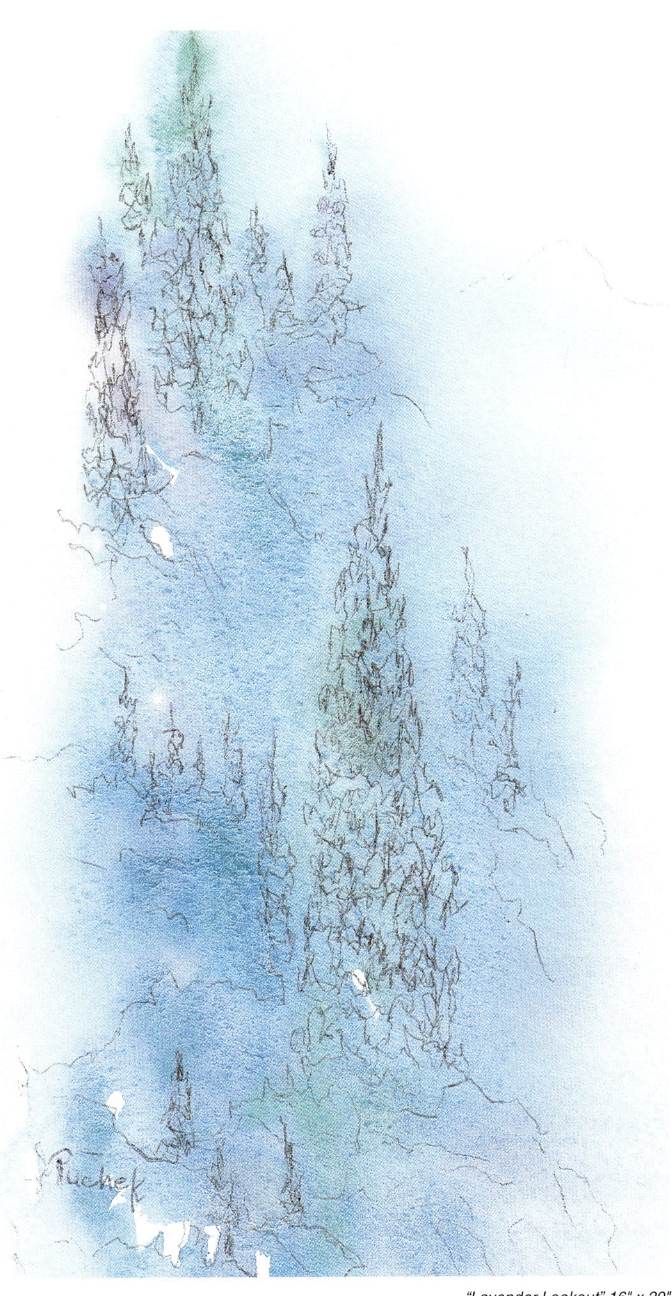

"Lavender Lookout" 16" x 20" Watercolor, Pen and Ink

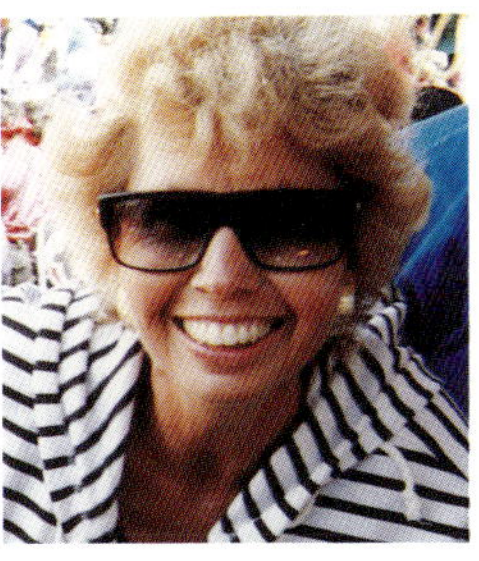

RUTH PUCHEK

Ruth Owen Puchek, a native of Golden, Colorado, began her career as a teacher-artist at Denver Art Museum.

In 1972, she ventured to the island of Lana'i, and fell in love with the beauty of this tiny island. Since then Ruth has trekked over most of the island wondering at the diversity of vegetation and climatic changes on an island so small.

These extreme changes from desert to jungle have never ceased to amaze Ruth. Although she has traveled to the other islands in the Hawaiian chain, it is Lana'i that has been the motivational force and source of inspiration for her paintings.

Puchek enjoys the spirit of nature's changing moods with color interpretations from earth tones to vibrant hues.

P.O. Box A118
Lana'i City, Lana'i, HI 96763
(808) 565-6902

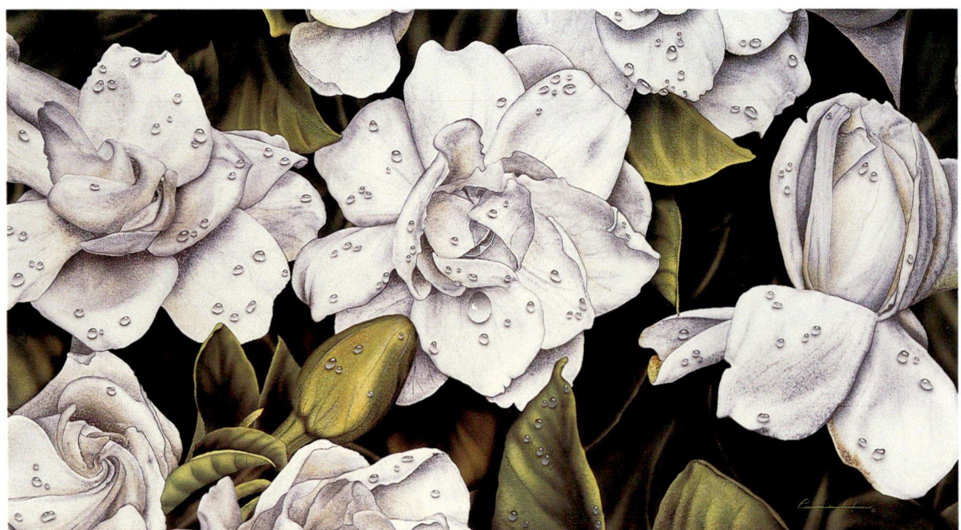

"Kiele III" 17" x 29"
Acrylic on Strathmore

It is not often that two individual artists are able to combine and express their talents to produce a single body of work. Peter and Madeline Powell have this rare creative alliance. Having met on Maui in 1976, they are presently working out of their Haiku Studio. They feel truly blessed in being able to live and work on Maui, while at the same time pursuing their dream of creating and sharing their art with others.

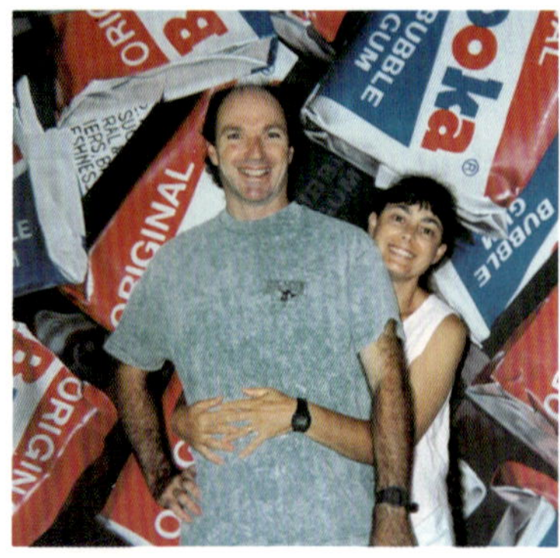

PETER & MADELINE POWELL
Powell Studios
141 Kapuai Road
Haiku, Maui, HI 96708
(808) 572-8105

Their diverse styles range from photo-realism to bold, colorful graphics, with many of their works having a touch of humor. Peter's varied painting techniques and Madeline's design and detail skills come together in a very unique partnership of versatility and expression.

"Looking for Mr. Goodbars" 96" x 144"
*Acrylic on Canvas *with 5 year old daughter Corinne.*

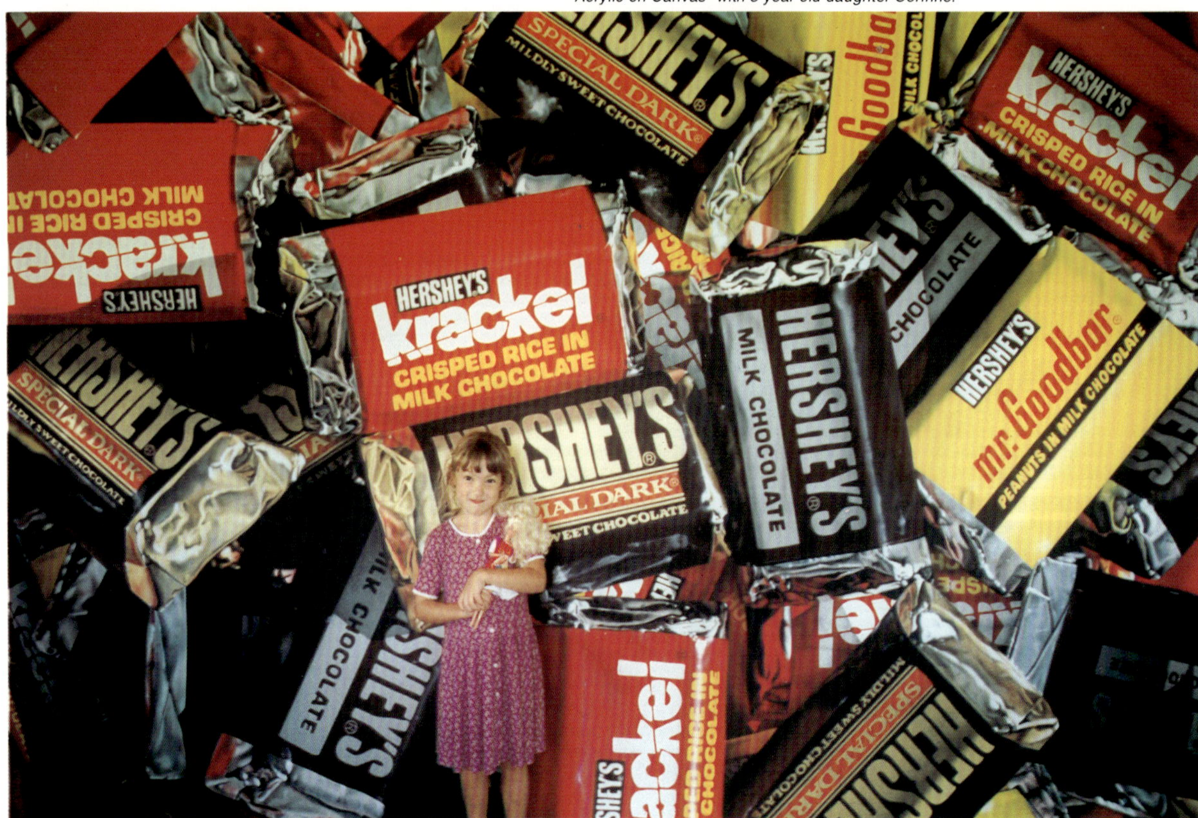

"First Day of School" 48" x 60" Acrylic on Canvas

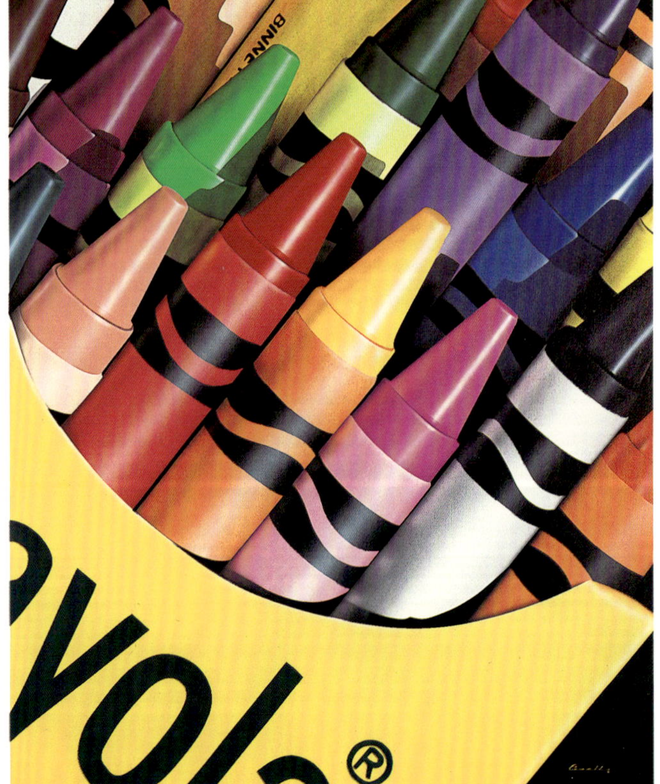

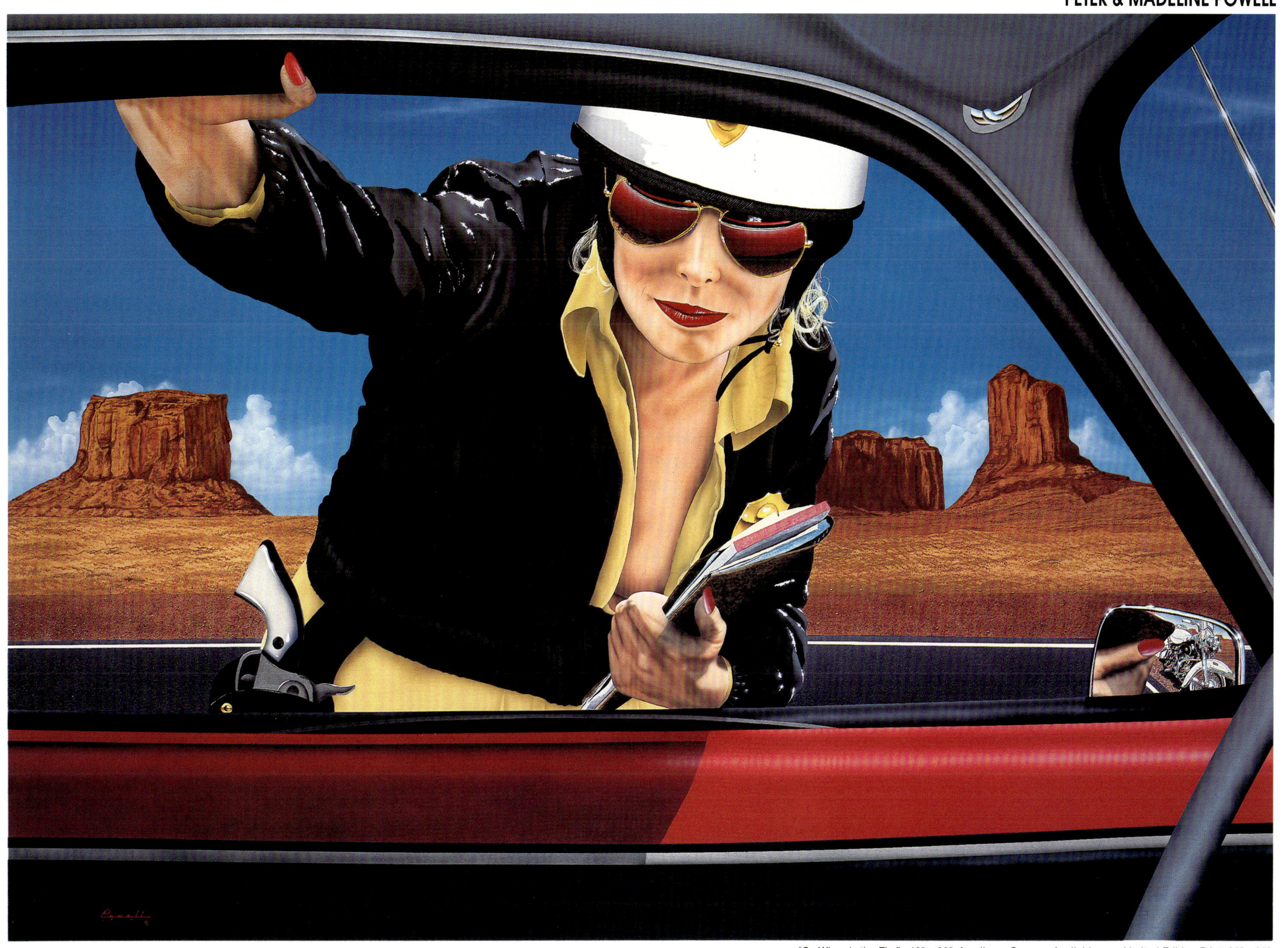

"So Where's the Fire" 48" x 60" Acrylic on Canvas. Available as a Limited Edition Print 35" x 25"

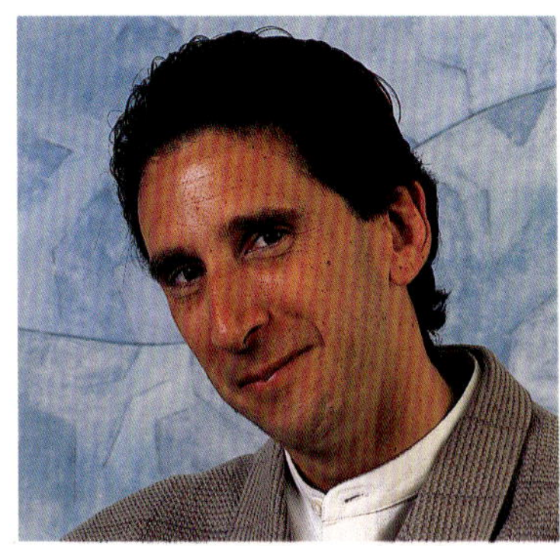

DAVID C. SACCO

3655 Baldwin Avenue
Makawao, Maui, HI 96768
(808) 572-6000 Fax (808) 572-6900
Mailing: P.O. Box 509
Makawao, Maui, HI 96768

David C. Sacco was born in Buffalo, New York, to a family of art, music, and technical genius. From this came an inherent love for working with his hands, and a talent for fine detail that manifested itself early in life. At the age of four, he was taking clocks apart and putting them back together. At the age of five, he says with a laugh, he could get them to work.

Exposed to New York's rich and diverse arts community, Sacco developed a passion for refinement and beauty. By the time he reached University, jewelry had captured his imagination.

Over the shoulder of an eccentric Yugoslavian, he learned how to set diamonds. But it was work of the Masters — the houses of Bulgari and Van Cleef and Arpels — that he found his enduring inspiration. He was drawn to their exquisite style, to the complexity of line and impeccable detail that demand from the jeweler's hand the utmost in skill.

Sacco delights in commissions that allow him to reveal the breadth of his creativity and he is committed to jewelry that is intelligently priced. As he believes that beauty is an expression of the soul, he is convinced that anyone who truly appreciates excellence should have the opportunity of possessing works of a calibre usually associated only with the well-to-do. Often, what intrigues him most in a commission is the challenge of taking a client's existing piece or several affordable stones and complementing them elegantly in an exquisite design.

"Why art and life are connected," he says, "is what my work is about. Therefore, I assume an appreciation of this sort, rather than wealth, to be the defining attribute of my customers. It is the affinity for fine things such as art that brings us a little closer to a more intimate experience of life."

Paying attention is integral to the spiritual practice he acquired while traveling in the East. That ability enables him to truly comprehend an individual's needs and desires and thus ensures that his custom pieces will delight both purchaser and wearer. Sacco says, "My goal is to incorporate the individual's taste and lifestyle, how often the jewelry will be worn, and what it will symbolize - something that is uniquely personal."

While David is happy to create jewelry for clients who communicate by telephone and mail, most of the pleasure he derives springs from face-to-face human interaction. When he greets clients at his Master Touch Gallery on the lush slopes of Maui's 10,000 foot dormant volcano, David extends to each individual a genuine warmth and attention.

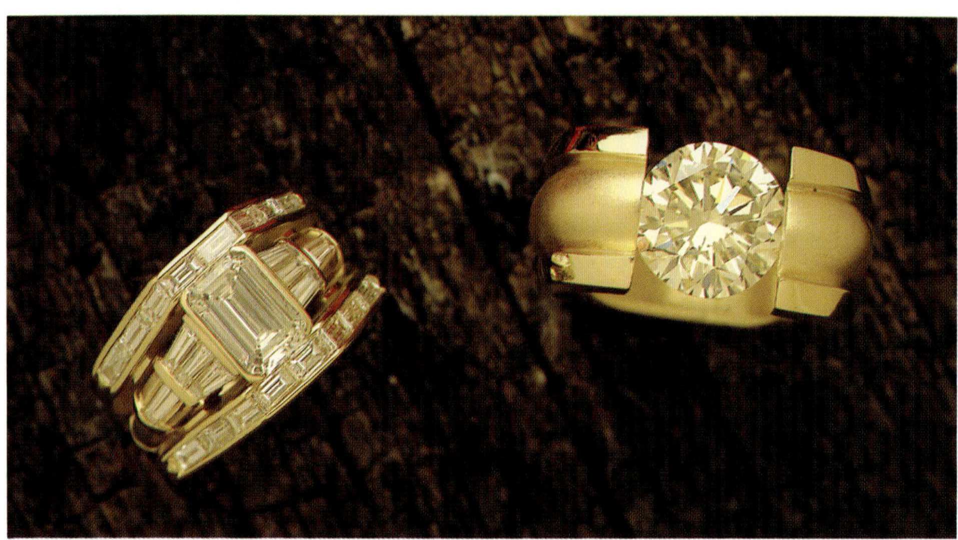

"The Wedding Set"
Emerald Cut Diamond and Baguettes
Gentleman's Solitaire, Both pieces in 18kt. Gold.

Ladies Cuff Bracelet with Pink Tourmaline,
Diamonds and Chalcedony Bullet.

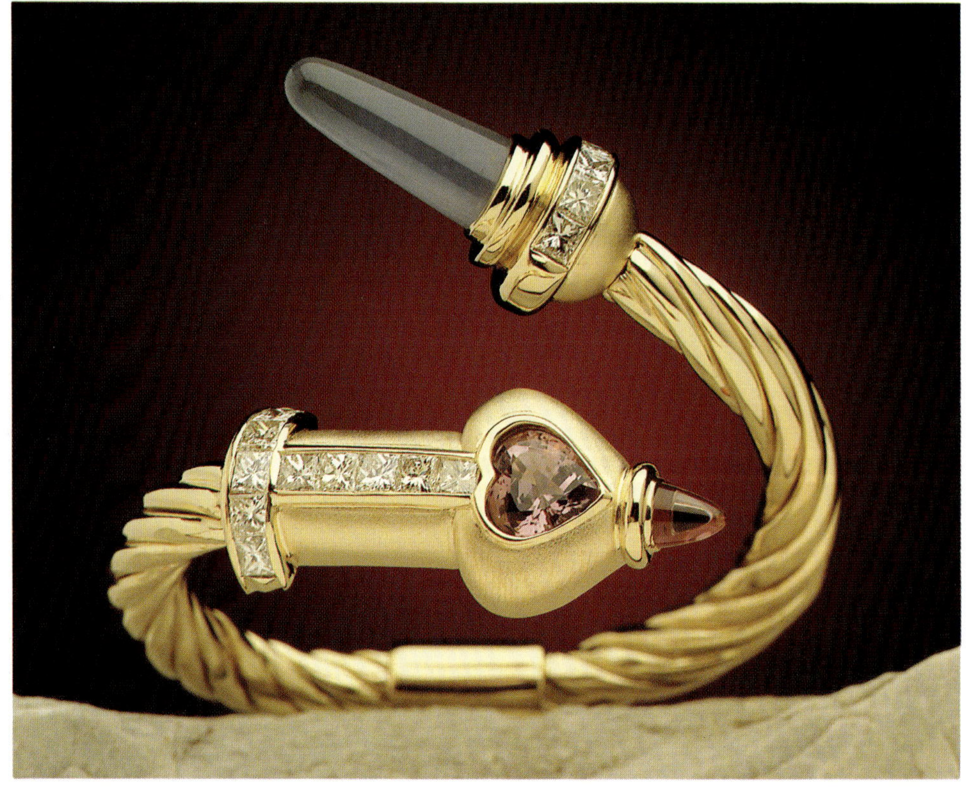

DAVID C. SACCO

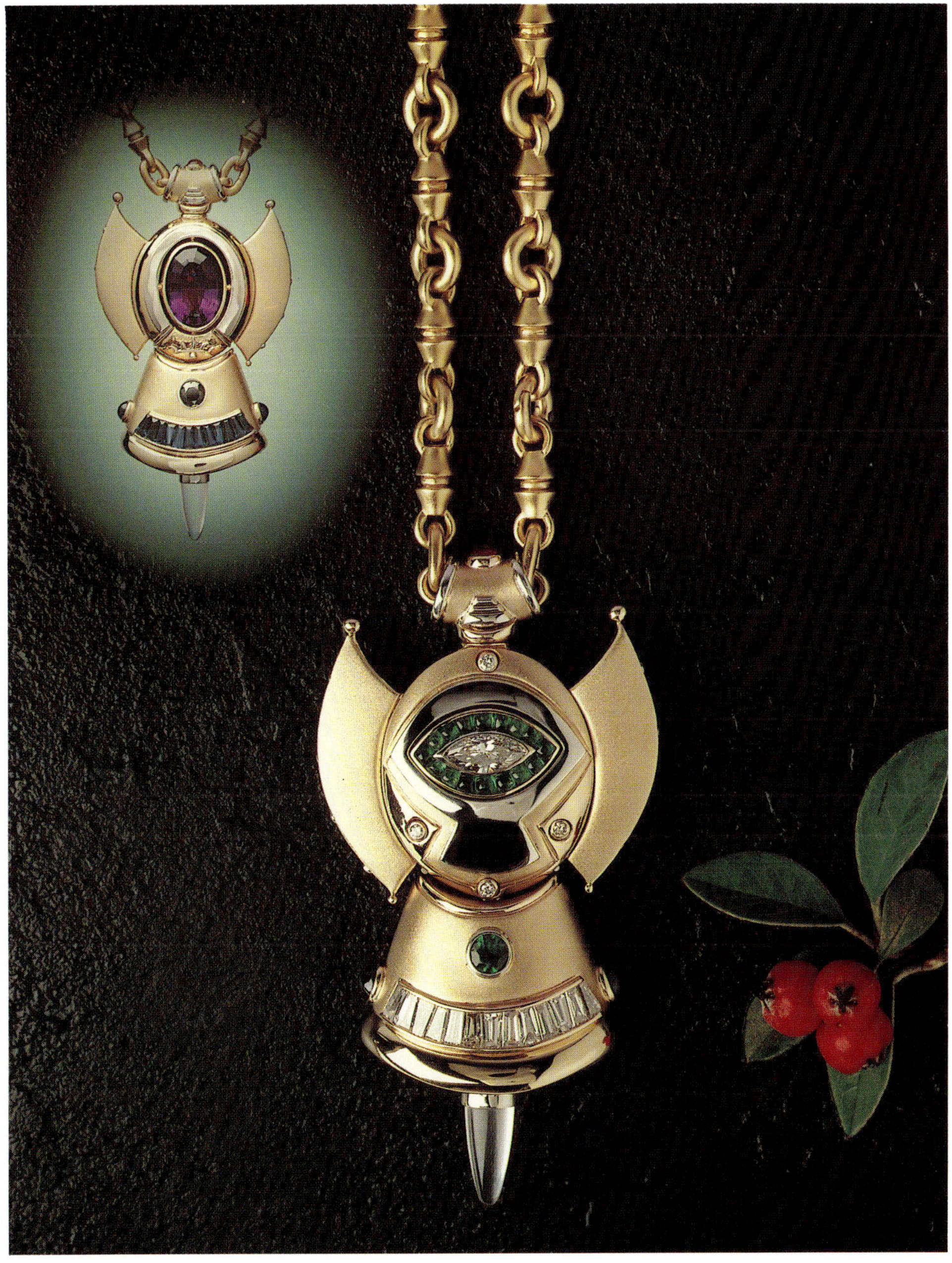

"Wings of Desire"
A Healing Amulet, Front and Back View (inset).

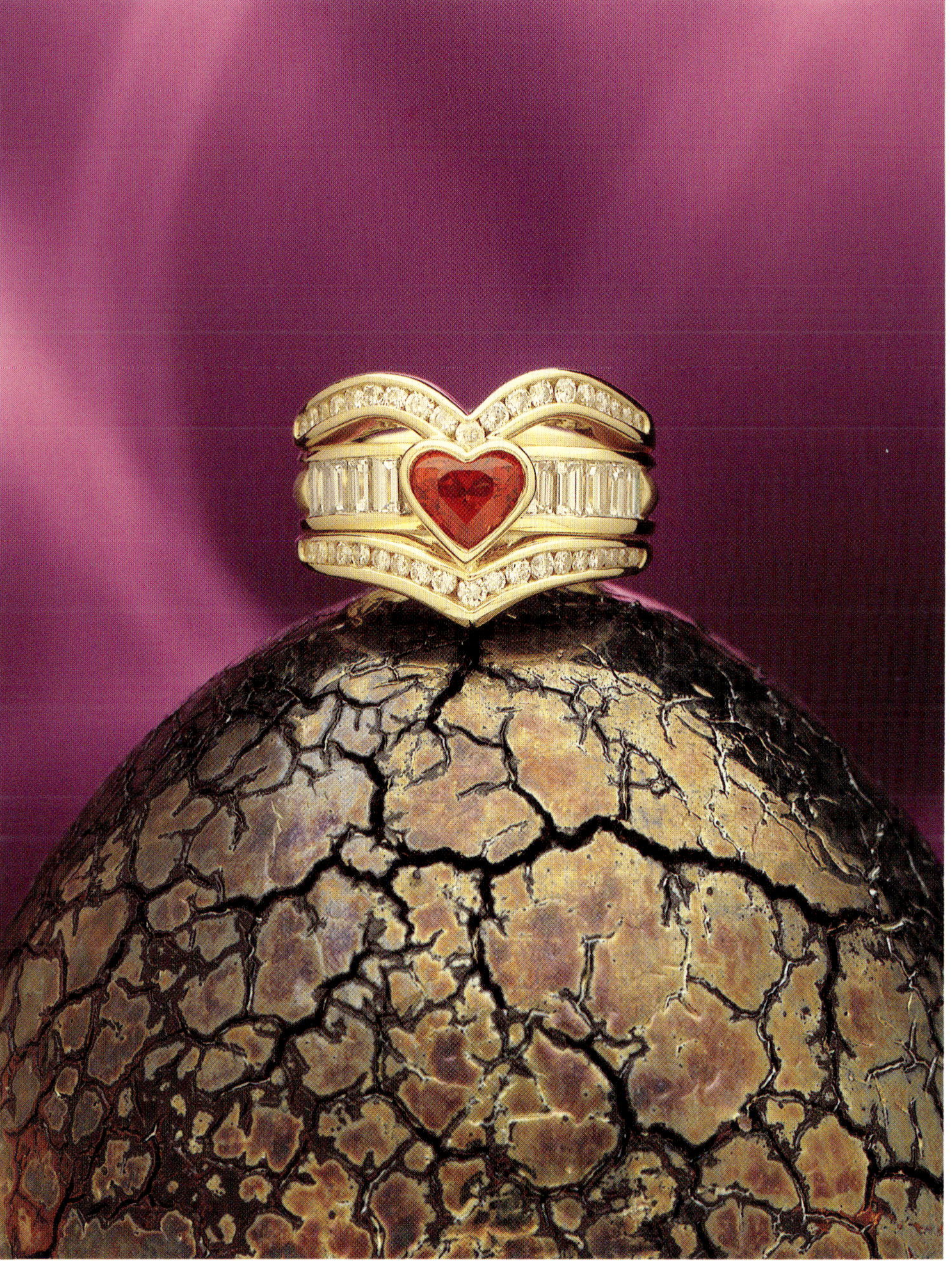

"Pomegranate Heart"
Artists Private Collection

DAVID C. SACCO

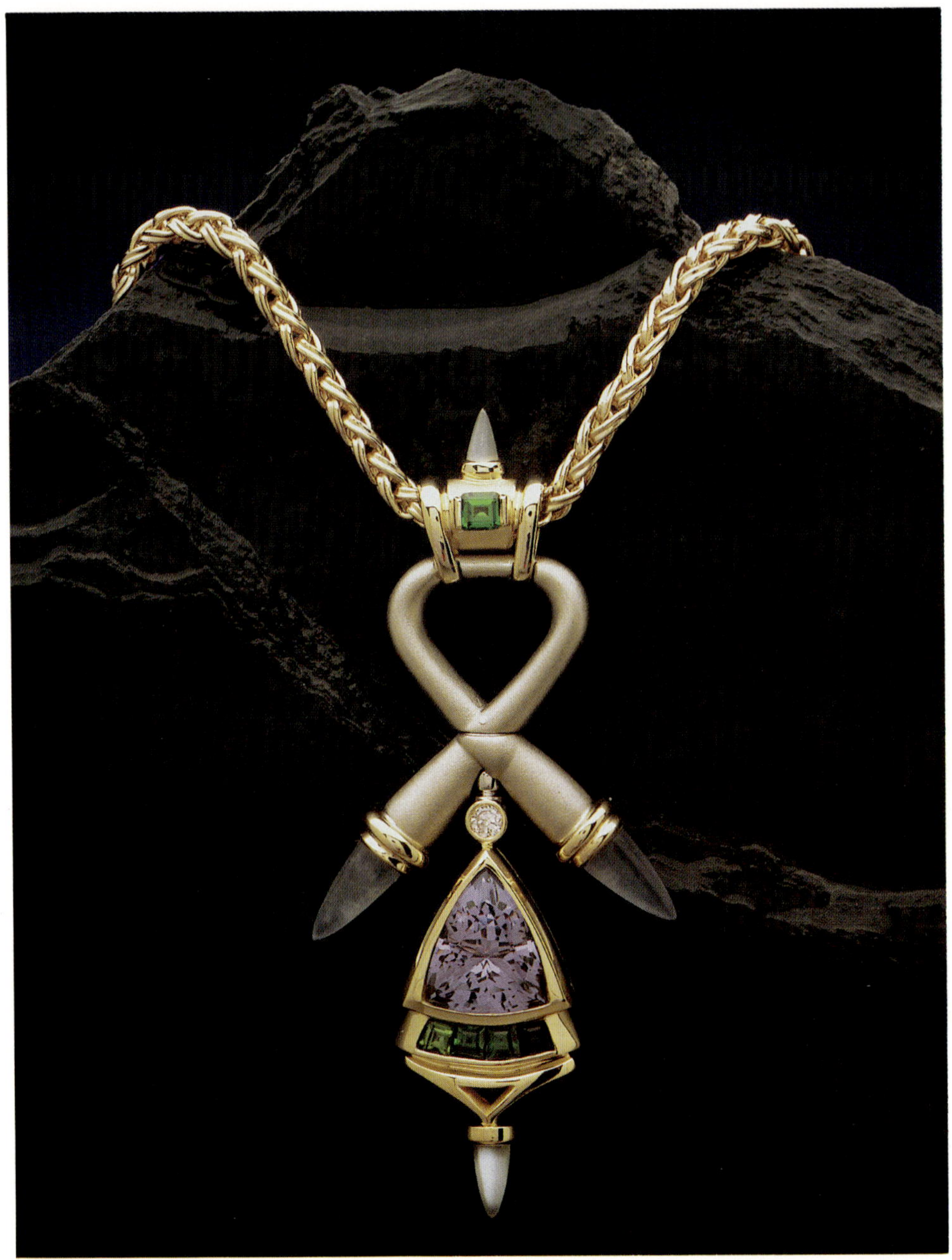

"The Love of Paul"
Tanzanite Amulet - Lavaliere with Colored Gems and Ball Bearing in 18kt. White and Yellow Gold.

"The Citadel"
Tanzanite and Colored Stone Neck Piece with Diamonds.

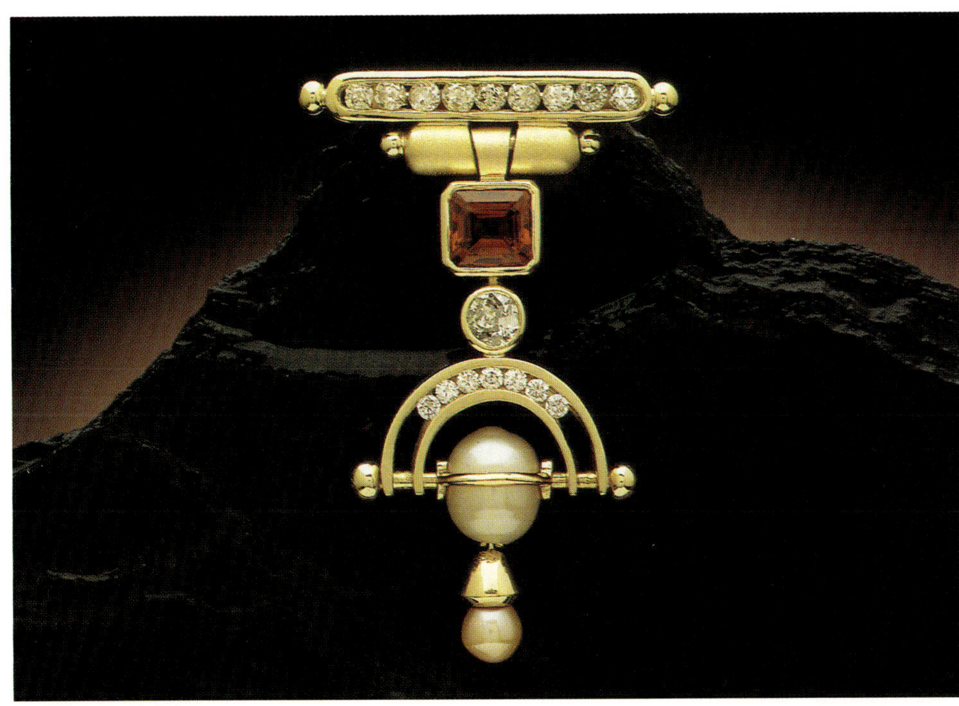

"Hessonite Garnet Broach
with Biwa Pearls and Diamonds.

"From the Ruins"
Ladies Diamond Solitare with Heart Shaped Accent.

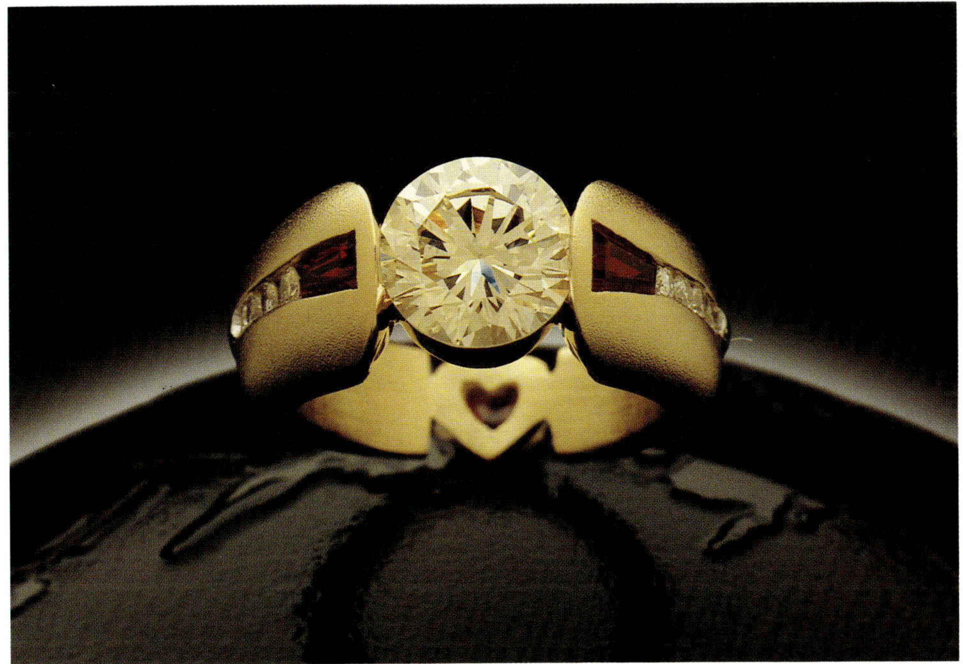

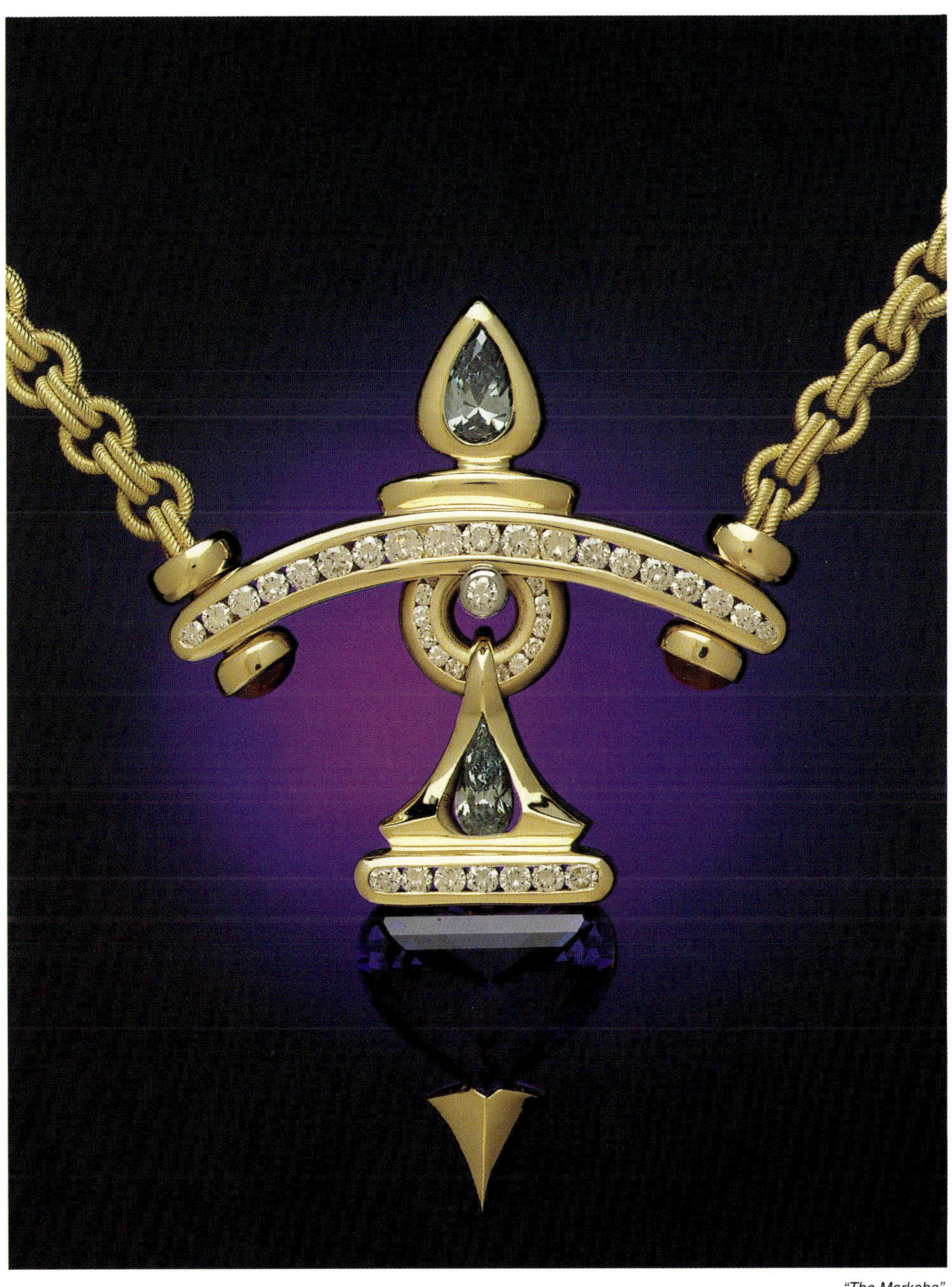

"The Markaba"
A Tanzanite Neckpiece with Blue and White
Diamond Accents in 18kt. Gold.

DAVID C. SACCO

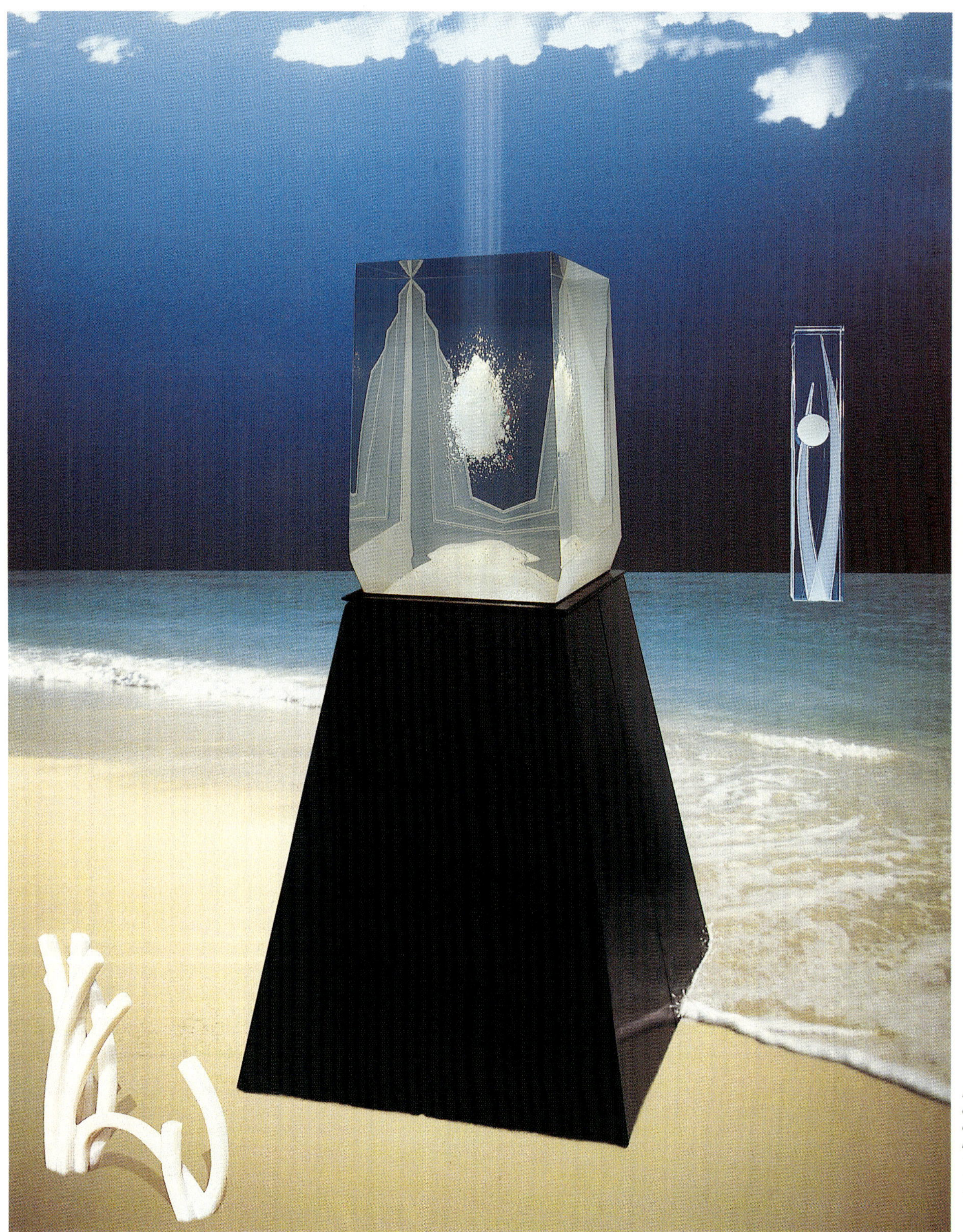

Limited Edition Lithograph 24" X 36"
or Cibachrome Print 16" X 20"
of original sculptures
named from left to right:
"Weilweil" (Scion)
"Pi'i Lani" (Ascention)
"Momilani" (Heavenly Pearl).

DAVID STILL

David Still's first inclination towards the creative came in his early childhood while growing up in Seattle, Washington. His artistic mind was gradually directed to architecture. After several years of study he felt too limited by its practical demands.

In his early twenties he moved to California where he began work with oils and collages, eventually turning to sculpture. David became a forerunner in the early 70's when he began experimenting with the use of Lucite, a relatively new medium to the art world. He found by adding color and definite design to the material, he was able to create pieces that possessed an ethereal quality, giving new definition to his use of light and space.

David now makes his home in Hawaii, where he feels most creative. His award winning sculptures have been exhibited by prominent art galleries and international collectors.

"Ascention", truly expresses David's feelings about his sculptures; that each piece should speak for itself and should capture the essence of limitless interpretations, an ascention of

1142 Auahi St., #3305
Honolulu, Oahu, HI 96814
(808) 593-3755
Cellular (808) 220-5212

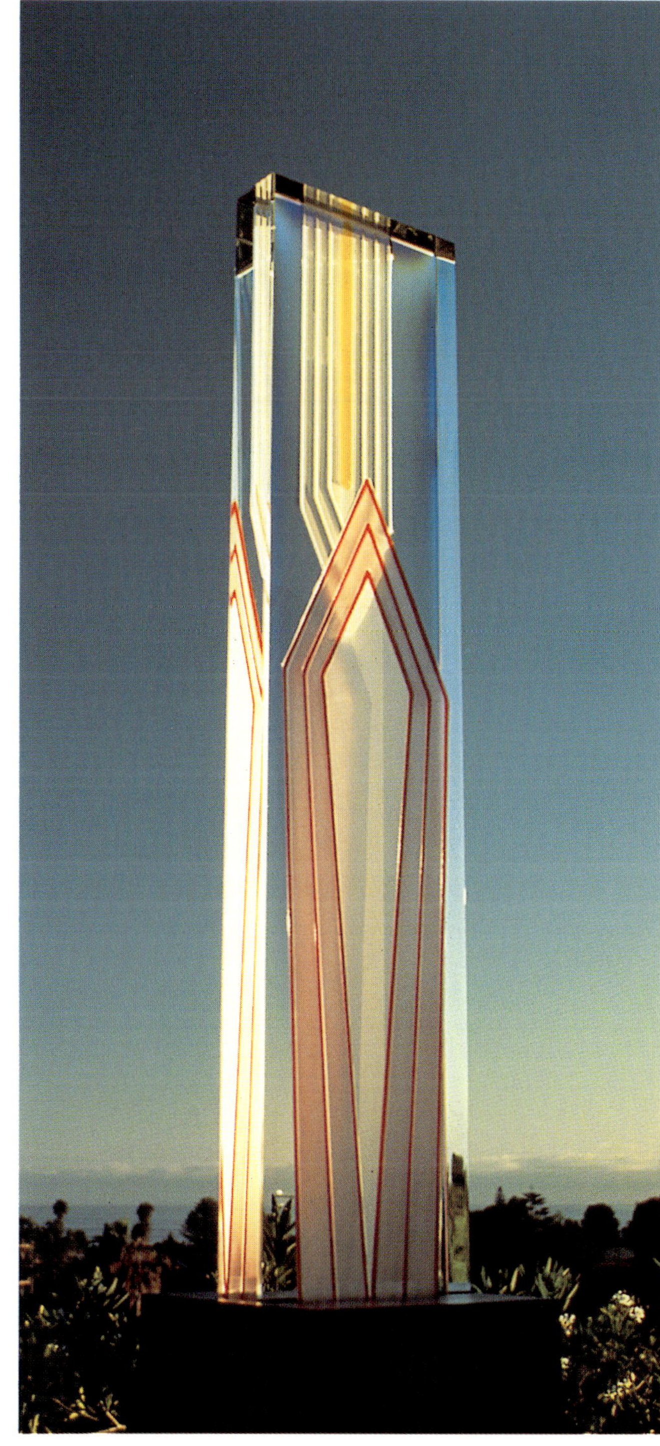

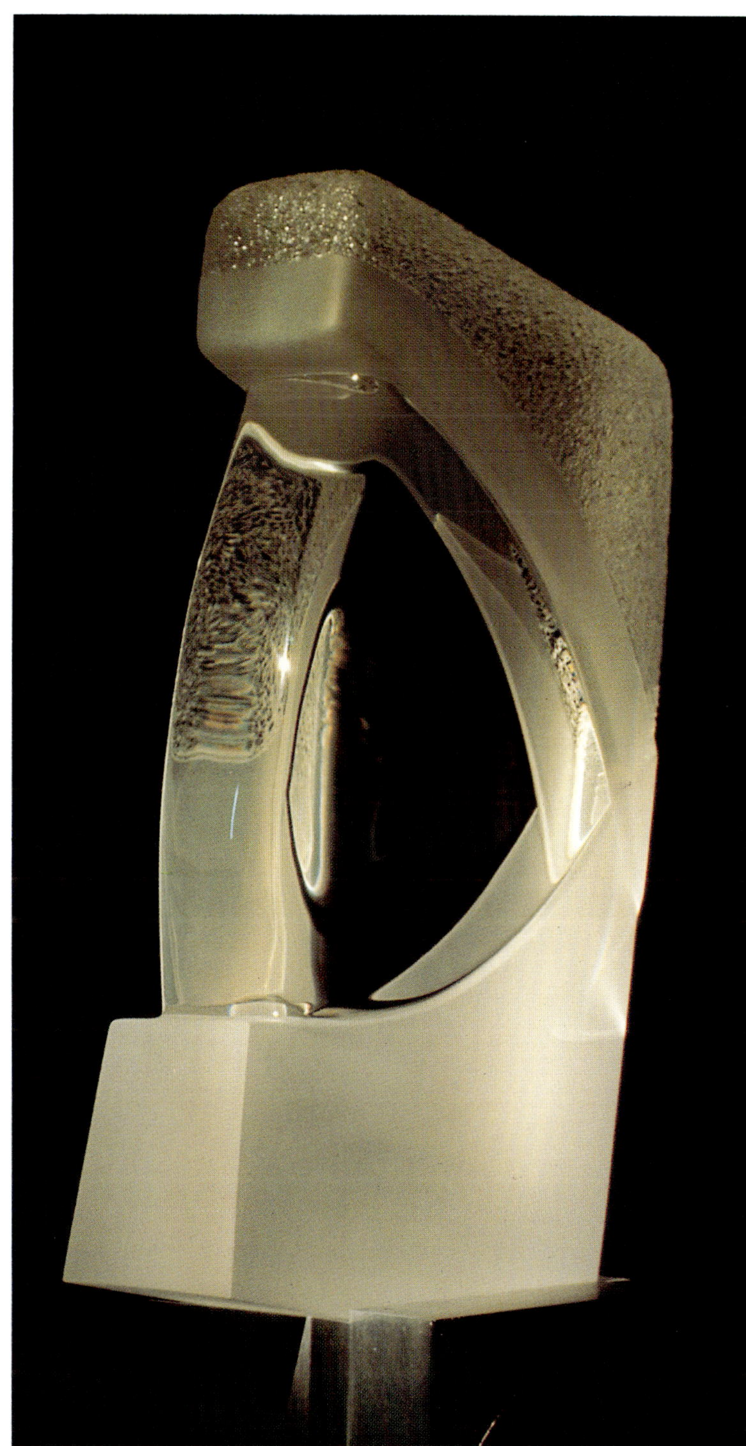

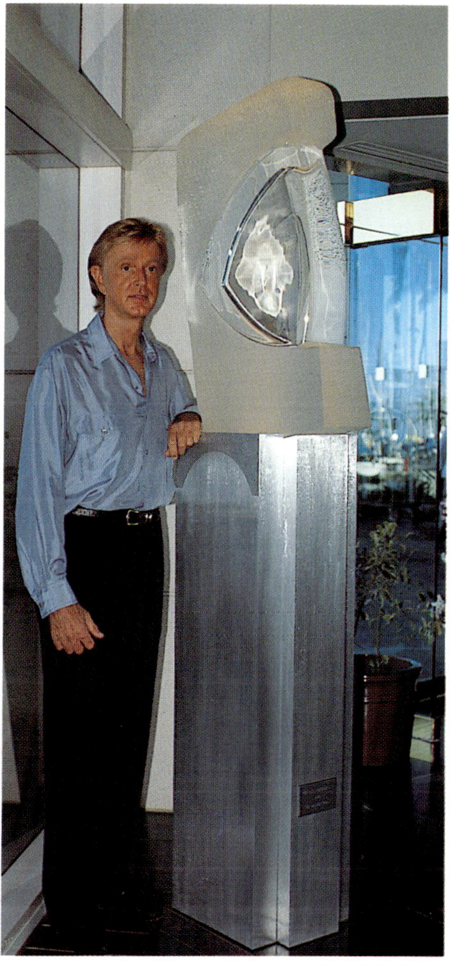

"Maka Iki" 88" High

mind and spirit. David's standards are high, his self expectations never wavering, his creations a true reflection of himself, and his vision.

Left: "Sculpture 90B" 48" High

Center: "Maka Iki" (All Seeing Eye)

DAVID STILL

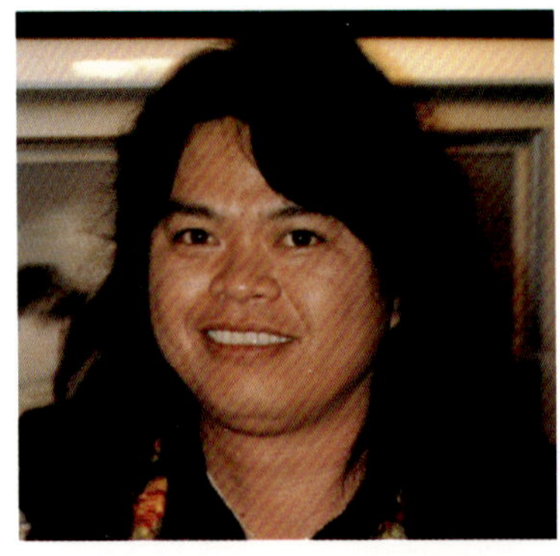

ROY GONZALEZ TABORA

Roy Gonzalez Tabora portrays the endless variations of Hawaii's beauty in his masterful seascapes. With works displayed in fine art galleries throughout the state, he is recognized as one of the islands' leading artists.

Tabora's work is a masterful blend of spontaneity and precision. Never content with merely recreating an observed scene or copying from a photograph, Tabora draws from his heart and his mind. Painting from a combination of memory and imagination, he creates realistic works alive with rolling surf, distant mountains, and radiant skies. He is a keen observer of light, color, and the continuous motion of the sea.

Each element offers endless variations of nature's dynamic design. In Tabora's art, every composition becomes a masterpiece of harmony, a poem of lyrical beauty.

Born on June 18, 1956, Tabora continues the legacy of generations of artists who populate his family tree. Growing up in Manila surrounded by art and artists, his earliest memories are of watching the creative process in action.

His lessons in the disciplines of drawing and painting began, as he recalls, at about age six. During his youth he was directed by his favorite uncle, Rick Gonzalez. As with all apprentices,

"Night Winds" 20" x 40" Original Oil Painting - Collection Mr. and Mrs. Tichy

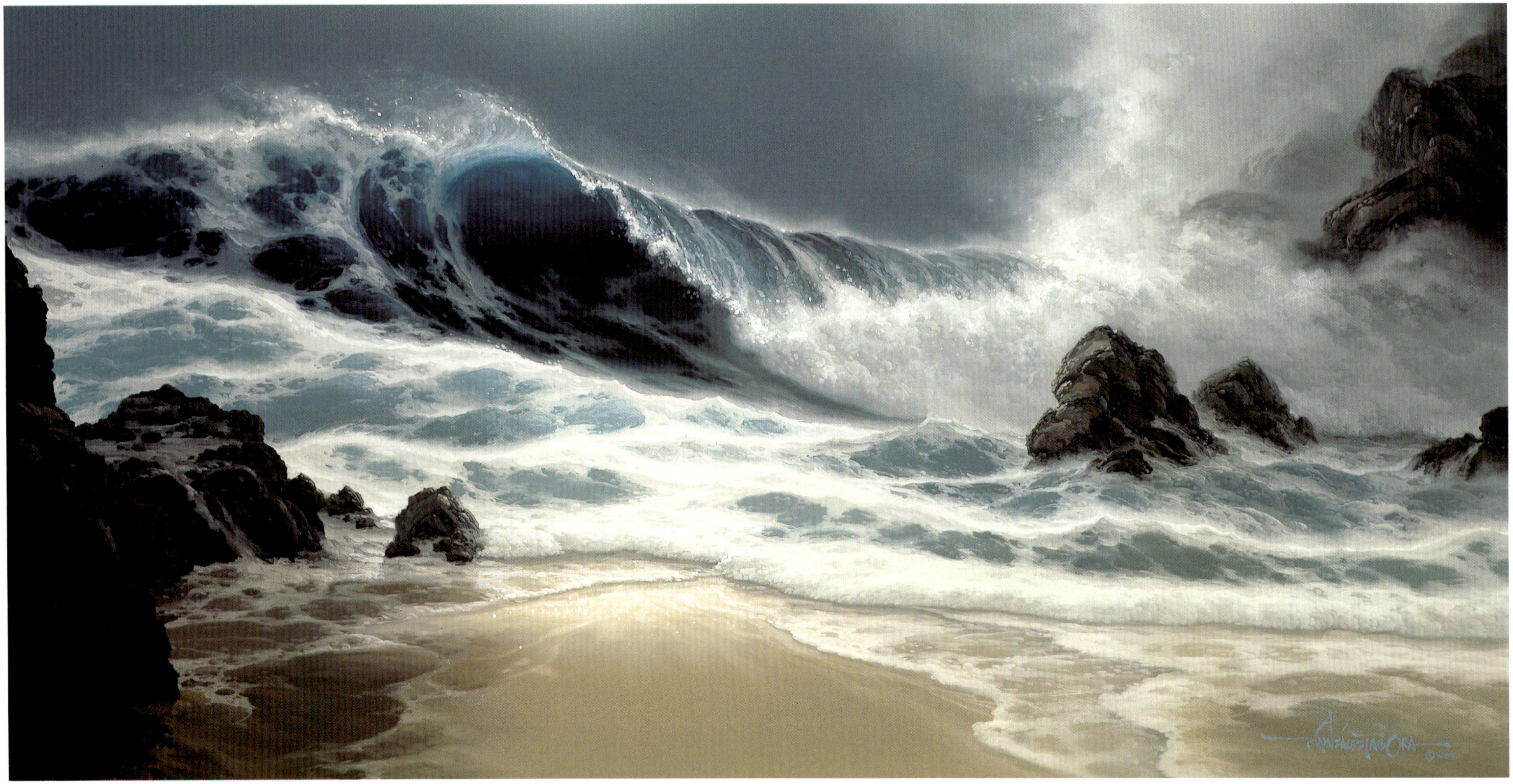

his days were occupied by sweeping floors, cleaning paint brushes and preparing painting materials, as well as receiving expert training in the traditional techniques of the old masters. In addition to learning his craft, his grandfather, Felix Gonzalez, played a pivotal role in molding his personal philosophy of art and what it means to be an artist. These early lessons are the foundations on which he has continued to improve and expand his art.

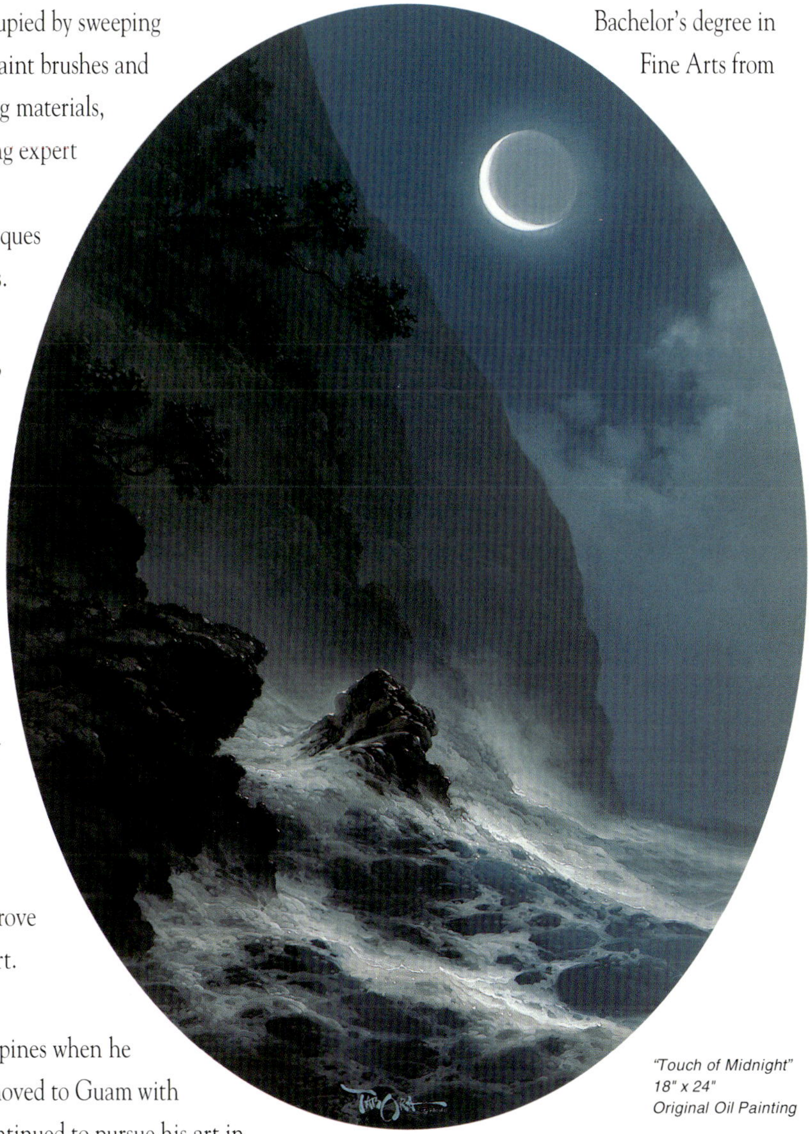

He left the Philippines when he was twelve and moved to Guam with his family. He continued to pursue his art in high school and at the advice of his teacher, enrolled at Washington State University. It was on his way to Washington that he first stopped in Hawaii. This short visit so impressed him that he vowed to return eventually. Already an accomplished realist at the age of twenty, he opted to continue his education and received his Bachelor's degree in Fine Arts from the University of Hawaii. He was soon discovered by Hawaii's leading art galleries and has since risen to great renown as one of the finest seascape painters in the world.

"Touch of Midnight"
18" x 24"
Original Oil Painting

The splendor of Hawaii's tropical shores is a constant source of Tabora's inspiration. Yet in his creative process, he relies even more on his heart than he does on his eye. "I romanticize," he says. "The scenes I portray are memories I have imagined… memories of when the footprints of men were not so prolific and deep. Nature alone is the subject of my work. Its allure is exquisitely pure. That's what I wish to convey. I see in Hawaii's land and sea the essence of beauty itself. It reaches me with a richness of emotion that I simply must express."

There is a magic in Tabora's work, a remarkable glow that seems to shine from an inner light. His colors are at once subtle and intense. This is achieved through a long and painstaking process of layering and glazing. Tabora begins with a wash of turpentine and color. Then using oils, he underpaints the image. This is followed with five to ten applications of colors he calls transparent - each to bring out a greater sense of depth or tonal value. Each layer builds luminosity and light within the transparent waves. Highlights and glazes complete his paintings, resulting in works that enter our minds and become our dreams.

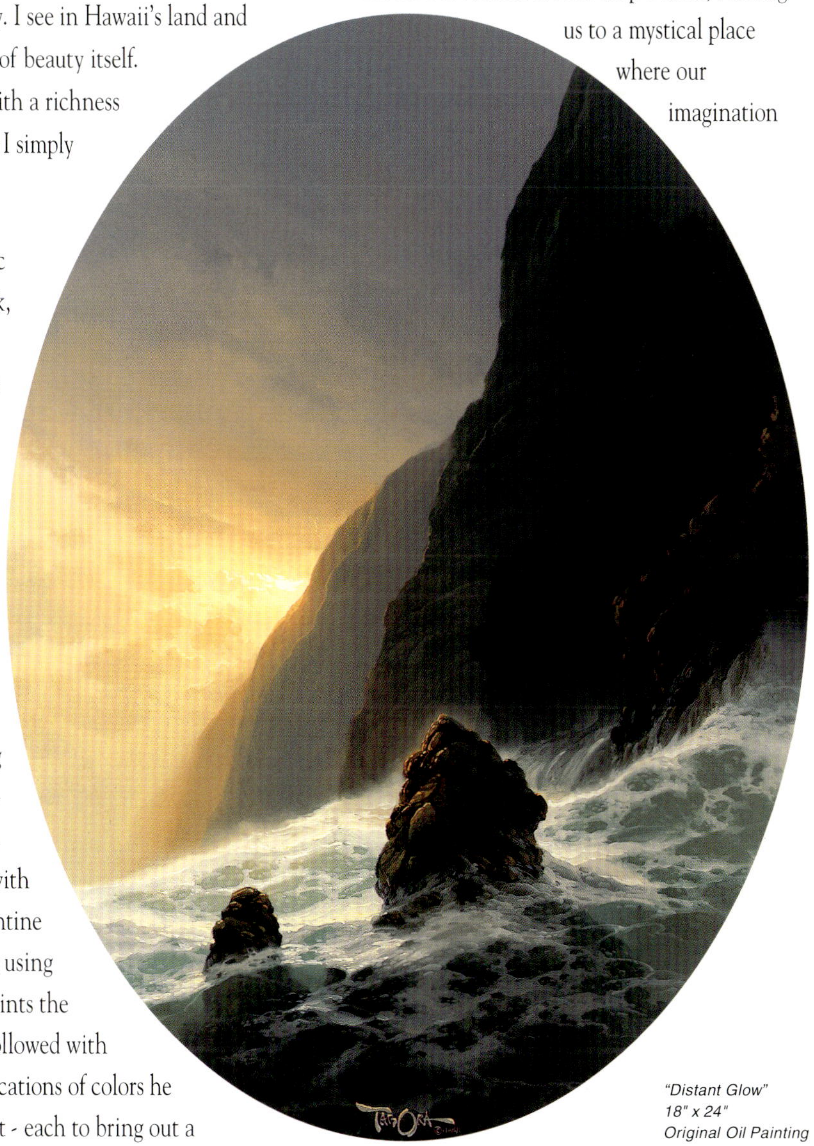

Tabora's art strikes a cord deep within, sending us to a mystical place where our imagination

"Distant Glow"
18" x 24"
Original Oil Painting

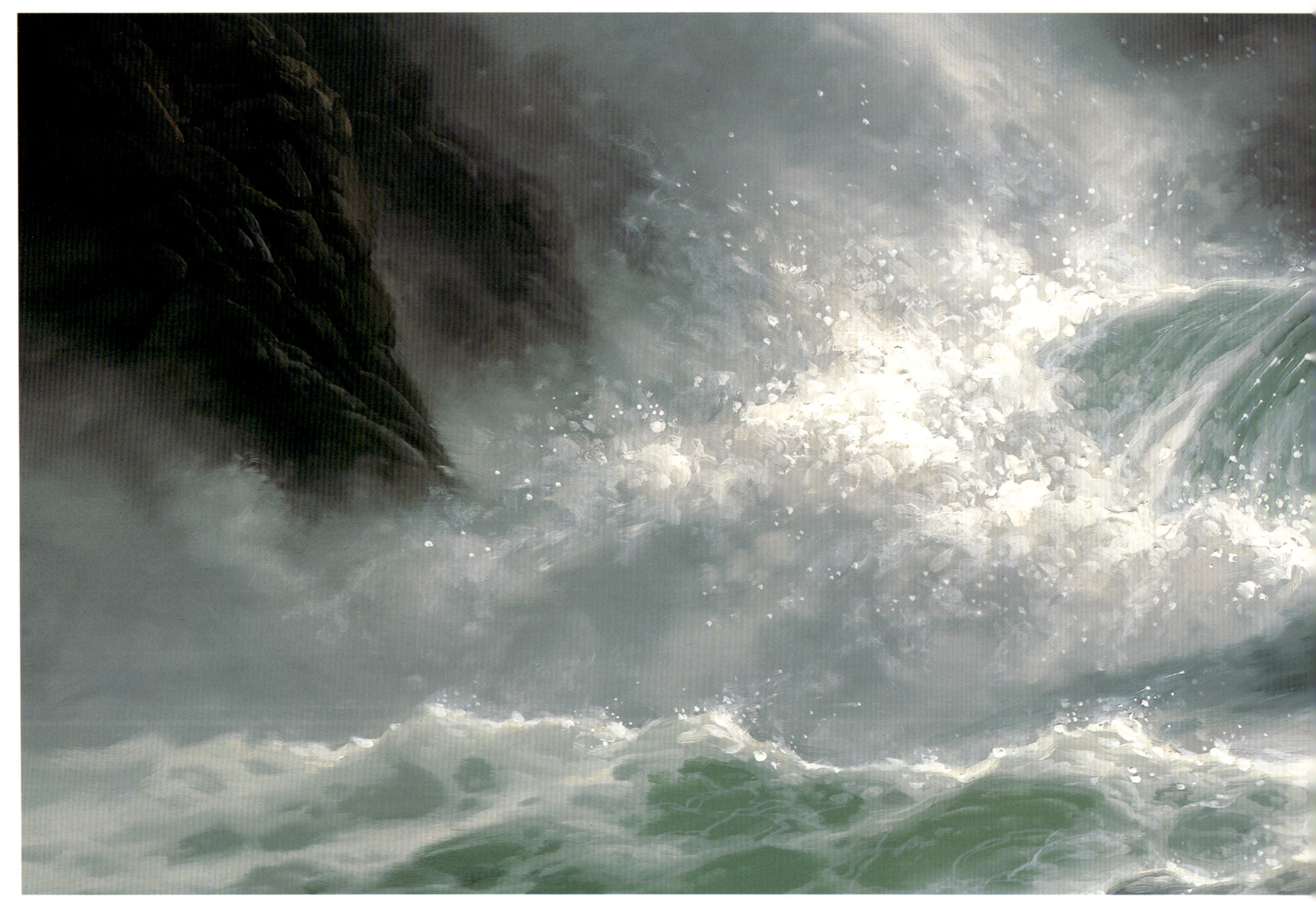

"Thundering Surf" 12" x 24" Original Oil Painting - Collection Dr. and Mrs. Davidhizar, Limited Edition Print

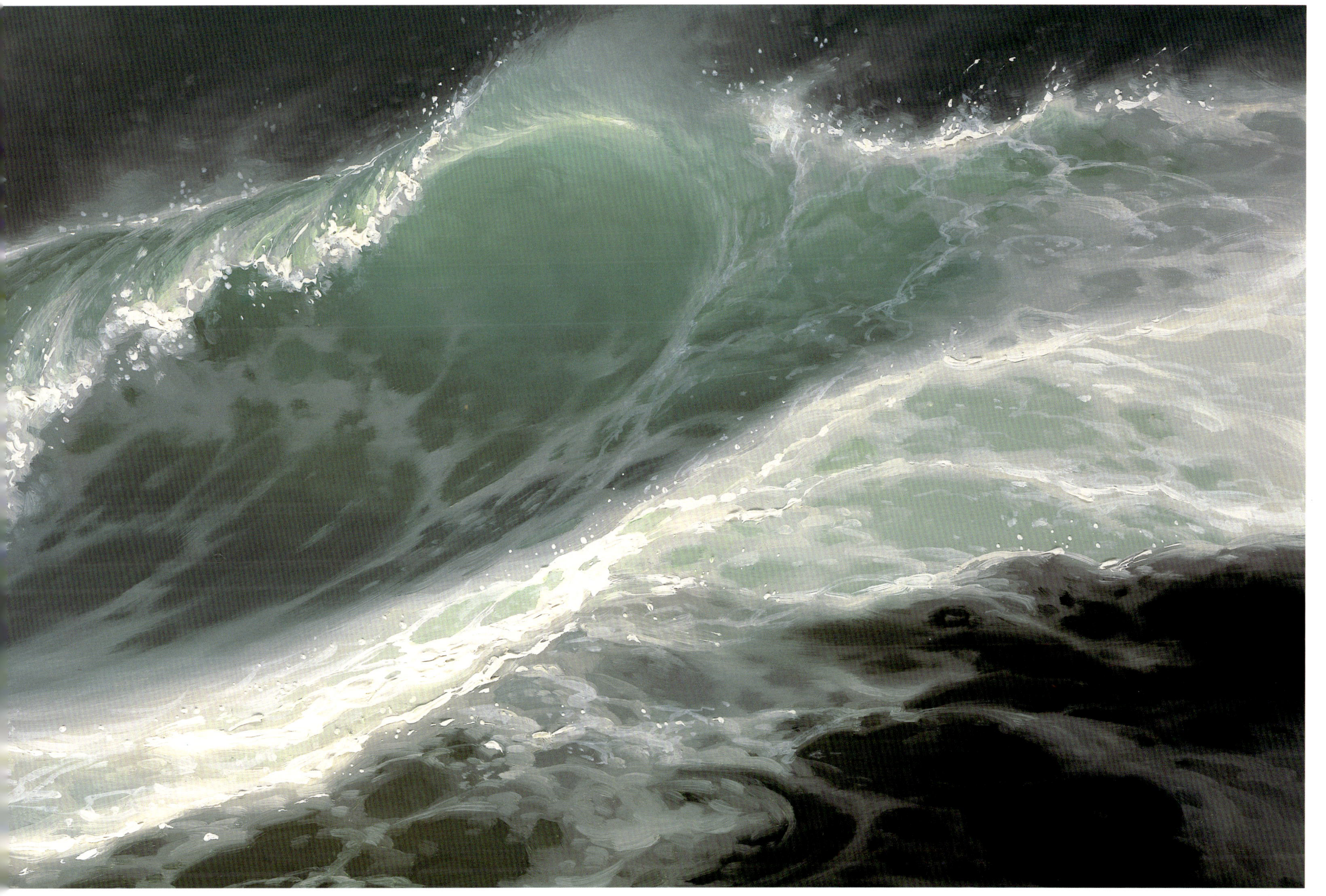

ROY TABORA

ROY TABORA

is free to wander amid our fondest memories. Ultimately we arrive at a moment of tranquility. To capture these moments and share them with his viewers is the artist's highest aim and this is the true essence of Roy Tabora's unforgettable seascapes. His original paintings and limited edition prints are highly prized by collectors for their irresistible qualities of majesty, mood, and meticulous perfection.

In his latest effort to realize the essence of the sea, he focuses on the one element he feels best conveys the sea's varied expressions, the breaking wave. The images that comprise his "Classic Waves" collection have been composed to convey the incredible range of moods and qualities of the sea as it swells, curls, and breaks into a foaming and misty roar. He chose to portray the ocean in its purest and most classic form - concentrating on the wave's basic components. The compositions are unadorned yet powerful. Unencumbered by mountains or trees, each is simply framed by a minimum of rocks and sky. From the curling lip to spraying foam, Tabora sought to capture the graceful movement and awesome power of the wave. "The ocean has always been a source of fascination and inspiration for me. With these images, it is my hope that those who view my work will find the same and more."

"Serenity" 20" x 40" Original Oil Painting - Collection Dr. V. Owen

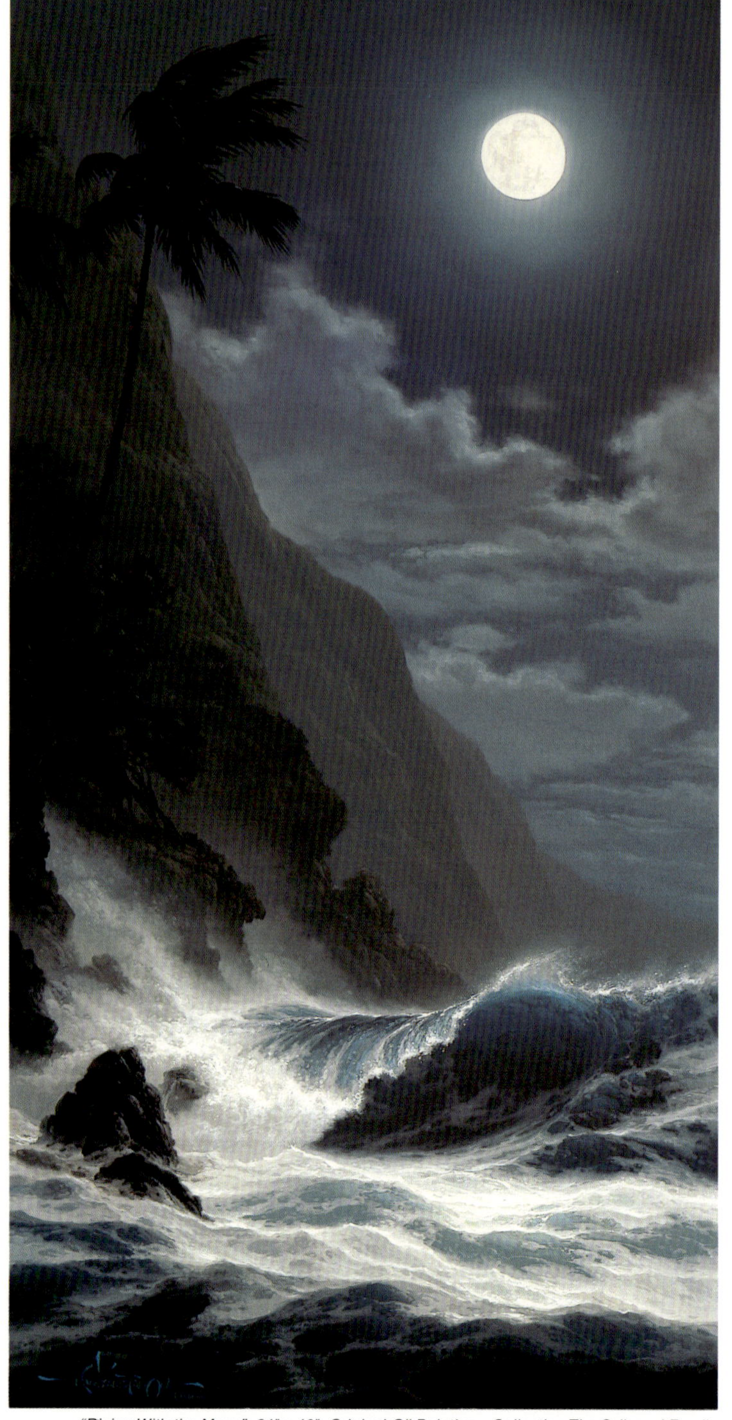

"Rising With the Moon" 24" x 40" Original Oil Painting - Collection The Szilvagyi Family

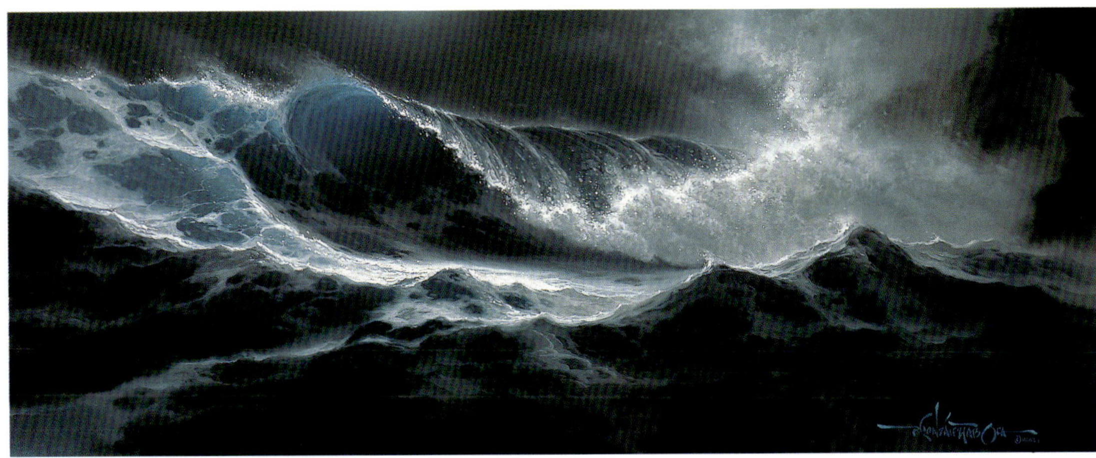

"High Midnight Surge" 12" x 30" Original Oil Painting - Collection Mr. Stewart M. Powers, Jr., Limited Edition Print

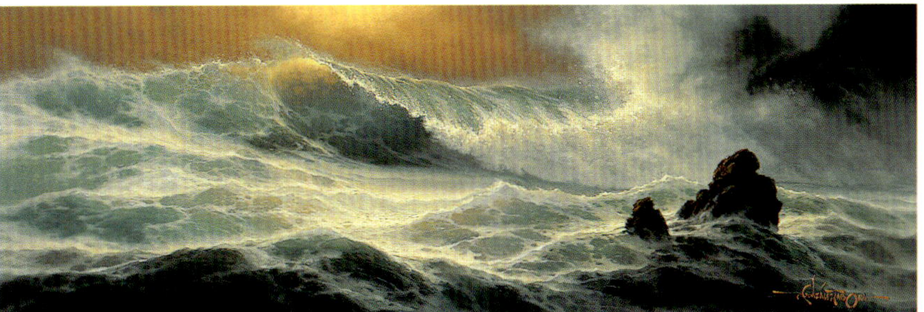

"Amber Afterglow" 12" x 36" Original Oil Painting - Collection The Biegertt Family, Limited Edition Print

ROY TABORA

Tabora Studio, Inc.
58-356B Kamehameha Highway
Haleiwa, Oahu, HI 96712
(808) 638-7881
FAX (808) 638-9505

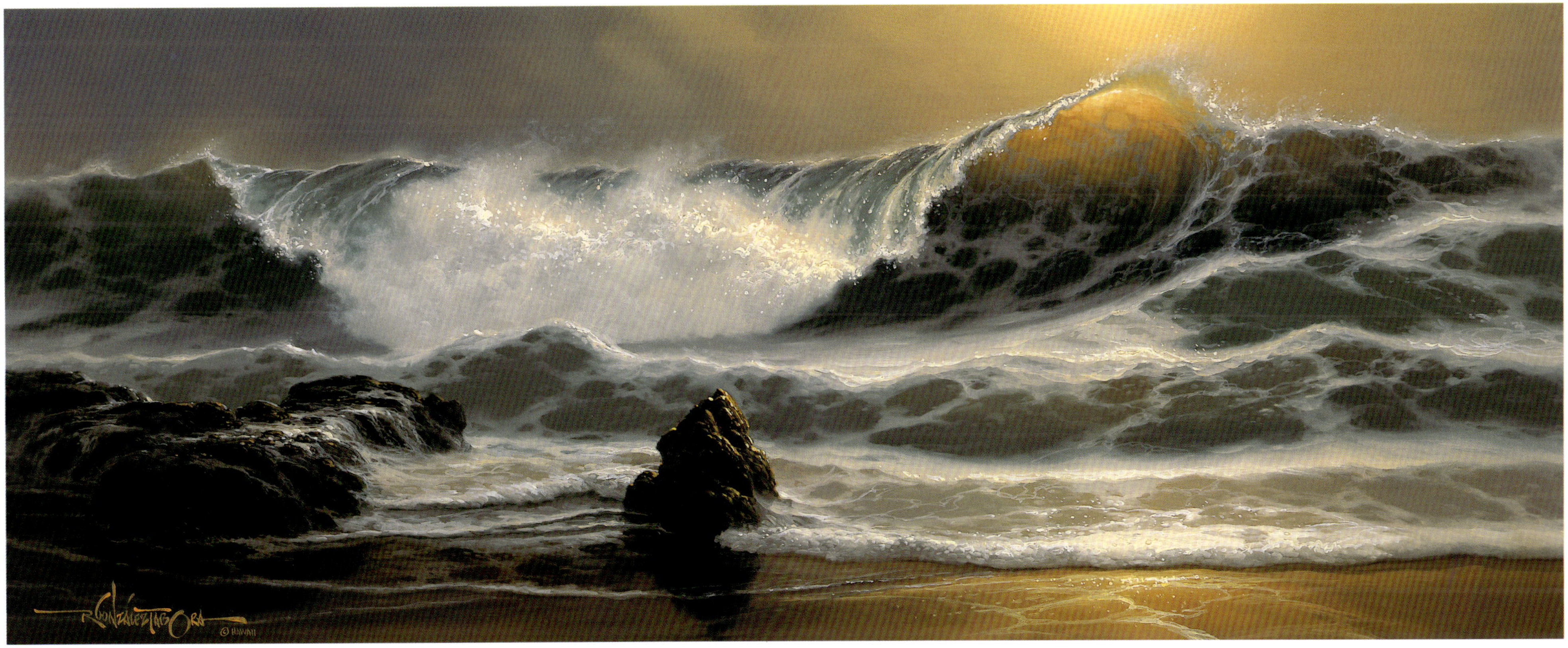

"Golden Moment" 12" x 30" Original Oil Painting and Limited Edition Print

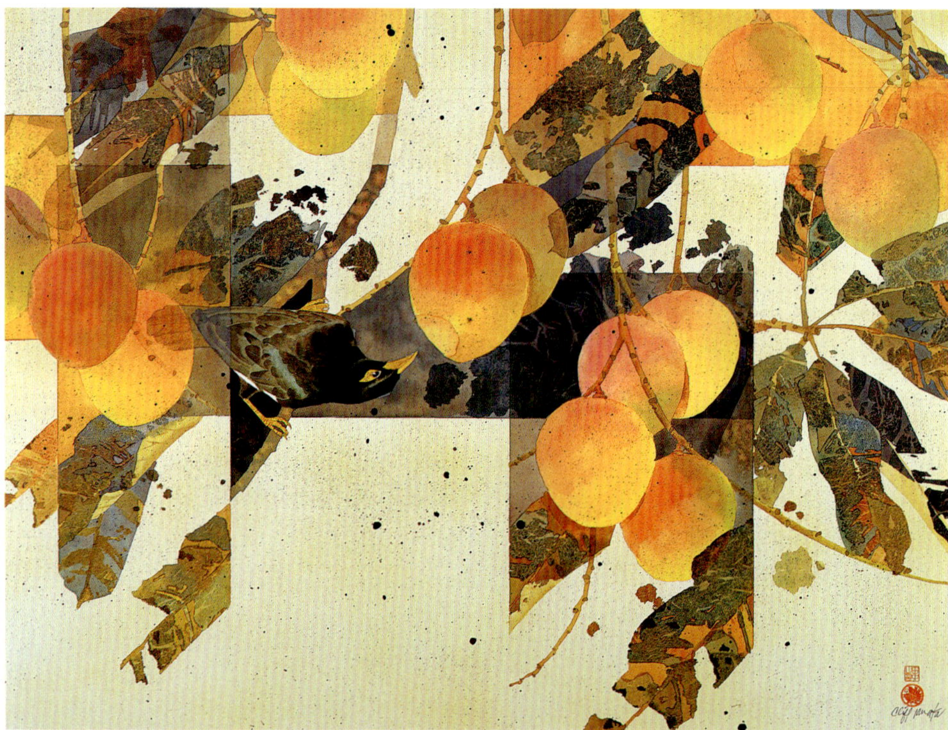

"Mango and Mynah" 22" x 30"
Limited Edition Print

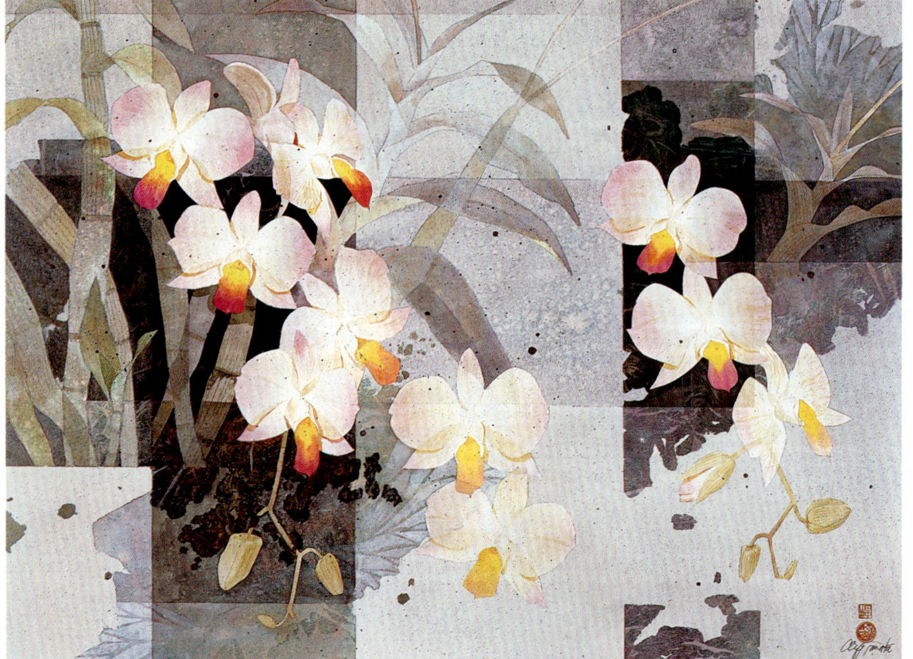

"Orchids" 30" x 40"
Original Artwork

CLIFF TANAKA

Cliff Tanaka was born in Paia, a small plantation town on Maui's windward coast. At an early age, his ability at drawing was quite apparent and by the eighth grade he was quite determined to become an artist. Upon graduation from Baldwin High School, he then attended Art Center and Chouinard Art Institute in Los Angeles to study graphic design and fine art. His childhood in the islands left an indelible influence on his art work which is still expressed to this very day.

After completing his formal art training, Mr. Tanaka served in the Army and was stationed in Germany. He had the opportunity then to visit the great museums of the world in France, Germany, Spain and Italy. Upon returning to the islands, he worked as a free-lance graphic artist and illustrator for the top advertising agencies in Honolulu.

Using watercolor inks, Mr. Tanaka creates a geometric grid on which his subjects are laced. The lines serve to give his paintings balance and continuity. He often will produce an interesting interplay of light and dark areas within his composition.

By combining only three primary colors, Mr. Tanaka can create all of the colors found in his work, from soft pastels to intensive saturated colors. Having worked as a graphic artist for over 15 years, he has a wide range of techniques at his fingertips. Cliff Tanaka's favorite hobby is raising and breeding koi fishes. His knowledge of their proportions, spotting and movement within the water has made him the premier koi artist in Hawaii.

Cliff Tanaka's unique ability to combine elements from his oriental heritage with the influences from his island upbringing, in a very contemporary manner is what makes his artwork so distinctive. Collectors are most fond of the originality and freshness of his paintings.

Hawaii Art Sales & Services
47-594 Nukupu'u Street
Kaneohe, Oahu, HI 96744
(808) 239-4027

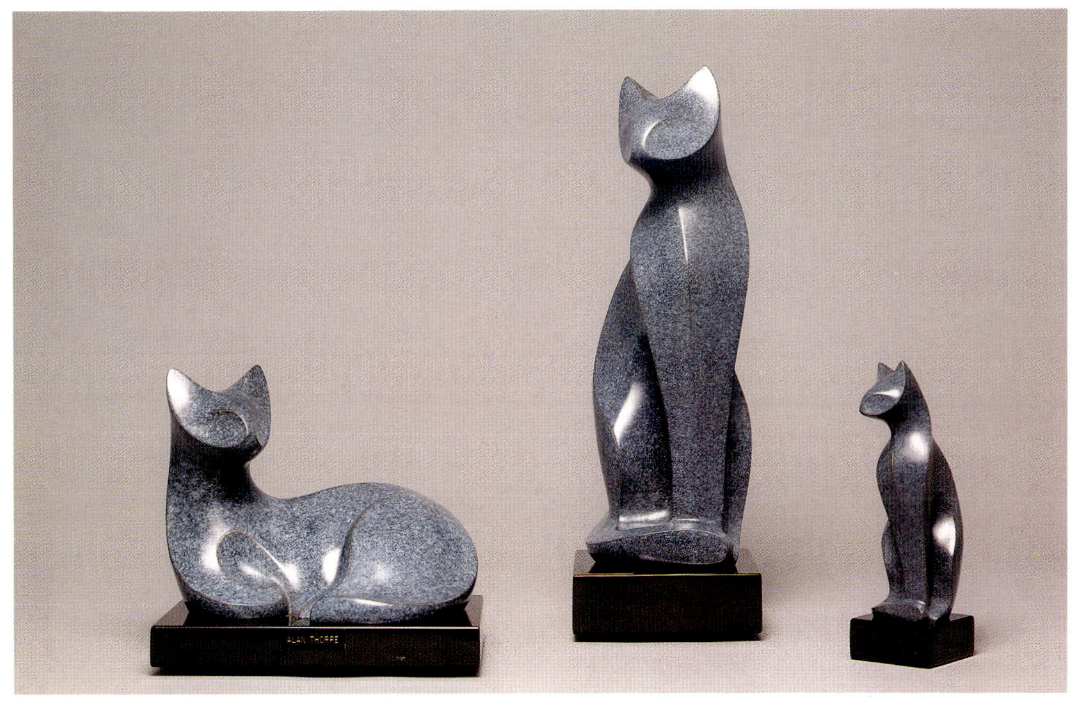

Above sculptures:
Bronze, (L to R) Reclining Cat, 10"x7" h
Seated Cats, 17 1/2" h and 8 1/2" h

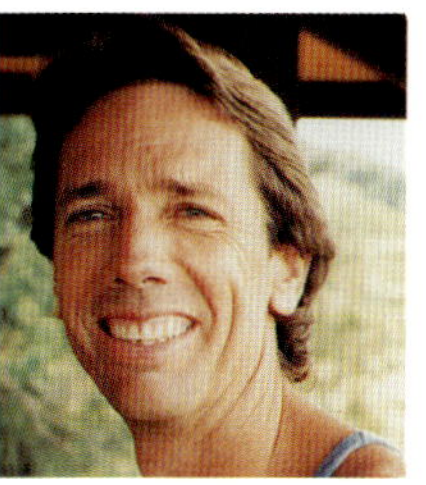

ALAN THORPE

Creating stunning, graceful lines in crisp, hard edge sculpture is Alan Thorpe's gift.

Thorpe was born in Oakland, California in 1948. His desire for freedom of expression prompted him to turn from traditional academic training and rely instead upon his own intuitive artistic sense.

In a world where originality is difficult to achieve, Thorpe's variety of subject matter has given his work a unique appeal and it is being sought after by knowledgeable collectors around the world.

Thorpe works with a wide variety of materials including bronze, wood, aerospace polyurethane and automobile lacquers.

The themes most common in his works are the female figure, dancers, mother and child, certain animals, and large floral designs.

Alan Thorpe
Kihei, Maui, HI 96791
(808) 779-4212

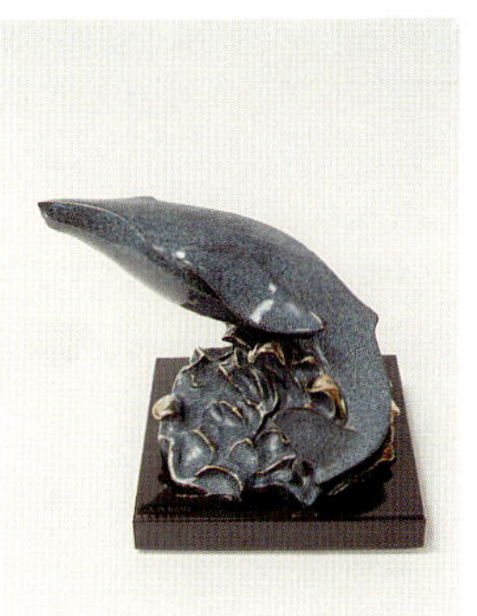

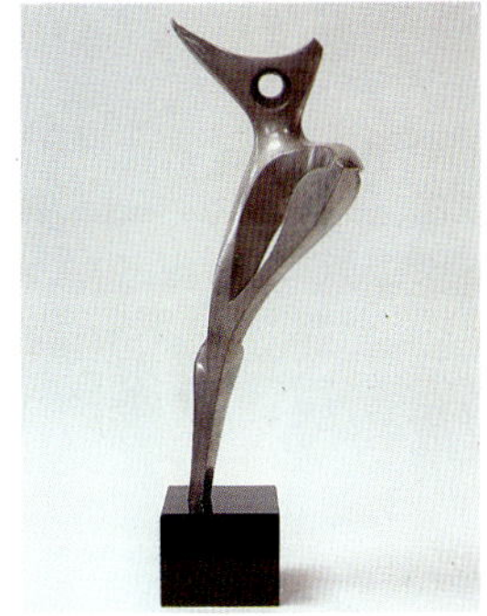

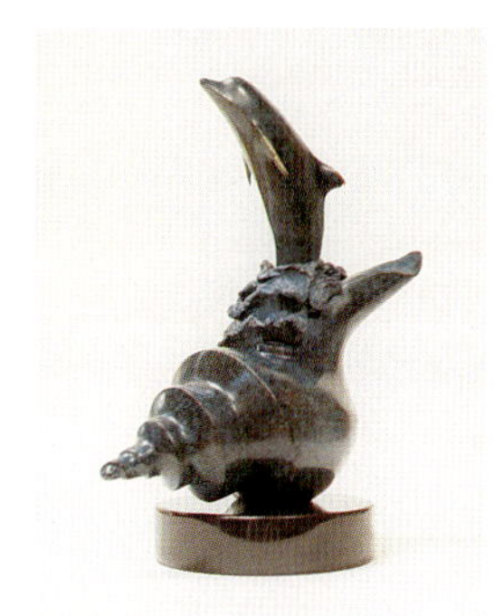

Center row : Bronze, (L to R)
Breaching Humpback, 8" h x 13" L
Flight of the Ballerina, 25" h
Dolphin Walk, 16 1/2" L x 18" h

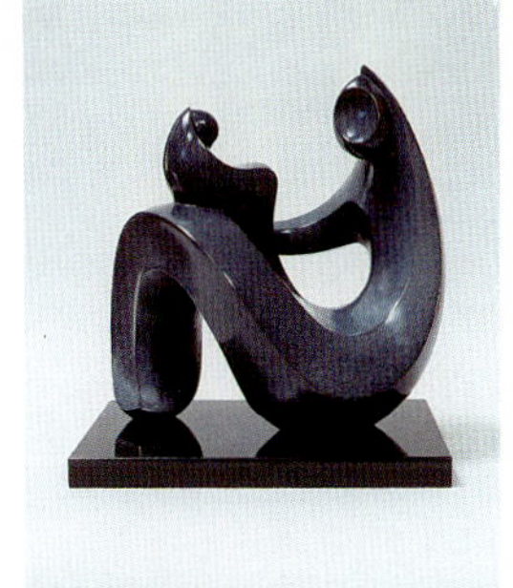

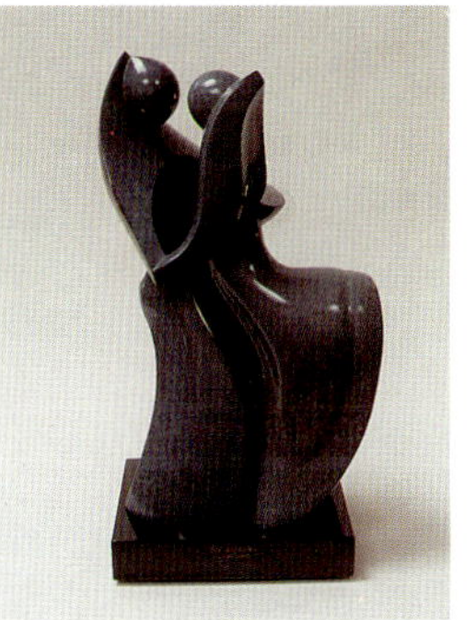

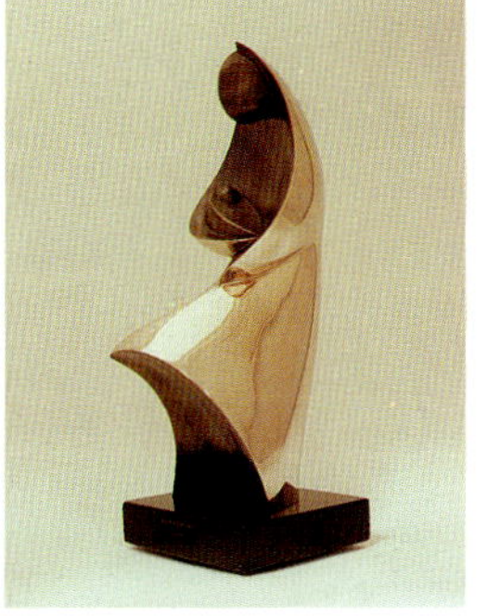

Lower sculptures: Bronze, (L to R)
Mother and Child, 18" x16" h
Dancers, 22" h
Mother and Child, 22" h

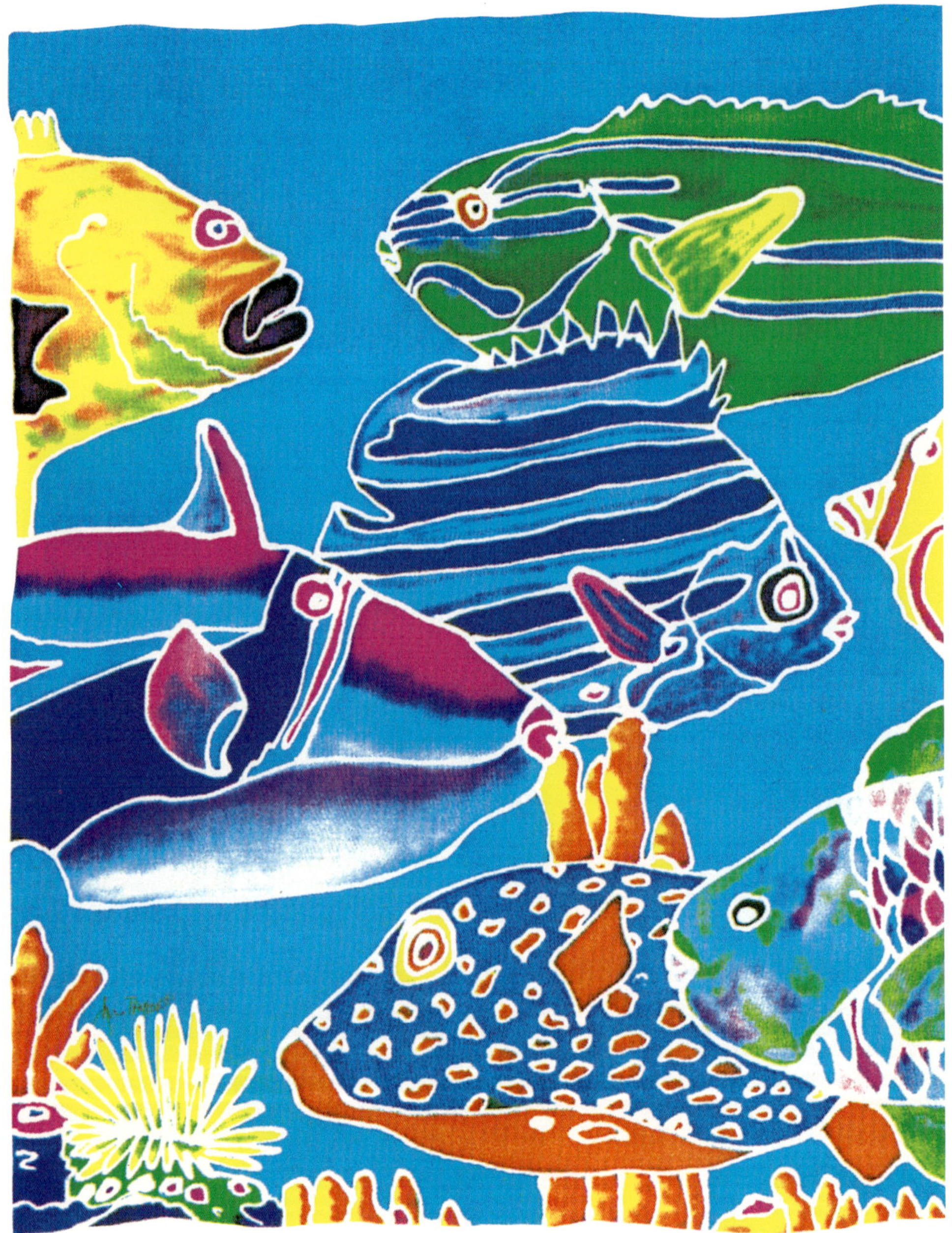

"E. Sea Street" 9" x 12"
Batik on Silk

As of July 30, 1994 Ann Taylor is newly married and creates her new work using her married name Ann Taylor-Vance.

An island girl from birth, Ann Taylor grew up on the Caribbean island of Tobago in the British West Indies. Ms. Taylor was educated at boarding school in Barbados, followed by college in Canada, where she specialized in early childhood and primary special education. Inspired by her work with young children, Ann Taylor's art captures the essence of her natural island surroundings. She paints with cheerful, vivid colors, utilizing the ancient Indonesian technique of Batik and silk painting, and is also known for her petite pen and ink watercolor paintings.

Ms. Taylor resides in Maui and works from her studio in Lahaina. She frequently ventures out of her creative workshop to teach classes in watercolor techniques for young children.

Her work can be found internationally in various arenas: original Batiks are available through Village Galleries in Lahaina. Island Heritage Publishing reproduces her work in the Island Heritage collection of art cards. Matted prints are available at selected gift stores and galleries in the islands. Ann Taylor art fabric designs are found on fabrics in the Cooke Street line of aloha wear and T-shirts on the islands also display her artwork.

Of her work, Ms. Taylor comments: "I enjoy being able to have visitors take home visual reminders of their stay on the islands, some illustration that stirs warm memories of happy times."

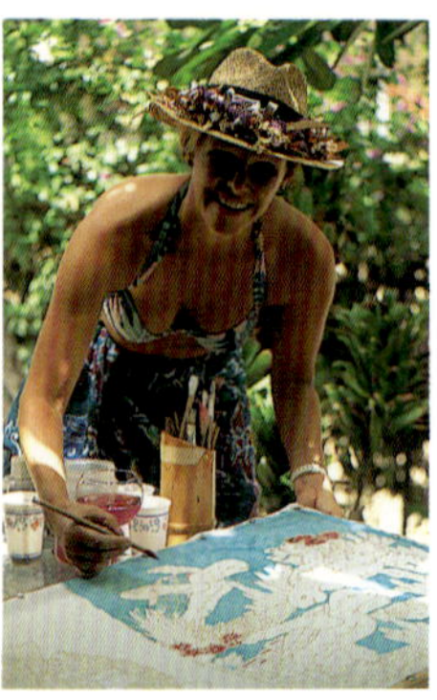

ANN TAYLOR-VANCE

Ann Taylor Art
P.O. Box 10444
Lahaina, Maui, HI 96761
(808) 661-7812
FAX (808) 661-7812 * 51

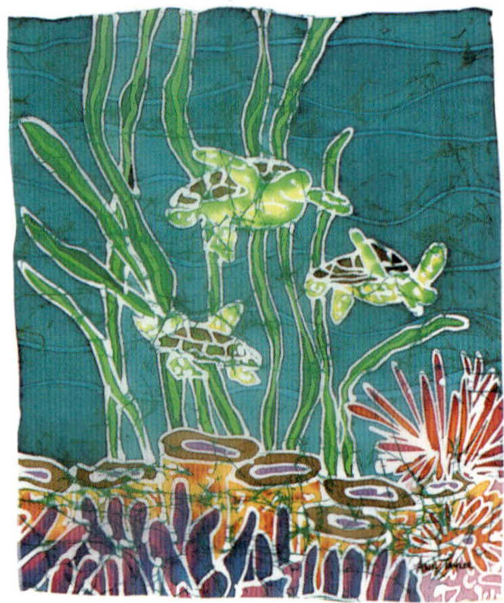

"Sea Turtles" 9" x 12" Batik on Silk

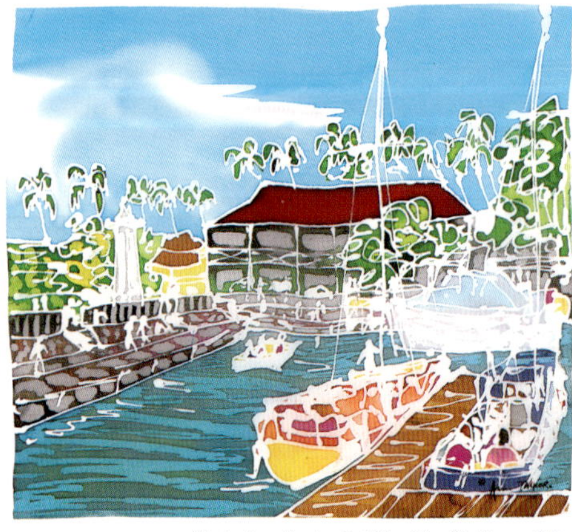

"Lahaina Harbor" 12" x 9" Batik on Silk

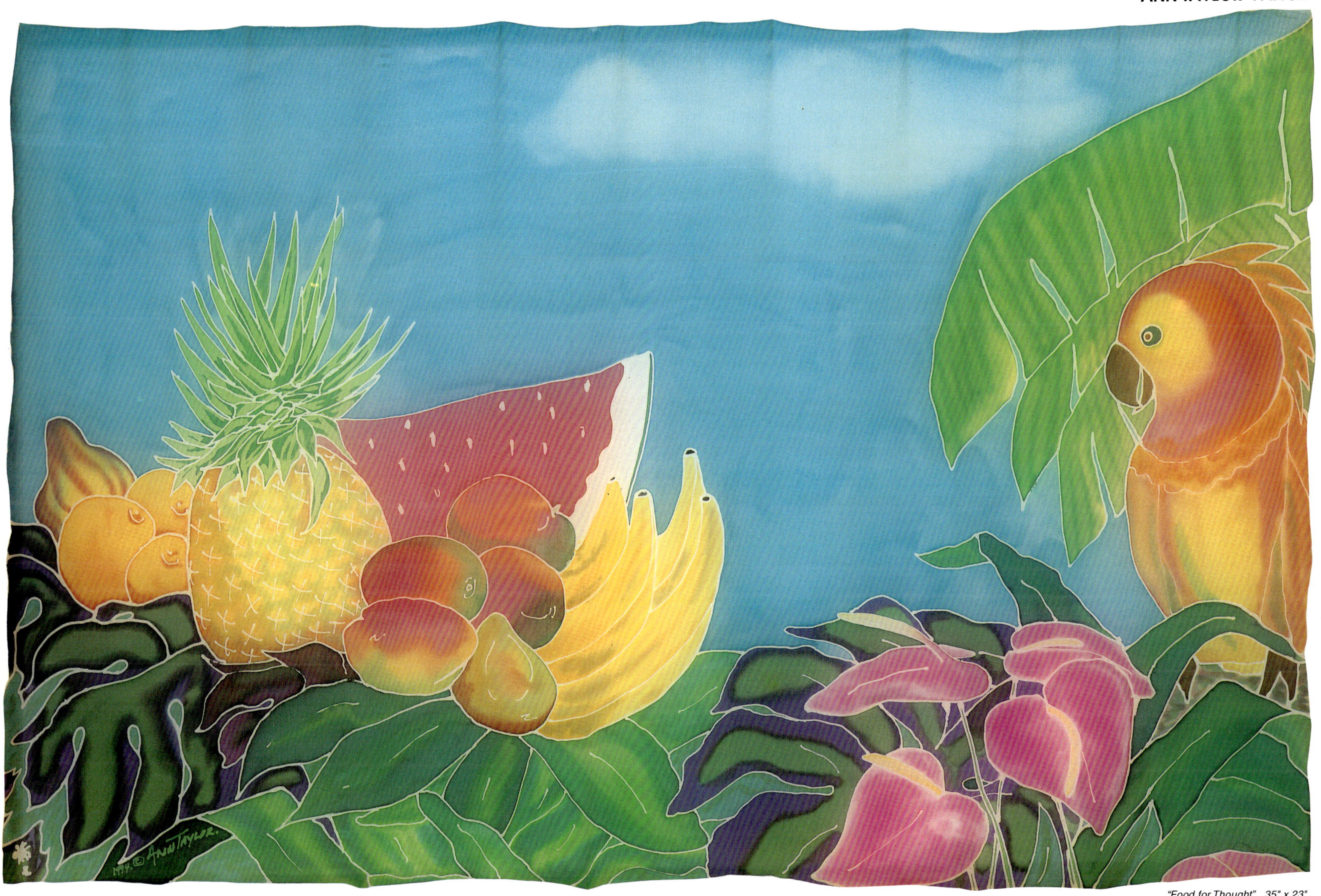

"Food for Thought" 35" x 23"
Batik on Silk

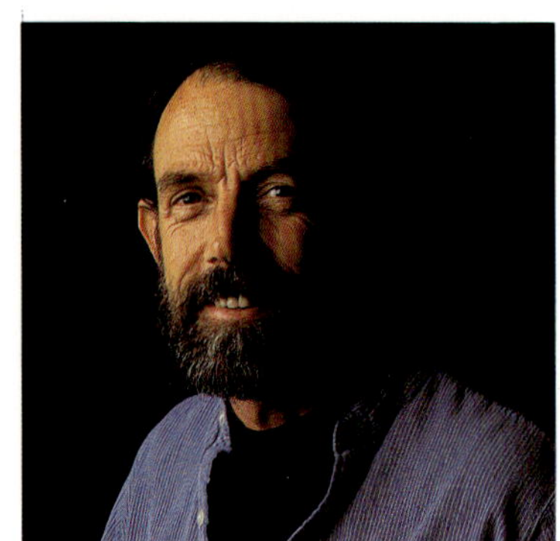

BRUCE TURNBULL

Sculpture Garden
R.R. 1, Box 151A
Wailuku, Maui, HI 96793
(808) 244-9838

Bruce Turnbull, for the better part of two decades, has lived and worked just a few miles from the rural village of Kahakuloa on Maui's rugged northeastern coast. It is the perfect setting for this master sculptor who takes his cues from nature and all things peaceful.

The clear, calm, disciplined oriental influence that is evident in the artist's demeanor is also evident in his work place. A subscriber to the Japanese concept of the importance of negative space, he purposefully leaves wood chips and sawdust on the floor of his studio. He tells us that "What you take away from a piece is as important as what's left when you're finished."

Turnbull's "dream" comes into focus in his sculpture garden. The land is, in fact, an ancient Hawaiian garden; the old stone walls almost hidden but still standing.

"I chose this place because of my alliance with nature. I need to fit in with nature, not exploit it. Everything fits out here. It's natural for me to live and work this way".

He moved to Maui in 1968, returning to San Jose State University in 1970 to study under renowned American sculptor Wendell Gates. The following year, Turnbull earned his Master's degree in Fine Arts, and his master's project - a dramatic bronze sculptor of a gymnast - today graces the government building in Wailuku, Maui's county seat.

It was during the time he returned to San Jose for his master's degree that Turnbull gathered the confidence one needs to make a living from art. And much of that confidence came from his teacher, Wendell Gates, who remained his advisor even after he had retired from teaching and Turnbull had returned to Maui. In December 1984, advanced Parkinson's disease forced Gates to retire from sculpting altogether. The following month, Turnbull received a gift: his teacher's tools; a kind of sculptor's torch being passed. Turnbull views it not only as an honor, but also as an awesome responsibility.

Of his work with wood, he says, "The design is already there. I simply bring it to life by taking away what hides it."

Because of its strength, Turnbull says, "Bronze allows me a greater range of interpretation. With bronze I can be more innovative. Bronze has a timeless quality which only improves with age". Written by Bonnie Friedman.

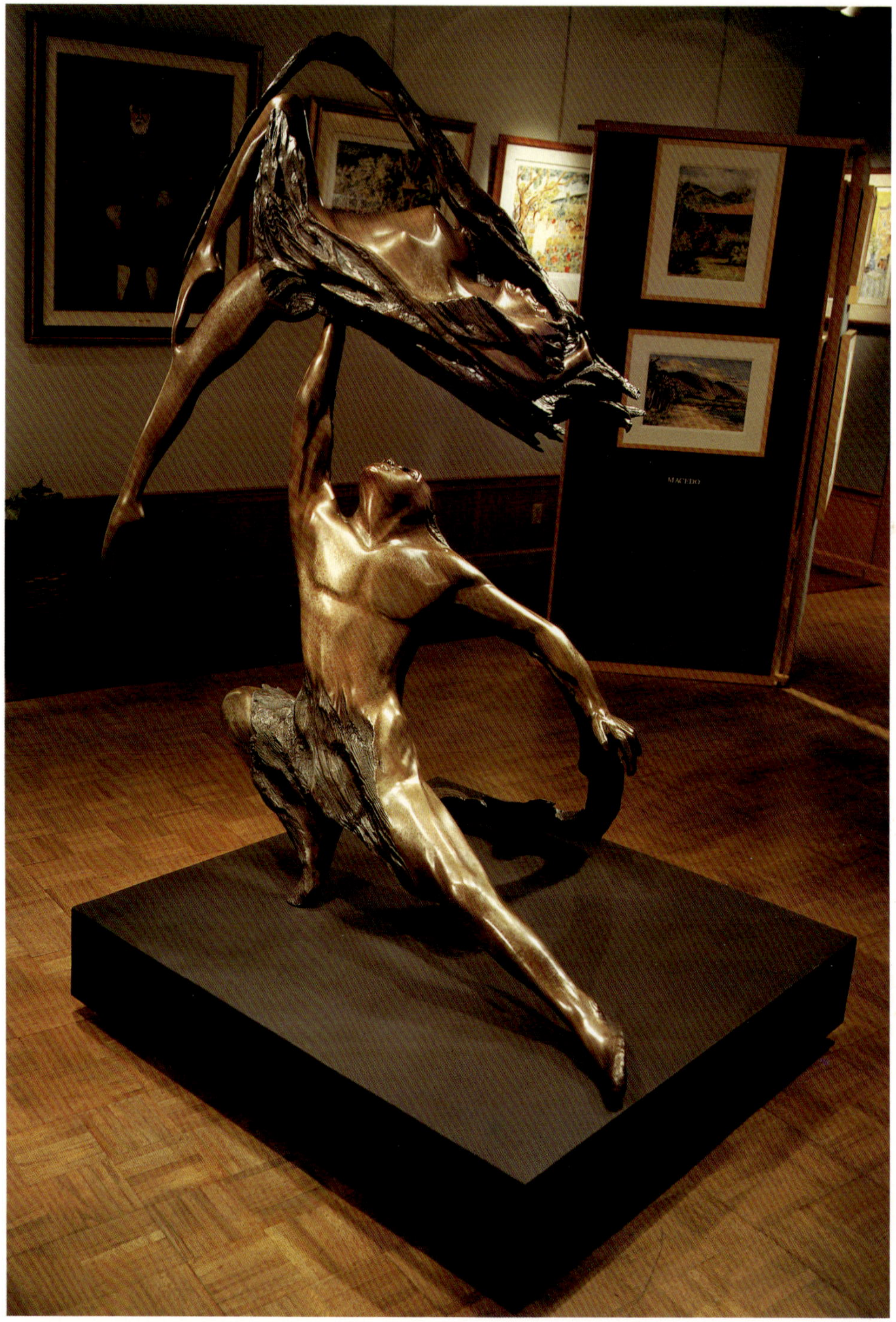

Photo By Steven Rea

"The Torch" Lifesize Outdoor Bronze Sculpture

"Snowcrane," Bronze, "Michiko" - (Top Figure) and "Garden Spirit" - (Kneeling Figure) Outdoor Lifesize Bronze Sculptures

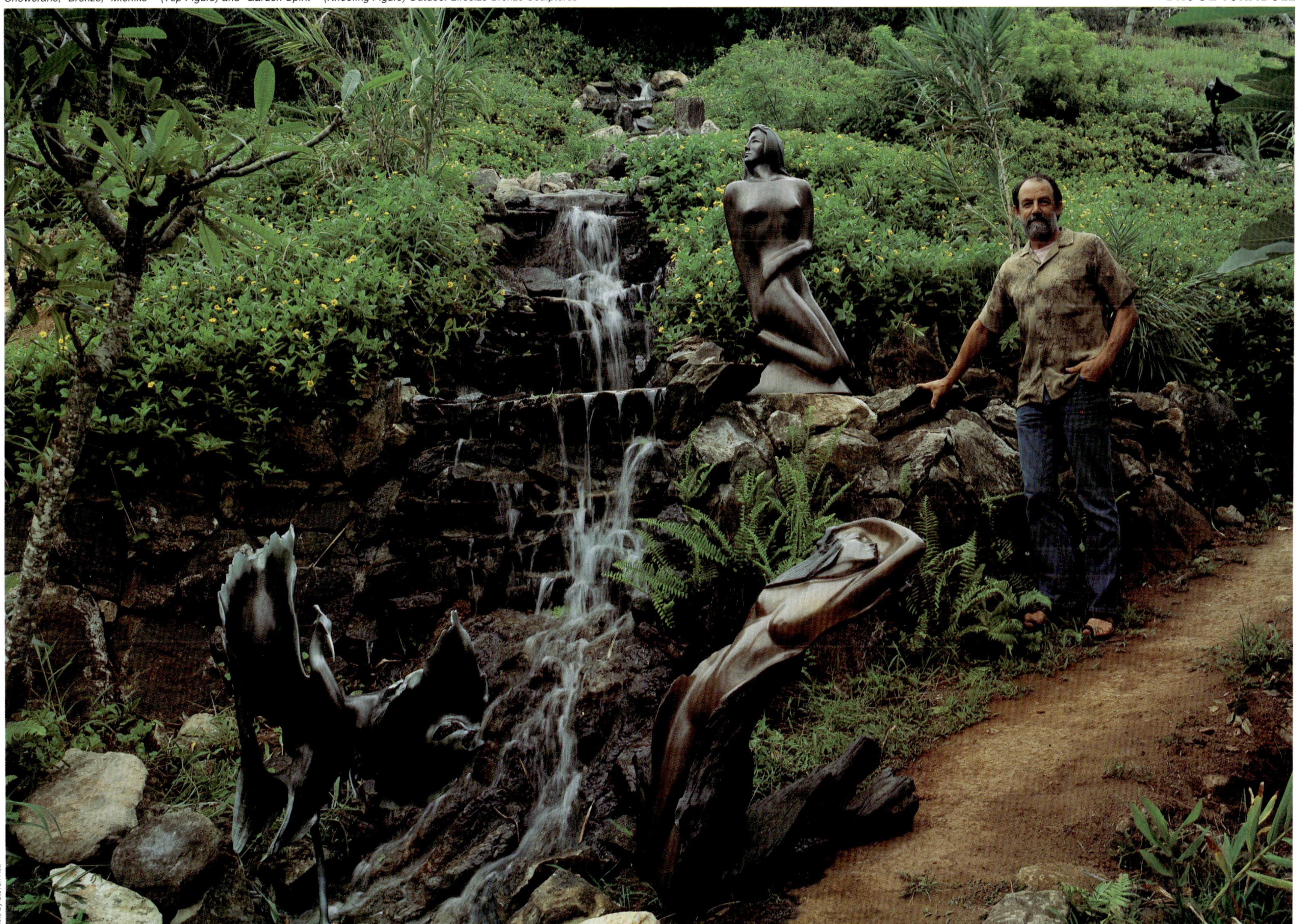

Photo By Steven Rea

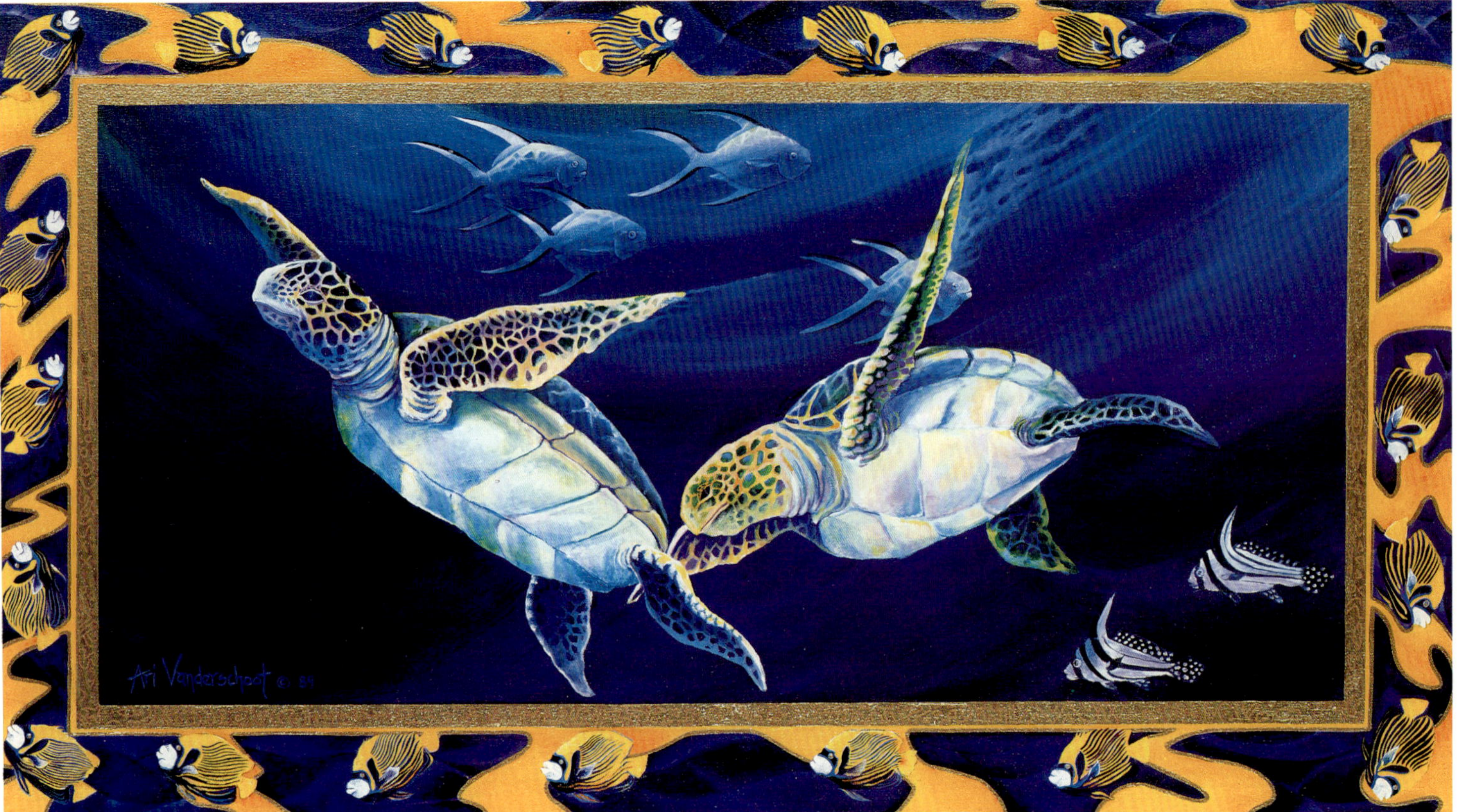

"First Love" 50" x 30" Original Acrylic Painting

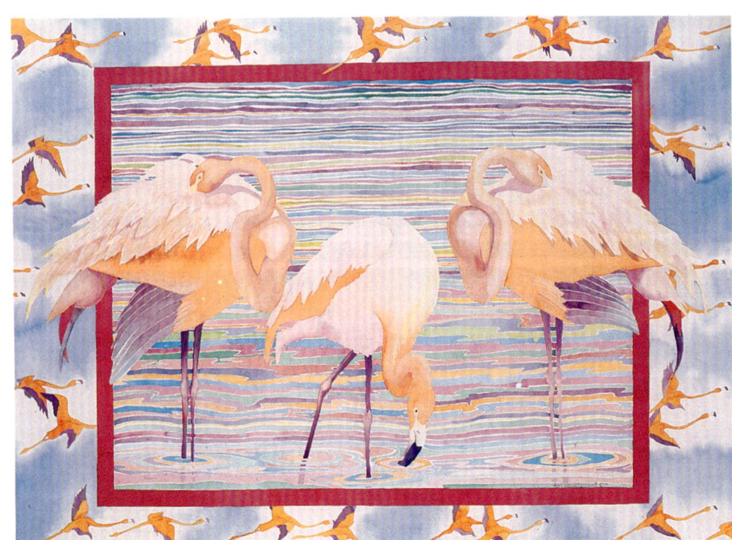

"Reflections of a Dream" 42" x 32" Original Watercolor Painting

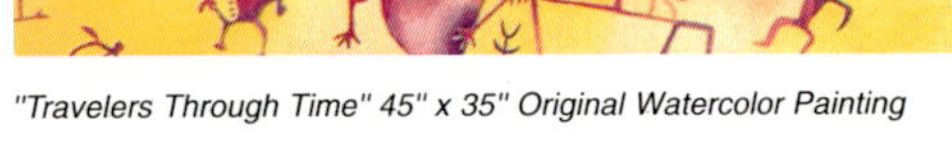

"Travelers Through Time" 45" x 35" Original Watercolor Painting

Opposite Page:
"Iao Valley" 40" x 45" Original Acrylic Painting, Posters Available

ARI VANDERSCHOOT

Ari Vanderschoot spent her childhood in the Bahamas where much of her time was spent roaming the islands on horseback and exploring the undersea world of fishes and fantasy. In her work today, this childhood freedom lives on.

Her paintings display a rich blend of a spicy Caribbean flavor and sweet Polynesian aroma that stimulates one's creative appetite. Love and fascination of life's infinite wonders are her inspiration. Her ultimate goal, she says, is to be balanced at all times, and to inspire others to attain this bliss so that together we can work towards bringing our one and only Earth back into balance as well.

"I've been painting a lot of marine art lately... expressing the ocean's timeless wisdom. Amazed by nature's power & beauty. I am beginning to understand. Moving towards the statement to divert it's destruction. I often use the animals as messengers of peace and balance."

Ari works with the environmental groups Green Peace, Cousteau Society, Pele'Defence and The Dolfin & Whale Foundation.

P.O Box 699
Makawao, Maui, Hawaii 96768
(808) 878-2690

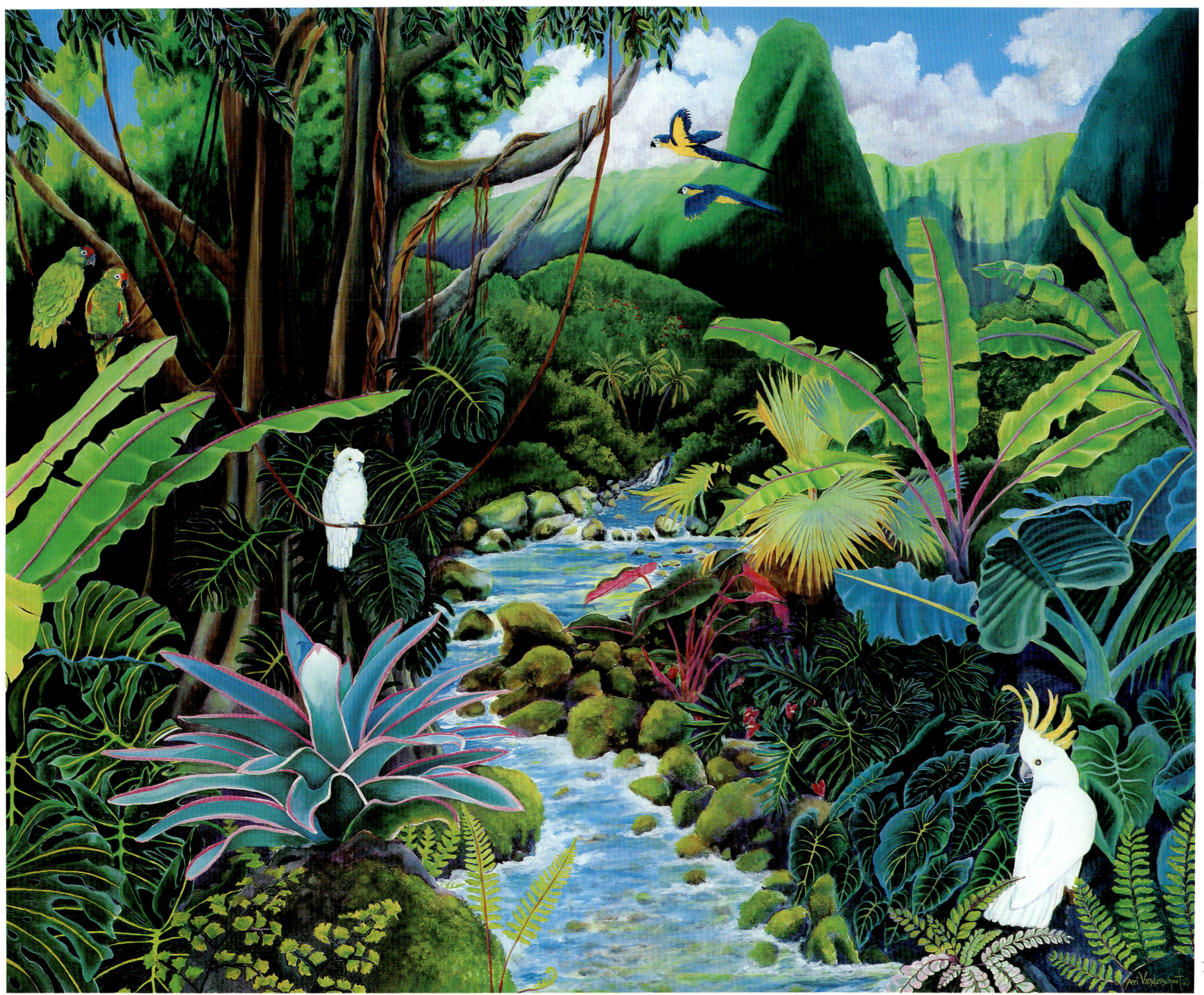

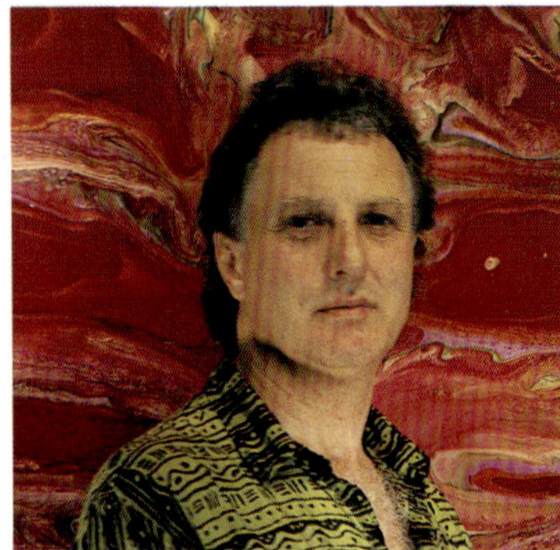

ÉLAN VITAL

The Creator of *Metarealism*, Élan Vital's creative genius has synergized in beautiful paintings which are alive with radiant organic colorfields of metarealistic visions that transport the viewer into and through magical, mystical, spiritual and energetic worlds that are both familiar and new.

Élan's metarealistic visions illuminate, examine and give honor to the underlying forces that cause things to be. If one found a photo taken through a telescope of the earth from outer space or a photo through a microscope focused on a single cell, one may think this is a photo of an abstract painting. However, these "abstractions" are truly an expanded view of macro and micro worlds beyond our normal vision.

Scientists can now determine the entire look of an organism or being by examining its DNA blueprint.

Élan believes that this vision of the underlying forces inherent in all things make it possible to

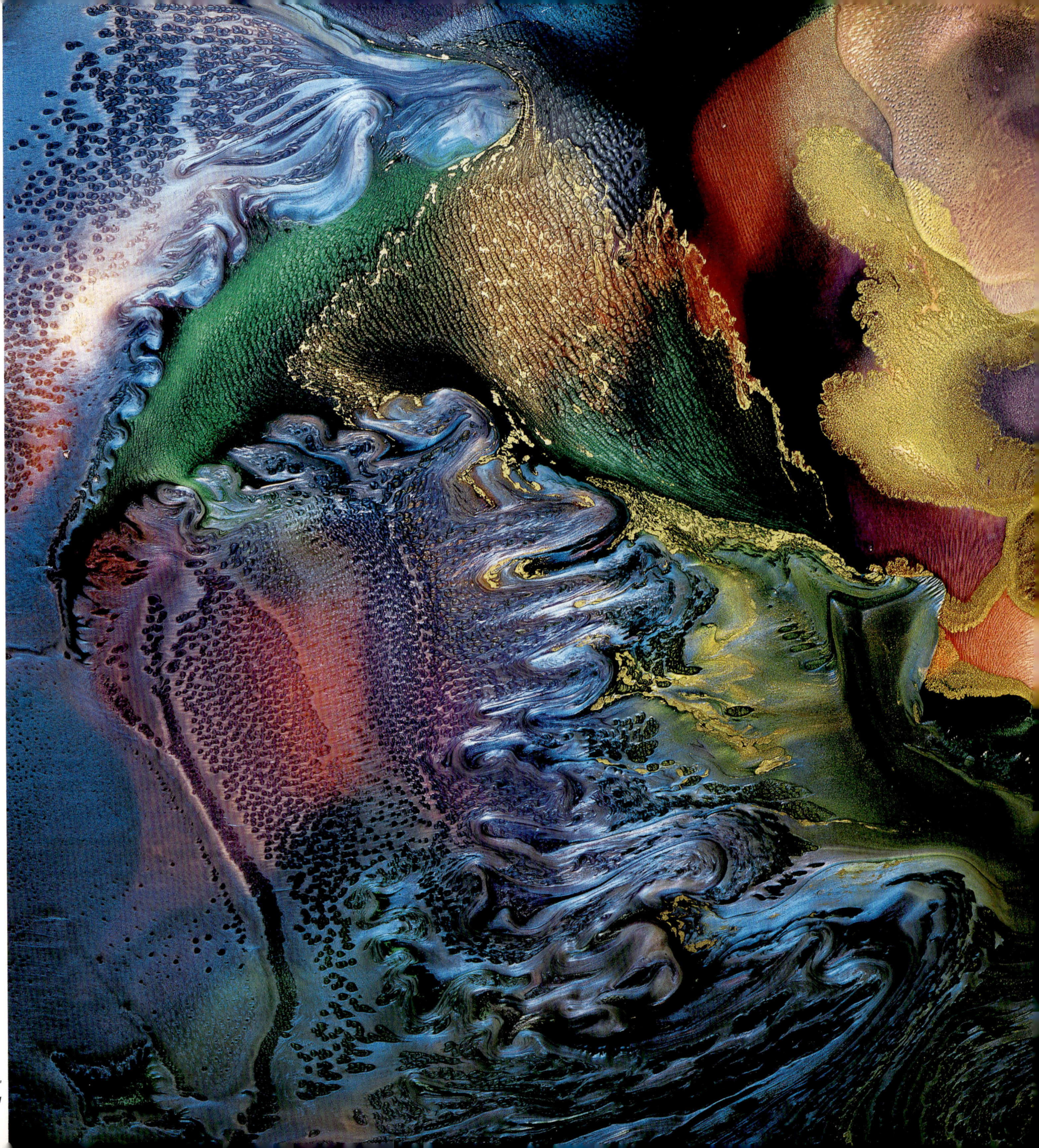

"Bliss" 40" x 40"
Original Oil Painting

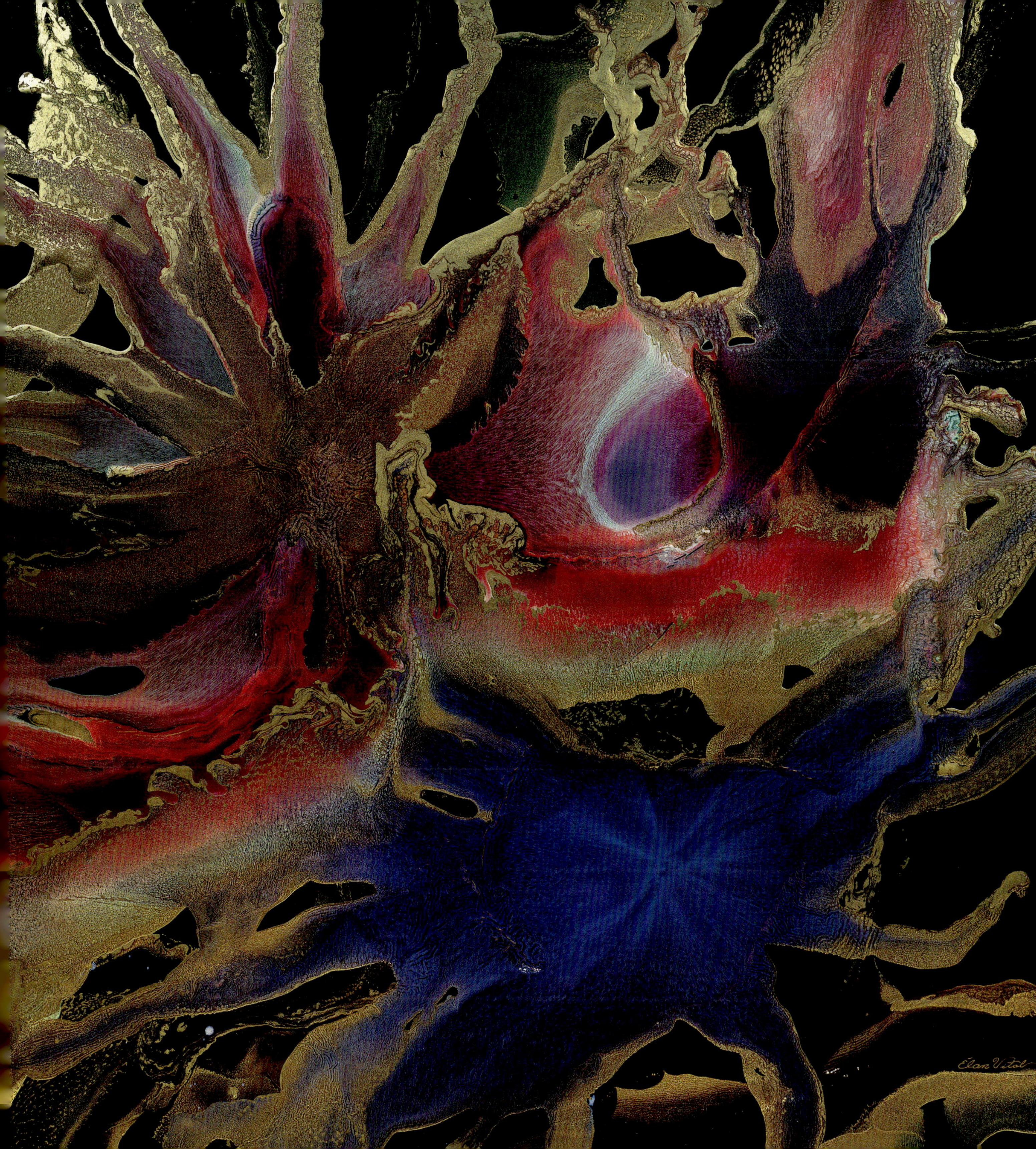

represent the river by its flow, the tree by the process of its growth, the mineral or organisms by its metamorphosis.

To further the concept of an expanded vision, Élan desired to look below the surface at beauty, hence The Creation of a... *Gemstone Palette.* Throughout the ages, the rare brilliance of gemstone colorations have motivated, challenged and eluded artistic efforts to capture and replicate the luminosity of emerald greens, ruby reds, sapphire blues, opalescence pearlessence, aquamarine, etc.

Élan noted that these wondrous colors existed only within depths of a jewel, through a transparent or translucent base. The colors are a combined effect of transparent layering and light passing back to the eye. A search to find a transparent base ended in a clear honey-thick *Aerospace Enamel* that allowed Élan to disperse and layer pigments of finely ground metals, copper bronze, mica, etc, just as nature does when creating gemstones.

Plaguerizing nature further, Élan created a technique called... *Interaction Painting*. Whereas action-painting impresses the semi-calligraphic signature of artists such as Jackson Pollack upon the canvas, Élan's technique takes into account the chemical actions and natural proclivities of the paint while he leads the paint in a "Dance of Creation".

"Golden Orchid" 40" x 40"
Original Oil Painting

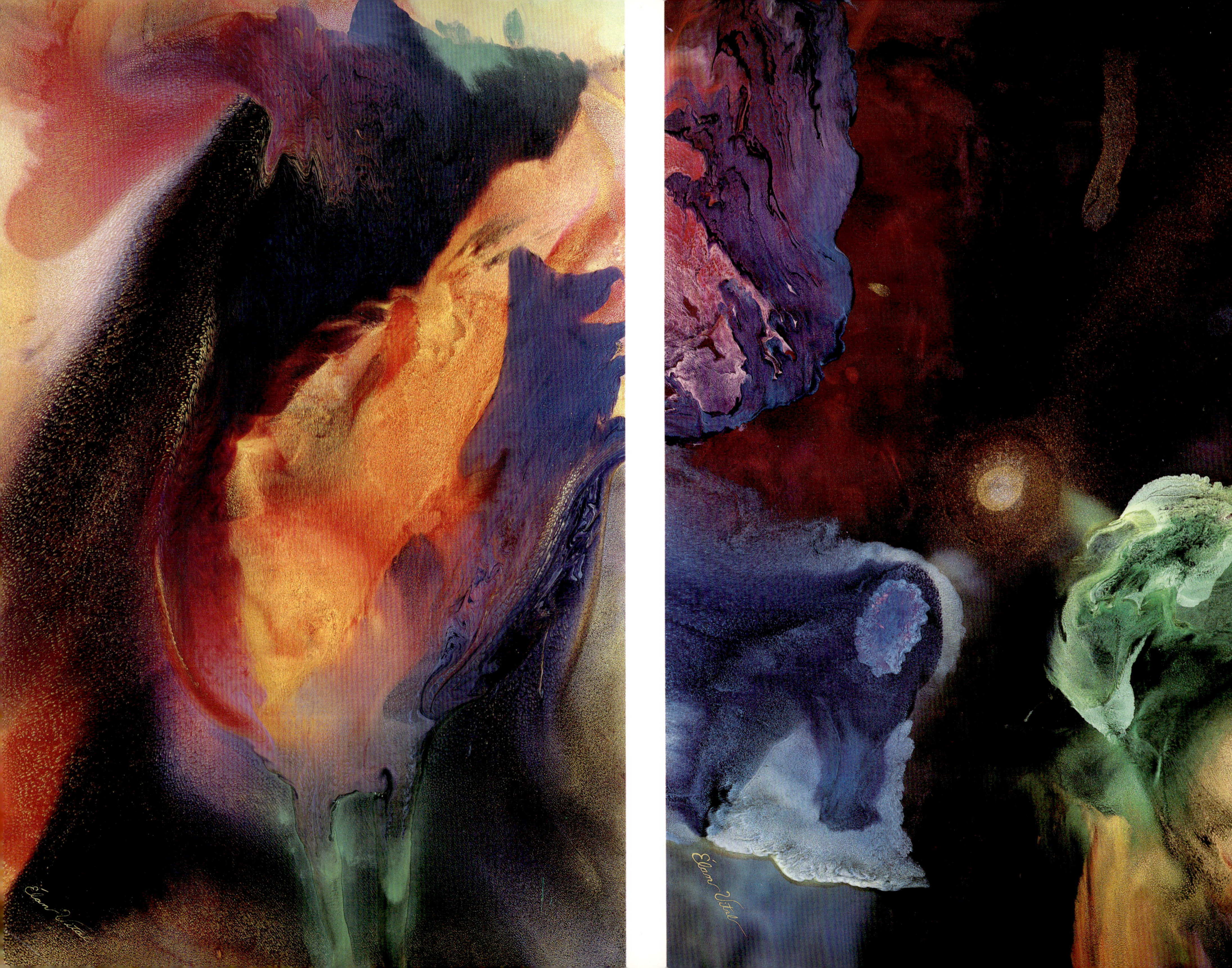

ÉLAN VITAL

"Wild Orchid" 40" x 40"
Original Oil Painting

The "Nectars of Gems" as Élan calls his paints are poured, dripped, sprayed, blown, squirted and injected onto a horizontal canvas by means of hypodermic needles, squeeze bottles, turkey basters, air guns, etc. The canvasses are often shaped from the back causing hills and valleys which assist the nectars to flow in desired paths naturally. The canvas is manipulated, shapes are added, and or removed as the work evolves and while lakes or rivers of liquid color harden and skin over, they can be further manipulated by infra-red light to elongate or stretch the "skin" or cellular structure.

Pigments are colorful chemicals which react in predictable ways when placed in proximity to one another. Some dominate , some accept, some repel, others blend.

Élan has studied these inter-actions and uses this knowledge to allow the paint to express itself without dominating his partner, the paint, in the "Dance of Creation" he leads. This "partnership" results in colors maintaining their own radiancy, never being muddied by being forced to mix with other colors as a brush would do.

Luminous Limited Editions... The problem of creating limited editions that vie with Élan's originals was solved by metal dyes which are photographically suspended in a mylar film producing rich vibrant colors that have a depth.

Opposite Page Left Side:
"After Glow" 40" x 60" Original Oil Painting

Opposite Page Right Side:
"Stardust Nebula" 40" x 60" Original Oil Painting

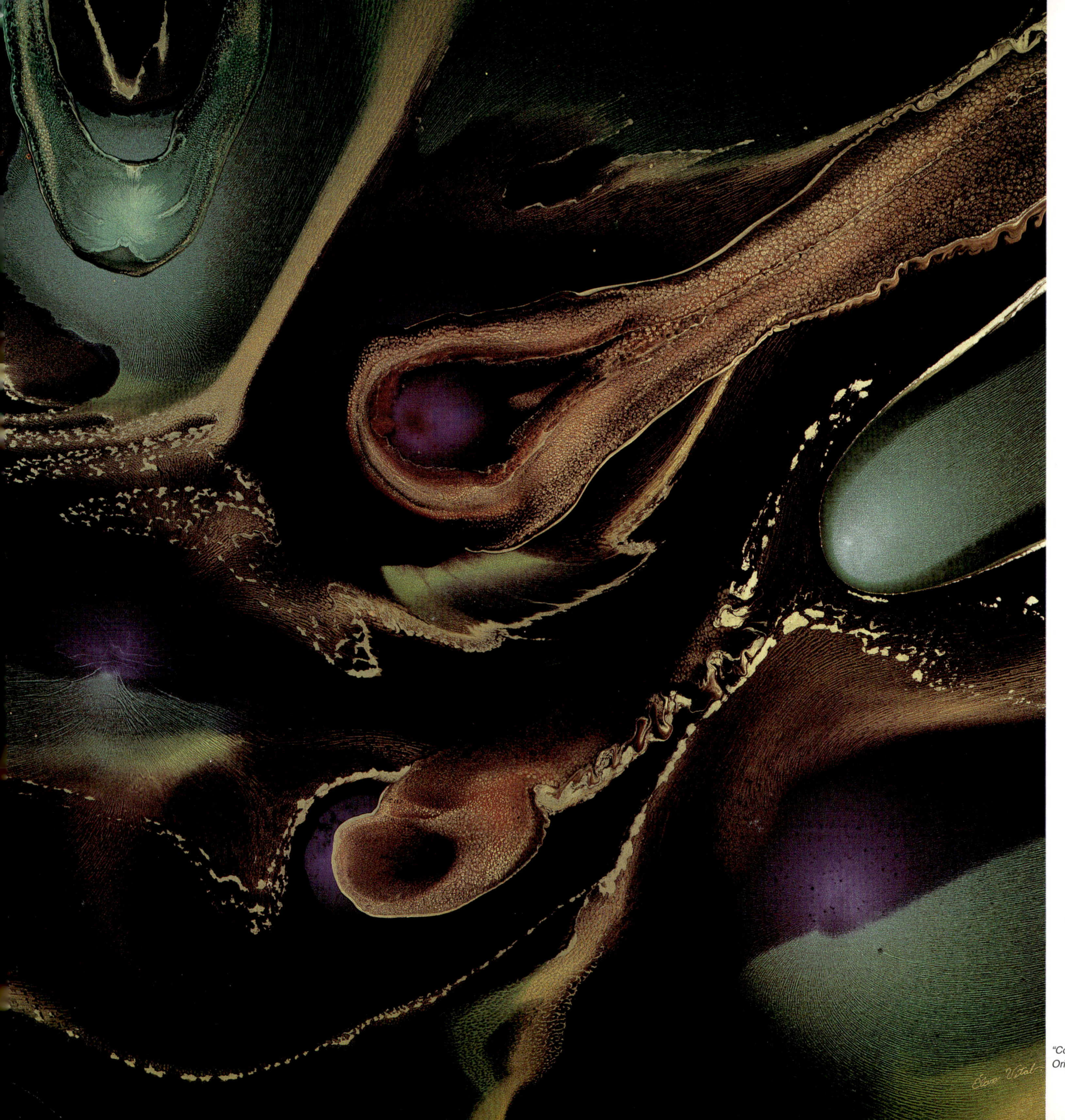

"Comets Tales" 40" x 40"
Original Oil Painting

ÉLAN VITAL

Élan is involved in every step from producing portraits of his originals with an 8"x 10" bellows camera, as well as darkroom work, enlargements and creating his own framing and formats.

LUMÉLANS... With his new signed and numbered backlit editions, he fulfills his philosophy of the healing quality of art. Full spectrum light is emanated by the interaction of light through transparent color-fast metai dye films stretched over a box frame containing special fluorescent bulbs. Understanding the healing power of light, the German government has a policy to use only full spectrum light in their hospitals, schools and institutions.

Élan Vital grew up in New York City, the son of a lithographer and as such was exposed to art color theory and process at an early age. His discovery of Leonardo DaVinci's renaissance diversity first touched Élan at the age of seven and became a major influence in Élan's life.

Élan went to a special high school for gifted children and graduated with the equivalency of an Associate degree in Engineering.

At 19 years old, Élan was hired by IBM Corporation as a computer diagnostics expert, then by ITT as design engineer for projects such as the Manila airport underground lighting system as well as designing towers for a hydroelectric dam in Pakistan.

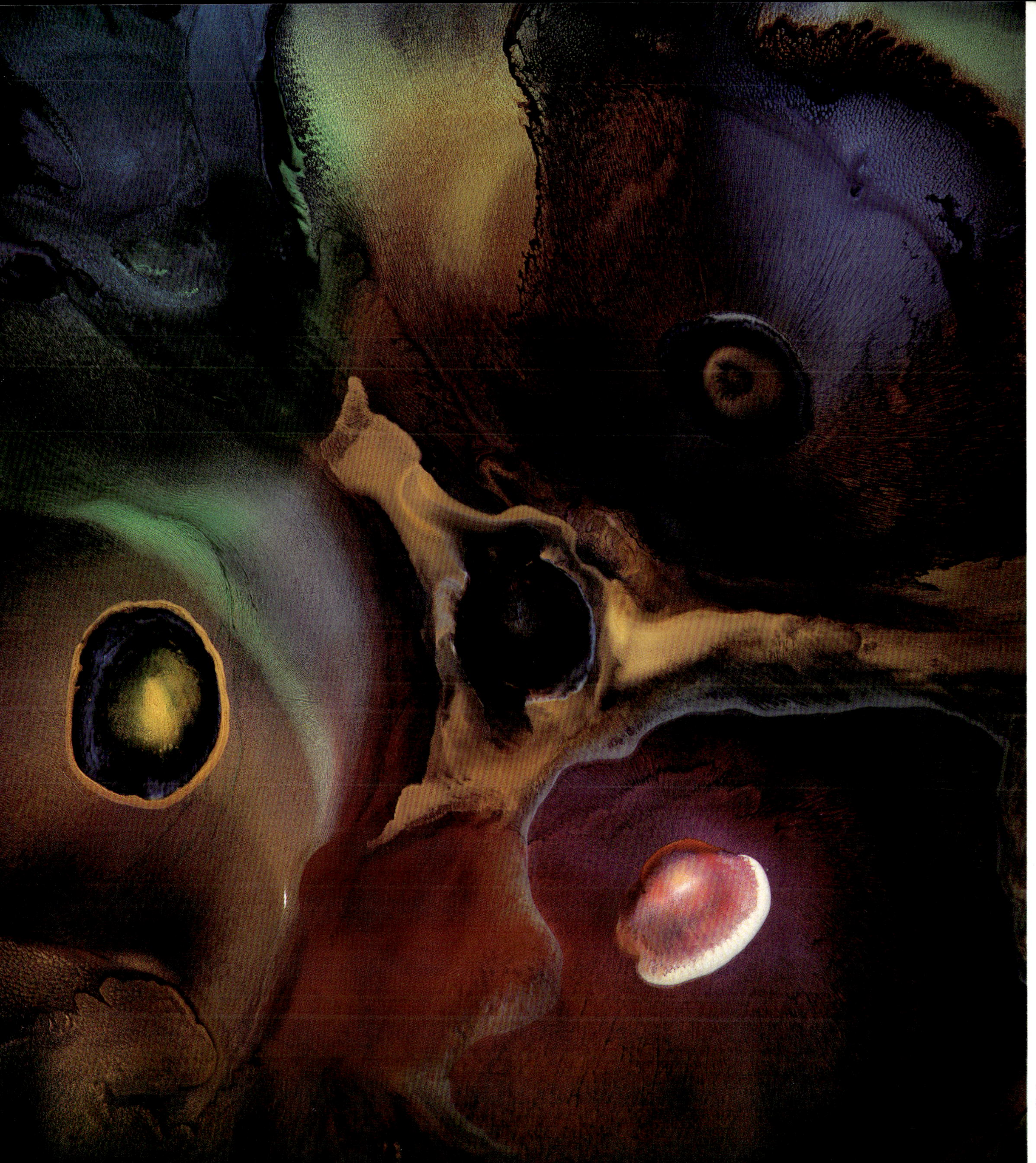

ÉLAN VITAL

The big switch toward art occurred after he dropped out and joined a commune in East Village, Manhattan. It was there while he was designing psychedelic lighting equipment, that he met Andy Warhol. Andy put up the money for Élan to design the first psychedelic discotheque on St. Marks Place, New York. This became the springboard for many artistic leaps combining invention and art which led to his moving to Maui in January 1988.

Élan's first major work here was to sculpt the largest sculpture in Hawaii - a 46' long, 10 ton, life size, humpback whale and donate this to establish Ecology Park in Kihei, Maui where it is now on permanent prominent display.

After completing this true to life monumental sculpture, Élan turned his attention to expanding the scope of Hawaii's art scene by successfully introducing cutting edge art.

During 1993-94, Élan Vital has sold more original oil paintings than any other artist on Front Street in Lahaina. When asked why? Élan Vital replied, "My patrons tell me it's the beauty of the life-force within that lifts their spirits and makes them want to share their home with it."

Represented by Addi Galleries -Lahaina, Maui and Collectors Fine Art, Hyatt Regency, Kauai.

171 Pauwela Road
Haiku, Maui, HI 96793
(808)575-9736 Tel/Fax (808) 242-0089

"Resurrection" 40" x 40"
Original Oil Painting

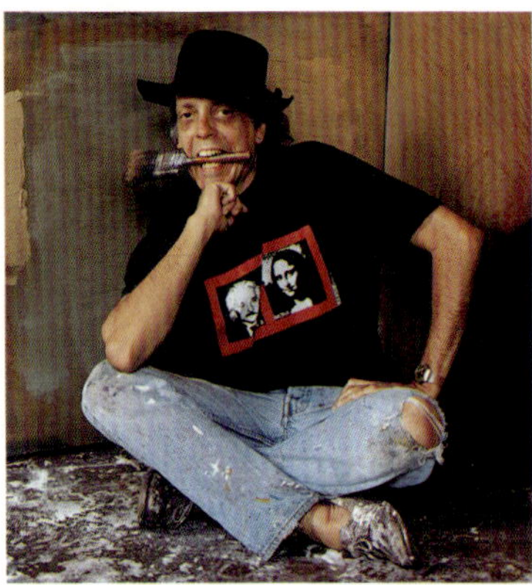

Tony Walholm

11 Ho'opalua Drive
Pukalani, Maui, Hawaii 96768
(808) 572-1543

This prolific painter, printmaker and teacher was born in Honolulu in 1945, the fifth generation of a Maui Portuguese family. Tony makes his home on the slopes of Haleakala on the island of Maui in a setting of rural beauty, close to the nature which forms such a strong inspiration for his abstract works of elegance and subtle evocative power. "If one can see past the beauty of the landscape you realize what an intensely strong and warm light there is here. It infuses everything, it is very similar to that of the Mediterranean. I absolutely love it!" states the artist; though as an artist, his references to nature or to landscape are never deliberate nor direct. Marcia Godinez, art writer for the Maui News, has written: "...for this artist has climbed inside his subject matter and reduced it to undiluted essence."

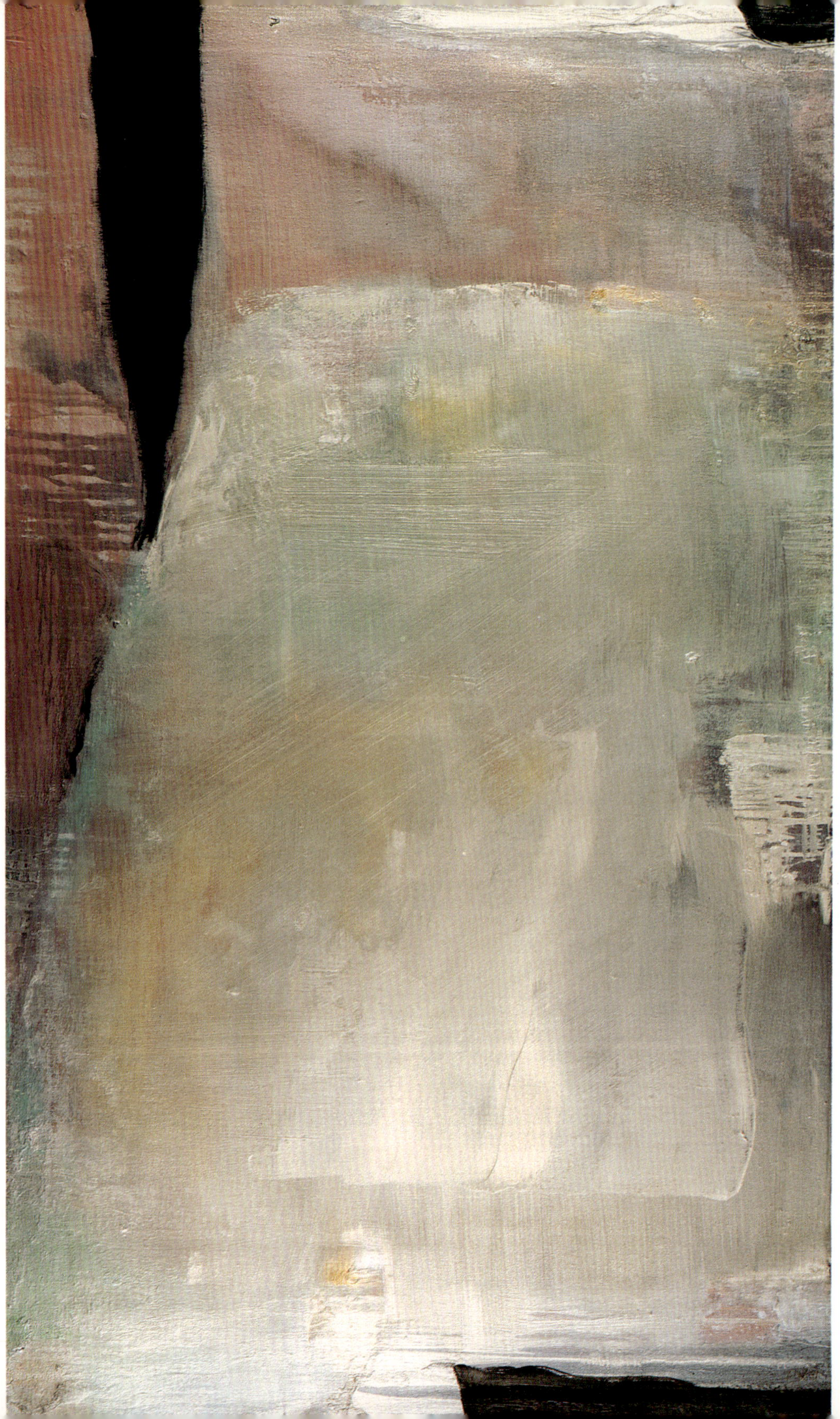

"Vessel #2, LASCAUX"
Original Oil Painting 5' x 3'

Tony Walholm

It can be said that Tony's a painter's painter. In his work the formal concerns of surface, picture plane, the velocity of the brush stroke, and the impact of color hold dialogue with artist and audience to reveal beneath this composite structure of the process of painting, an image that connects with our common humanity. Though highly charged, aesthetically, this is not mere decoration, but fraught with the struggles and victories life affords. "I think works of art can be seen as 'footprints' left behind by one who lives a conscious and examined life" he suggests. The combined influences of his abiding interest in psychology, mythology and poetry are apparent in his work, which drew the attention of Joseph Campbell who stated, "I see that you, too, are in the service of the White Goddess." Duane Preble, Professor Emeritus at the Department of Art, University of Hawaii, and author of the book *Artforms* has said that Tony has achieved one of the most difficult things to achieve in art today, that is, to have mastered the visual language of Abstract Expressionism; yet having found his own voice, he reveals a style immediately recognizable as his own, resulting in powerfully strong works of "substance, subtlety and beauty."

"Vessel #3, TANG"
Original Oil Painting 4' x 4'

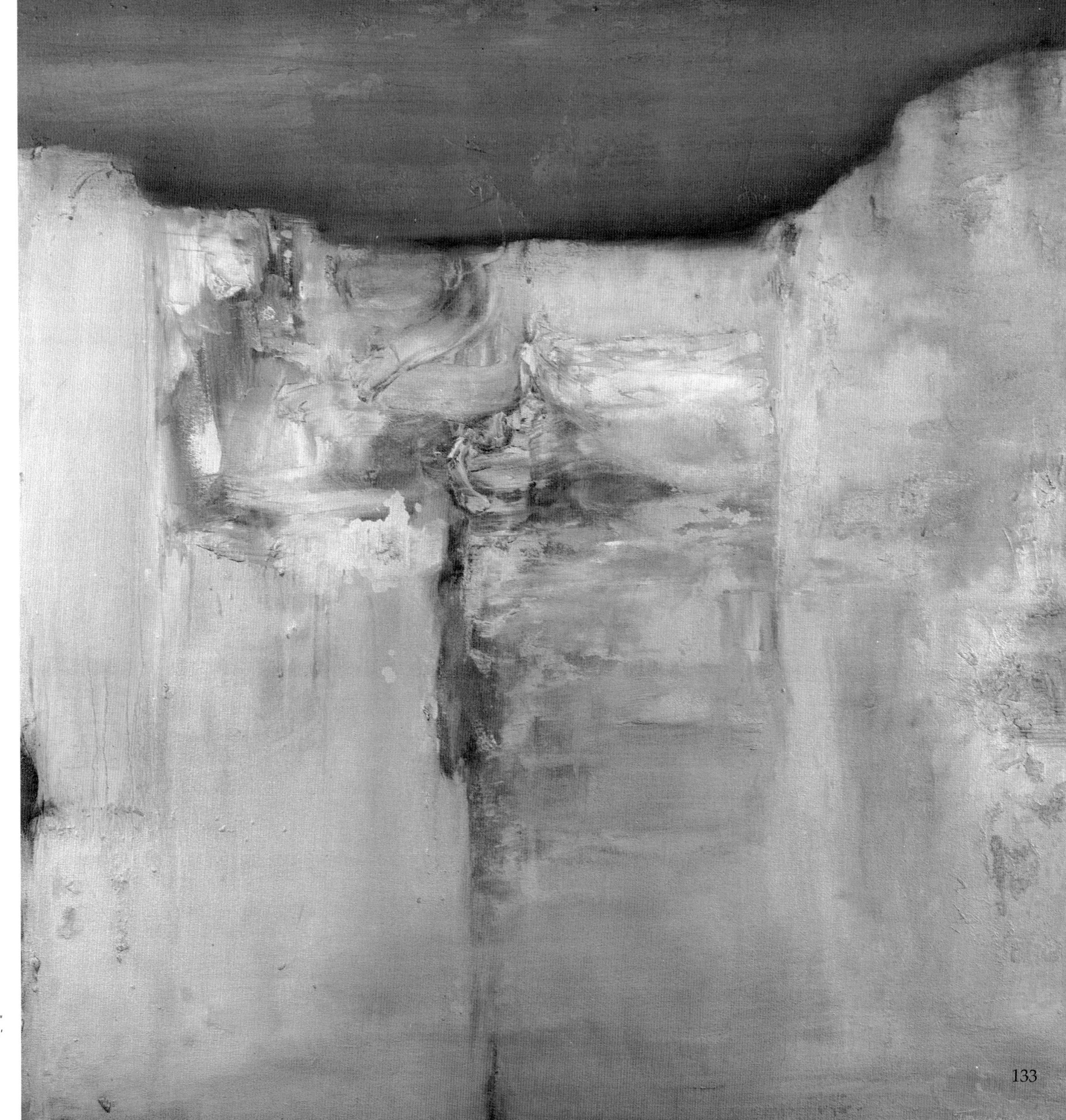

Tony Walholm

"Red, Gold, Blue" 3' 10" x 5' Original Oil Painting

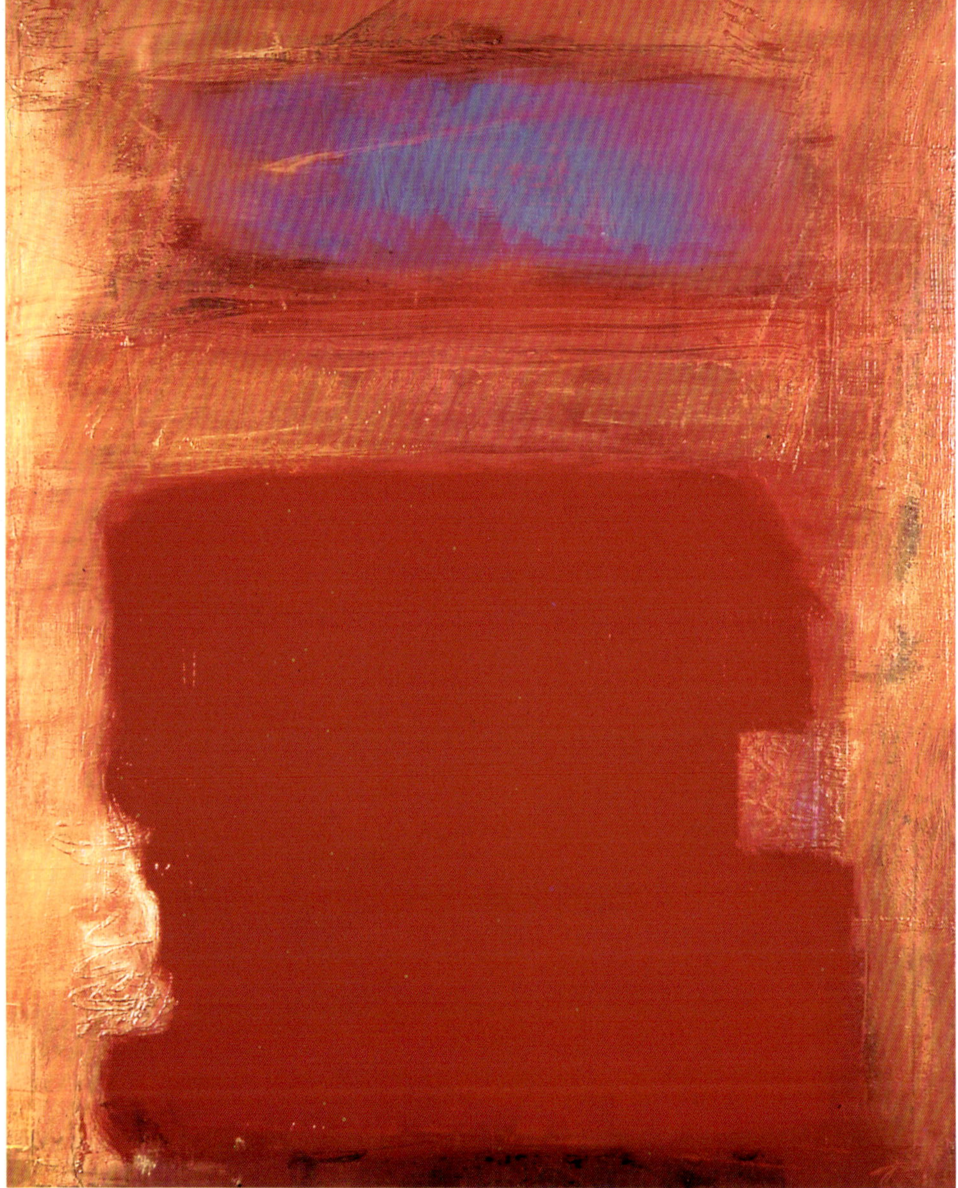

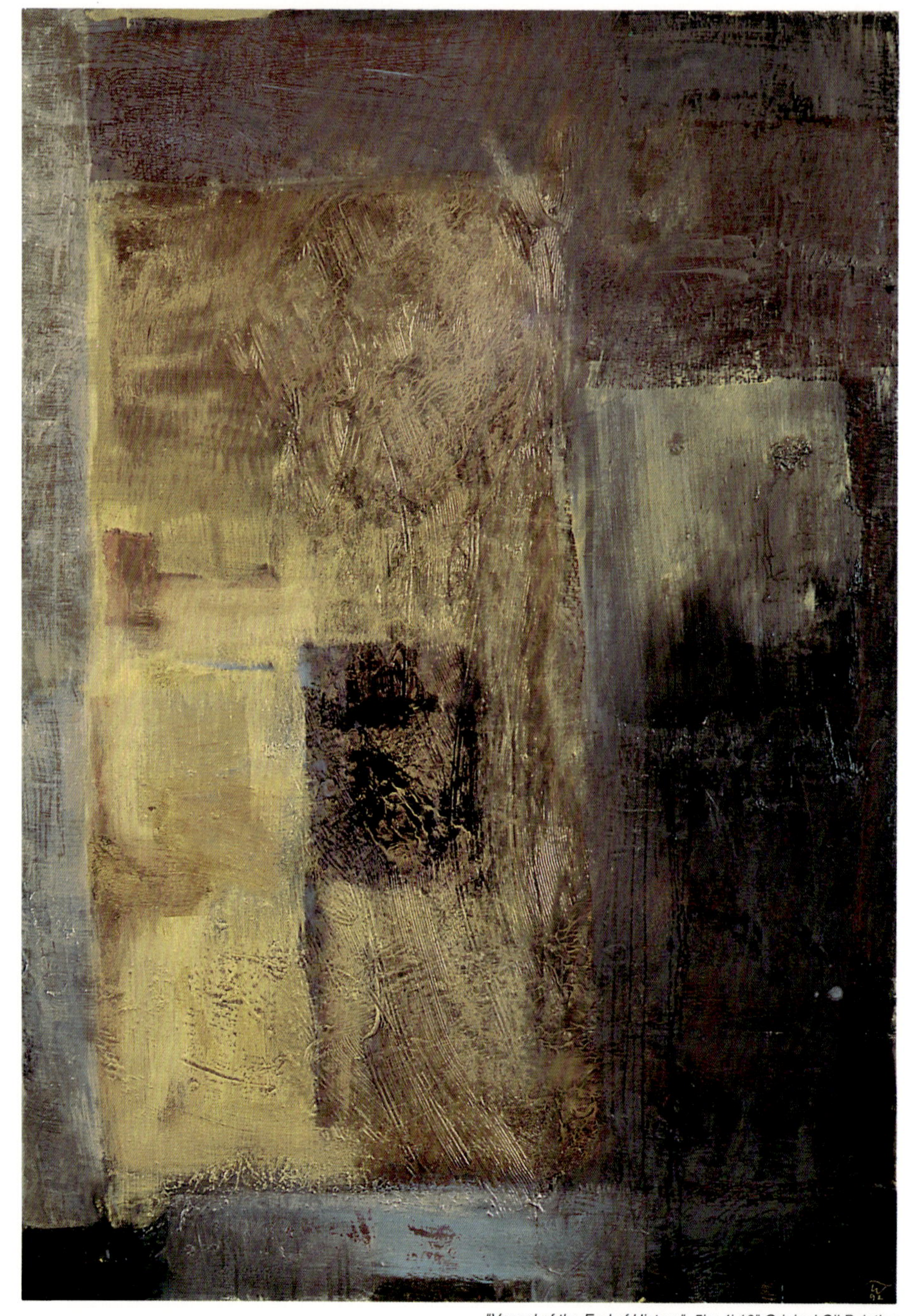

"Vessel of the End of History" 5' x 4' 10" Original Oil Painting

Tony feels he made a breakthrough in 1992 with the series of paintings known as the Vessel Series. "It was not so much a breakthrough in technique or approach so much as a shift in how I saw these works as relating to me and to the viewer outside my studio. I saw the work not on a metaphoric or a symbolic level, but as being a vessel, a container of energy, which is to be

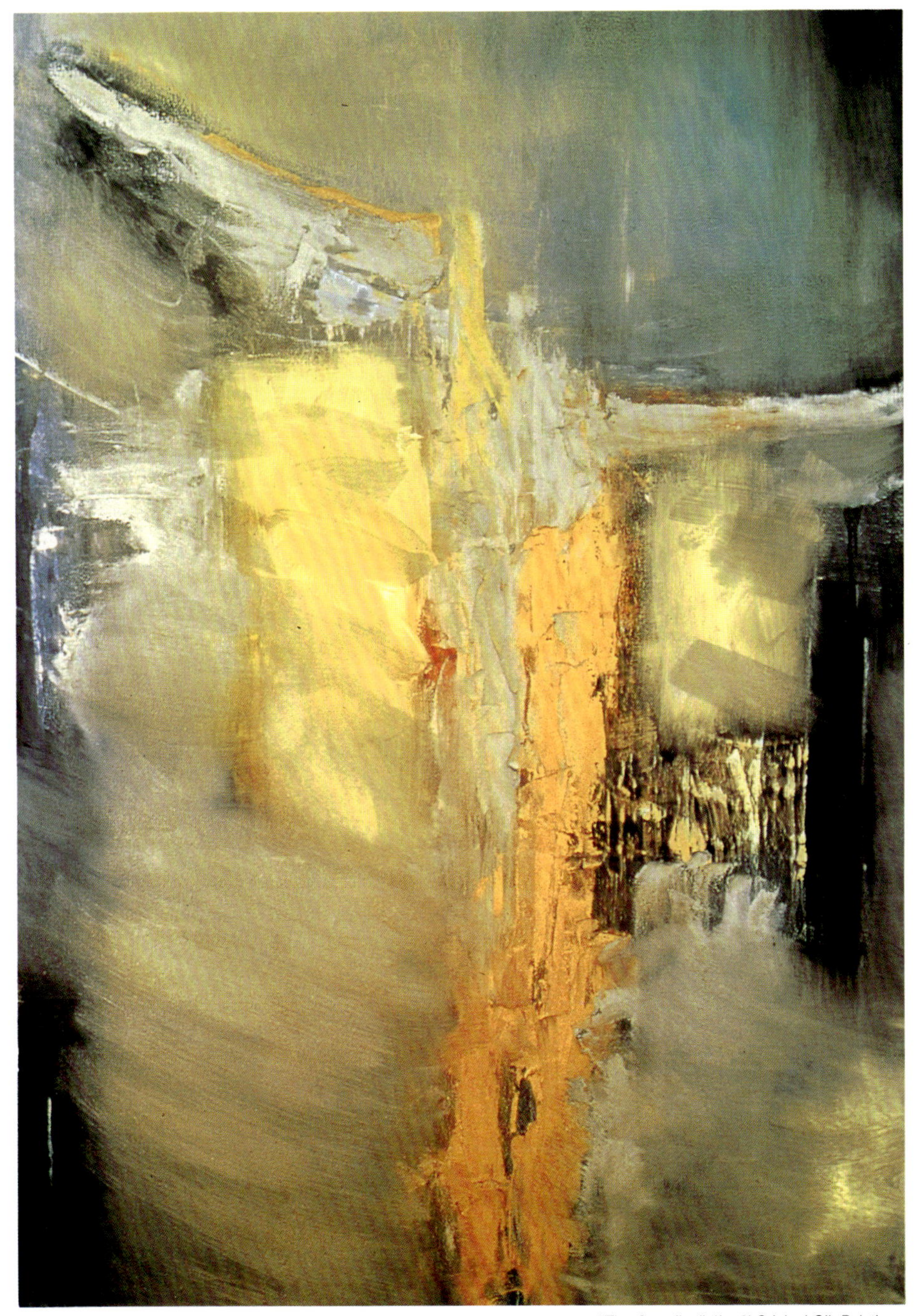

"The Guardian" 4' x 6' Original Oil Painting

"Red with Black Dot" 4' x 6' Original Oil Painting

transmitted to the viewer through active perception of color and form." As such, the artist saw the possibility for art opening up a sacred space with none of the trappings of the past.

When a monumental painting was needed to grace the mezzanine landing of the Maui Community Arts and Culture Center's main

Tony Walholm

Tony Walholm

"Quartet For The End Of Time" Original Oil Painting, Four Panels 2' x 6' 8", L to R "Shrine", "The Well At The World's End", "Night Sea Journey", "Mediteranian"

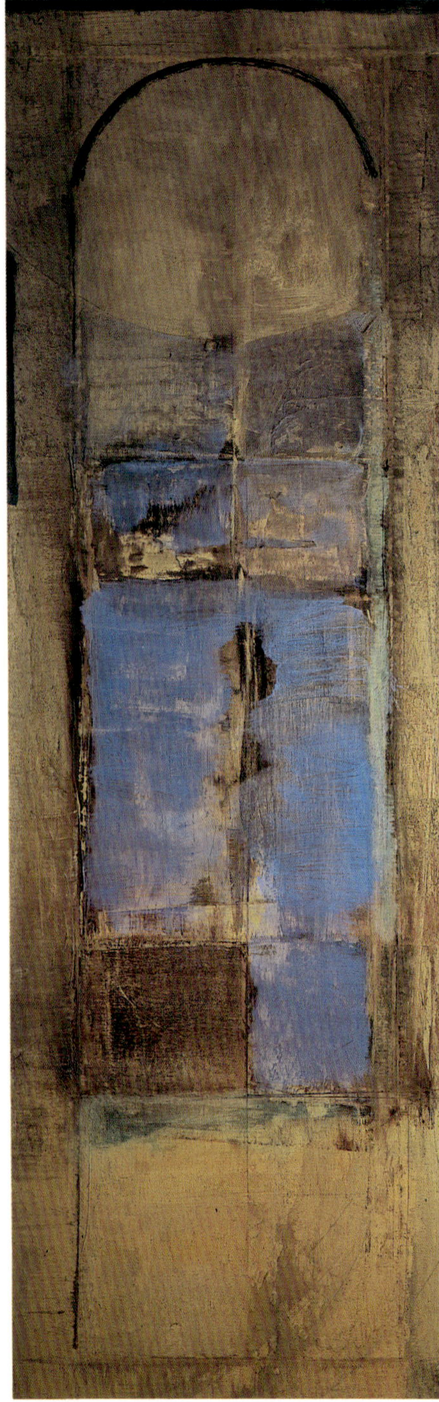

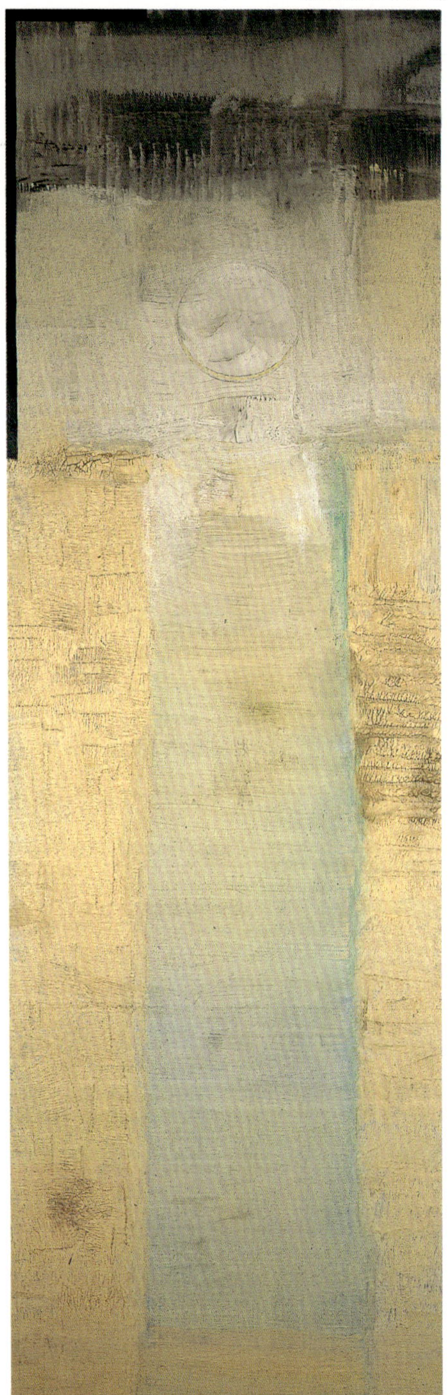

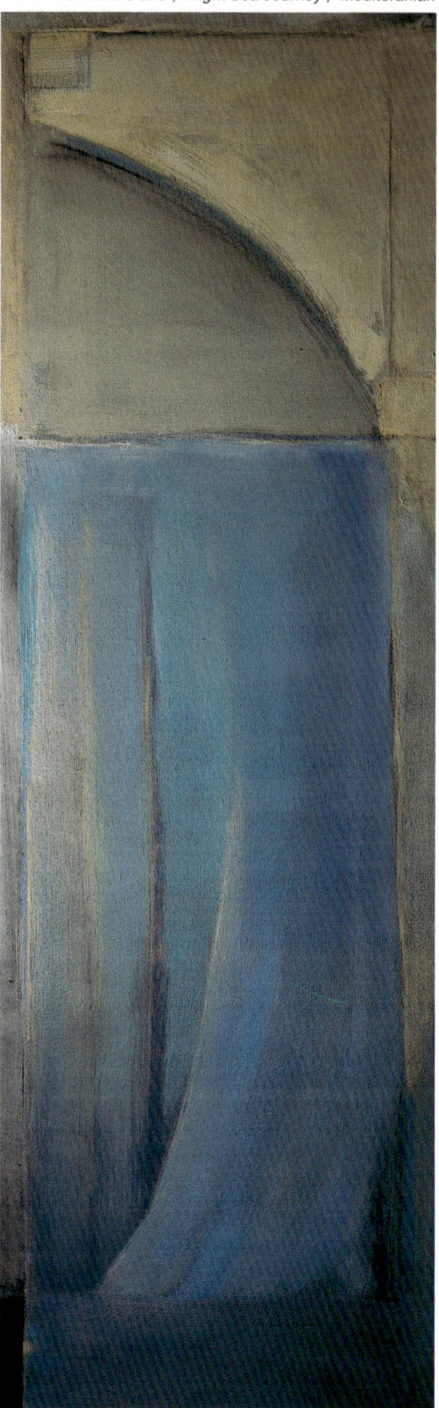

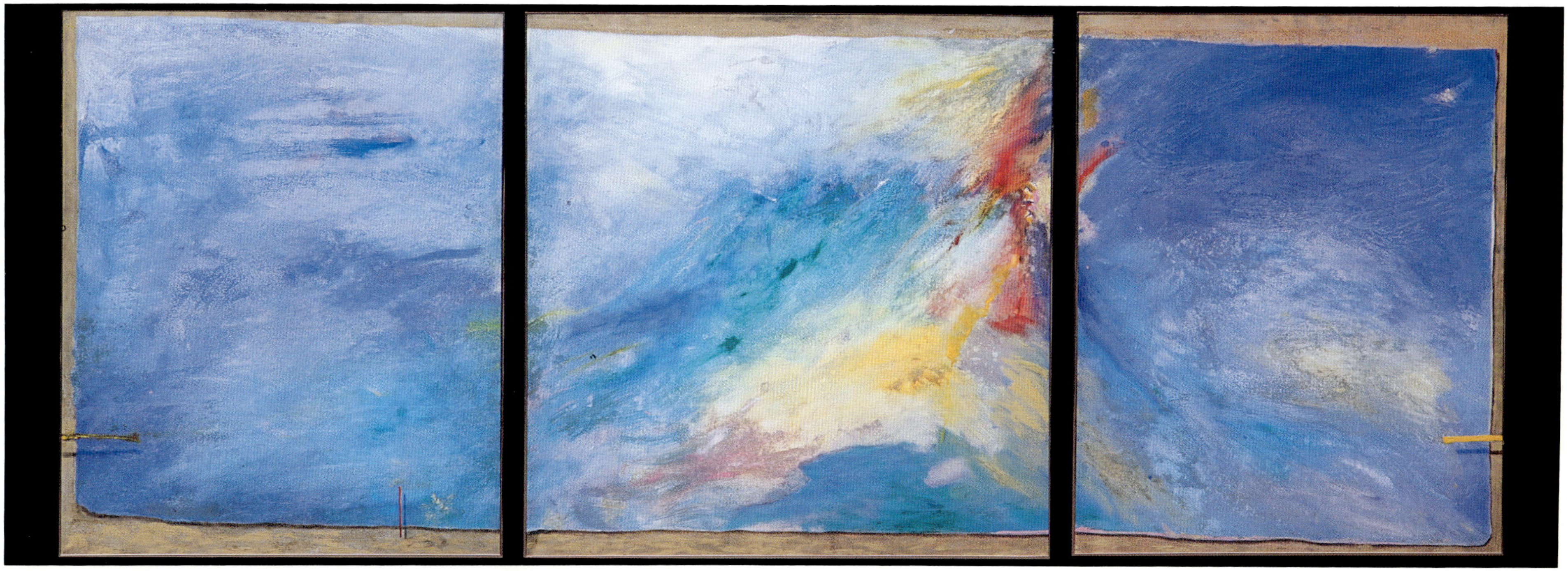

"Pacifica Tryptych"
3' x 10' 6" Original Oil Painting

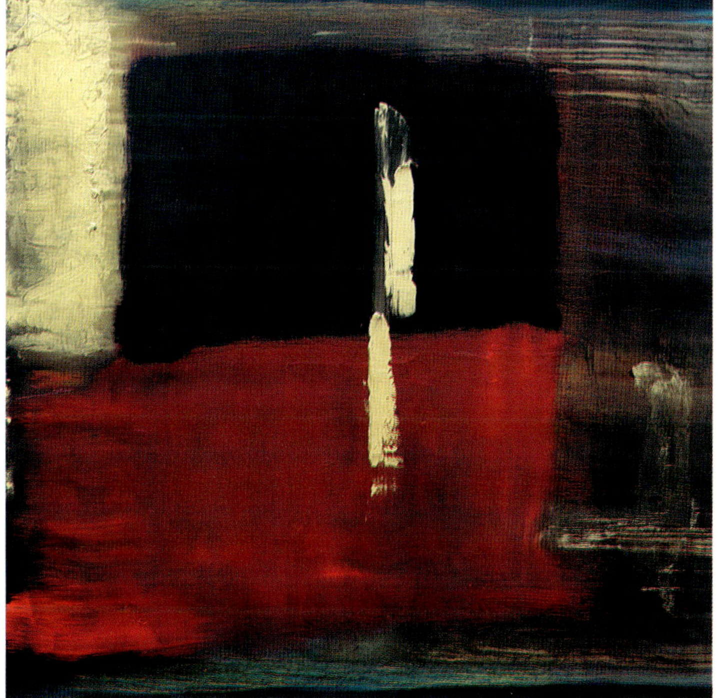

"The Hero Speaks"
4' x 4' Original Oil Painting

theater, it was Tony who was selected for the commission, even before the building existed. The painting was installed in May of 1994, adding to the list of major collections that hold examples of the artist's work, including the State of Hawaii. Tony's success has not changed his close relationship with his community, however, where he works closely with the cultural needs of Maui's children, working with the Department of Education on integrating art as part of the core curriculum, speaking, and giving demonstrations.

Tony Walholm

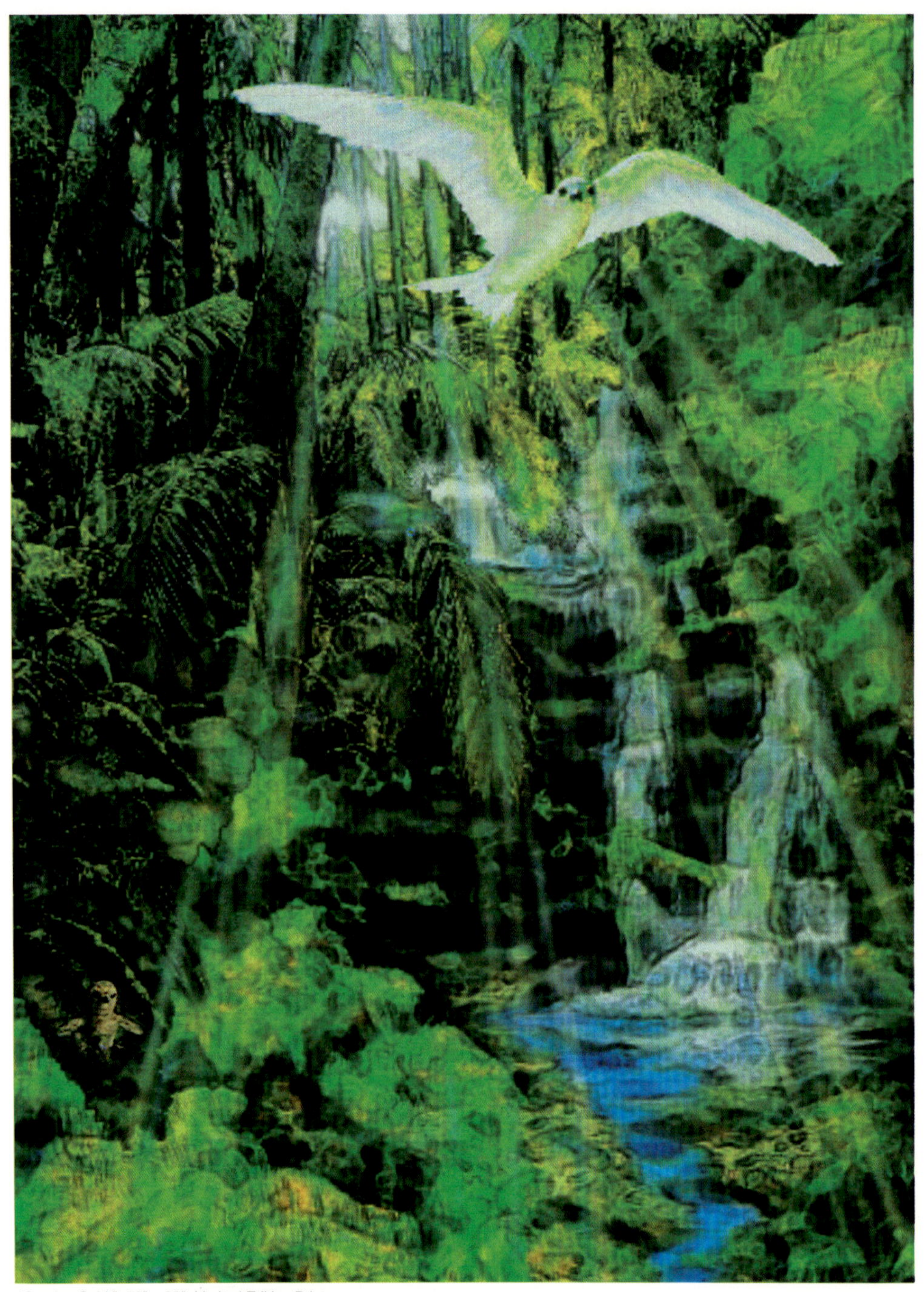

"Soaring Spirit" 22" x 30" Limited Edition Print

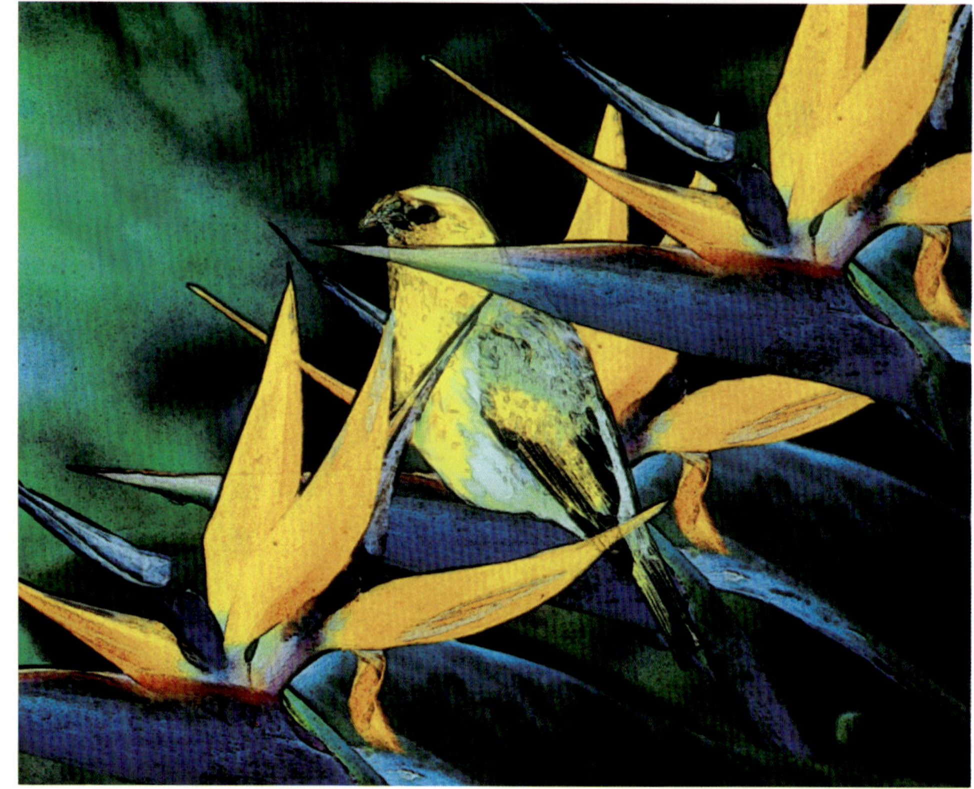

"Birds Of Paradise" 30" x 24" Limited Edition Print

MARILYNN WHEATLEY

Moving to Hawaii has had a major influence on Marilynn Wheatley. After a lifetime of painting sporadically, at 60 she now feels this is her time to show her "mind's eye" to the world.

Marilynn finds inspiration everywhere in the exotic beauty of Hawaii. Its vastness, she feels, affords a lifetime of painting inspiration. Her art portrays incredible scenes from above jungles to below the water's surface. Her style is so unique it's difficult to describe.

Waterfalls are one of her favorite subjects as she paints in the lush outdoor setting that her husband Mike has created. Kiawe, the family golden retriever, keeps her company; (that is until the waterfalls outside the studio become a refreshing escape from the afternoon sun).

When viewing her paintings you feel you are there. "You dare not make any sudden moves lest you startle the bird perched on the *Birds of Paradise*".

MARILYNN WHEATLEY

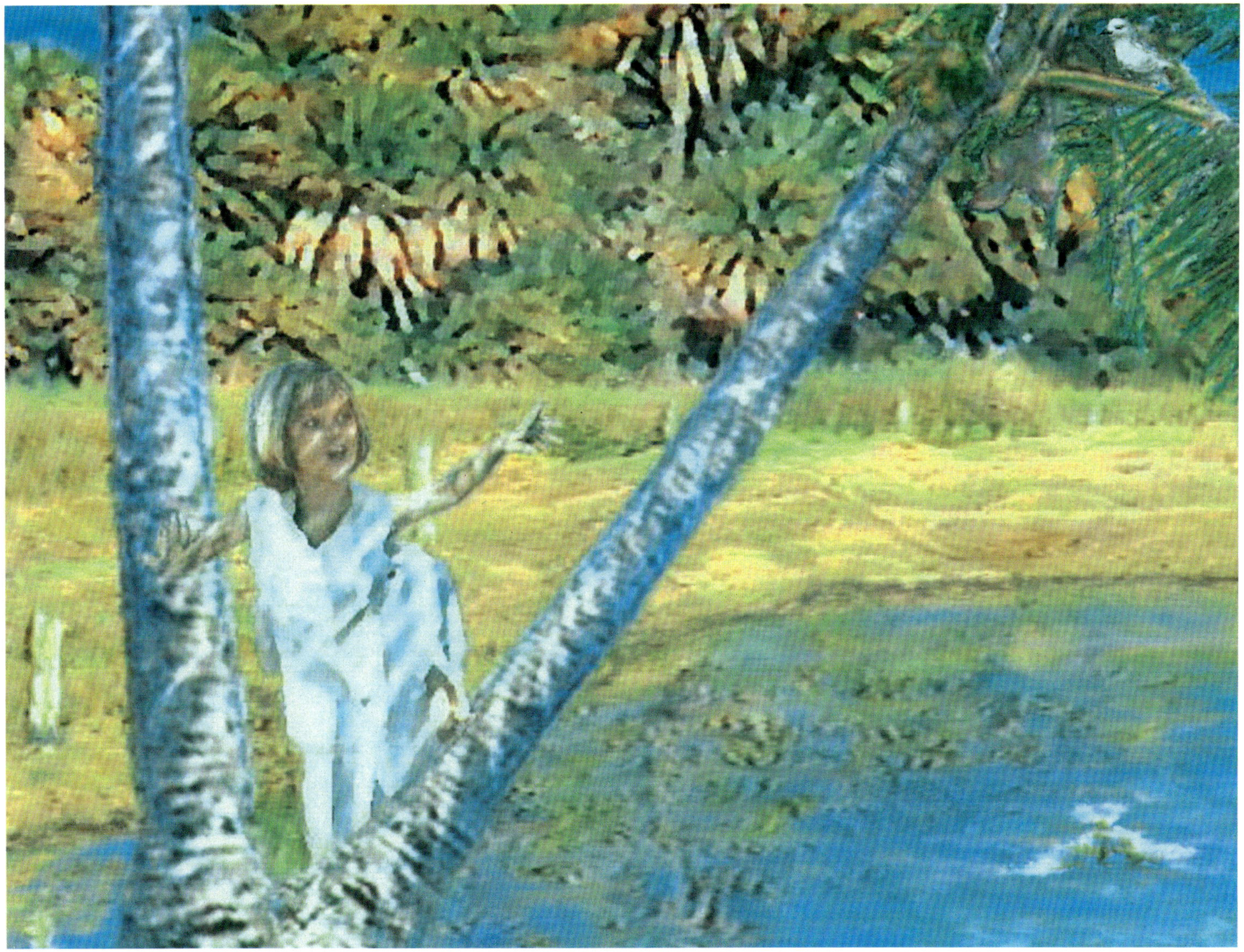

"Up There!" 40" x 30" Limited Edition Print

Marilynn Wheatley's love of children is apparent in her paintings. "Up There" and the historic "Queen's Bath", both evoke the wonder and innocence of childhood; a place from where we all come and where most would like to spend time again. Often while viewing her art people feel they re-experience this moment of joy.

Marilynn's techniques come from exploration and self-teaching. Her unique brush work and color style are all her own

Marilynn's art is full of hidden elements. You sense that the fairy tern nesting in "Up There" is being watched from above as you encounter the mother bird's reflection in the water below.

The astounding beauty of nature in Hawaii makes subject choice a pleasant dilemma. Marilynn depicts colorful birds, verdant rain forests and breathtaking waterfalls in many of her works. While painting these magical scenes Marilynn often wonders: "How could I live anywhere but Hawaii."

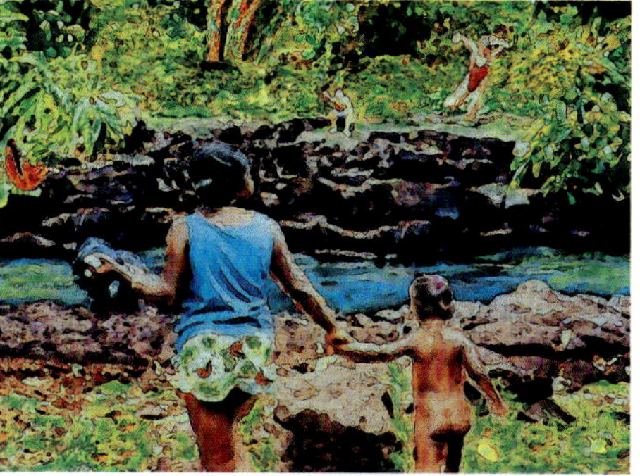

"Queens Bath" 40" x 30" Acrylic On Canvas

Despite growing demand for her work, Marilynn still finds time to do portrait paintings for her clients. She excels at creating art that is beautifully decorative as well as being a reminder of a special time shared with a loved one.

"Self Portrait" 30" x 20" Acrylic on Canvas

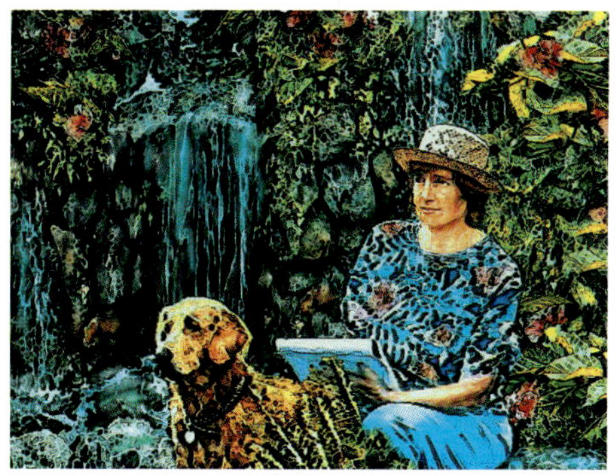

Spectrum Fine Art
75-909 Hiona Street
Holualoa, Hawaii, HI 96725
(808) 329-9999
FAX (808) 326-5444

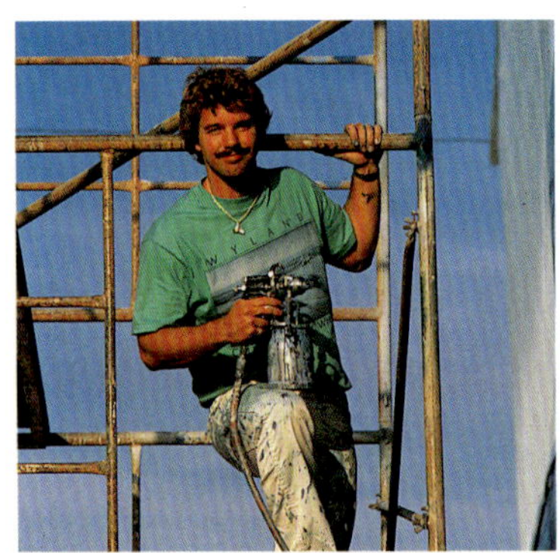

WYLAND

Wyland Galleries Hawaii
94-130 Leokane Street, Penthouse
Waipahu, Oahu, HI 96797
(808) 676-7407 FAX (808) 676-7004

Wyland, The World's Finest Ocean Artist, has been a pioneer in the marine art movement since 1971. The painter, sculptor, muralist and writer is one of the most prolific and celebrated artists of our day. Wyland's name has become synonymous with whales and man's efforts to save these magnificent creatures from extinction.

Considered to be the world's leading environmental marine life artist, Wyland's art has raised our consciousness of the plight of whales and the beautiful oceans in which they live. Even more importantly, he has exposed the world to his cause through a series of incredible Whaling Walls, life-size murals that transform giant walls into living oceans featuring brilliant portraits of great whales, dolphins and other marine life.

Over one billion people a year see his landmark murals throughout the U.S., Canada, Japan, Australia and Europe. His vision over the last 25 years has inspired people all over the world to become more aware of the struggle faced by all ocean life. "I try to not only capture the great whales, but also the great spirit they possess", Wyland says.

In 1992 he completed Whaling Wall XXXIII, "Planet Ocean" in Long Beach, California. Eleven stories high and 1,280 feet in circumference, it is the largest mural in the world as acknowledged by the Guinness Book of World Records. He topped that feat in 1993 by completing a whirlwind tour along the eastern seaboard of the United States, completing 17 murals in 17 weeks in 17 cities from Maine to Florida.

Always a leader, Wyland and his brother, Bill Wyland, have established the largest and most successful fine art gallery in the state of Hawaii's history. Wyland Galleries Hawaii features the art of Wyland at 13 locations on four islands along with three Wyland Collection Stores featuring Wyland's art on retail merchandise.

Wyland's original oil paintings, water colors and sculptures reflect Wyland's first-hand experiences diving with whales and dolphins all over the world. His ability to capture the true spirit of his subjects and offer a look into their souls separates his work from other artists in his genre.

To date, Wyland has completed over 60 Whaling Walls since painting his first life-size mural in Laguna Beach, California in 1981. Never resting from "planetary duty", Wyland plans to complete 100 walls by the year 2011. Each wall is dedicated to the great whales and life in our oceans.

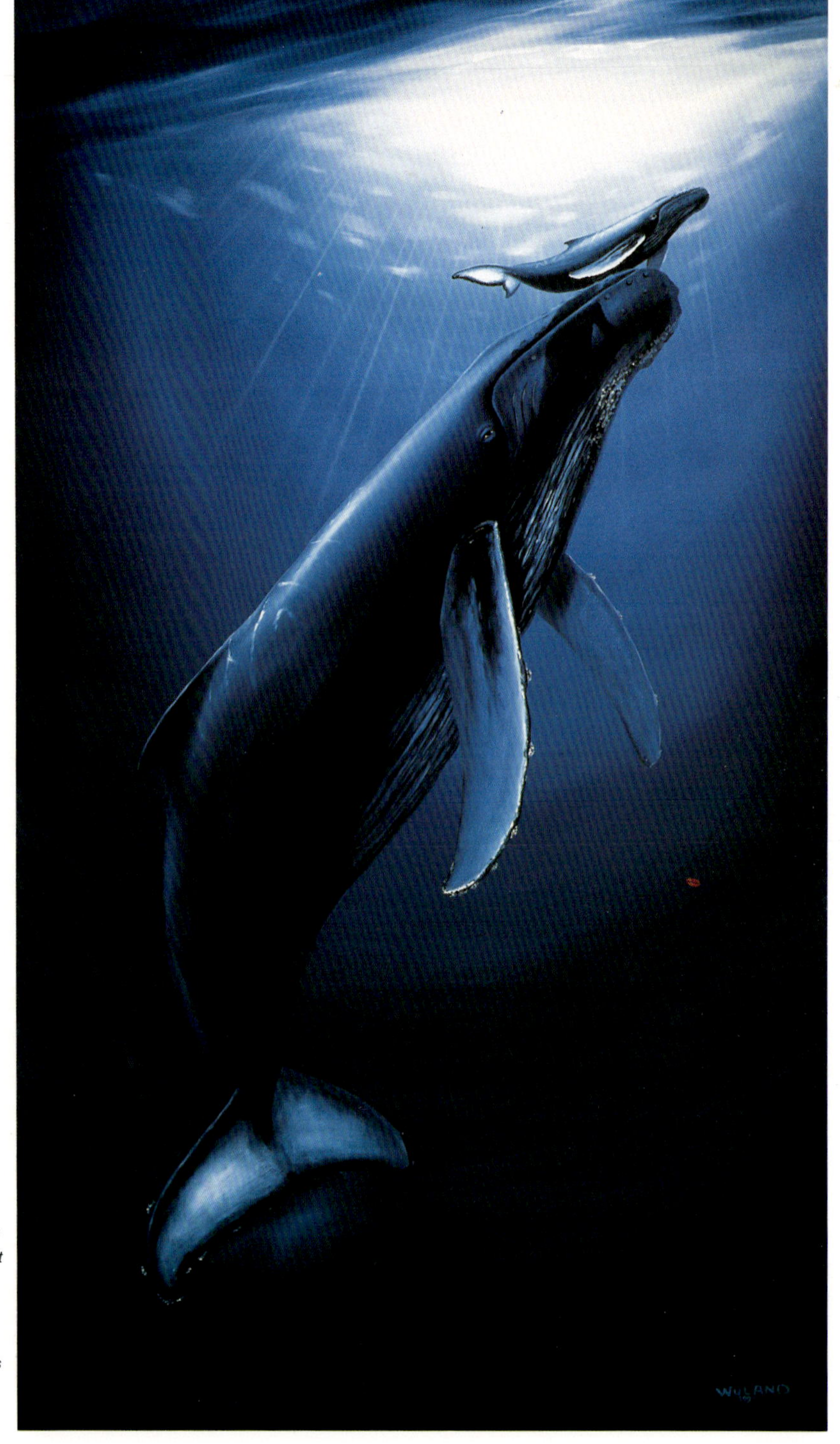

"First Breath"
Original Oil Painting,

and 18" x 26" Limited Edition Prints - Offset S/N 950 & Proofs,

and 30" x 50" Cibachrome®-Limited Edition Prints S/N 295 & Proofs

WYLAND

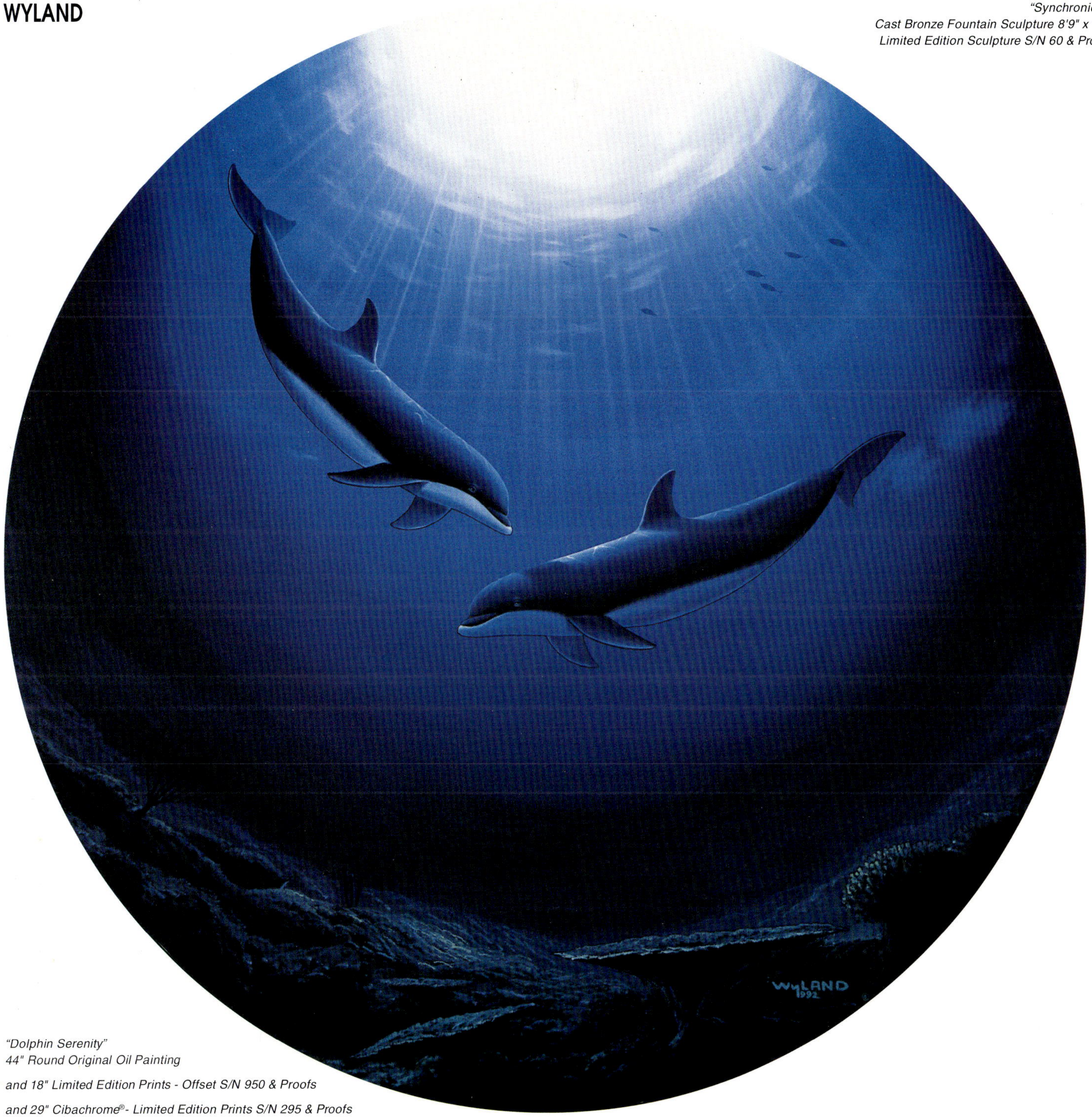

"Synchronicity"
Cast Bronze Fountain Sculpture 8'9" x 8'9"
Limited Edition Sculpture S/N 60 & Proofs

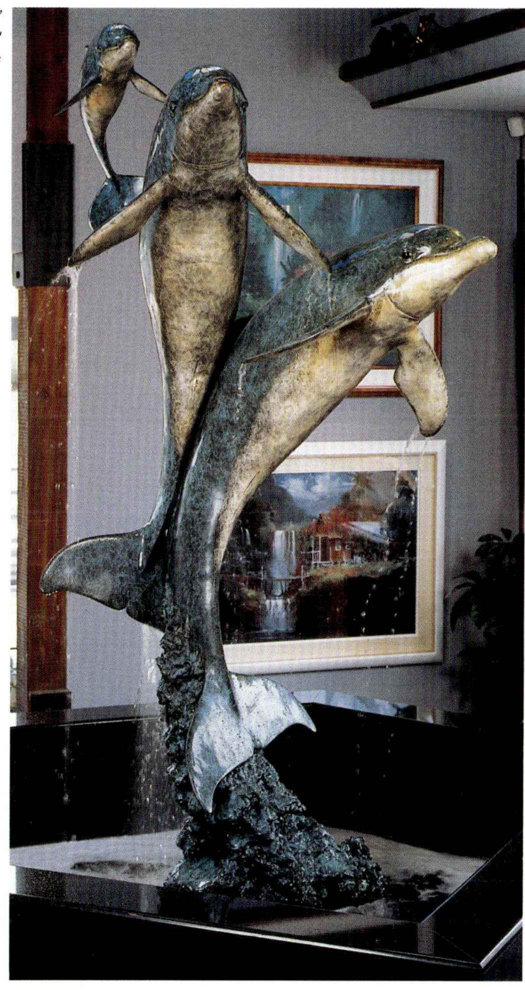

Whaling Wall XXXIII

"Planet Ocean" Certified As The World's Largest Mural By The Guinness Book Of World's Records.

110' High x 1225' Long 360° Dedicated July 9, 1992

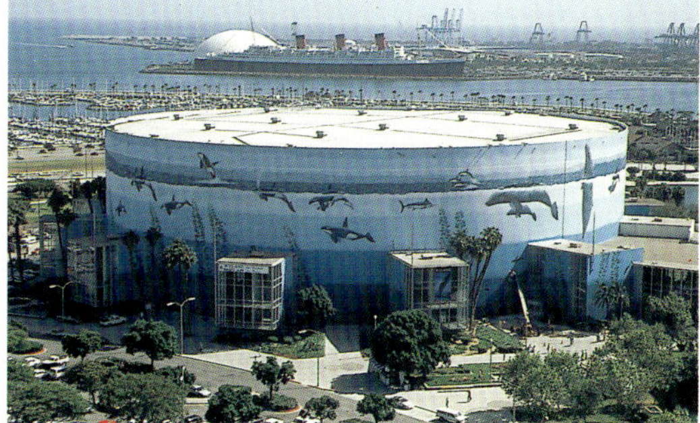

"Dolphin Serenity"
44" Round Original Oil Painting

and 18" Limited Edition Prints - Offset S/N 950 & Proofs

and 29" Cibachrome®- Limited Edition Prints S/N 295 & Proofs

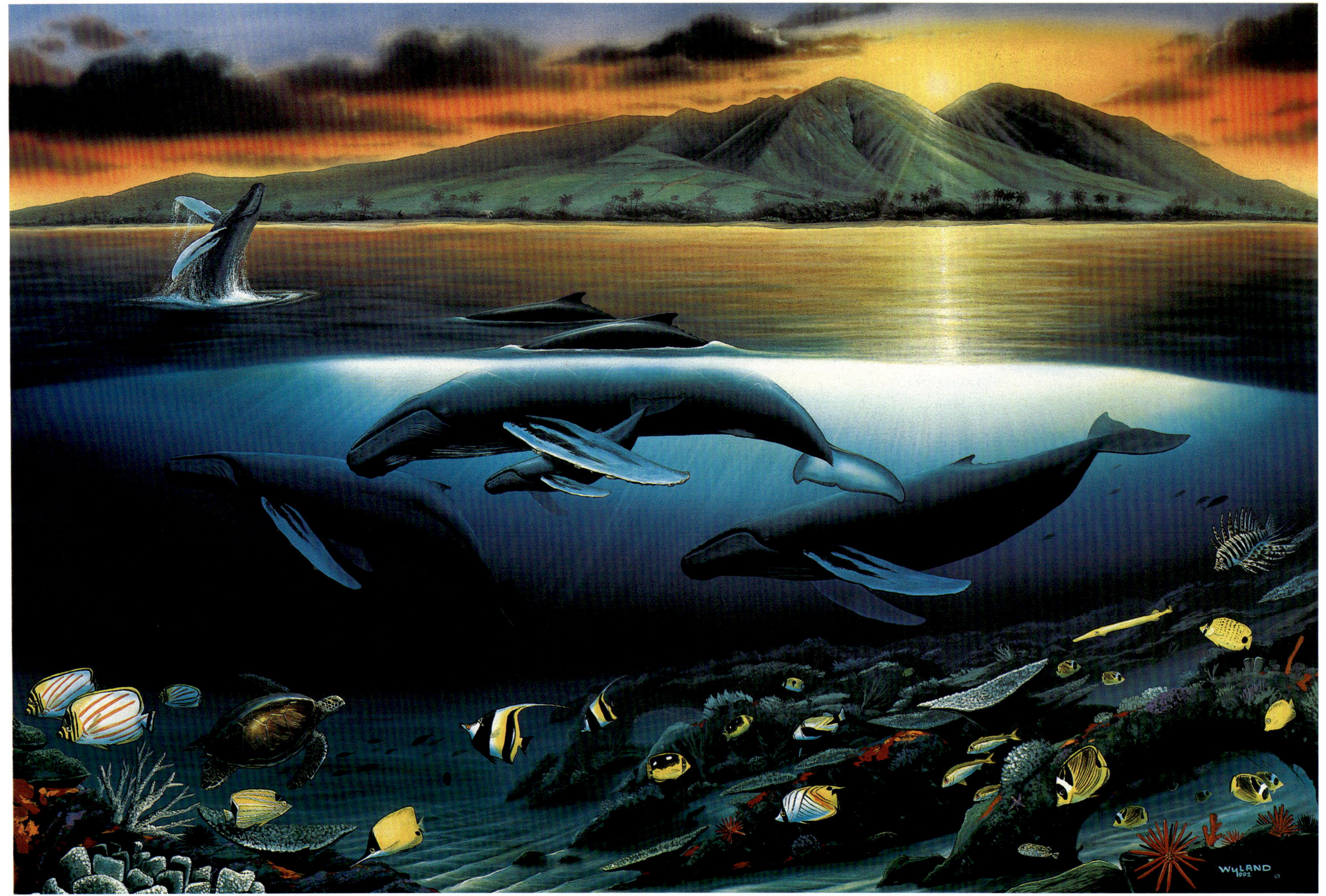

"Maui Dawn" 72" x 48" Original Oil Painting and 26" x 39" Limited Edition Prints - Offset S/N 750 & Proofs and 33" x 50" Cibachrome®- Limited Edition Prints S/N 75 & Proofs

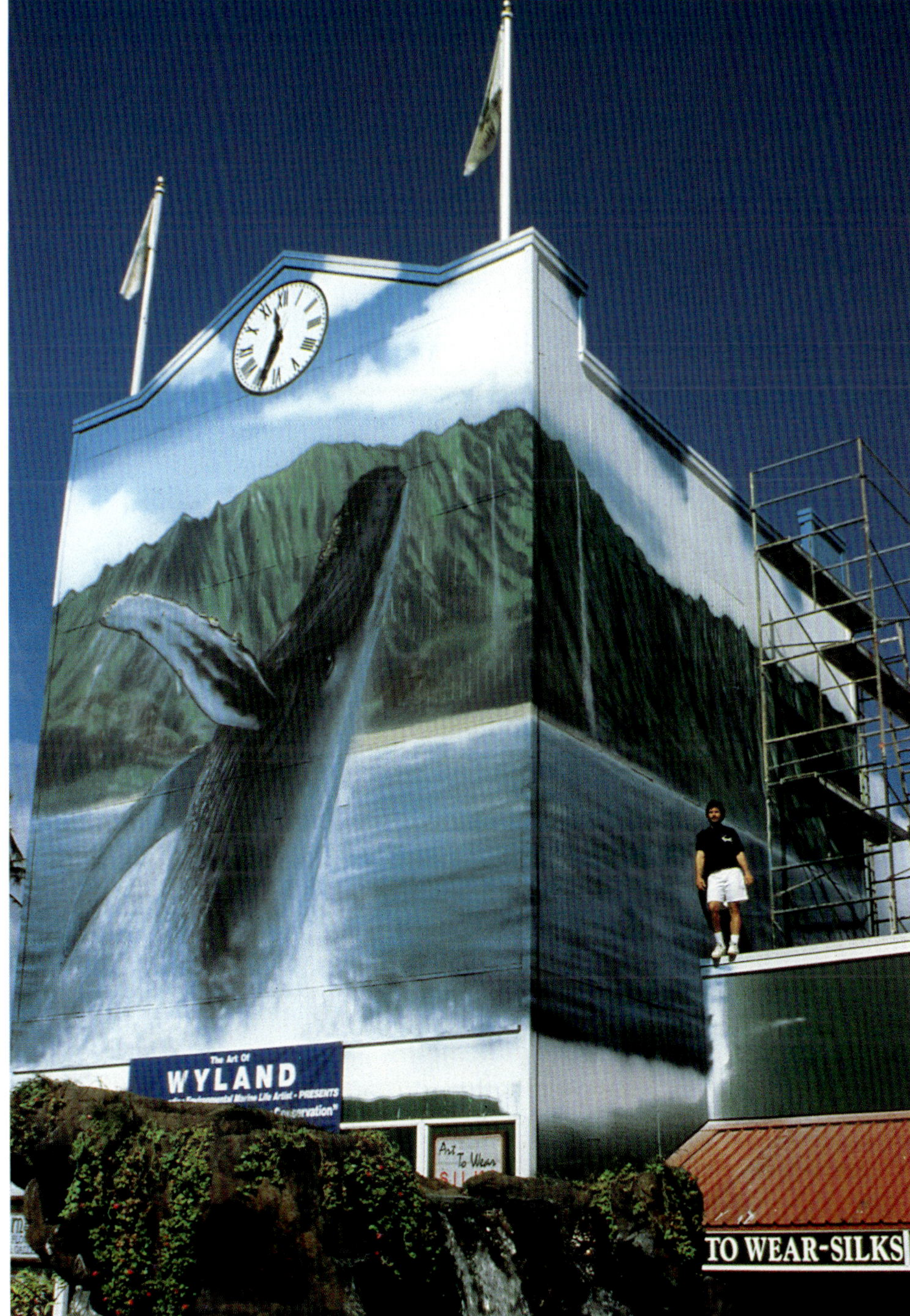

Whaling Wall XXVIII "A Time For Conservation" 44' High, 360°
Dedicated January 8, 1991 Kauai Village, Kauai, Hawaii

Collaborative Painting by Wyland & Walfrido

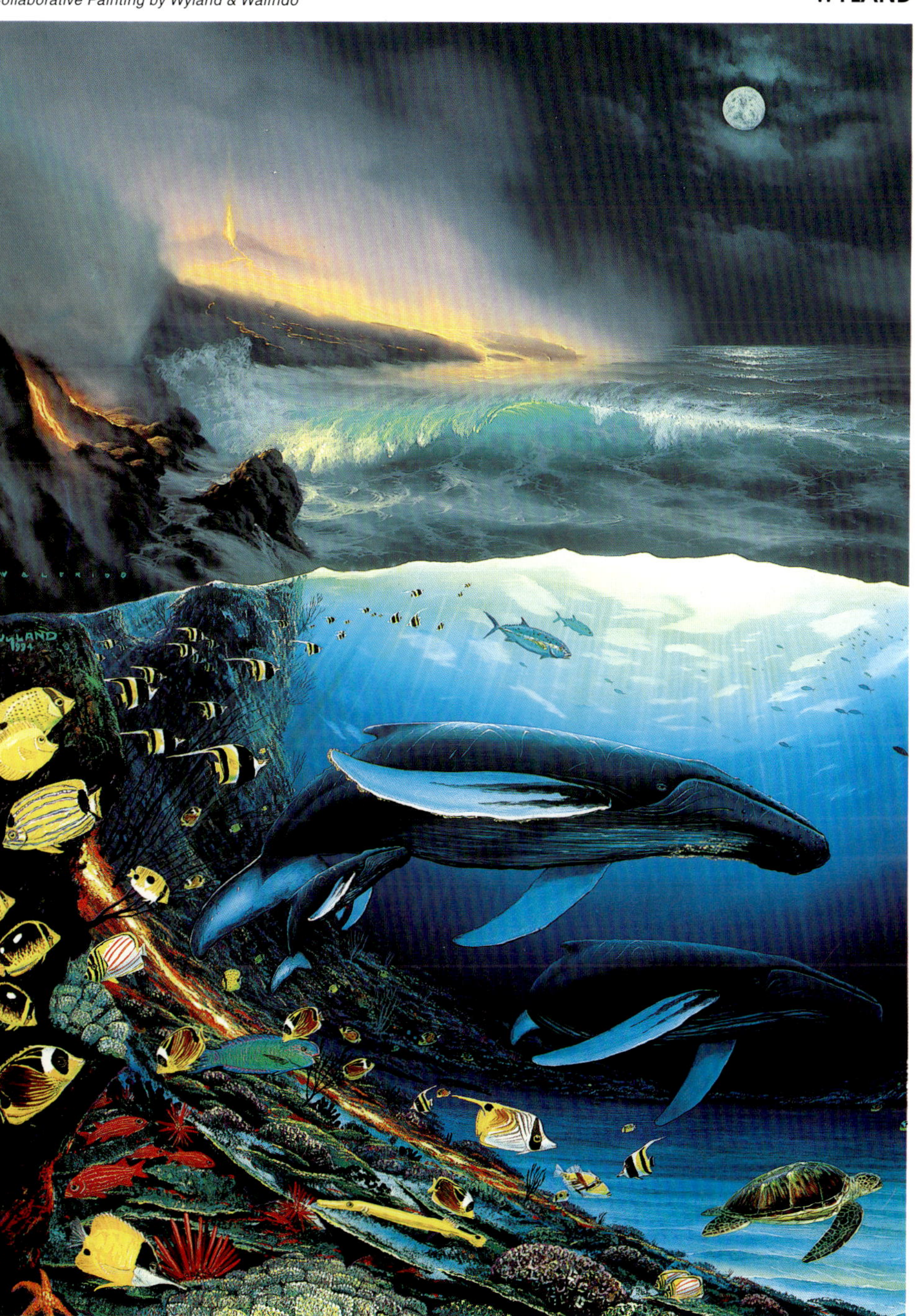

"Two Worlds of Paradise" 24" x 36" Original Oil Painting
and Limited Edition Prints S/N & Proofs and Cibachrome®- Limited Edition Prints S/N & Proofs

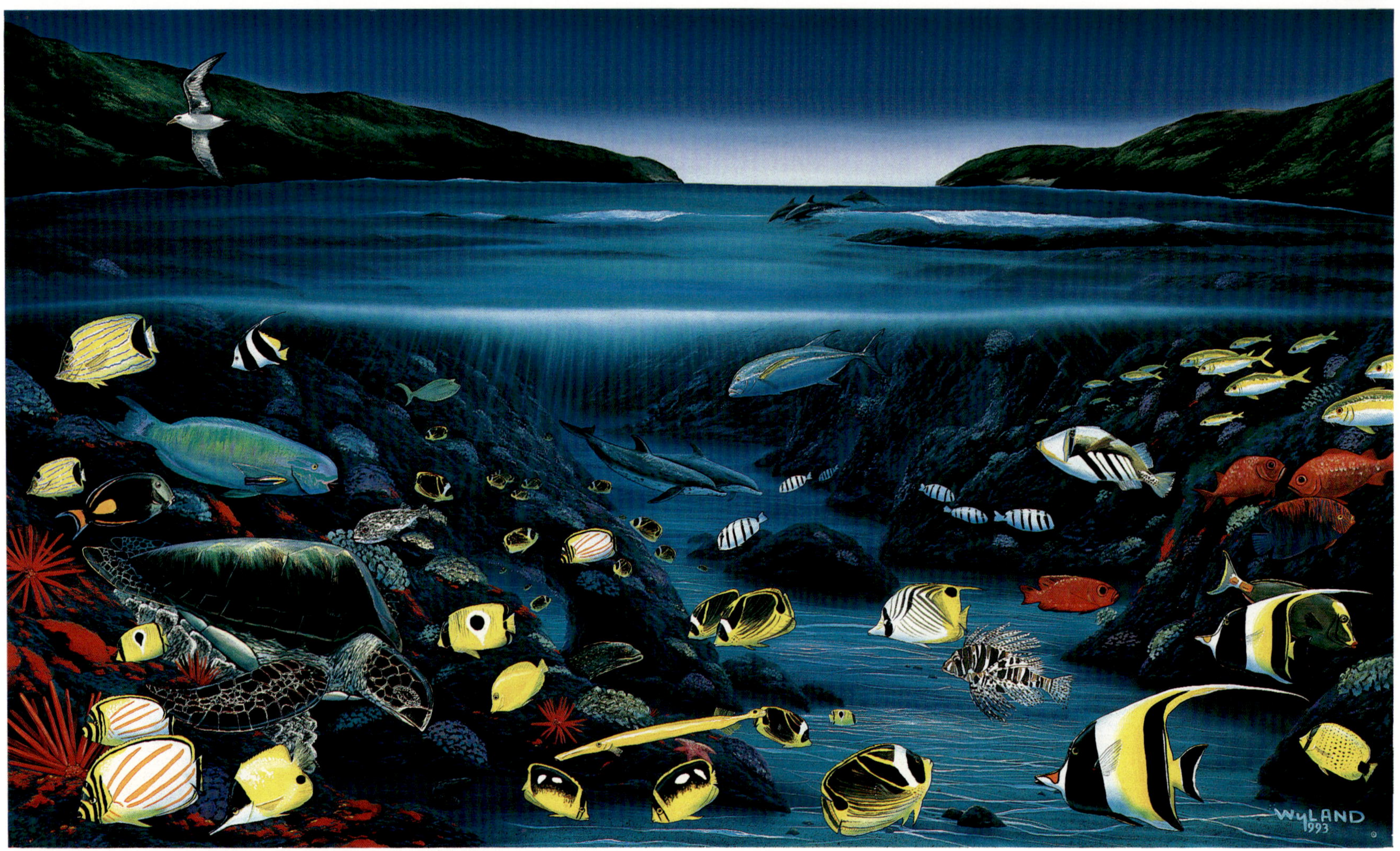

"Hanauma Bay" 72" x 48" Original Oil Painting and 17" x 30" Limited Edition Prints - Offset S/N 950 & Proofs and 29" x 50" Cibachrome®- Limited Edition Prints S/N 295 & Proofs

DIRECTORY OF ARTISTS

Jack Adams
1415 Kalakaua Avenue, Room 204
Honolulu, Oahu, HI 96826
(808) 955-6100

Loren D. Adams
Loren D. Adams Studio
880 Front Street, #881
Lahaina, Maui, HI 96761
(808) 572-0239

George Allan
37 Haliu Street
Lahaina, Maui, HI 96761
(808) 669-8271

Linda Andelin
752 Front Street
Lahaina, Maui, HI 96761
(808) 667-1982

Rae Andrews
1941 S. Kihei Road
Kihei, Maui, HI 96753
(808) 879-4181

Andrew Annenberg
Annenberg Masterworks
P.O. Box 778
Kula, Maui, HI 96790
(808) 878-3010

Arna Johnson
P.O. Box 4277
Kaneohe, Oahu, HI 96744
(808) 236-0009

Margaret Bedell
Kihei, Maui, HI 96793
(808) 879-9911

Gayle Bright
Kihei, Maui, HI 96791
(808) 875-0862

Mary Brong
738 Menehune Lane, Suite 4
Honolulu, Oahu, HI 96826
(808) 942-0156

Susie Brooks
Arts of Paradise Gallery
2330 Kalakaua Avenue
Waikiki, Oahu, HI 96815
(808) 924-2787

Kirsten Bunney
P.O. Box 638
Makawao, Maui, HI 96768
(808) 572-8118

Joelle Chicheportiche Perz
256B Front Street
Lahaina, Maui, HI 96761
(808) 667-5561

Douglas Chun
Douglas Chun Studio
116 Holopuni Road
Kula, Maui, HI 96790
(808) 876-0142

Lau Chun
Gallery Lau Chun
2259 Kalakaua Avenue
Honolulu, Oahu, HI 96815
(808) 922-8818

James Coleman
2397 Laurel Park
Thousand Oaks, CA 91360
(805) 373-2990

Gregory Craft
The Art of Gregory Craft
148-E Mokauea Street
Honolulu, Oahu, HI 96819
(808) 525-1884 Pager

Michael David
Spectrum Fine Art
75-909 Hiona Street
Holualoa, Hawaii, HI 96725
(808) 329-9999

Lance Fairly
53-839 Kamehameha Highway
Punaluu, Oahu, HI 96717
(808) 293-9009

Tom Faught
2927 Kaluanui Road
Makawao, Maui, HI 96768
(808) 572-8904

Mary Lucas Faustine
P.O. Box 831
Paia, Maui, HI 96779
(808) 572-3718

Betty Hay Freeland
439 Front Street
Lahaina, Maui, HI 96761
(808) 661-5766

Scott Hanson
Hanson Studio
4962-1 Kilauea Avenue
Honolulu, Oahu, HI 96816
(808) 737-4309

Loretta Hera
P.O. Box 794
Lana'i City, Lana'i 96763
(808) 565-6115

Ho Hung Wong
Robyn Buntin of Honolulu
900-A Maunakea Street
Honolulu, Oahu, HI 96817
(808) 523-5913

Brian Ibaan
94-167 Kiaha Loop
Mililani, Oahu, HI 96789
(808) 623-3365

Jan Kasprzycki
P.O. Box 277
Makawao, Maui, HI 96768
(808) 572-0585

Avi Kiriaty
Pacifica Prints
P.O. Box 37
Honomu, Hawaii, HI 96728
(808) 963-6706

Elisabeth K.
Atelier EK
2999 Kalakaua Avenue, Suite 601
Honolulu, Oahu, HI 96815
(808) 923-1711

Mary Koski
P.O. Box 1349
Kamuela, Hawaii, HI 96743
(808) 885-6912

Terry McDonald
R.R. 2 Box 230C
Kula Highway
Kula, Maui, HI 96790
(808) 878-6906

The Makk Family
1515 Laukahi Street
Honolulu, Oahu, HI 96821
(808) 373-2772

Joshua Miller
Rolling Fire Studio
P.O. Box 1361
Kehena Beach, Hawaii, HI 96778
(808) 965-7345

Susie Monroe
P.O. Box 1208
Kula, Maui, HI 96790
(808) 878-3804

Niles Nakaoka
284 Mananai Place, #R
Honolulu, Oahu, HI 96818
(808) 487-4009

Roy Okamoto
P.O. Box 949
Lana'i City, Lana'i HI 96763
(808) 565-6221

Peter & Madeline Powell
Powell Studios
141 Kapuai Road
Haiku, Maui, HI 96708
(808) 572-8105

Ruth Puchek
P.O. Box A118
Lana'i City, Lana'i HI 96763
(808) 565-6902

David Sacco
P.O. Box 509
Makawao, Maui, HI 96768
(808) 572-6900

David Still
1142 Auahi Street, #3305
Honolulu, Oahu, HI 96814
(808) 593-3755

Roy Tabora
Tabora Studio, Inc.
58-356B Kamehameha Highway
Haleiwa, Oahu, HI 96712
(808) 638-7881

Cliff Tanaka
Hawaii, HI Art Sales & Services
47-594 Nukupu'u Street
Kaneohe, Oahu, HI 96744
(808) 239-4027

Ann Taylor-Vance
Ann Taylor Art
P.O. Box 10444
Lahaina, Maui, HI 96761
(808) 661-7812

Alan Thorpe
Kihei, Maui, HI 96791
(808) 779-4212

Bruce Turnbull
Sculpture Garden
R.R.1, Box 151A
Wailuku, Maui, HI 96793
(808) 244-9838

Ari Vanderschoot
P.O. Box 699
Makawao, Maui, HI 96768
(808) 878-2690

Elan Vital
171 Pauwela Road
Haiku, Maui, HI 96708
(808) 575-9736

Tony Walholm
11 Ho'opalua Drive
Pukalani, Maui, HI 96768
(808) 572-1543

Marilynn Wheatley
Spectrum Fine Art
75-909 Hiona Street
Holualoa, Hawaii, HI 96725
(808) 329-9999

Wyland
Wyland Galleries Hawaii
94-130 Leokane Street, Penthouse
Waipahu, HI 96797
(808) 676-7407

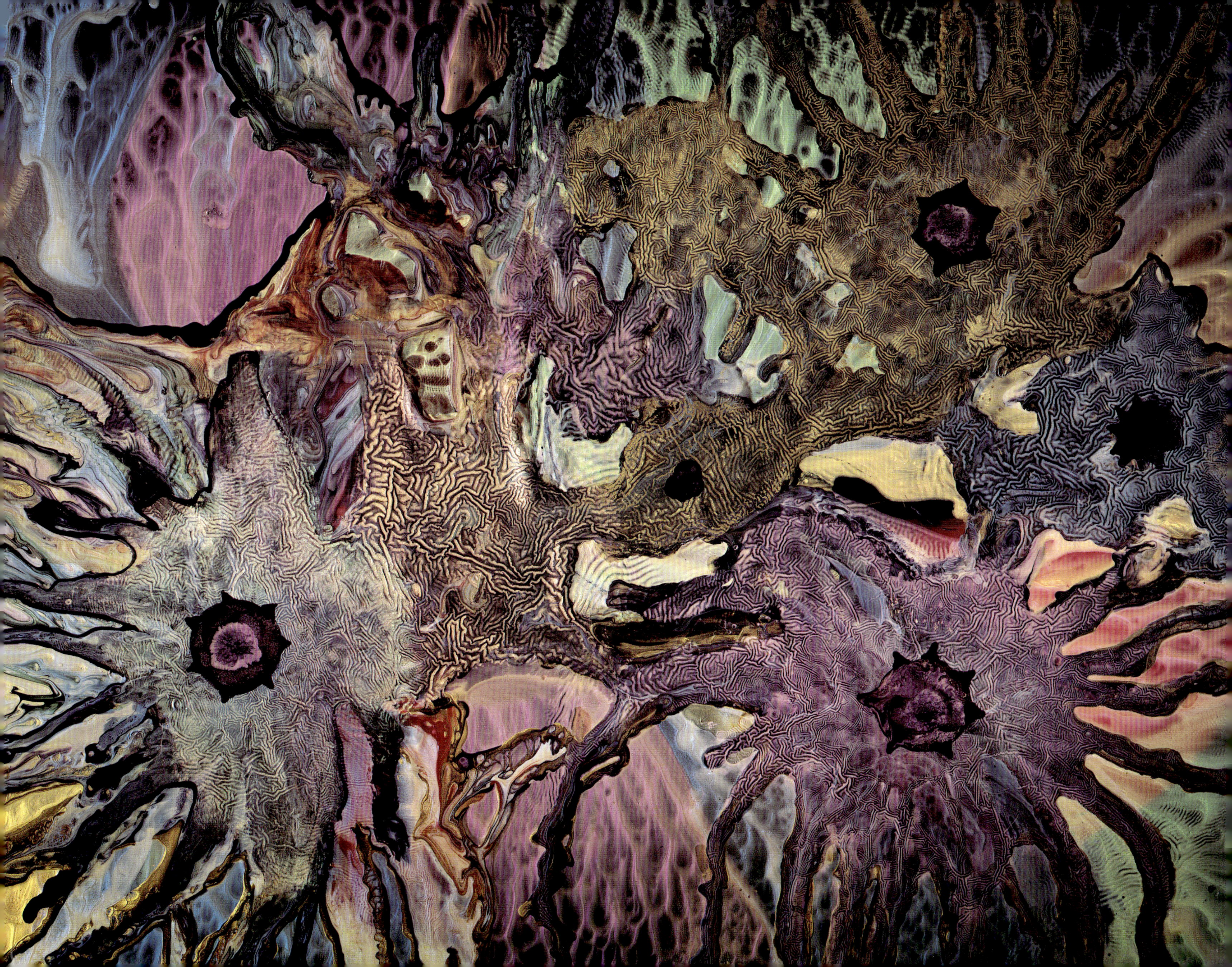

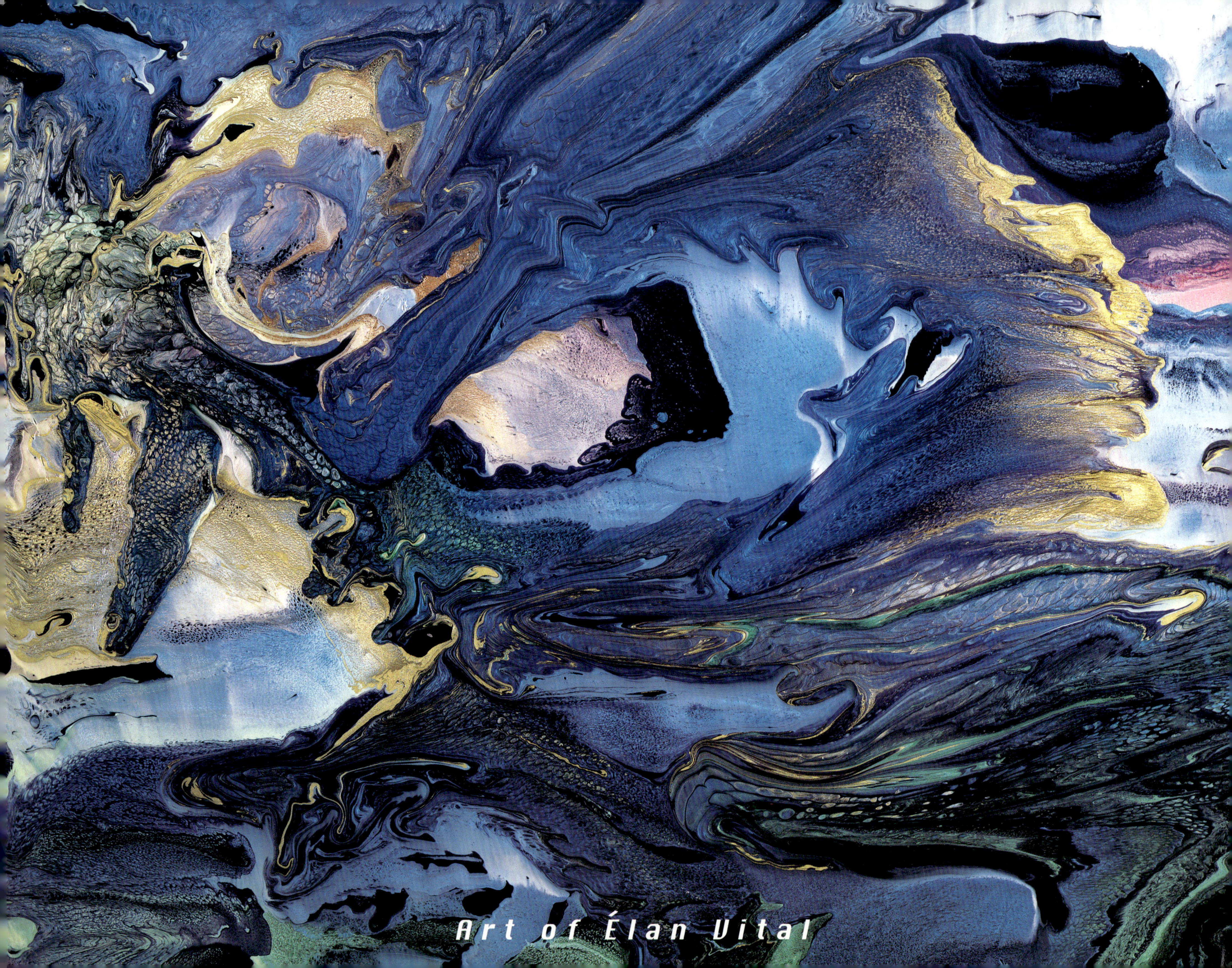
Art of Élan Vital